NetWare Training Guide: Managing NetWare Systems

2nd Edition

First book in the four-part NetWare Training Guide *series*

Debra Niedermiller-Chaffins

with

Dorothy Cady

New Riders Publishing, Indianapolis, Indiana

NetWare Training Guide: Managing NetWare Systems, Second Edition

By Debra Niedermiller-Chaffins

Published by:
New Riders Publishing
201 West 103rd Street
Indianapolis, Indiana 46290 USA

All rights reserved. No part of this book may be reproduced or transmitted in any form or by any means, electronic or mechanical, including photocopying, recording, or by any information storage and retrieval system, without written permission from the publisher, except for the inclusion of brief quotations in a review.

Copyright © 1994 by New Riders Publishing

Printed in the United States of America 1 2 3 4 5 6 7 8 9 0

Library of Congress Cataloging-in-Publication Data

```
Niedermiller-Chaffins, Debra R. 1963-
NetWare Training Guide : Managing NetWare Systems/ Debra R.
Niedermiller-Chaffins with Dorothy L. Cady -- 2nd ed.
     p.       cm.
Includes index
ISBN 1-56205-305-1 : $69.95
1.   NetWare (Computer file)
2.   Operating systems (Computers)
3.   Local area networks (Computer networks)
I.  Cady, Dorothy L., 1953-
II. Title
QA76.76.063N535        1994
005.7'1369--dc20                                     94-2113
                                                        CIP
```

Warning and Disclaimer

This book describes courses and tests developed by Novell, Inc. for use in their Certified NetWare Engineer program. Novell, Inc. does not endorse this book, and is not responsible for the accuracy of any material contained herein.

Every effort has been made to make this book as complete and as accurate as possible, but no warranty or fitness is implied. The information is provided on an as is basis. The author and New Riders Publishing shall have neither liability nor responsibility to any person or entity with respect to any loss or damages arising from the information contained in this book or from the use of the disks or programs that may accompany it.

Publisher	**Lloyd Short**
Associate Publisher	**Tim Huddleston**
Manager of Acquisitions	**Cheri Robinson**
Managing Editor	**Matthew Morrill**
Marketing Manager	**Ray Robinson**

NetWare Training Guide: Managing NetWare Systems, 2nd Edition

Product Director
Drew Heywood

Production Coordinator
Lisa D. Wagner

Senior Editor
Tad Ringo

Editor
Suzanne Snyder

Acquisitions Editor
Alicia Krakovitz

Acquisitions Coordinator
Stacey Beheler

Publisher's Assistant
Melissa Lynch

Editorial Assistant
Karen Opal

Book Design
Roger Morgan

Imprint Manager
Juli Cook

Production Team
Nick Anderson
Lisa Daugherty
Steph Davis
Rich Evers
Dennis Clay Hager
Angela P. Judy
Stephanie J. McComb
Shelly Palma
Michelle M. Self
Ann Sippel
Elaine Webb

Proofreaders
Ayrika Bryant
Kim Cofer
Kim K. Hannel
Jamie Milazzo
Nanci Sears Perry
Linda Quigley
Ryan Rader
Beth Rago
Kris Simmons
Tonya R. Simpson
SA Springer
Suzanne Tully
Dennis Wesner
Donna Winter

Indexers
Charlotte Clapp
Jennifer Eberhardt
Rebecca Mayfield

About the Authors

Debra R. Niedermiller-Chaffins is Education Director for Computer Data, Inc. in Madison Heights, Michigan. Ms. Niedermiller-Chaffins started the education department at Computer Data in 1988 to help organizations develop autonomy and self-sufficiency in training future Certified NetWare Engineer (CNE) operations. She is a Certified NetWare Instructor (CNI) and a CNE, specializing in training future CNEs. In addition to teaching, Ms. Niedermiller-Chaffins also supports a small client base, which provides her with a background of real-world networking scenarios. She is the author of *Inside Novell NetWare*, Special Edition, and *Inside NetWare Lite*, also published by New Riders Publishing.

Dorothy L. Cady is a senior technical writer for Novell, Inc., in Provo, Utah. Mrs. Cady started with Novell in 1990 as the team leader for the Software Testing Department's Document Testing Team, helping to assure the quality of the documentation that ships with Novell's NetWare 2, 3, 4, NetWare Lite, and Personal NetWare products. She is a Certified NetWare Instructor (CNI), Certified NetWare Engineer (CNE), and Certified NetWare Administrator (CNA). In addition to her duties as a technical writer, Mrs. Cady also is a member of the adjunct faculty at Utah Valley State College and a free-lance writer. Mrs. Cady has over 20 years of experience in the computer industry, including both the private and public service sectors. Mrs. Cady also is the author of *Inside Personal NetWare*, also from New Riders Publishing.

Acknowledgments

I want to dedicate this book to the many people who helped and supported me through this project. Thanks to my parents for always believing in me and my endeavors. A special thanks to my husband, Brian, without whom this book would not be possible. I also want to thank Computer Data partners and my boss, Jim Weyand, for his support in my education projects. Finally, to the fantastic group of people at New Riders, a special thanks for their guidance. I appreciate all your help.—*Debra Niedermiller-Chaffins*

The authors specifically want to thank the following individuals for their contributions to this book:

Rose Kearsley of Novell, Inc., for her promptness, responsiveness, and occasional bits of detective work, without which this book would have been considerably less comprehensive.

Peter Jerram of Novell, Inc., for his generous support for this project in its early phases.

Drew Heywood, for his developmental work and attention to detail during the author review stage of the book.

NetWare Training Guide: Managing NetWare Systems, 2nd Edition

Kurt Schernekau, for ensuring the technical accuracy of the first edition.

Lisa Wagner, for her contributions as production editor and for tracking the book through the production process; and Suzanne Snyder, for her ruthless pursuit of perfection as a copy editor.

Karen Opal, for editorial assistance wherever needed.

The Prentice Hall Computer Publishing production, illustration, and indexing staffs, for the design and expeditious handling of materials.

Trademark Acknowledgments

New Riders Publishing has made every attempt to supply trademark information about company names, products, and services mentioned in this book. Trademarks indicated below were derived from various sources. New Riders Publishing cannot attest to the accuracy of this information.

ARCnet is a registered trademark of Datapoint Corporation.

CompuServe is a registered trademark of CompuServe, Incorporated.

IBM and Micro Channel are registered trademarks and NETBIOS is a trademark of International Business Machines Corporation.

Lotus and 1-2-3 are registered trademarks of Lotus Development Corporation.

Microsoft Windows is a registered trademark of Microsoft Corporation.

NetWare, NetWare Name Services, and Novell are registered trademarks of Novell, Inc.

Trademarks of other products mentioned in this book are held by the companies producing them.

Contents at a Glance

Introduction	**1**
Part One: Deciding on a Path	**7**
1 Novell's Certification Programs	9
2 Studying for the Certification Exams	27
Part Two: NetWare Basics	**45**
3 Moving Around NetWare Directory Structures	47
4 Understanding NetWare Security	97
5 Utilities	125
6 Printing on a Novell Network	213
7 Customizing the User's Environment	273
Part Three: NetWare 2.2	**351**
8 NetWare 2.2 System Manager	353
9 NetWare 2.2 Advanced System Manager	375
Part Four: NetWare 3.1*x*	**423**
10 NetWare 3.1*x* Administration	425
11 NetWare 3.1*x* Advanced Administration	469
Part Five: Appendixes	**565**
A Answers to Review Questions	567
B Test Objectives	573
C Comparison Charts	601
D NetWare 2.15	605
Index	**617**

Table of Contents

Introduction — 1
   Who Should Read this Book? — 2
   What Is Covered in this Book? — 2
   What Topics Are Not Included? — 3
   The Details of this Book — 3

Part One: Deciding on a Path — 7

1 Novell's Certification Programs — 9
   Choosing the Right Certification — 10
      CNE: The Certified NetWare Engineer — *11*
      ECNE: The Enterprise Certified NetWare Engineer — *16*
      CNA: The Certified NetWare Administrator — *17*
   Taking the Certification Tests — 21
      Form Tests — *22*
      Adaptive Tests — *22*
      Self-Evaluation Tests — *22*
      NAECs and NEAPs — *23*
   Summary — 24

2 Studying for the Certification Exams — 27
   Using the Progress Maps — 28
      CNE Progress Map — *28*
      ECNE Progress Map — *30*
   Elective Tests — 31
      Electives Map — *32*
   Preparing To Study — 37
   Choosing a Certification Path — 39
   Using Study Techniques — 41
      Repetition — *41*
      Linking — *41*
      Mnemonics — *42*
   Testing Covered in this Book — 43
   Summary — 44

Part Two: NetWare Basics — 45

3 Moving Around NetWare Directory Structures — 47

- Creating File Server Names — 48
- Accessing NetWare Volumes — 49
  - *Volumes, NetWare, and DOS* — 49
- Naming and Setting Up Volumes — 51
- Understanding Required Directories — 52
  - *SYS:LOGIN* — 52
  - *SYS:MAIL* — 55
  - *SYS:PUBLIC* — 57
  - *SYS:SYSTEM* — 58
- Managing Required Directories — 60
- Using Recommended Directories — 62
  - *HOME Directories* — 62
- Using DOS Commands in NetWare — 67
- Using NetWare Commands on the Directory Structure — 68
  - *CHKDIR* — 68
  - *CHKVOL* — 69
  - *LISTDIR* — 69
  - *NCOPY* — 71
  - *NDIR* — 72
  - *RENDIR* — 77
  - *VOLINFO* — 77
- Mastering Drive Mappings — 79
  - *Networks and Drive Mappings* — 79
  - *Networks and Search Drives* — 81
- Setting Up Drive Mappings — 82
  - *Using Local Drive Mappings* — 82
  - *Using Network Drive Mappings* — 83
  - *Using Search Drive Mappings* — 85
  - *Deleting Drive Mappings* — 86
- Using the DOS CD Command on Drive Mappings — 87
- Review Questions — 89
- Case Study — 94

Table of Contents

4 Understanding NetWare Security — 97

- Defining Security Levels — 97
  - *The Supervisor* — 99
  - *The Supervisor Equivalent* — 99
  - *The FCONSOLE Operator* — 99
  - *The Workgroup Manager* — 100
  - *The User Account Manager* — 100
  - *The PCONSOLE Operator* — 100
  - *The End User* — 101
- Exploring NetWare Security Levels — 102
  - *Login/Password-Level Security* — 102
  - *User Rights* — 103
  - *File-Level Security* — 105
- Using Command-Line Utilities — 107
  - *The RIGHTS Command* — 108
  - *The TLIST Command* — 108
  - *The GRANT Command* — 109
  - *The REVOKE Command* — 109
  - *The REMOVE Command* — 110
- Understanding NCP Packet Signature — 111
  - *The NCP Packet Signature Process* — 112
  - *NCP Packet Signature Security Levels* — 113
  - *Change or Disable Packet Signing* — 116
- Review Questions — 117
- Case Study — 122

5 Utilities — 125

- Navigating the Menus — 126
- Exploring SYSCON — 127
  - *The SYSCON Accounting Option* — 127
  - *The Change Current Server Option* — 136
  - *The File Server Information Option* — 136
  - *The Group Information Option* — 137
  - *The Supervisor Options* — 144
  - *The User Information Option* — 148
- Exploring the FILER Menu Utility — 165
  - *Current Directory Information Menu* — 165
  - *Directory Contents Menu* — 167

Select Current Directory Menu	*170*
Set Filer Options Menu	*170*
The Volume Information Menu	*172*
Exploring the MAKEUSER Utility	173
MAKEUSER Keywords	*176*
Exploring the USERDEF Utility	178
Introducing ROUTEGEN	181
Nondedicated Protected Mode	*181*
Dedicated Real Mode	*182*
Dedicated Protected Mode	*182*
Examining NBACKUP	187
Enhanced Backup Using SBACKUP	193
Using the HELP Utility	195
Understanding the SESSION Menu Utility	197
Change Current Server	*198*
Drive Mappings	*198*
Group List	*200*
Search Mappings	*200*
Select Default Drive	*200*
User List	*201*
Using WSUPDATE	202
Review Questions	204
Case Study	210
6 Printing on a Novell Network	**213**
Understanding Network Printing	214
Examining and Defining Queues Using PCONSOLE	216
Current Print Job Entries	*217*
Current Queue Status	*223*
Currently Attached Servers	*224*
Print Queue ID	*224*
Queue Operators	*224*
Queue Servers	*224*
Queue Users	*225*
Installing Print Servers	225
One Printer Servicing Multiple Queues	226
One Queue Using Identical Printers	227
RPRINTER	*236*

Table of Contents

Directing Printer Output	236
The CAPTURE Command	*237*
The ENDCAP Command	*238*
The NPRINT Command	*239*
CAPTURE and NPRINT Flags	*239*
Controlling the Print Server	246
Customizing the Printers Using PRINTDEF	251
Print Devices	*251*
Forms	*255*
Creating Print Jobs Using PRINTCON	256
The PSC Command	*260*
Printing Under OS/2	264
Review Questions	264
Case Study	270

7 Customizing the User's Environment — 273

Choosing and Installing an Application	274
Ascertaining Software Network Support	*274*
Creating a Directory Structure	*276*
Installing the Application	*277*
Flagging the Files	*277*
Granting Access to Users	*278*
Developing Login Scripts	279
System Login Scripts	*279*
User Login Scripts	*280*
Default Login Scripts	*281*
Script Parameters	*281*
Login Script Commands	*282*
Creating Custom Menus	297
Menu Format	*298*
Menu Requirements	*301*
Menu-Calling Procedures	*302*
Techniques for Setting Up Menus	*304*
Input Variables	*308*
NetWare 3.12 Menuing System	*311*
Logging In to the Network	316
Running WSGEN To Generate IPX	*316*
Logging In through DOS	*323*

Logging In through ODI Drivers	*327*
Using the NetWare VLMs	*333*
NetWare 3.12 Environment Enhancements	337
Packet Burst	*338*
Large Internet Packet (LIP)	*339*
Using the ATTACH Command	339
Using the LOGOUT Command	340
Review Questions	340
Case Study	349

Part Three: NetWare 2.2 — 351

8 NetWare 2.2 System Manager — 353

Exploring the NetWare 2.2 File Server	355
File Server Memory	*356*
Value-Added Processes	*356*
NetWare 2.2 Disk Storage	*357*
System Fault Tolerance	*358*
File Server Console Commands	*359*
Exploring Network Security	360
Directory Rights	*361*
Effective Rights	*362*
Examining Network Printing	363
Setting Up Core Printing in a v2.2 Server	*364*
Review Questions	366
Case Study	372

9 NetWare 2.2 Advanced System Manager — 375

Installing NetWare 2.2	375
Module 1: Operating System Generation	*376*
Module 2: Linking and Configuring	*376*
Module 3: Track Zero Test	*377*
Module 4: File Server Definition	*377*
Starting the INSTALL Program	377
-E: Expert—Advanced Installation	*378*
-L: Linked or Linking Complete	*378*
-N: No Linking	*379*
-C: Configuration Complete	*379*
-M: Maintenance	*379*

-F: File Server Definition	*379*
-U: Upgrade	*379*
Investigating the INSTALL Options	380
Basic Installation	*380*
Filling in the Blanks	381
Basic Installation Demonstration	*382*
Advanced Installation Demonstration	*385*
Managing NetWare 2.2 Using FCONSOLE	393
Using FCONSOLE for Management Operations	*394*
Cache Statistics	*398*
Disk Statistics	*399*
File Server Statistics Summary	*400*
Exploring File Server Memory	404
NetWare 2.2 Memory Model	*407*
File Service Process	*412*
Dynamic Memory Pools	*413*
Review Questions	414
Case Study	420

Part Four: NetWare 3.1*x* — 423

10 NetWare 3.1*x* Administration — 425

Exploring NetWare 3.1*x*	425
Understanding NetWare 3.1*x* Security	429
User Rights	*430*
Combining IRMs and Trustee Rights	*433*
Understanding Attributes	435
Archive Needed	*436*
Execute Only	*436*
Hidden File	*436*
Read Audit and Write Audit	*437*
Read Only and Read/Write	*437*
Shareable and Nonshareable	*437*
System File	*438*
Transactional	*438*
Copy Inhibit	*438*
Delete Inhibit	*438*
Rename Inhibit	*439*
Purge	*439*

Using Directory Attributes	439
Hidden Directory	439
System Directory	439
Purge Directory	440
Using NetWare 3.1*x* Documentation	440
Understanding Workstation Utilities	441
ACONSOLE	442
Modified Utilities	449
Learning File Server Console Commands	452
ABORT REMIRROR	452
ADD NAME SPACE name TO VOLUME volume	452
BIND, UNBIND	452
CLS	453
ENABLE TTS, DISABLE TTS	453
DISPLAY NETWORKS	453
DISPLAY SERVERS	454
EXIT	455
DOWN	455
LIST DEVICES	455
LOAD path NLM parameter	455
MAGAZINE	456
MEDIA	456
MEMORY	456
MIRROR STATUS	456
MODULES	456
PROTOCOL	456
REGISTER MEMORY	457
REMIRROR PARTITION	457
REMOVE DOS	457
RESET ROUTER	457
SCAN FOR NEW DEVICES	457
SEARCH	458
SECURE CONSOLE	458
SET	459
SET TIME ZONE	459
SPEED	459
VERSION	459
VOLUMES	459

Table of Contents

Understanding NetWare Loadable Modules	459
Review Questions	460
Case Study	466
11 NetWare 3.1x Advanced System Manager	**469**
Providing Protocol Support in NetWare 3.1x	469
Discovering Other Protocol Options	470
NetWare Requester for OS/2	*471*
Transport Control Protocol/Internet Protocol (TCP/IP) and Network File System (NFS)	*471*
NetWare for Macintosh	*471*
Exploring the ODI Configuration Files	471
NET.CFG Driver Configuration Options	*472*
SHELL.CFG Parameters	*479*
Protecting Your Network	482
SBACKUP	*483*
Backup Hardware	*488*
Interface Adapters	*489*
Media and Drive Types	*491*
Optical Drives	*492*
Software	*494*
Backup Plans	*499*
Rotation Methods	*500*
Off-Site Backups	*503*
Testing	*504*
Disaster Recovery	*504*
Support Issues	*507*
Training	*508*
Consultants	*509*
Fixing Volumes Using VREPAIR	*509*
Exploring the NetWare 3.1x Memory Model	511
File Cache Buffer Memory Pool	*512*
Cache Movable and Non-Movable Memory Pools	*513*
Permanent Memory Pool	*514*
Semi-Permanent Memory Pool	*514*
Alloc Short Term Memory Pool	*514*
Understanding NetWare 3.1x Memory Configuration	516
NetWare Tables and Buffers	*518*
Directory Entry Table (DET)	*518*

File Allocation Table (FAT)	518
Directory Cache Buffers	519
Packet Receive Buffers	519
Optimizing Memory and Performance	520
Total Cache Buffers	521
Dirty Cache Buffers	521
Packet Receive Buffers	522
Directory Cache Buffers	522
Service Processes	522
File Server Statistics	522
Resource Tags	523
System Module Information	523
Resource Utilization	524
Processor Utilization	524
Using Console SET Parameters	525
Communications	525
Memory	527
File Caching	529
Directory Caching	530
Defining NetWare Name Service (NNS)	532
Domains	532
Profiles	532
Synchronization	532
Name Service Database	533
NETCON	534
Modified Utilities	535
The First NNS Server	536
Understanding Remote Management	537
ACONSOLE	541
RSETUP.EXE	541
EDIT.NLM	542
Installing and Upgrading NetWare 3.12 Server and Client	543
Installing a NetWare 3.1x Server	543
Upgrading Existing NetWare Servers	549
Installing a DOS Client	554
Review Questions	556
Case Study	564

Table of Contents

Part Five: Appendixes		**565**
A	**Answers to Review Questions**	**567**
	Chapter 3	567
	Chapter 4	568
	Chapter 5	568
	Chapter 6	568
	Chapter 7	569
	Chapter 8	569
	Chapter 9	570
	Chapter 10	570
	Chapter 11	570
	Appendix D	571
B	**Test Objectives**	**573**
	NetWare 2.2 System Manager: Test #50-20	573
	NetWare 2.2 Advanced System Manager: Test #50-44	576
	NetWare 3.11 System Manager: Test #50-91	579
	NetWare 3.1*x* System Administration: Test #50-130	582
	NetWare 3.11 Advanced System Manager: Test #50-82	586
	NetWare 3.11 OS Features Review Rev. 1.02: Test #50-45	589
	NetWare 3.1*x* Advanced Administration: Test #50-131	591
	NetWare 2.2 Certified NetWare Administrator: Test #50-115	594
	NetWare 3.11 Certified NetWare Administrator: Test #50-116	596
C	**Comparison Charts**	**601**
D	**NetWare 2.15**	**605**
	Exploring v2.15 and v2.2 Similarities	605
	Binderies	*606*
	Mapping and Directory Structure	*606*
	Major Utilities	*606*

xvii

System Fault Tolerance and Memory Management	*606*
Security	*607*
Login Scripts and Menus	*607*
Exploring NetWare 2.15 Security	607
Access Rights	*608*
Default Rights	*609*
Exploring Printing in NetWare 2.15	610
Using Backup and Restore	610
LARCHIVE and LRESTORE	*611*
NARCHIVE and NRESTORE	*611*
BACKUP and RESTORE	*612*
MACBACK	*612*
Third-Party Support	*612*
Review Questions	613
Case Study	615
Index	**617**

INTRODUCTION

The need for well-trained, competent individuals in today's computer industry is greater than ever. Novell, Inc., has seen the need to educate users who support NetWare products and has created the following certifications to meet the industry's needs:

- ◆ Certified NetWare Administrators (CNAs) have been tested to ensure basic competence with managing a specific NetWare operating system.

- ◆ Certified NetWare Engineers (CNEs) are tested for their knowledge of a wide variety of NetWare server products, as well as for their understanding of LAN hardware, software, and communication technologies. This certification is in high demand by systems engineers, consultants, and administrators of NetWare products.

- ◆ Enterprise CNEs are additionally certified for their competence with a variety of NetWare products, which might include network management and diagnostic tools, UNIX or Macintosh support products, or communication and gateway products.

Candidates for these certifications must pass one or more tests. A variety of preparation methods are available, including classroom instruction from Novell Authorized Education Centers (NAECs) and self-study kits available from Novell. The test objectives for each test are public, and candidates can choose to study by using their own materials. Novell, Inc. also provides assessment disks with sample test questions to help users prepare for taking the necessary tests. These disks can be acquired through most NAECs, as well as through the NetWire forum on CompuServe.

Introduction

Most candidates use a variety of these training methods, and many feel the need for additional training help. The *NetWare Training Guide* series from New Riders Publishing is intended to provide supplemental study information to help you pass the tests required to achieve Novell certification.

Who Should Read this Book?

NetWare Training Guide is written for individuals who need to learn more about Novell NetWare because of a job responsibility and for those who need to know more about system administration and the operating system. The following chapters guide you through the various revisions of the NetWare product in an effort to acquaint you with the variety of security and functionality that NetWare offers.

What Is Covered in this Book?

Managing NetWare Systems is the first volume of NRP's *NetWare Training Guides*. It addresses the following NetWare certification requirements:

- NetWare 2.2 System Manager
- NetWare 2.2 Advanced System Manager
- NetWare 3.11 System Manager
- NetWare 3.11 Advanced System Manager
- NetWare 2.15 System Update
- Certified NetWare 2.2 Administrator
- Certified NetWare 3.1*x* Administrator

What Topics Are Not Included?

Managing NetWare Systems covers the test material with regard to the Operating Systems only.

CNE candidates also will be interested in the companion volume, *NetWare Training Guide*: *Networking Technologies*, which covers these core courses for the CNE curriculum:

- DOS/microcomputer concepts
- NetWare service and support
- Networking technologies

This volume does not include coverage of NetWare 4.*x*. If you are seeking certification as a NetWare 4 administrator, you will be interested in two other titles in NRP's *NetWare Training Guide* series:

- *NetWare 4 Update* enables those who are currently certified on NetWare 2.*x* and 3.*x* to efficiently upgrade their certifications for NetWare 4.*x*.
- *NetWare 4 Administration* is a complete course in NetWare 4 administration for the new NetWare administrator. This book will meet the needs of those who are seeking a CNA certification for NetWare 4 or who are pursuing a CNE on a NetWare 4 track.

The Details of this Book

You can flip quickly through this book to get a feel for its organization. The book is organized into five parts that lay the foundation on which you can build an understanding of the current NetWare operating systems. Each chapter is introduced, then the topics are covered in depth. At the end of each chapter are review questions in the form of multiple-choice answers and case studies that help you apply each of the concepts presented in the chapters. Specific answers to the multiple-choice questions are given, but the case studies can have multiple answers.

Introduction

The following section provides an overview of each chapter in this book.

Part One describes the certification process:

- ◆ Chapter 1 introduces the CNE, ECNE, and CNA programs. This chapter teaches you about the requirements and benefits of certification.

- ◆ Chapter 2 describes the different types of tests and also explains how to register for the tests. You also learn about the various tests involved in becoming certified.

Part Two describes the features common to current NetWare versions:

- ◆ Chapter 3 teaches you about directory structures, drive mappings, and moving about the network.

- ◆ Chapter 4 discusses security concepts. In this chapter, you learn about the different user types and how to create and manage users and groups. This chapter discusses rights and attributes for files and directories.

- ◆ In Chapter 5, you learn about NetWare menu utilities and several command-line utilities that enable you to create and manage users and files on the network.

- ◆ Chapter 6 comprehensively covers the topic of printing. In this chapter, you learn to navigate the menu utilities that apply to printing and learn about the printing command-line utilities.

- ◆ Chapter 7 is all about customizing the environment for the user. In this chapter, you learn about loading applications on the network, creating login scripts and menus, and creating the proper files for the workstation so that a user can log in to the network.

Part Three describes the features specific to NetWare 2.2:

- ◆ Chapter 8 deals with basic v2.2 administration skills. In this chapter, you learn the ways in which v2.2 is different from v2.15 and v3.11.

The Details of this Book

- Chapter 9 deals with advanced v2.2 topics, such as memory management and accounting.

Part Four describes the features specific to NetWare 3.11:

- In Chapter 10, you learn about the features of v3.11 that make this operating system so unique and well-liked. Here you learn about the features that the system administrator has at his disposal for security and functionality.

- Chapter 11 covers the advanced topics that deal with v3.11, such as memory management, SBACKUP, and NetWare Naming Service.

Part Five contains four appendixes:

- In Appendix A, you find the answers to the multiple-choice questions.

- In Appendix B, you find a listing of the testing objectives.

- In Appendix C, you find comparison charts that you can use to study for the tests. These charts quickly point out many similarities and differences between the different NetWare versions.

- Appendix D describes the features of NetWare 2.15, a version that you might still encounter in many NetWare LAN environments.

Deciding on a Path

Chapter 1
Novell's Certification Programs

Chapter 2
Studying for the Certification Exams

Novell's Certification Programs

Networking knowledge is a commodity that is in ever-increasing demand in the computer industry. Every day, corporations with local-, municipal-, and wide-area networks discover the value of relying on current staff to maintain the network's integrity. Security issues, reliability concerns, and general maintenance problems all need to be resolved quickly and efficiently.

Companies always have been concerned with the ways in which they best can address the needs that arise from using a network. Rarely is the best solution to skip over current staff and hire an outsider to fit the bill. Hidden somewhere in most computer departments is an individual with the aptitude and drive to manage the network. A program that trains this individual on the company's specific operating system is valuable. Of even greater value to the business is a way to assess the knowledge this person has obtained.

Occasionally, the need arises to look beyond the in-house staff for a network support person. When shuffling through resumes, employers cannot always ascertain the exact amount of network knowledge applicants have. The applicants might have a broad knowledge of service, support, administration, and more; or they might only have expertise in administering specific versions of

Chapter 1: Novell's Certification Programs

operating systems. An established method for employers to spot the type of individual for which they are searching definitely eases the difficult task of filling network support positions.

Novell, Inc. recognized these problems and instituted several certification programs to help place the necessary information in the hands of the people supporting the network. If you have a Novell network that needs a competent administrator or technician, Novell's certification programs can help you get the best-quality people into those positions. If you are responsible for managing a NetWare network, Novell's certification programs can help enhance the knowledge and skills you need. If you are considering a career as a network manager, Novell's CNA, CNE, and ECNE certifications can make it easier for you to get started in that career.

This chapter provides the following information about Novell's certification programs:

- Overview of the CNE, ECNE, and CNA programs
- Understanding candidates' requirements
- Discovering the benefits of earning certification
- Exploring the tests' characteristics
- Beginning the certification process
- Finding additional training

Choosing the Right Certification

Each company has special needs. Some companies need people who can troubleshoot hardware and software problems; others simply need people capable of installing applications and solving user complaints. Novell offers several levels of certification, each with a different area of expertise. These certifications include the following:

- Certified NetWare Engineer (CNE)
- Enterprise Certified NetWare Engineer (ECNE)
- Certified NetWare Administrator (CNA)

CNE: The Certified NetWare Engineer

The Certified NetWare Engineer program was created by Novell so that NetWare customers easily can distinguish people committed to learning about NetWare. Achieving CNE status means that you have passed Novell's rigorous testing requirements. Through the certification programs, you can establish a special relationship with Novell Technical Support (NTS) not available to the general public.

Anyone who works with PC hardware and Novell products is a candidate for the CNE program.

Certification Requirements

The certification process begins after you take the first test. The CNE program revolves around your ability to pass the required tests, which you can take in any order. Chapter 2 contains an easy reference chart to help you map your progress with the tests. From the time you take your first test, whether or not you pass that test, you have one year to complete the program.

The Novell certification process generally requires the following skills and knowledge:

- CNE candidates must have a thorough understanding of DOS and microcomputer concepts. The certification programs become ineffective when the CNE candidate memorizes the material without learning the basic information. For the CNE program, the essential information is a fundamental understanding of what DOS does and what hardware makes up a personal computer.
- CNE candidates are responsible for planning their own curriculum within Novell guidelines. Tests are taken at

Chapter 1: Novell's Certification Programs

Drake Authorized Testing Centers (DATC). After taking a test, you receive a printed copy of your test results. Retain this copy as proof that you took the test. Although Drake is very reliable, test results occasionally are lost. Keep your test results easily available to verify your progress.

◆ Novell has individual classes that relate to all tests except DOS and micro hardware. These courses are offered through Novell Authorized Education Centers (NAEC) nationwide. Test material is taken directly from the course material provided by the NAECs. If you decide to take NetWare courses from an NAEC or NEAP, Novell recommends that you take the related certification exam within six weeks of completing that course. Novell only guarantees that the exam questions relate directly to the course objectives if you take the exam within the recommended six-week period. This statement does not mean that the exam will definitely change, only that it is subject to change. Call 800/233-3382 for more information about NAECs in your area.

◆ As NetWare makes advancements in networking technology, CNEs are responsible for fulfilling continuing education requirements. You have one year to complete these requirements. Unless you meet all continuing requirements within the required time frame, your certification expires. To become recertified, you must retake all the certification exams. In addition, if you completed only some recertification requirements, they are voided. You must start over, and you must complete the program within one year, just as you did the first time that you became certified.

Novell mails you notification of continuing education requirements, so make sure that you send any address changes to the following address:

Novell CNE/ECNE/CNA Administration
Mail Stop E-31-1
122 East 1700 South
Provo, UT 84606

You also can fax address-change information to 801/429-5565.

Certification Benefits

The biggest benefit to becoming a CNE is industry recognition. The network computing industry recognizes individuals who have earned the Certified NetWare Engineer credential as LAN technicians capable of providing superior network support.

Some less obvious benefits also are available. After you become NetWare certified, for example, you own the certification even if your employer paid for it. A company cannot become certified—only an individual. You can, therefore, take your certification with you no matter which company you choose to work for. Novell NetWare certifications can enhance your resume and your chance of being hired if you plan to search for a NetWare networking position.

Other more tangible benefits also come with the CNE certification, including the following:

- The Network Support Encyclopedia
- Novell Technical Support
- Authorization to use the CNE logo
- Eligibility as a CNEPA member

Network Support Encyclopedia

All CNEs receive a free copy of the *Network Support Encyclopedia* (*NSE*). The *NSE* is an electronic information database that contains valuable technical information. The *NSE* is intended to help you install or maintain your network. It is available in two volumes (Standard and Novell Professional), and on tape or CD-ROM. The Novell Professional volume, however, is available only on CD-ROM.

The *NSE* contains the following information:

- Novell "Technotes" and bulletins
- Novell product documentation (the manual set that ships with the Novell product)

Chapter 1:   Novell's Certification Programs

- Novell press releases, success stories, and reseller bulletins
- A copy of the *NetWare Buyers Guide*
- Novell NetWare files, patches, and fixes
- Additional device drivers
- Special utilities such as printing and print server diagnostics
- Education information on NAEC course offerings and Certified NetWare Instructor information

The *NSE* also includes third-party information that is of value to you as a NetWare system administrator or manager. In addition, it is compatible with Folio Views. If you have Folio Views, you can create your own information databases to add to your *NSE* copy. The Folio Previews that ships with the *NSE* lets you browse, search, and retrieve text from the original *NSE* database and any other database you might create using Folio Views.

The *NSE* is updated periodically. These updates are available to you if you purchase a subscription to the *NSE*. CNEs and CNEPA members receive discounts on the *NSE* update. For more information on the *NSE*, call or write as follows:

> Novell, Inc.
> 122 East 1700 South
> Provo, UT 84606
> 800/NETWARE in the US and Canada
> 801/429-5588 outside the US and Canada

To place an order:

> Novell, Inc.
> P.O. Box 5205
> Denver, CO 80217
> 800/377-4136 in the US and Canada
> 303/297-2725 outside the US and Canada
> Fax: 303/294-0930

Technical Support Provided by Novell

CNEs receive two free support incidents and the ability to purchase additional support incidents for a 50-percent discount. The two free support calls are good for one year from the date you receive your certification. An *incident* is the identification, follow-up, and resolution of a problem. The support is provided by Novell Technical Support (NTS) and is available 24 hours a day, seven days a week.

Utilizing the CNE Logo

After you have achieved CNE status, you can use the CNE logo on your business literature. This identifier lets your customers know that you are a Novell-certified service provider.

When you receive your CNE welcome-aboard kit, you also receive CNE logo copies. Three types of logos are available. One is intended for use in advertising that you might place in your local phone company's yellow pages. Another is for use on business cards and letterhead. Another, slightly modified variety is intended to accommodate those of you who live in a state that does not enable you to use the word "Engineer" in your CNE designation.

If you are a CNE and you need additional logos or a copy of the logo-usage guide, you can obtain these items by calling 800/377-4136. You need to give them your certification number when you call, so keep it handy.

CNE Professional Association Membership

Novell encourages all CNEs to join the CNE Professional Association (CNEPA). The CNEPA is a nonprofit organization created to help you keep your technical skills current. Only CNEs can join this organization. With your membership, you can access a special CNE forum on NetWire. *NetWire* is a special-interest group on CompuServe.

After you begin the CNE certification process, you are eligible to join the CNEPA as an associate member. The membership fee is approximately two-thirds the regular membership fee and enrolls you as an associate member for six months. If you complete your CNE requirements within six months of joining the CNEPA, the associate membership fee that you paid is applied to your regular membership fee, if you apply for full membership. Full membership is renewed annually.

Becoming a CNEPA member includes many benefits, one of which is its publication, *Network News*. The *Network News* keeps you up to date on important issues such as continuing certification requirements and chapter news. In addition, it helps you keep your technical knowledge current by providing technical information on Novell product changes. In addition, *Network News* often provides troubleshooting tips and tactics and includes classified advertisements for companies looking to hire NetWare-certified people.

CNEPA chapters can be found across the country including Arizona, California, Colorado, Connecticut, District of Columbia, Florida, Georgia, Hawaii, Illinois, Kentucky, Louisiana, Massachusetts, Maryland, Mississippi, Minnesota, Missouri, North Carolina, New Hampshire, New Jersey, New Mexico, New York, Oklahoma, Ohio, Oregon, Pennsylvania, South Carolina, Texas, Utah, Virginia, Vermont, Washington, and Wisconsin. In addition, four international chapters in Australia, British Columbia, England, and Ontario also are available.

For more information on joining the CNEPA, contact the CNEPA executive offices at 801/429-7227, or write to the following address:

> CNEPA
> 122 East 1700 South, MS E-31-1
> Provo, Utah 84606

ECNE: The Enterprise Certified NetWare Engineer

The Enterprise Certified NetWare Engineer (ECNE) program is a significant level above the CNE program. This certification enables the CNE to specialize in several different areas of networking, including TCP/IP, Communication, and Troubleshooting.

Certification Requirements

- To become an ECNE, you already must be a CNE, which means that you already have CNE program benefits. If you have had your CNE certification for some time, make sure that your status is current. You must be a CNE in good standing to begin the ECNE program.

- The ECNE program requires you to earn 14 credits of elective tests. Please refer to the chart in Chapter 2 to determine which electives are available.

Certification Benefits

The network computing industry recognizes individuals who have earned the Enterprise Certified NetWare Engineer credential as LAN specialists: the greatest benefit in spending the time to become an ECNE. NetWare clients recognize that the ECNE belongs to individuals who have surpassed the level of CNE and possess a wide range of networking expertise.

You also can use the ECNE logo. This logo helps you advertise the fact that you successfully completed the rigorous testing regimen that Novell requires of ECNEs.

CNA: The Certified NetWare Administrator

The CNA program is Novell's entry-level certification program. It is designed to show that an individual has obtained a minimum level of knowledge about networking by using one of Novell's NetWare products—NetWare 2.2 or NetWare 3.1*x*.

The CNA program also is Novell's newest certification program. Since its inception in late 1992, over 3,500 individuals have successfully met the program's requirements and been granted the status of Certified NetWare Administrator.

Chapter 1: Novell's Certification Programs

The Certified NetWare Administrator program is for individuals who manage a NetWare network and are responsible for its day-to-day operation. The CNA is responsible for system administration and fine-tuning. If you are skilled at administering a v2.2 or v3.1x NetWare LAN, then this program is the one you should pursue.

The CNA path is appropriate for the person who manages the LAN but not for the hardware technician. Though the CNA program is not intended as a stepping stone to the CNE program, it helps you learn valuable information that can assist you later if you choose to get your CNE certification. In fact, many of the CNA candidate's NetWare 2.2 and 3.1x course objectives are identical to CNE program objectives. As a CNA, however, you are not required to meet many of the advanced networking course objectives that the CNE candidate is required to meet.

Certification Requirements

As a CNA candidate, you must know DOS and basic microcomputer concepts. Although you are not specifically tested on these concepts, you need a working knowledge in these areas in order to successfully administer a NetWare LAN. The basic concepts to be mastered in these areas include the following:

- Basic functions of DOS
- Computer boot process
- Internal and external DOS commands and their related syntax and switches
- Disk drive operations including formatting and partitioning of both fixed and floppy disks
- DOS file-naming rules and conventions
- DOS directory structure and command search order
- Purpose, creation, process, and commands used in batch files
- Purpose and function of DOS configuration files, their related commands, and system board configuration settings

- Major hardware components of a microcomputer
- Basic functions of a microcomputer
- Types of microprocessor chips and differences between them
- Basic data bus characteristics
- Purpose and function of interrupt, memory, and I/O address settings
- Main function and types of memory
- Video display types and elements
- Parallel and serial port communications using external devices or peripherals

Because you are expected to have a working knowledge of DOS and microcomputers before you take the CNA test, Novell does not provide courses on DOS and microcomputers. Novell does provide an alternative, however, if you need training in these areas and are unable to find it elsewhere, or if you simply prefer to study DOS and microcomputer concepts using Novell materials. Novell has authorized workbooks for both DOS and microcomputer concepts.

 You can purchase these Novell-authorized education workbooks from any NAEC or NEAP (if the course is currently offered).

In addition, New Riders Publishing's book entitled *Networking Technologies*, the companion volume to this *NetWare Training Guide*, also covers DOS and microcomputer concepts.

CNA candidates take only one test. The test you take depends on which version of NetWare—2.2 or 3.1*x*—you plan to support. Each test is comprehensive and is designed to measure your level of networking skill and knowledge. These tests cover the following areas:

Chapter 1: Novell's Certification Programs

- Adding and deleting users and groups
- Configuring printers
- Modifying configuration files
- Creating and modifying user menus
- Managing basic mail services
- Making Novell ElectroText available to users
- Creating and debugging login scripts
- Loading applications
- Maintaining network security
- Managing workstation shells and requesters
- Backing up the file server
- Troubleshooting

Certification Benefits

Estimates indicate that approximately three million LANs exist today. Most LANs need someone to administer them, whether that individual is a dedicated or part-time LAN administrator. Your CNA certification gives you industry recognition. The computer networking industry recognizes that Novell has set a standard of competence for network administration. Your CNA certificate proves that you have made a commitment to learning ways to manage NetWare.

You also gain improved job performance through increased knowledge. When you learn about the network's intricate workings, you automatically learn ways the network can best function in your own customized environment. This knowledge makes your network easier to manage and makes you more productive.

Your increased networking knowledge and the CNA designation tell your current or future employers that you are qualified to handle the tasks of administering a NetWare network. They also increase your potential for career advancement and make you more eligible for a position as a NetWare administrator in another company. Your certification also might contribute to increases in your current or future salary.

Taking the Certification Tests

Drake Training and Technologies provides the testing and delivers the results for the certification programs. Drake has many sites throughout the country at which you can take the certification tests. When you are ready to take a test, call 800/RED-EXAM. The Drake certification personnel will ask for your name, address, Social Security number, and billing method. After payment is received, you can schedule a specific date at the testing center of your choice. If you are using a credit card, you can complete the entire process in two working days. Each center has different schedules, which Drake can provide to you.

At the testing center, you need a picture ID with a signature as well as one other piece of identification that has your signature. A proctor shows you to the testing room, which generally is protected from outside disturbances. You have 30 to 90 minutes to complete the test, depending on the type of test and the number of questions.

The tests are computerized; questions are answered by using the keyboard or mouse, and some testing centers provide touch-screen capabilities. The tests are downloaded to the testing center from Drake the night before the test, and results are automatically sent via modem to Drake at the end of each day. Novell receives the results from Drake within 48 hours.

When you finish taking the test, you immediately get your results on the computer screen. The proctor also presents a printed copy to you. The printed copy must have the Drake embossed seal on it to be valid. Retain this copy as proof that you passed the test.

You can take primarily two types of exams: adaptive and form.

Chapter 1: Novell's Certification Programs

Form Tests

Form tests are the older style of testing. As new tests are developed, they first appear as form tests until enough answers are gathered to devise an adaptive test.

Form tests have a set number of questions for each test, and you are given a set amount of time to answer all the questions. In this type of test, you can mark and review your answers if you have enough time. All questions are multiple-choice.

Adaptive Tests

This book prepares you for adaptive tests. In an *adaptive test*, each question you are asked depends on the answer you gave to the preceding question. You cannot, therefore, review your answers after you are finished.

The first question is of medium difficulty. If you answer the question correctly, the next question is more difficult. If you answer it incorrectly, the next question you receive is easier. This way, in as little as 10 or 15 questions, the test can determine what your experience level is. If it is higher than the score that Novell has predetermined, then you pass the test. Adaptive tests consist of 10 to 25 questions. The newer the test, the more questions you are asked.

Much effort has been put into developing adaptive testing. This type of test's main benefit is that it is less stressful than other methods. Your testing experience is briefer, and the test is tailored to you individually. Before taking the actual certification exams, you also can take computerized self-evaluation tests.

Self-Evaluation Tests

Novell has prepared a Certification Assessment Diskette to help you determine your level of NetWare knowledge. The disk contains sample certification test questions designed to give you practice at answering questions of a format similar to questions on the actual certification exams.

The questions on this disk cover the concepts that you need to know in order to pass the CNA, CNE, or ECNE test you are preparing to take. The higher you score on the assessment test, therefore, the more likely you are to pass the actual test. The self-evaluation test, however, is intended primarily to help you determine where you might need more study or more preparation. A high score on the assessment test does not guarantee that you can pass the actual certification exams, but does give you a feel for what is expected of you and the types of questions you can anticipate when you take the actual tests.

The disk contains several tests. You can take all the tests or only the tests of interest to you. When you complete a test, your score appears along with recommendations for additional study (called "prescriptions"). All recommended study materials are available from your local NAEC, and also might, in many instances, be available from your local NEAP.

The Novell Certification Assessment Diskette is made available to NAECs and NEAPs at no charge. Most NAECs and NEAPs copy and distribute them as needed. Novell owns the rights to the disk, but copying and distributing is permissible as long as it is *not* distributed for resale. Thus, you should be able to get a Novell Certification Assessment Diskette copy, at no charge, from your local NAEC.

NAECs and NEAPs

If you decide that, in addition to the self-study preparation that this book provides, you also want to obtain Novell reference materials or take a NetWare course, your local NAEC or NEAP can supply your needs.

Some people find that taking a course or two helps answer their questions and brings together all their acquired knowledge into a form that is practical for them to use. If that description fits you,

Chapter 1: Novell's Certification Programs

and you want to take a course or obtain additional study materials, you can contact one of the more than 1,000 NAECs and NEAPs worldwide.

You often can find your local NAEC by checking the yellow pages of your phone book for a school that has the official Novell NAEC designation. Authorized NAECs can use the official NAEC logo in their advertisements. Check with your local community college or university to see if it is an NEAP. If neither method is sufficient for you, you can call 800/233-3382 in the United States and Canada or 801/429-5508 elsewhere to get a list of NAECs or NEAPs in your area.

After you locate an NAEC or NEAP near you, you can enroll for a course or, in many cases, purchase additional materials without enrolling in a course. If you take a course through an NAEC or NEAP, you can be assured of quality. Novell guarantees complete customer satisfaction for all its courses. It offers this guarantee because NAECs and NEAPs are required to meet a rigorous set of standards before they become authorized to teach Novell courses. These standards include the following:

- All courses must include Novell-developed course materials
- The facility must meet equipment and student-comfort standards set by Novell
- Courses at either facility must be taught by a Certified NetWare Instructor (CNI)
- Courses must meet (or exceed, as many NEAPs frequently do) the time guidelines for the course as set by Novell

Summary

At this time, you should have a good understanding of what is expected of you when you enter Novell's certification program. Each program has different requirements and benefits.

CNA is for the system administrator and requires knowledge of managing the network's software portion, fine-tuning the network, and setting up printing capabilities.

Summary

CNE is for the network engineer. The CNE must understand the same items as the CNA, but also know ways to install and support the most popular Novell operating systems and add-on products.

ECNE is for the CNE who wants recognition as a NetWare specialist. The ECNE can select areas of expertise and must pass the test required by Novell for each specialty.

After you decide which certification process is right for you, Chapter 2 explains methods you can use to study for the appropriate tests.

Studying for the Certification Exams

CHAPTER 2

Chapter 1 introduced you to the certification programs, their requirements, and their benefits. This chapter helps you prepare to study and take the tests.

In this chapter, you learn several methods of studying for the tests. Each person taking these tests can, of course, develop his or her own methods for remembering information. This chapter provides some alternative ways to study.

In this chapter, you find the following:

- ◆ Maps to chart your progress through the certification process
- ◆ Information to help you decide when you are ready to take the tests
- ◆ Memorization techniques
- ◆ A list of the exams for which this book helps you prepare

The first thing you need to see is the progress map.

Chapter 2: Studying for the Certification Exams

Using the Progress Maps

Included in this manual are three maps to help you chart your progress as you become a CNE and ECNE.

- The first map shows the prerequisite, operating system, and core requirements for obtaining your CNE.

- The second map shows the core requirement (CNE certification) and operating system requirements for obtaining your ECNE.

- The third map shows the elective credits you can take to complete the requirements for the CNE and the ECNE, with the differences noted.

Because the CNA only needs to take one test, no chart is necessary.

Record the date when you pass each test. CNE requirements are tracked automatically by Novell. After you have completed your ECNE requirements, notify Novell.

CNE Progress Map

Prerequisite Requirement: 2 credits

Date Passed	Test Name	Test Number	Credits
_____	DOS/Microcomputer Concepts	50-15	2

Operating System Expertise: 5 Credits

You must have 5 credits from the NetWare 2.2 or the NetWare 3.1x operating system courses. If you choose to test your operating system expertise in NetWare 2.2, complete the following tests:

Using the Progress Maps

	v2.2 System Manager	50-20	3
	and		
	v2.2 Advanced System Manager	50-44	2

If you choose to test your operating system expertise in NetWare 3.1*x*, select one combination from among the four shown below:

	v3.11 System Manager	50-91	3
	and		
	v3.11 Advanced System Manager	50-82	2

or

	v3.11 System Manager	50-91	3
	and		
	v3.1*x* Advanced Administration	50-131	2

or

	v3.1*x* Administration	50-130	3
	and		
	v3.11 System Manager	50-91	3

or

	v3.1*x* Administration	50-130	3
	and		
	v3.1*x* Advanced Administration	50-131	2

Chapter 2: Studying for the Certification Exams

The NetWare 3.1x Administration and v3.1x Advanced Administration tests (#50-130 and #50-131) will eventually replace the NetWare 3.11 System Administrator and v3.11 Advanced System Administrator tests (#50-91 and #50-82). The last day, therefore, that you can register for tests #50-91 and #50-82 is May 24, 1994. In addition, the last day you can take either test is June 30, 1994. After those dates, you must register for and take the NetWare 3.1x tests #50-130 and #50-131.

Core Requirement: 8 credits

_____	NetWare Service and Support	50-46	5
_____	Networking Technologies	50-80	3

ECNE Progress Map

Core Requirement

_____	CNE Certification

Operating System Expertise: 5 credits

You must have 5 credits from v3.11 System Manager and v3.11 Advanced System Manager, or from v3.1x Administration and v3.1x Advanced Administration. You can have these credits in any combination as shown on the CNE Progress Map. If you choose this path for your CNE, you do not need to take these tests again. You must, however, take two tests if you took the v2.2 OS expertise track.

_____	v3.11 System Manager	50-91	3
	or		
_____	v3.1x Administration	50-130	3

Using the Progress Maps

	and		
_____	v3.11 Advanced System Manager	50-82	2
	or		
_____	v3.1x Advanced Administration	50-131	2

The NetWare 3.1x Administration and v3.1x Advanced Administration tests (#50-130 and #50-131) will eventually replace the NetWare 3.11 System Administrator and v3.11 Advanced System Administrator tests (#50-91 and #50-82). The last day, therefore, that you can register for tests #50-91 and #50-82 is May 24, 1994. In addition, the last day you can take either test is June 30, 1994. After those dates, you must register for and take the NetWare 3.1x tests #50-130 and #50-131.

If you are interested in NetWare 4.0, a NetWare 3.11 to 4.0 Update option is available. This test is #50-124. Choosing this option when seeking a NetWare 3.11 or v3.1x OS track changes your elective credit requirements from 10 to 7. The *NetWare Training Guide: NetWare 4 Update* book provides information regarding certification in NetWare 4.0.

Elective Tests

You must earn four elective credits to obtain your CNE and 10 (or 12, see preceding note) elective credits to complete the ECNE certification requirements. Elective credits obtained during your CNE certification process can apply to your ECNE. NetWare 3.1x and v3.11 elective credits do not apply, however.

Electives Map

CNEs must take four credits of electives and ECNEs must take 10 (or 12 as previously noted) credits of electives to fulfill the electives requirements of the program.

 CNEs must take four credits of electives. NetWare 2.2, NetWare 3.11, and NetWare 3.1x tests can be counted as electives if they were not taken to meet the operating system requirements, as noted in the following two paragraphs.

ECNEs must have 10 (or 12) elective credits chosen from the following list. NetWare 2.2 tests can be counted as electives for the ECNE program, even if they were taken to meet the operating system requirements for the CNE, because the ECNE program's required NetWare 3.11 or 3.1x tests can be applied to ECNE operating system requirements.

Novell plans to add ECNE operating system tracks for other operating systems in 1994. If you select alternate operating system tests to meet your operating system requirements for the CNE program, you can apply NetWare 2.2, 3.11, and 3.1x tests as elective credit.

Operating Systems
(Please note all conditions for operating systems tests)

If you did not meet operating system requirements using NetWare 2.2 tests, the following tests count toward certification:

Date Passed	Test Name	Test Number	Credits
_____	v2.2 System Manager	50-20	3
_____	v2.2 Advanced System Manager	50-44	2

Elective Tests

If you did not meet your operating system requirements by taking the NetWare 3.11 or 3.1x tests, you can use two of the following tests to meet elective requirements for certification:

_____	v3.11 System Manager	50-91	3
_____	v3.11 Advanced System Manager	50-82	2
_____	v3.11 OS Features	50-45*	2
_____	v3.1x Administration	50-130	3
_____	v3.1x Advanced Administration	50-131	2

Note Test 50-45 cannot be counted as elective credit if you took and passed tests 50-91 or 50-82.

Reseller Authorization Tests

You can count *one* of the following tests:

_____	Product Information	50-100	1

Elective credit for this test is granted only if you complete your certification before August 6, 1994.

_____	Product Info for Gold Authorized Resellers	50-19	2

Elective credit for this test is granted only if you complete your certification before April 9, 1995.

Chapter 2: Studying for the Certification Exams

TCP/IP

_____	NetWare TCP/IP Transport	50-86	2
_____	LAN WorkPlace for DOS 4.1 Administration	50-104	2
_____	NetWare NFS	50-87	2
_____	NetWare NFS Gateway	50-119	1

Troubleshooting

_____	NetWare for SAA Installation and Troubleshooting	50-85	3
_____	LANtern Services Manager	50-89	3
_____	LANalyzer for Windows	50-105	1

Connectivity

_____	NetWare for Macintosh Connectivity	50-93	2
_____	NetWare Dial In/ Dial Out Connectivity	50-112	2

Internetworking

_____	Fundamentals of Internetwork and Management Design	50-106	2
_____	NetWare Internetworking Products	50-117	2

Elective Tests

UNIX

_____	UNIX OS Fundamentals for NetWare Users	50-107	2
_____	UnixWare Personal Edition Installation and Configuration	50-102	2
_____	UnixWare Application Server Installation and Configuration	50-103	2

Other

_____	NetWare Management Systems for Windows	50-128	2
_____	NetWare Global MHS	50-108	2
_____	NetWare 4.0 Installation and Configuration Workshop	50-126	2
_____	Btrieve: An Overview	50-127	1
_____	Programming with Btrieve v2.0	50-129	2

If you complete your CNE certification before the dates noted in the following list, and you have already taken the following discontinued tests, the indicated tests still count as elective credits toward your CNE.

Chapter 2: Studying for the Certification Exams

June 25, 1994:

_____	Product Information for Authorized Resellers	50-18	2
_____	v2.2 System Update	50-35	2
_____	v2.15 to v2.2 Update	50-37	2

August 6, 1994:

_____	Advanced LANalyzer for Token Ring	50-97	3
_____	LANalyzer Basics	50-110	3
_____	Advance LANalyzer for Ethernet	50-111	3

October 29, 1994:

_____	LAN WorkPlace for DOS Administration	50-95	2

November 30, 1994:

_____	NetWare Internetworking Products	50-109	2

Note To get additional information regarding the Novell Certified CNE/ECNE programs, call 800/NETWARE or 801/429-5508. In Europe, you can call +49/211/5277-744.

Preparing To Study

Two principles apply when you are studying for the certification exams. If you follow these maxims, the process of studying and actually learning the material is easier and less fatiguing:

- You must completely and thoroughly understand, in the context in which it is presented, any fact that you must remember.
- You must consciously decide that you want to remember the information and know why it is important.

The information presented in this book is here for two reasons. First, the information is important to anyone who needs to understand the way Novell NetWare works, specifically in the following areas:

- Security
- Printing
- Memory configuration
- Hardware and software basics
- Utilities
- Backup
- Login scripts
- Applications installation
- Prevention and maintenance

This information comprises the fundamental knowledge on which everything else you learn about NetWare is based. This book is the first step to ensuring your success in administering a network.

Second, the information contained in this book is not trivial. It includes all the objectives stated by Novell on which the tests are based. Everything presented in this book is based on a hierarchy of knowledge. Each small piece of information contributes to the total concept that must be learned.

Chapter 2: Studying for the Certification Exams

Studying for the certification tests is not to be taken lightly. On the adaptive tests, you are asked between 10 and 25 questions per test. If you take three tests, you encounter between 30 and 75 unique questions. You cannot predict which questions you will get or even which specific topics will be covered. The questions are designed so that you must understand the entire concept to answer the selective questions. Ultimately, you need to know and understand all the information in this book not only for the test, but for the sake of any network with which you come in contact.

This book is filled with ways to remember concepts. As you read through the material, notice that many items are emphasized or denoted in such a way as to catch your attention. These notes are key concepts to which you should pay special attention. They are shown in such a way as to provide quick study notes. If you review these items before the test, you can increase your familiarity with the information.

You can use several methods to take the certification exams. The first is to study the information for one test, and then take that test. Although this method works for many people, it forces the tester to memorize the information, spew it back for the exam, and then forget it while studying for the next test.

This book is designed to teach you the whole concept from beginning to end, then the specifics for each operating system. The method in this book helps you learn all the information, then take the tests all together.

Even though maps were included in this chapter for the ECNE program, this book focuses on the information you need to successfully pass the exams for CNA or CNE certification. The ECNE maps were included because some CNEs choose to continue the certification program and obtain their ECNE as well. If you decide upon this course of action, choosing CNA tests wisely can reduce the total number of tests you take for the ECNE program.

Other volumes provide additional information to help you toward your ECNE.

Choosing a Certification Path

This book is divided into five parts to help you easily locate and study the material you need for the specific certification path you select (see fig. 2.1).

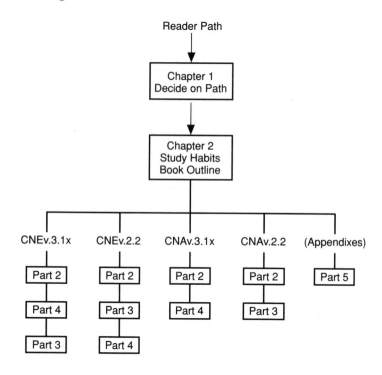

Figure 2.1

Study this book's parts that apply to your specific certification path.

If you select the CNE path in v3.1x, for example, study Part 2 then Part 4. The tests you take first (after passing the DOS Microcomputer Concepts test) are the v3.11 System Manager or the v3.1x Administration exams, and the v3.11 Advanced System Manager or the v3.1x Advanced Administration exam. Next, learn Part 3 and review Part 2 to pass v2.2 electives tests. This method gives

Chapter 2: Studying for the Certification Exams

you the best overall understanding of the way each piece of information relates to all the NetWare operating systems. When you pass these tests, the operating system requirements and the four elective credits are fulfilled. The core requirements are all that remain.

If you take the CNE path in v2.2, you still begin with Part 2 of this book. Next, you need to learn Part 3. These chapters enable you to pass the v2.2 System Manager and v2.2 Advanced System Manager tests. Then study Part 4 to pass the v3.1x elective tests. Again, after you pass these tests, the operating system requirements and the four elective credits are fulfilled. The core requirements are all that remain.

If you take the CNA path, you must learn Part 2 and then Part 3 or Part 4, depending on the operating system for which you are testing. Parts 2 and 3 supply the information you need to pass the v2.2 Certified Administrator's test; Parts 2 and 4 enable you to pass the v3.1x Certified Administrator's test.

After you have chosen the path you want to take, make sure that you are comfortable with the information before you schedule the tests. The more stress you are under, the more difficult it becomes to pass the tests. Study the sample questions after each chapter. These sample questions are similar to the question format on the certification tests, and you can understand the way in which the test questions are phrased. The most frequent complaint of persons taking the tests is that they did not like the way the questions were asked. The questions in this book touch on major points. Make sure that you do not just memorize the answers, but understand why the correct answer is correct and the wrong answer is wrong.

Finally, before you take the tests, thumb through this book looking for areas in which you feel least prepared. This review helps place details in your short-term memory that might come in handy during the test.

Using Study Techniques

Many techniques for remembering things are available. This section introduces you to several techniques used throughout this book to aid you in remembering key topics.

Repetition

Repetition is an incredibly strong method for retaining information. In this book, you read about a concept and are asked questions about items relating to that topic. You might also notice that some key concepts are discussed several times throughout the book. This repetition helps you understand the topic's details.

To further enhance your learning by using repetition, consider making NetWare flash cards. On one side of a 3-by-5 card, write a question; write the answer on the other side. This method differs from the review question procedure, because you do not give yourself multiple-choice answers. It also ensures that you are learning the concept, not simply making an educated guess. The more cards you create, the less likely you are to be surprised by a test question.

Another way to create questions for flash cards is to develop fill-in-the-blank questions. When creating these questions, replace key words with a blank. Write the key words on the cards' backs. You also can reverse this study method by looking at the key words and placing them in a sentence that describes their function.

Linking

When you need to remember something elusive, try relating it to something with which you are familiar. This process is called *linking*. The more outrageous the comparison, the easier it becomes to remember. Take a look at the following examples for Hot Fix and bridge.

To remember what Hot Fix means, picture yourself moving a hot pan from a fire that has gone out to a new fire. Imagine slightly singeing your fingers on the pan handles. You have just "fixed a hot problem," or "hot fix." In NetWare terms, *Hot Fix* involves moving a piece of data written to a bad hard drive block over to a good hard drive block.

To remember what a bridge does, think of why concrete bridges are created. Normally, a bridge is built to connect two or more roads that otherwise cannot be connected. The Mackinac Bridge was built to connect Michigan's upper and lower peninsulas. In networking, a *bridge* connects two similar network topologies.

Mnemonics

Another type of linking is *mnemonics:* a method of remembering a list of items by assigning the first letter of each word to a common word and linking the words together to form an easily remembered sentence.

A common mnemonic in Novell's Networking Technologies class is used to remember the Open System Interconnect (OSI) model's seven layers. A list of these seven layers follows:

- Application
- Presentation
- Session
- Transport
- Network
- Data Link
- Physical

When you take the first letter of each word, you have APSTNDP. Next, each letter is assigned to a word that makes up a sentence that you can remember easily:

All

People

Seem

To

Need

Data

Processing

This simple, pertinent sentence helps you remember the seven layers in order.

Keep a notebook handy as you go through this book. Keep any notes you take in one place; you can use them as a quick reference of points important to you.

Testing Covered in this Book

The material presented to you in this book helps you pass the following exams:

- NetWare 2.2 System Manager   50-20
- NetWare 2.2 Advanced System Manager   50-44
- NetWare 3.11 System Manager   50-91
- NetWare 3.11 Advanced System Manager 50-82
- NetWare 3.11 OS Feature Review   50-42
- NetWare 3.1x Administration   50-130
- NetWare 3.1x Advanced Administration 50-131

Appendix B lists the objectives for each test and the chapters in which you can find the information.

Chapter 2: Studying for the Certification Exams

Summary

In this chapter, you learned about the paths you can take that lead to certification. By using the charts supplied in this chapter, you can track your progress through the program you have chosen.

You also learned some time-tested tips that can help you study and pass the certification tests.

In Part 2 of this book, you learn about the elements common to NetWare 2.2 through 3.1x. Chapter 3 begins your certification studies by providing an overview of ways in which information is stored on a network and which utilities are available to retrieve this information.

PART 2

NetWare Basics

Chapter 3

Moving Around NetWare Directory Structures

Chapter 4

Understanding NetWare Security

Chapter 5

Utilities

Chapter 6

Printing on a Novell Network

Chapter 7

Customizing the User's Environment

Moving Around NetWare Directory Structures

CHAPTER 3

In this chapter, you become familiar with the basic structure of a Novell NetWare network from the viewpoint of a system administrator. You learn to do the following:

- Identify the levels of a NetWare directory structure
- Name the required NetWare volume and the system-created directories, their contents, and their location in the directory structure
- Organize an efficient directory structure
- Write a NetWare directory path using the proper syntax
- Identify the DOS and NetWare command functions related to directory structures
- Identify default drive pointers
- Differentiate between network drive mappings and search drive mappings
- Identify all MAP parameters and syntax

At this chapter's end, you find review questions and case studies to help you reexamine the information presented.

Chapter 3:   Moving Around NetWare Directory Structures

The most basic element common to all NetWare versions through v3.1*x* is the directory structure. NetWare enables DOS directory structures to exist on the network much as they would on a stand-alone computer running DOS. Most of the commands available in DOS to manipulate and manage the directory structure also are available in NetWare. In addition, NetWare includes many other utilities to control the directory structure and provide greater functionality.

In DOS, you can name a storage device, whether it is a hard drive or a floppy disk. NetWare requires you to name storage device portions: the file server and its volumes. The next section discusses file server names and volumes.

Creating File Server Names

File servers must have unique names to "talk" to other file servers. Computers do not recognize nonverbal communication. If you are in a room full of people named Chris, for example, you expect some confusion. Gestures and eye contact can help you single out one of the individuals with little difficulty. Computers do not have the capability to see and interpret visual clues. If you try to access two computers with the same name, the system locks up, because NetWare cannot figure out which system you want.

Before you name a file server, consider its intended use and how easily you want users to access it. In most NetWare training classes, the first generic file server is referred to as FS1 and the second as FS2. Some NetWare students are so comfortable with these file server names that they use them in their offices. You can give servers names of two to 45 characters in length. For this reason, most companies use some form of their names or department names for their file servers.

A NetWare file server's structure begins with the file server name, which launches the full directory path. The shorter the name, the easier the users can move among file servers. File server names resemble DOS labels for hard drives or floppy disks, and like drives or floppy disks, file server names usually indicate the type of information the drive contains.

A full *directory path* in NetWare uses the following syntax:

```
FILESERVER\VOLUME:DIRECTORY\SUBDIRECTORY
```

The directory path CDI\SYS:PROGRAMS\DATABASE, for example, begins with a file server name (CDI) and then a volume name (SYS:). The file server name and the volume name are separated with a backslash (\). The volume name always is followed by a colon (:). After the volume name, the first-level directory, or *parent* directory (named PROGRAMS), appears followed by a secondary directory, or *subdirectory*, called DATABASE. The full directory path indicates your location on a network or your desired location. If your network plans do not include connecting to another file server, you can name your server anything you want.

In a single server environment, you can leave the file server name out of the directory path. Because you did not specify another server, the system assumes that you want to address this file server. That assumption, however, does not mean that you can leave the file server unnamed after you install it. All file servers require a server name, even in a single-server environment.

Accessing NetWare Volumes

Volumes are the next level in a full directory path. Unlike file server names, volumes are essential to the full directory path.

Volumes, NetWare, and DOS

Volumes are to NetWare what root drives are to DOS. In a DOS directory tree, the highest level you can access is the root drive.

Chapter 3: Moving Around NetWare Directory Structures

Root drives are identified by a backslash after the drive indicator. The root drive of C is shown as C:\. To get to this directory structure level, tell the system to change the directory to the root by typing **CD**.

One of the most common mistakes users make when they change directories is to improperly use the backslash. After you type the backslash directly after the CD command, as in **CD**, the system is instructed to find the root directory. If the directory you want to change to is really the current directory's subdirectory, insert a space rather than the backslash after the CD command, followed by the subdirectory's name. For example, to change to the subdirectory called DBASE1 from your current path of CDI\SYS:PROGRAMS\DATABASE, type **CD DBASE1**. A directory beginning with a backslash is located below the root; a directory without a backslash is located below the current directory. In the following example, the directory DATABASE is represented by the following directory structure:

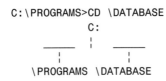

```
C:\PROGRAMS>CD \DATABASE
           C:
           |
     _____|_____
     |           |
  \PROGRAMS   \DATABASE
```

In the next example, DATABASE is a subdirectory of PROGRAMS. The directory structure that applies to this example is as follows:

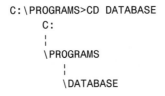

```
C:\PROGRAMS>CD DATABASE
     C:
     |
     \PROGRAMS
           |
           \DATABASE
```

This information on DOS applies to both a stand-alone DOS workstation and DOS used on a network. Keep the directory structure in mind when changing directories.

Comparison Note NetWare 2.2 can have up to 32 volumes, and NetWare 3.1*x* can have up to 64 volumes.

Naming and Setting Up Volumes

When you create and name volumes in NetWare, remember that the volume name must follow certain conventions. The following rules apply to all NetWare volume names:

- You can assign volume names of one to 15 characters.

- Except for the characters *, /, \, ?, and @, you can use almost any keyboard character for volume names. The @ sign is new to the unavailable characters list and is reserved for designations made by the NetWare Naming Service (NNS) product, which came out with v3.1. Novell offers this product for simplifying the login process in multiple-server environments. Chapter 11 discusses NNS in more detail.

- You can use a period (.) in a file server name as long as the period is not the first character.

- The first volume on the first drive always is called SYS:.

- Volume names always are followed by a colon (:).

In NetWare 2.2, the largest volume that you can access is 255M. If you have a drive larger than 255M, use the remaining space for additional volumes. If you have a 650M drive, for example, one option is to break the drive into three volumes—two volumes that contain 255M and another volume that contains 140M.

NetWare 3.1x breaks the 256M limitation, enabling you to create a single volume of up to 32 terabytes. A *terabyte* (T) is a number that has 12 zeros after it (1T equals 1,099,511,627,776).

Chapter 3: Moving Around NetWare Directory Structures

Understanding Required Directories

When you install NetWare, four directories are created that are essential to an efficient and reliable system. The LOGIN, MAIL, PUBLIC, and SYSTEM directories are established in the SYS: volume. These directories are very important to network functionality and should never be deleted. The next few sections describe these directories and show you the way they work within the NetWare environment.

SYS:LOGIN

LOGIN is the first directory you can access on a network. It contains the SLIST.EXE and LOGIN.EXE files. SLIST.EXE displays all the file server names of which the routing table is aware.

Figure 3.1 illustrates one network's response to the SLIST command. As you can see, servers are listed in alphabetical order by server name. Each server's network, node address, and status also are shown.

Figure 3.1

Server list using SLIST.

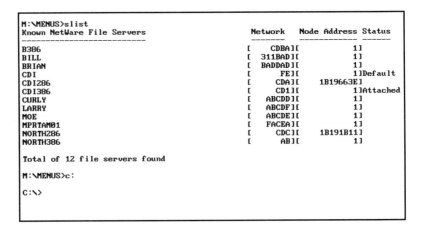

Understanding Required Directories

A status appears for each listed file server. Three status types are displayed: Blank, Default, and Attached. The status field displays the workstation's relationship (status) to the listed file server. It does not reflect the actual status of the server itself, as is commonly first assumed.

A *Blank* status means that this workstation has no relationship established with the server other than the fact that it can see that server on the network.

The *Default* status means that after the workstation loaded the files necessary to communicate with the network, this server was the first server on which it found a LOGIN directory containing files with which it could log in to the network.

If you have a PREFERRED SERVER = statement in your workstation's NET.CFG file, the default server is the same as the server named in the PREFERRED SERVER = statement unless the preferred server could not be found on the network.

The *Attached* status means that this workstation has logged in to or attached to this file server.

Little difference exists between logging in to a server and attaching to a server. The two processes' results, however, can differ substantially.

After you log in to a server (by typing the LOGIN command), available system and user login scripts are run. If no system or user login script is found, a default login script runs instead.

After you attach to a server, no login script of any type is run. Because you can establish or change drive mappings, attachments to other servers, batch files, and other elements of your networking environment using login scripts, the result of a login can differ substantially from that of an attachment.

continues

Chapter 3: Moving Around NetWare Directory Structures

continued

The other main difference between logging in to a server and attaching to a server can have significant consequences as well. If you attach to a server after having previously logged in to another server, existing drive mappings and other workstation configuration information remains unchanged. After you log in to a server, however, a log out of all other connected servers is assumed and run. Your workstation, therefore, loses all its previously set connections and drive mappings.

As noted previously, by entering **SLIST** from a workstation, you can see a list of file servers from which you can select. SLIST is particularly useful for three reasons.

First, if you attempt to log in to the network without typing the exact name of the file server you want to log in to, the system attempts to log you into the first available server. If you do not have a user identification on that server, you are prompted for a password, then denied access. NetWare's security system does not tell you that you are not a user on the server. You might not, therefore, immediately realize what went wrong.

Second, you can see at a glance to which servers you already are attached. This command is a quick way to find out this type of information.

Third, if you cannot remember the exact name of a file server, you can use the SLIST command with a wild-card character. Using the servers listed in figure 3.1, for example, to see all servers that begin with the letter B, type **SLIST B*** and press Enter. Only servers B386, BILL, and BRIAN appear.

Before you can attach to a file server and access the LOGIN directory, you must load some client files on your workstation. These files announce your presence on the cable system and communicate to NetWare that you want to connect to the server. The file server returns a response similar to, "I recognize you as a node. You can use this directory to attempt logging in to a server in the server list." At this point, changing to the F drive or to the first available network drive specified in your workstation's NET.CFG file points you to the SYS:LOGIN directory. You then can view and read any file in this directory.

If your workstation is a *diskless* workstation (one without a hard disk or a floppy disk drive), your workstation now can access the boot image file it requires to log in to the network. The boot image file for logging a diskless workstation into the network resides in this directory. If you have multiple file servers, place this image file in each server's login directory so that each workstation can find its proper boot file in any server to which you attach. You can learn more about this process in *NetWareTraining Guide: Networking Technologies*, the companion volume to this book.

Use caution after you place files in the SYS:LOGIN directory. Anyone who has access to the SYS:LOGIN directory can use files placed here. A user can get access to SYS:LOGIN after loading the necessary client files.

SYS:MAIL

This directory takes its name from a simple mail program that Novell provided with previous versions of NetWare. This program introduced users to electronic mail by saving messages in each user's ID directory. NetWare no longer includes this program. The SYS:MAIL directory still is used, however.

Each user has a MAIL_ID directory, as NetWare refers to the user's MAIL directory, which is created after the user is added to the network. These directories hold the user's personal login script. They also contain the PRINTCON.DAT file if the user has print jobs created through PRINTCON.

The MAIL_ID directories reside under the SYS:MAIL directory. The MAIL_ID directory names are up to eight hexadecimal digits long.

Chapter 3: Moving Around NetWare Directory Structures

The system SUPERVISOR ID has the distinct name of SYS:MAIL\1.

Two screens in NetWare enable you to view MAIL directories and their corresponding users. Both screens are options in the SYSCON menu utility.

If you select the User Information option in the SYSCON menu and then specify a user, two menu options enable you to view ID information (see fig. 3.2). The first option, the Other Information Option, shows a User ID number. The User ID number is the same as the name of the user's mail directory, but with the preceding zeros deleted.

Figure 3.2
SYSCON, User Information, and other information windows.

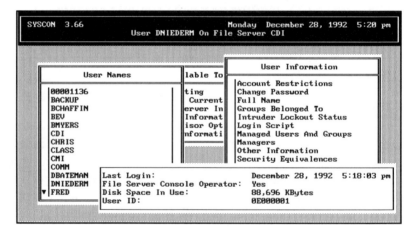

Another place that lists ID information is in the Trustee Directory Assignments list illustrated in figure 3.3. After you become a new user on the network, you automatically are granted all rights by NetWare under your USER_ID directory except for Access Control in v2.2 and Supervisory in v3.1*x*. Use this option to see the directory under SYS:MAIL in which you have rights. Notice the manner in which the system automatically truncates the preceding zeros as SYSCON displays this information.

Users have rights to their own MAIL_ID directories, and system managers also have rights to user MAIL_ID directories. By default, system supervisors have rights to all directories. This privilege enables supervisors to create personal login scripts and PRINTCON printing jobs for users.

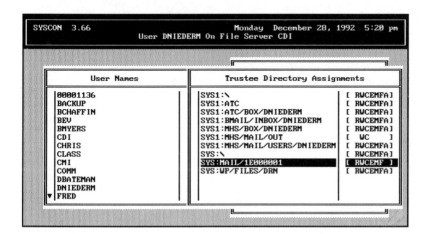

Figure 3.3
SYSCON, User Names, and Trustee Directory Assignments windows.

SYS:PUBLIC

The SYS:PUBLIC directory contains all the network management command files that network users need to access. Each menu utility and the command-line utilities available to network users appear in this directory. Printer definition files (PDF) and overlay files reside in the SYS:PUBLIC directory. These overlay files are NetWare Operating System subroutines brought in and out of file server memory as needed. The help files (HLP) also appear in this directory and provide you with an on-line reference guide to NetWare.

Although NetWare creates the SYS:PUBLIC directory for NetWare utilities, the system administrator should create a directory structure beneath this directory for COMMAND.COM files used on DOS machines. Follow the procedure in the Chapter 7 section entitled "Login Scripts" to ensure that each workstation is capable of finding the appropriate COMMAND.COM files.

SYS:SYSTEM

This directory contains the command-line utilities that only network supervisors and users with supervisor rights (privileges) can access. A few of the most frequently used utilities put into the SYS:SYSTEM directory are accessed by using the following commands:

- **ATOTAL.** Computes the aggregate totals for the system if you are using NetWare's accounting feature. These totals are shown as per day and per week values. Figure 3.4 illustrates the result of running this command.

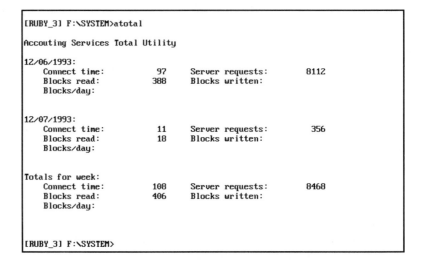

Figure 3.4
ATOTAL accounting screen.

- **PAUDIT.** Lists individual entries for each user who logs in to or out of the system. Figure 3.5 illustrates the result of running this command.
- **SECURITY.** Compares your system to the NetWare recommendations for securing a system (see fig. 3.6). SECURITY displays system supervisor, manager accounts, and user accounts that have not been used recently.

Understanding Required Directories

```
[RUBY_3] F:\SYSTEM>paudit

12/6/93 17:59:23  File Server TSARINA
    CHARGE: 220 to User SUPERVISOR for File Server services.
    Connected 97 min.; 8112 requests; 1590016 bytes read; 0 bytes written.
12/6/93 17:59:23  File Server TSARINA
    NOTE: about User SUPERVISOR during File Server services.
    Logout from address 01D0C300:00001B045C70.
12/7/93 8:40:34  File Server TSARINA
    NOTE: about User SUPERVISOR during File Server services.
    Login from address 01D0C300:00001B045C70.
12/7/93 8:51:57  File Server TSARINA
    CHARGE: 9 to User SUPERVISOR for File Server services.
    Connected 11 min.; 356 requests; 73008 bytes read; 0 bytes written.
12/7/93 8:51:57  File Server TSARINA
    NOTE: about User SUPERVISOR during File Server services.
    Logout from address 01D0C300:00001B045C70.
12/7/93 9:25:55  File Server TSARINA
    NOTE: about User SUPERVISOR during File Server services.
    Login from address 01D0C300:00001B045C70.
[RUBY_3] F:\SYSTEM>
```

Figure 3.5

PAUDIT accounting screen.

```
SECURITY EVALUATION UTILITY, Version 2.23
Group NFSGROUP
    No Full Name specified

Group NOGROUP
    No Full Name specified

User NFSDEMO
    Has [ R    F ] rights in SYS:SYSTEM (maximum should be [         ])
    Has [ R    F ] rights in SYS:MAIL (maximum should be [    C    ])
    Has no login script
    Is not required to change passwords periodically
    Can have passwords that are too short (less than 5)
    No Full Name specified

User NOBODY
    Has [ R    F ] rights in SYS:SYSTEM (maximum should be [         ])
    Has [ R    F ] rights in SYS:MAIL (maximum should be [    C    ])
    Has no login script
Press any key to continue ... ('C' for continuous)
```

Figure 3.6

A sample report from SECURITY.

- ◆ **BINDFIX.** Attempts to repair bindery problems. This utility creates new bindery files and renames the previous files with OLD extensions. Use BINDFIX if you suspect bindery file corruption.

- ◆ Bindery files contain security information regarding users and groups on the system. This security information includes password requirements, station and time restrictions, trustee rights, and security equivalencies. If these files are corrupted, random portions of the user and group accounts cannot be modified.

Chapter 3: Moving Around NetWare Directory Structures

NetWare 2.2 contains two bindery files, NET$BIND.SYS and NET$BVAL.SYS. NetWare 3.1*x* contains three bindery files, NET$OBJ.SYS, NET$PROP.SYS, and NET$VAL.SYS. These files are hidden system files that reside in the SYS:SYSTEM directory.

- ◆ **BINDREST.** Deletes the newly created binderies created by BINDFIX, renames the OLD files to SYS files, hides the new files, and then makes them system files. Use BINDREST if the BINDFIX command does not fix corrupted files and you need to put the binderies back to their original state.

In NetWare 3.1*x*, an additional directory is added to the list of required directories. This directory is called SYS:ETC. This directory contains files for use with TCP/IP connectivity. In Chapter 11, you learn more about multiple protocol options in NetWare.

Here is an easy way to remember the required directories. It is SiMPLE!

SYSTEM
i
MAIL
PUBLIC
LOGIN
ETC

Managing Required Directories

When you work with NetWare directories, remember that these directories are created by the NetWare installation procedure. In other words, DOS plays no part in their creation. After NetWare networks are installed, the operating system sets up these directories for its own use. If a user tries to delete or rename these directories within DOS, the results can produce difficulties for

Managing Required Directories

the network. For this reason, follow these guidelines when you work with NetWare directories:

- ◆ Keep these directories clean. Leave these directories for the network. Do not add programs and data files to the default NetWare directories. Place program and data directories elsewhere on the system. Even though you might find it convenient to place program directories in the SYS:PUBLIC directory, you do not gain any performance advantage by doing so.

- ◆ Do not modify the installed NetWare directories. If you change a NetWare MAIL ID directory name, the directory becomes unusable because NetWare uses hexadecimal names, not logical names. Although you might find it inconvenient to try and match hexadecimal-named subdirectories with logical names in the MAIL program, the system uses these different naming methods to match user names and directories. For this reason, do not change the subdirectory names in NetWare or they might not work.

- ◆ Do not move default NetWare directories. NetWare looks in only one place for the four installed directories. The place for these directories is SYS:.

Do not modify or move the LOGIN, MAIL, PUBLIC, and SYSTEM directories. You can effectively improve network performance if these directories are left alone, because NetWare does not need to sort through data to find the information it seeks.

If an application insists on installing itself in one of the essential directories, however, you can leave the program in the directory. Whenever possible, load the application in something other than an essential directory.

In some instances, you can successfully install a program that requires installation at the root directory. You might have to install it from a workstation rather than directly from a DOS prompt at the file server console, using a drive that has been mapped using the MAP ROOT command. To see the exact syntax for using this command, log into a NetWare server from a workstation, type **MAP /?**, and press Enter.

Do not be afraid to create directories. A good directory structure tells a story about your network. A well-constructed directory tree enables anyone who views it to know instantly the location of utilities, programs, and data directories for each program.

 When you create directories in NetWare, remember a rule applied to creating DOS directories: not too deep and not too wide. In other words, do not create directories that have too many subdirectories or files. Network users notice that the system slows down when more than 500 files exist in a directory. Backup programs have been known to choke and fail if a directory has more than 1,000 files.

For easier security administration, create categories of directories. The following section examines some categories for directories.

Using Recommended Directories

NetWare supplies the directories it needs for proper operation. The system administrator must decide the manner in which she wants to manage programs and data directories. This section examines several options to help you determine where to place new directories.

The preceding section discussed the directories that NetWare needs to operate. This section examines other directory types not mandatory to NetWare operation. The following three categories of directories can help you organize your system: HOME directories, application directories, and data directories.

HOME Directories

Network structures that include HOME directories for end users can help you monitor network usage. Although they are optional,

Using Recommended Directories

Novell recommends the use of HOME directories to help keep your network running smoothly. HOME directories are useful on your network for other reasons as well.

HOME directories are set up for the user to store personal files. Users can, for example, determine if any of their files should be shared with others and control access within their own directories.

Many companies set up a directory off SYS: called \USERS. Each user has a directory with a login name. Users usually have all privileges at their HOME directory level. This type of setup works well if user names are eight characters or less, because DOS sets an eight-character limit for directory names.

You can create user names that are a maximum of eight characters, which then ensures that users' HOME directory names are no longer than eight characters. Companies use different approaches to solving this problem.

Some companies, for example, assign user names based on the employees' first and last names. A user is assigned a network identification name using the first initial of the user's first name and the first seven characters of the user's last name.

Another option is to use only the first eight characters of a user's first or last name. This approach is only effective when the company has a limited number of employees and no one has the same last or first name.

If the company is too large for either of these options, use a variation of one or more of these approaches. For duplicate names, you can add a user's middle initial, thus limiting the first or last name characters to a maximum of seven.

If your network has a user named John C. Smith and one named Jane R. Smith, using JSMITH as a

continues

continued

user name can cause a conflict. You can, however, use JCSMITH and JRSMITH successfully, as well as JOHN and JANE, or JOHNS and JANES.

You can use any method for assigning user names. As long as these names do not exceed eight characters, you also can use them to create user HOME directories.

 In v3.1*x*, you can limit directory structure branches to a specific amount of file server disk space allowed for the users. In other words, system administrators can decide the amount of space each user can have for his own work. In both v2.2 and v3.1*x*, you can limit space per user for the entire volume. Both features enable system administrators to monitor file server disk consumption.

Network protection provides another reason to give users their own separate HOME directories. Supplied with their own directories on the file server, users can control their files and subdirectories. Given a structural branch that they can modify, users are less likely to cause system damage. If you provide directories that users can manipulate, they tend to stay in those directories rather than wander around the system.

From an administrator's point of view, knowing where to look for expendable files saves time. If the system supervisor instructs users to place only nonessential data in HOME directories, he can delete files easily and safely in the event that the system runs out of storage space.

Application Directories

The placement of *application directories* (directories required by an application) depends on where the program designers want the program to be located. The installation procedure for an

Using Recommended Directories

application largely dictates the placement of its directories in the NetWare directory tree. Other applications can be placed anywhere. The designer of your system's security structure ultimately determines where application directories are installed on the network.

You can locate application directories in any volume on the network, which provides you, the system administrator, with several options. If a volume is going to be used primarily by the accounting department, and the accounting programs are used only by the accounting staff, for example, then place the application among directories that pertain to those users. In other words, place applications within the directory for the department that uses the programs. Figure 3.7 shows this type of directory structure.

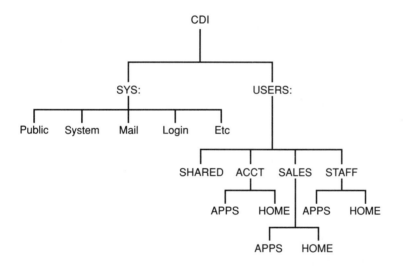

Figure 3.7

Structure for applications on the network.

Another option is to place application directories under the SYS: volume, because everyone has rights to these directories.

You can put application directories anywhere. The placement of application directories, however, factors into any security plans for a network. Whichever method you select, remember that the best planned systems always clearly label the directory's contents.

Data Directories

Never mix applications and data in the same directory. The main responsibility of system administrator is to ensure that end users can work without a system failure. The extra burden of determining which files are data and which contain applications is a task that can and should be solved early in the network's life.

If a program needs to be deleted or upgraded, a well-planned directory structure prevents wasting the administrator's time sorting through directories for data files. By placing data in a separate directory, administrators easily can update the application without losing data.

Numerous options are available for data directories. One option, called a *shared data directory*, places the data directory with the program. This method enables anyone who uses the program to place the data files in a common directory.

Another possibility for organizing data is to create *departmental directories*. Each member of a department then has a place to put his data files. Departmental directories often are used when departments work mostly on their own.

One other popular method for organizing network data is to have users place their data files in their own HOME directories. This method usually includes a single shared directory in which users place files that other users need. Many corporations that employ tight security use this method for their data directories.

Finally, creating a separate volume for data is a practical solution if you have disk drives with large amounts of memory storage. This method maintains a high level of security, but also requires that users have more system knowledge.

The directories discussed in this section are only suggestions to help you organize your network. You cannot use every option on every system. Before you configure a network structure, try it on paper so that you can better understand what your structure should look like. Your network users will let you know quickly what needs to be changed. Fortunately, you can move most applications and modify the system without many problems.

In the next section, you are introduced to several commands used both in DOS and NetWare. You also are shown several commands used in NetWare to manipulate the DOS directory structure and to view statistics about the directories.

Using DOS Commands in NetWare

NetWare enables many commands created for DOS to be used on the network. The following list contains the most common commands used by the average network user.

- **COPY CON.** This command enables the user to create a file on the network when this command is followed by a file name. The F6 function key or Ctrl+Z quits and saves the file. In the following example, a simple file called DATA.TXT is created with a row of Xs.

    ```
     >copy con DATA.TXT
    XXXXXXXXXXXXXXXXXXXXXXXXX
    ^Z
         1 file(s) copied
    C:>
    ```

- **CD.** Change Directory. This command enables you to change from one directory to another.

- **RD.** Remove Directory. You also can use RMDIR. This command enables you to get rid of empty directories.

- **MD.** Make Directory. You also can use MKDIR. This command enables you to create new directories.

- **DEL.** Delete. This command enables you to remove files from a directory.

- **COPY.** This command enables you to copy a file to another location. See the next section to learn the difference between using DOS's COPY command and NetWare's NCOPY command.

Using NetWare Commands on the Directory Structure

This section discusses several commands that can help you learn about and manage an existing directory structure.

CHKDIR

CHKDIR is used to view information about a volume or directory. CHKDIR displays space limitations for a particular file server, volume, and directory.

This command displays the maximum storage capacity of a volume or directory if a space limitation has been placed on it. CHKDIR is useful to determine the amount of free space a directory has.

If space limitations have been placed on users, the CHKDIR utility enables them to keep track of the amount of space they have left. To use CHKDIR, simply enter the command by itself or enter the command plus the path of the directory you are checking. Figure 3.8 shows a CHKDIR command example.

Figure 3.8
Displaying CHKDIR information.

```
[RUBY_3] Z:\PUBLIC>chkdir

Directory Space Limitation Information For:
TSARINA\SYS:PUBLIC

     Maximum      In Use     Available
     30,888 K     18,372 K   12,516 K    Volume Size
                  9,828 K    12,516 K    \PUBLIC

[RUBY_3] Z:\PUBLIC>
```

CHKVOL

The CHKVOL utility displays total volume space. This space includes total space used by files, deleted files, FATs, and directories. All CHKVOL information is presented in kilobytes and is useful when complete volume information is required.

The information provided by CHKVOL is presented in a simple, two-column format. CHKVOL displays the following information:

- File server name
- Volume name
- Total volume space
- Total space used by files, FATS, and directory tables
- Space in use by deleted files
- Space available from deleted files
- Space remaining on volume
- Space available to user

As with CHKDIR, you can use CHKVOL with or without a directory path. You also can use the standard DOS wild cards (* and ?) with CHKVOL. The command CHKVOL *, for example, displays information for all volumes, and CHKVOL */* displays information for all volumes on all the file servers to which you are attached. Figure 3.9 is a sample of the information available by using CHKVOL.

LISTDIR

LISTDIR is similar to the DOS TREE command. As shown in figure 3.10, each subsequent subdirectory is indented to show the hierarchy. You can use this command to view your directory structure:

```
LISTDIR /S
```

Chapter 3: Moving Around NetWare Directory Structures

Figure 3.9
Displaying CHKVOL information.

```
F:\>chkvol

Statistics for fixed volume CDI/SYS:

Total volume space:                     628,120  K Bytes
Space used by files:                    505,292  K Bytes
Space in use by deleted files:           44,636  K Bytes
Space available from deleted files:      44,636  K Bytes
Space remaining on volume:              122,828  K Bytes
Space available to DNIEDERM:            122,828  K Bytes

F:\>
```

The LISTDIR command has other options that you can use:

LISTDIR *path option*

Figure 3.10
A sample SYS1: volume directory tree.

```
The sub-directory structure of CDI/SYS1:
Directory
─────────────────────────────────────────
->DELETED.SAV
->DATABASE
->  DBASE
->  DBTOOLS
->NCDTREE
->DATA
->MHS
->  MAIL
->     PUBLIC
->     PARCEL
->     OUT
->     QUEUES
->     USERS
->        -PM4WARD
->           POSTMAST
->           IPARCEL
->        00001136
->           POSTMAST
->           IPARCEL
->     ADMIN
Press any key to continue ... ('C' for continuous)
```

Remember to use a backslash (\) for path names and a forward slash (/) for options.

Options

LISTDIR also can use several command-line switches. The following switches are available. Be sure to place a space after LISTDIR and the switch.

- ◆ **/R.** Lists directory rights and inherited rights masks.
- ◆ **/E.** Lists effective rights.
- ◆ **/D** or **/T.** Lists both creation date and time.
- ◆ **/S.** Lists all subdirectories. Subdirectories show up as indented line items.
- ◆ **/A.** Lists all available information.

NCOPY

The NCOPY command is similar to the DOS COPY and XCOPY commands. NCOPY has two advantages over the DOS commands. The first advantage is that NCOPY is faster. If you want to copy all the files from the path of P:\DATA\NEW to M:\DATA\OLD using the DOS command, enter the following:

    COPY P:*.* M:

The command first passes to the file server and grabs the necessary tables from memory. These tables then are downloaded to the workstation (pass 2), and the changes in file placement are written to the tables. The tables then go back to the file server (pass 3). Finally, the token returns to the workstation for further instructions (pass 4). The DOS COPY command takes four passes on the cable to complete the action.

Token is a file server process that tells a workstation to transmit information to the network. The process of sending a token from one *node*, either a workstation or a file server, to another is called a *pass*.

If you want to transfer files, use the same syntax, but add the letter N in front of the copy command, as follows:

    NCOPY P:*.* M:

Chapter 3: Moving Around NetWare Directory Structures

NCOPY goes straight to the file server to manipulate its memory tables rather than the workstation's. This process takes only two passes, one to the file server and one back to the workstation. The result is two passes less than the DOS COPY procedure. The difference between COPY and NCOPY is minimal for small amounts of files, but the time saved is substantial when copying large directory structures.

The second advantage to using NCOPY rather than COPY or XCOPY is that NCOPY displays the source and destination directories. This information is helpful if you often use shortcuts when you copy files, and you mistakenly copy dozens of files to the wrong place. Figure 3.11 shows the NCOPY command that copies all files with the OVL extension in the U:\PROGRAMS\UTILS directory to the directory to which G points, SYS1:\STORE. You see the destination directory because of the way NCOPY works. DOS does not give you this information.

Figure 3.11

An example of using the NCOPY command.

```
G:\STORE>ncopy u:*.ovl g:
From CDI/SYS:\PROGRAMS/UTILS
To   CDI/SYS1:\STORE
     IBM$RUN.OVL    to IBM$RUN.OVL
     $RUN.OVL       to $RUN.OVL
     NDOS.OVL       to NDOS.OVL

     3 files copied.

G:\STORE>
```

NDIR

NDIR stands for *Network Directory Search*. You can use the NDIR command to search the network for file or directory parameters.

Using NetWare Commands on the Directory Structure

Figure 3.12 shows available information about files and subdirectories in the G:\STORE directory. This information includes file name, file size, last update (the last time the file was modified), flags (attributes), and owner (who created the file). In addition, you see the subdirectory name, inherited and effective rights (discussed in Chapter 7), and the date and time it was created or copied. Finally, you see the number of files NDIR found and the amount of space they occupy.

```
G:\STORE>ndir
CDI/SYS1:STORE

Files:              Size      Last Updated        Flags             Owner
-------             ----      ------------        -----             -----
$RUN       OVL      2,288     3-27-86  9:38a   [RoS-----------DR]  DNIEDERM
IBM$RUN    OVL      2,288     3-27-86  9:38a   [RoS-----------DR]  DNIEDERM
NDOS       OVL     73,510     8-05-91  6:01a   [RoS-----------DR]  DNIEDERM

        78,086 bytes in    3 files
        81,920 bytes in   20 blocks

G:\STORE>
```

Figure 3.12

An example of using the NDIR command.

You also can use NDIR to search for specific information. The syntax for the NDIR command is as follows:

    NDIR path /options

Path

You can replace this option with a directory path, wild cards, or up to 16 file names. Use a backslash to specify path names and a forward slash for the options.

Sort Parameters

Sort parameters alter the order in which files and subdirectories are displayed to the user.

73

Chapter 3: Moving Around NetWare Directory Structures

- **/SORT** *(parameter)*. Enables you to sort the directory on selected parameters by using the parameters described in the following section. The parameter you specify is substituted into the parameter variable after you type the SORT option.
- **/REV /SORT** *(parameter)*. Reverses the SORT according to the parameters you specify after the SORT option.
- **/UN.** Leaves list unsorted.

Parameters

A complete list of parameters for the NDIR command is given in this section. You can use these parameters to gather specific information about files and subdirectories.

Parameter	Description
OW	Owner
SI	Size
UP	Update (Last Modified Date)
CR	Created Date
AC	Last Accessed Date
AR	Last Archived Date

Display Formats

NDIR displays whatever you request. The following switches describe specific conditions that you can meet by using NDIR.

- **/FO.** Displays file names only
- **/DO.** Displays directories only
- **/SUB.** Searches all subdirectories
- **/DATES.** Lists last modified, last archived, last accessed, and created dates

- **/RIGHTS.** Lists inherited and effective rights
- **/MAC.** Lists Macintosh files and subdirectories
- **/LONG.** Lists the long file names for Macintosh, OS/2, and NFS
- **/HELP.** Lists NDIR options

Attribute Searches

If you need to look for files flagged with specific attributes, the following list shows each switch and the attribute it represents.

Attribute Search	Limitation
/A	Archive Needed
/CI	Copy Inhibit
/DI	Delete Inhibit
/H	Hidden
/I	Indexed
/N	Normal
/P	Purge
/RI	Rename Inhibit
/RA	Read Audit
/RO	Read Only
/S	Shareable
/Sy	System
/T	Transactional
/WA	Write Audit
/X	Execute Only

To search for select attributes, place the /NOT option before the attribute.

Restricted Displays

NDIR enables you to restrict displays according to specified conditions.

- **/OW EQ** *name*. Enables you to search for files or directories created by the user's name.

- **/OW NOT EQ** *name*. Enables you to search for file and directory owners, not the user name specified.

- **/SI operator** *nnn*. Finds all files of a certain size. The *nnn* parameter specifies the number of bytes in a file.

- **/SI NOT** *operator nnn*. Finds all files that do not fall into the category of requested information. To look for files no bigger than 10K, for example, type **NDIR /SI NOT GR10**.

- **/UP** *operator mm-dd-yy*. Finds all files updated before, after, or on a certain date.

- **/UP NOT** *operator mm-dd-yy*. Finds all files not updated before, after, or on a certain date.

- **/CR** *operator mm-dd-yy*. Finds all files created before, after, or on a certain date.

- **/CR NOT** *operator mm-dd-yy*. Finds all files not created before, after, or on a certain date.

- **/AC** *operator mm-dd-yy*. Finds all files accessed before, after, or on a certain date.

- **/AC NOT** *operator mm-dd-yy*. Finds all files not accessed before, after, or on a certain date.

- **/AR** *operator mm-dd-yy*. Finds all files archived before, after, or on a certain date.

- **/AR NOT** *operator mm-dd-yy*. Finds all files not archived before, after, or on a certain date.

Using NetWare Commands on the Directory Structure

Operators

Operators, or basic math concepts, are available when using the NDIR command. NDIR does not accept the > or < characters. These operators are used to connect parameters to form specific conditions for NDIR to search.

Operator	Description
GR	Greater Than
LE	Less Than
EQ or =	Equal To
BEF	Before
AFT	After

RENDIR

The RENDIR command enables you to rename a network subdirectory without affecting users' rights to that directory.

In the following example, the SYS:APPS directory is renamed to SYS:PROGRAMS.

    F:\>RENDIR APPS PROGRAMS

 RENDIR works only in the Parent directory when renaming. You cannot include a path.

VOLINFO

The VOLINFO (Volume Information) utility is probably the administrator's most commonly used command. The VOLINFO utility presents in table form the total space, free space, and

Chapter 3: Moving Around NetWare Directory Structures

directory entries in all volumes (see fig. 3.13). The VOLINFO command is the simplest way to view volume free space.

Figure 3.13
Volume Information main screen.

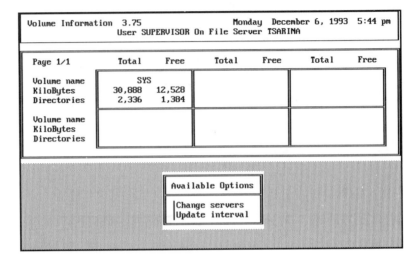

Novell also has made available a Windows version of VOLINFO. Figure 3.14 is an example of VOLINFO for Windows. This utility is part of the NetWare tools program provided by Novell. It provides a standard Microsoft Windows interface and enables space to be presented in megabytes or kilobytes.

Figure 3.14
Windows 3.1 Volume Information screen.

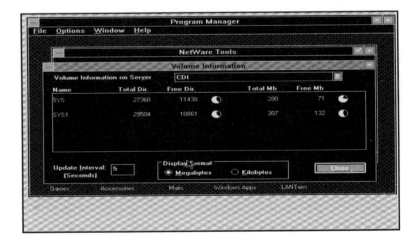

In the next section, you learn about mapping drives and their uses on the network.

Mastering Drive Mappings

NetWare uses drive mappings to enable users to quickly access commonly used directories. Drive mappings are necessary for all NetWare networks. This section discusses the following types of mappings available in NetWare and ways you can use them to customize your network:

- Mappings to local drives
- Mappings to network data directories
- Search mappings to network program directories

You can think of drive mappings as bookmarks in NetWare. If you are reading a textbook or reference manual, for example, the easiest way to access useful data quickly is to mark the pages with bookmarks. Then, whenever you need to access this information, you easily can flip to the pages by using the bookmarks. Drive mappings in NetWare enable the user to quickly find the needed directory.

Networks and Drive Mappings

Networks have 26 available mappings. By pointing these bookmarks to frequently used directories, you can move to any directory in three keystrokes. Suppose, for example, that the directory structure shown in figure 3.15 is on the hard drive of a PC shared by several part-time employees. The morning-shift user, USERAM, needs to access several directories, marked A, B, and C.

Figure 3.15

A sample directory structure.

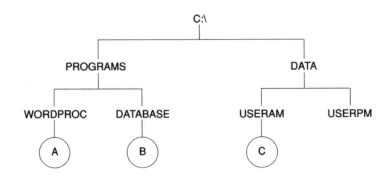

Now, suppose that USERAM boots the PC and begins the workday. First, USERAM needs to go to the word processing directory. At the DOS prompt, he types **CD PROGRAMS\WORDPROC**. If you include typing the space and pressing Enter, 21 keystrokes are used.

Next, USERAM needs to go to his HOME directory. From the C:\PROGRAMS\WORDPROC directory, USERAM types **CD\DATA\USERAM**. This takes a total of 15 keystrokes. USERAM'S manager now asks USERAM to print a database report, so USERAM must type **CD\PROGRAMS\DATABASE**, which again is 21 keystrokes. These procedures can add up to a substantial number of keystrokes typed during the workday.

By using the same directory on a network, C:\ becomes the volume level. By assigning drive letters to each directory, USERAM can get to any of the directories in three keystrokes. Suppose, for example, that drive letter W is assigned to the \PROGRAMS\WORDPROC directory, drive letter X is assigned to the \PROGRAMS\DATABASE directory, and drive letter H is assigned to the \DATA\USERAM directory. To get to any directory, USERAM simply types **H:** , **W:** , or **X:** and presses Enter—just three keystrokes each time. Later in this chapter, you learn the requirements for setting up drive mappings on your network.

Networks and Search Drives

To make finding files in directories even easier, you can use *search drives*. These drive mappings enable you to place yourself in a directory created to store data and call the program from the searched drive. Most programs, unless otherwise configured, dump data into the same directory from which they were called. In NetWare, you can use search drives to help you locate certain files. NetWare performs the following basic steps whenever you ask for a file: the system searches for the file in the current directory; then, if the system fails to find the file in the current directory, the system searches each established search drive in order.

In NetWare, a maximum of 16 search drives are available out of a possible 26 drive mappings. Because of the method used for searching for files, the more search drives you use, the longer searches can take. Suppose, for example, that you have 16 search drives and are currently in a directory not set up as searchable. If you request a file that does not exist in any directory, the system searches through 17 directories before you receive a `File not found` error message. Another problem is that the system allocates file server RAM for search drives. The more search drives users have on the system, the more memory is taken away from the server.

Each user can create and use his or her own set of up to 26 drive mappings. The drive mappings that USERAM sets up, for example, have no effect on the mappings that USERPM creates. Figure 3.16 shows the way you can map all 26 drive mappings in NetWare. NetWare offers several options for assigning drive letters to a directory. These options are discussed later in this chapter.

Figure 3.16

NetWare's default drive mappings.

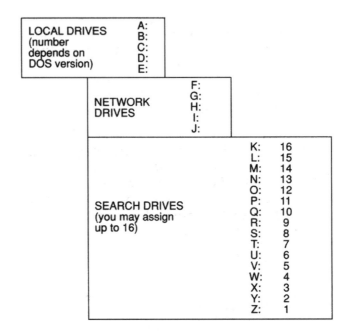

Setting Up Drive Mappings

You can set up drive mappings in several places on the network. Two places are considered temporary; three places are permanent. To set up drive mappings temporarily, type the command at the DOS prompt or from a menu called Session. Whenever you log out, these mappings are discarded. To set up drive mappings always available for use, use a system login script, user login script, or menu option.

With the exception of using SESSION and NWUSER, the syntax for defining drive mappings is the same. The syntax for drive mappings is discussed in the next few sections.

Using Local Drive Mappings

NetWare automatically allocates the letters A through E for local hardware. The drive letter A refers to the first floppy drive, and B refers to the second floppy drive. The drive letters C, D, and E refer to local hard drives. Even if your workstations do not have all this local hardware, these drive letters are reserved. You can, however, redirect any drive letter to refer to a network drive. If a local drive is remapped to a network drive and then deleted, the drive letter reverts back to referring to the local drive. The following example shows a way you can redirect the local drive E to the network drive SYS:DATA:

```
MAP E:=SYS:DATA
```

Using Network Drive Mappings

You usually use network drive mappings with data directories. Several parameters are used when you map to a directory on the network. The following is the syntax for mapping network drives:

```
MAP options A-Z: = fileserver/volume:path
```

You can use the following options in the preceding syntax:

- **NEXT.** This option enables you to map the next available network drive letter. You can use this option when you are not sure which drive letters are not being used. End users using the DOS LAST DRIVE command can use this option to find the next open drive letter. When using this option, you do not specify a drive letter. To map the next available network drive to file server CDI, PUBLIC directory, APPS subdirectory, type the following:

    ```
    MAP NEXT CDI\SYS:PUBLIC\APPS
    ```

- This option also helps to prevent mapping over a drive letter that already has been mapped. When you map a drive letter that has been mapped previously, the original mapping is scrapped without an error message. By using the NEXT option, you preserve any existing mappings.

- ***#:.** This option is used only in login scripts and works in the same way as the NEXT option. *#: searches for the next unused drive letter and maps it to the directory.

Chapter 3: Moving Around NetWare Directory Structures

◆ **ROOT.** Some older programs and many single-user programs require all rights in the root directory, which is an unacceptable request. To get around this, NetWare enables you to specify a false root drive. A false root drive appears to be a real root directory to the user and the computer. A *false root drive* displays as a drive letter with a backslash, indicating that it is a root drive. When you use the CD\ command, you return to the false root, not the real root. To return to the real root, the user must type **CD** *volume*:, which returns the user to the volume's true root. To map drive K as a root drive to the APPS directory in the PUBLIC directory on file server CDI, type the following:

```
MAP ROOT K:=CDI\SYS:PUBLIC\APPS
```

Using the DOS CD\ command takes the user to the "false" root, not the "real" root. To get back to the "real" root directory, type **CD** *volume*:.

False root drives appear differently when you use the MAP command to display the drives. In figure 3.17, for example, S: is mapped to the false root of \APPS\SS. The user sees only part of the directory, in this case \DATA.

The choice of letters is up to you. Generally, a letter that mnemonically represents the directory path is chosen. This type of drive mapping should be done with directories that hold data. Program directories should be search drives. You might, for example, map the drive letter M: to point to the \MENUS directory, as discussed in the following section. The following is an example syntax of this mapping:

```
MAP M:=SYS:MENUS
```

If you are logged in to only one file server, you can skip the MAP command's portion that refers to the file server name. Using the volume name always is recommended.

84

Setting Up Drive Mappings

```
S:\DATA>MAP

Drive  A:    maps to a local disk.
Drive  B:    maps to a local disk.
Drive  C:    maps to a local disk.
Drive  D:    maps to a local disk.
Drive  E:    maps to a local disk.
Drive  F: = CDI286\SYS:      \SHELLS
Drive  G: = CDI286\SYS:      \USERS\DAVE
Drive  S: = CDI286\SYS:APPS\SS    \DATA
       ---
SEARCH1:  = Z:. [CDI286\SYS:   \PUBLIC]
SEARCH2:  = Y:. [CDI286\SYS:   \PUBLIC\IBM_PC\MSDOS\V3.30]
SEARCH3:  = X:. [CDI286\SYS:   \APPS\SS]

S:\DATA>
```

Figure 3.17

An example of a MAP screen.

Using Search Drive Mappings

Search drive mappings are used with program directories to enable users to access programs while actually being at a data directory. The syntax for mapping regular drives follows:

MAP *options S1-16:* = *fileserver/volume:path*

You can use the following options in the preceding syntax:

♦ **INSERT.** This option puts a search drive mapping into a specific slot. INSERT ensures that an existing drive is not overwritten and that the new drive is put in the order specified.

If you require path statements to your local drives, always use INSERT for search drives. This procedure ensures that previous path statements to local drives are not overwritten.

By using this method, you can retain your DOS PATH statement when you log out of the network.

♦ **ROOT.** This option is the same as the ROOT option used for network data drive mappings. This option enables you to set false root directories. The command CD\ returns the user to the false root. To return to the real root, the user needs to type **CD** *volume:*, which returns the user to the volume's true root.

85

Chapter 3: Moving Around NetWare Directory Structures

When mapping a search drive, specify S*n*, in which *n* is replaced by the desired search drive number, and NetWare automatically assigns the next available drive letter beginning at Z and working up the alphabet. You also can insert a search drive, if you need that drive to be searched in a particular order. If, for example, you set up a root search drive to a directory that contains a quirky application, and it requires that it be the first search drive, you can accommodate the program by entering the following:

```
MAP INS S1:=CDI\SYS:PUBLIC\APPS
```

In the preceding example, the first existing search drive becomes the second search drive, the second becomes the third search drive, and so on. The search drive you inserted becomes the first search drive. No search drive mappings are lost. Their order simply is changed.

Deleting Drive Mappings

You might find that you are not using all your current drive mappings. By eliminating these excess drive mappings, you can increase your file server performance by returning memory used for tracking search drives to the file server. Also, when a user exits an application and does not need access to a directory, you can maintain system security by deleting the drive mapping. This makes it more difficult to get to the directory through an existing mapping.

To delete a mapped data drive, use the following syntax:

```
MAP DEL drive letter:
```

To delete a mapped search drive, use the following syntax:

```
MAP DEL Sdrive number:
```

These commands remove the mapping from the list. You do not need to specify the full path to delete the drive mappings. NetWare is concerned only with the label, or drive letter.

Setting Up Drive Mappings

 If you MAP DEL a search drive by using the letter rather than the S#:, the following message appears:

    This is a SEARCH DRIVE, are you sure you want to
    Delete? (Y/N)

If you make it a habit to delete all drive mappings by drive letter, including search drive mappings, you are less likely to accidentally delete a search drive mapping that you really need, such as the drive mapped to SYS:PUBLIC.

If you accidentally delete the SYS:PUBLIC drive mapping, you cannot run network commands. You must use DOS to CD through the directory structure until you again have a drive mapping to SYS:PUBLIC. Then you can use the MAP command to remap the deleted search drive.

Using the DOS CD Command on Drive Mappings

Drive mappings are *dynamic*, which means that they change. When you use the DOS CD command, drive mappings follow you around. As you learned in the previous sections, the MAP command establishes a drive letter and where that letter initially points. After the letter is initially set, you can determine where the letter points. To do this, use the CD command. This makes the mapping point to the new location. Drive mappings match the DOS prompt path; if it changes, the mapping reflects the change. Consider the following drive mapping shown when **MAP** is entered at the DOS prompt:

    Drive M: = CDI386\SYS: \UTILS\MENUS

This mapping uses the following syntax:

    MAP M: = SYS:UTILS\MENUS

Chapter 3: Moving Around NetWare Directory Structures

By entering **M:** at the DOS prompt, you are taken to the UTILS/MENUS directory. If you type **CD\LOGIN** at this directory, you are taken to the LOGIN directory. If you type **MAP** again, you see the following entry for M:

```
Drive M: = CDI386\SYS: \LOGIN
```

Changing directories using CD changes the location shown to you using MAP.

 You might find that using the CD command is a disadvantage if you issue it to a search drive. Possible inconveniences include searching a drive that does not need to be searched, or losing the path to a directory needed to run a program. If you find that you are lost, simply log in again. This procedure resets your mappings to the way they were set up in the login scripts.

Figure 3.18 shows the screen Windows provides for doing your mappings. Novell's Windows utilities follow the traditional point-and-shoot method of choosing a directory.

Figure 3.18
The Windows mapping screen.

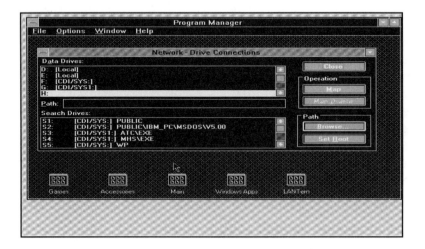

Review Questions

1. File servers must have unique names.

    a. This is required at all times.

    b. This is required only when communicating with another file server.

    c. This is optional.

    d. This cannot be done.

2. Which of the following is the correct syntax for a path pointing to the server B386, volume APPS, and subdirectory PROGRAMS under directory DATA?

    a. B386:SYS\PROGRAMS\DATA

    b. B386\SYS:APPS\PROGRAMS

    c. B386\APPS:DATA\PROGRAMS

    d. B386\DATA:PROGRAMS\DATA

3. NetWare 3.1x can have ___ volumes.

    a. 16

    b. 32

    c. 64

    d. 128

4. Which of the following is a legal volume name?

    a. TAX.VOL:

    b. SYS\VOL:

    c. VOL@COM:

    d. *STARCOM:

Chapter 3: Moving Around NetWare Directory Structures

5. Which of the following is not a required directory?
   a. LOGIN
   b. HOME
   c. SYSTEM
   d. MAIL

6. Which directory belongs to the user SUPERVISOR?
   a. SYS:SYSTEM\1
   b. SYS:MAIL\1
   c. SYS:LOGIN\SUPERVISOR
   d. SYS:MAIL\00000001

7. What gets put into a user's MAIL_ID directory?
   a. PRINTCON.DAT and LOGIN
   b. PRINT.CON and QUEUE.DAT
   c. PRINTCON.DAT and LOGIN.EXE
   d. PRINT.LOG and INFO.LOG

8. Which of the following is a true statement?
   a. The required directories must appear in every volume.
   b. You should not move the required directories, because the operating system depends on their location.
   c. Because Novell no longer includes an electronic mail package, you can delete the SYS:MAIL directory.
   d. To make it easier to spot the MAIL_ID directories, you can change the hexadecimal name to the user's login name.

Review Questions

9. Which utility is most closely related to the DOS TREE command?

    a. DIR /S

    b. LIST /A

    c. DIRLIST /S

    d. LISTDIR /A

10. Which utilities give you statistical information about the volumes?

    a. LISTDIR, VOLINFO, CHKDSK

    b. VOLINFO, CHKVOL, VOLDIR

    c. VOLINFO, CHKDIR, CHKINFO

    d. VOLINFO, CHKVOL, CHKDIR

11. Which of the following is not a valid option?

    a. LISTDIR /T

    b. NDIR SYS:*.dat /OW=SUPERVISOR /SUB

    c. LISTDIR /O

    d. NDIR \may.?? /FO /AC NOT BEF 2/5/92

12. Which command should you use to map a drive to the PROGRAM directory on the server NORTH386 on the SYS: volume?

    a. MAP INSERT S3:=NORTH386:\SYS\PROGRAMS

    b. MAP INSERT S3:NORTH386\SYS:PROGRAMS

    c. MAP INSERT 3:=NORTH386\SYS:PROGRAMS

    d. MAP INSERT S3:=NORTH386\SYS:PROGRAMS

Chapter 3: Moving Around NetWare Directory Structures

13. Where are you not allowed to map a drive?

    a. At the DOS prompt

    b. In FILER

    c. In a menu

    d. In a login script

14. Which command is added to the MAP statement to map a false root?

    a. DEL

    b. FALSEROOT

    c. ROOT

    d. NEXT

15. DOS reserves certain drive letters to use for local devices. Which of the following is a reserved drive letter for the local disk?

    a. E

    b. f

    c. s1

    d. z

16. How many search drives are available for each user as the default?

    a. 26

    b. 16

    c. 13

    d. 5

Review Questions

17. When a first search drive exists, which command should you use to add a new first search drive?

    a. MAP NEXT

    b. MAP BEFORE

    c. MAP S1

    d. MAP INSERT

18. Which of the following portion of a path name does not have to be used in a single-server network?

    a. SERVER

    b. VOLUME

    c. DIRECTORY

    d. SUBDIRECTORY

19. Which statement about using DOS commands on the network is not true?

    a. DOS commands should never be used on the network.

    b. You can use DOS commands on the network to access DOS system files.

    c. You can use DOS commands from drives A through E without affecting network drive mappings.

    d. DOS commands such as CD can be used to reestablish a drive mapping when it has been accidentally changed and NetWare commands cannot be accessed.

20. The NetWare directory structure's volume level is equivalent to which of the following?

    a. A NetWare search drive

    b. The root directory of a DOS directory structure

    c. A mapped root drive in a local DOS directory

    d. No equivalent exists

Case Study

Create a network environment for the following scenario.

You are setting up a network for the BDHOME company. They have two servers and 60 users. They use the following applications:

- Accounting
- Inventory
- Word Processing
- Spreadsheet
- Name and Address Database

The key people, listed by login name, are as follows:

- BD, the owner
- MYERS, the system administrator
- KMURPHY, the controller
- GDALL, quality control supervisor
- TERESA, the administrative assistant

The file servers each have one 650M drive.

Based on this information, answer the following questions.

1. Create a directory structure for the BDHOME company, keeping the following points in mind:
    - The Inventory and Accounting databases are the largest.
    - The key people want their own directories.
    - Accounting wants to make certain that their people are the only ones with access to the accounting software.

Case Study

- ◆ Everyone can access the Inventory database.
- ◆ The programs and the data must be kept separate from each other.

2. Discuss the difference between using NetWare 2.2 and 3.1x for this installation.

Understanding NetWare Security

CHAPTER 4

In Chapter 4, you learn about the security elements common to all versions of NetWare up to v3.11. In addition, you learn about the packet security enhancement—released for NetWare 3.11 servers and clients, and added to NetWare 3.12. The items covered in this chapter include the following:

- User types and what they can accomplish
- Levels of NetWare security
- Security functions at each level
- Security attributes
- Command-line utilities that affect security
- NetWare 3.12 NCP Packet Signature security enhancement

Defining Security Levels

NetWare has seven different types of network users. You can combine many of these types with other types to fine-tune what a user can do on the system. The following list shows the different NetWare user types, ranging from the highest level to the lowest level:

- Supervisor
- Supervisor equivalents

Chapter 4: Understanding NetWare Security

- ◆ FCONSOLE operators
- ◆ Workgroup managers
- ◆ PCONSOLE operators
- ◆ Account managers
- ◆ End users

 The user supervisor is an actual login account, while a supervisor equivalent is a user account that can perform all the same functions as the supervisor.

Workgroup managers have the power to create users and are, therefore, more authoritative than account managers.

Most users can be managed by a different type of user. By combining user types, you can create the administrators and users to fully utilize your network. Figure 4.1 illustrates the hierarchy of network administration.

Figure 4.1
NetWare's subsets of the security divisions and their domains.

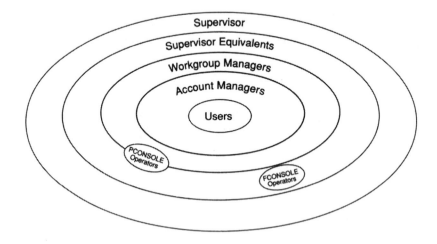

Defining Security Levels

The Supervisor

The *supervisor*, who has rights to every utility and file on the network, is the highest-level network user. Only one user named supervisor is permitted on the network. This user is given all rights and privileges. The supervisor can be viewed as having a "back door" into the network, meaning that he or she can get into the network in case of an emergency. Because of the supervisor's high status, he or she is exempt from deletion by other users on the network. This capability does not, however, give the supervisor full rights to all files on the network. If, for example, a file is marked as read-only, the supervisor cannot delete the file until the attribute is changed to Read/Write.

The supervisor password can be changed by the supervisor or by the supervisor equivalents (discussed in the following section). Many third-party network management programs that have system security still require the login ID of the supervisor and do not function for the supervisor equivalent users.

The Supervisor Equivalent

The *supervisor equivalent* user is a regular end user who has the same authority on the system as the supervisor. Supervisor equivalent users have the capability to create other supervisor equivalent users and can change the supervisor account, including the password.

The FCONSOLE Operator

NetWare's FCONSOLE utility enables you to view certain information about the network. FCONSOLE operators have certain privileges depending on whether they also are supervisor equivalents.

FCONSOLE operators who have supervisor equivalence can use all options available in FCONSOLE. FCONSOLE operators who do not have supervisor equivalence, however, cannot clear connections or down the file server from FCONSOLE. Users who are not FCONSOLE operators or supervisor equivalents can use FCONSOLE but are severely limited in the types of information they can see.

 Novell often refers to FCONSOLE operators as CONSOLE operators.

Chapters 9 and 10 walk you through all the FCONSOLE options and point out the features of FCONSOLE that are limited to FCONSOLE operators.

The Workgroup Manager

Workgroup managers can be users or a group of users. Workgroup managers can create, delete, and manage user accounts. They also can change passwords, account restrictions, and login scripts for users. Workgroup managers, however, can manage only those users and groups assigned to them or that they create. They cannot modify users or groups not in their list of managed users and groups.

The User Account Manager

User account managers can be users or groups. User account managers can manage and delete accounts assigned to them. Unlike workgroup managers, user account managers cannot create users and groups.

The PCONSOLE Operator

NetWare has two types of PCONSOLE operators. One type, the *print queue operator*, manages and deletes print queues. The other type, the *print server operator*, manages and deletes print servers.

Defining Security Levels

The only type of user, however, that can create print servers and queues is the supervisor.

Table 4.1 lists the functions that administrators and end users can use on the network and helps you visualize which types of users on the network can accomplish different management tasks.

Table 4.1
Security Domains

	Create/Delete Supervisor Equivalent	Create/Delete Workgroup Managers	Create Account Manager	Create/Delete Users	Inherits All Rights To Network	Create/Delete Print Queues and Servers	Manage Print Queues (by default)	Manage Print Servers (by default)	Use FCONSOLE (LIMITED) Access	Use FCONSOLE (UNLIMITED) Access
Supervisor	●	●	●	●	●	●	●	●		●
Supervisor Equivalent	●	●	●	●	●	●	●			●
Workgroup Manager		●	●						●	
User Account Manager			●						●	
Print Queue Operator							●			
Print Server Operator								●		
FCONSOLE Operator									●	

The End User

End users make up the majority of NetWare users. End users can perform only the functions given to them by the other six categories of users.

Exploring NetWare Security Levels

This section examines the various layers of NetWare security. In the process, you learn why NetWare can reliably provide the right level of protection for any company.

Four levels of security exist. The following list ranks these levels in order from lowest to highest:

- Login/Password
- Rights
- Attributes
- File Server Console

Login/Password-Level Security

NetWare enables you to use passwords as a measure of security. At least a dozen parameters are available for this feature; each parameter can be set for individual users or as a default for all users.

NetWare offers a defense measure before the password ever comes into play. Suppose, for example, that you want to log in to a network. Because most small to mid-sized companies use first names for login names, you might assume that a login name is "Ann" and try to log in with that name. The system responds to this request by asking for a password. You try using common passwords, but each time the network denies access.

You can try different passwords continually, but NetWare never tells you whether a user named Ann is on that system. This feature is NetWare's first line of defense against *hackers* (unauthorized users). Instead of responding with a message that Ann is not a valid user name, NetWare simply asks you for a password.

User Rights

Trustee rights are the rights users or groups have in a directory. These rights also are referred to as *privileges*. Seven trustee rights exist in v2.2, and eight trustee rights exist in v3.11. Trustee rights are the keys each user has for a directory. Table 4.2 lists the seven rights common in both v2.2 and v3.11.

Table 4.2
Rights Common to NetWare 2.2 and 3.11

Right	Function
Read	Enables the user to see the contents of a file and to use the file
Write	Enables the user to alter the contents of a file
Create	Enables the user to make new files and directories
Erase	Enables the user to delete existing files and directories
File Scan	Enables the user to view files and subdirectories in a directory; without this right, you cannot see files
Modify	Enables the user to change the attributes of a file; the user can change a file from Read/Write to Read-Only or from Nonshareable to Shareable
Access Control	Enables the user to give any of the preceding rights to other users on the network

In v2.2, you still can see subdirectories, even if you are denied rights; v3.11 hides subdirectories from the user.

In v3.11, Modify also enables the user to change the attributes for directories; v2.2 does not enable you to set attributes for directories.

Version 3.11 has an eighth right, Supervisory, which gives all the other rights to the user or group. This right makes the user a *directory supervisor*, someone who has control over what happens to a directory structure's branch. Version 2.2 only has seven rights.

Effective Rights

You can think of directory rights as locks that every directory has on your system. NetWare gives each directory a full set of locks by default.

Trustee rights act as keys that fit the directory locks. Each user can have his or her own set of unique keys. As an example, think of your own key ring. You have your own house key, car key, and so on. Chances are that no one has the same keys as you. Everyone has different locks that need to be opened. The same concept applies to networks. You have specific needs in directories. Some users have the same needs; others have different needs. Each user can have his or her own set of keys, or rights.

Effective rights are the trustee rights (keys) that actually match available directory rights (locks). If a lock exists and you do not have a key, you cannot perform the function. The only way you can use a right is to have matching locks and keys.

Trustee rights include all rights you have been given individually combined with all the rights given to any groups to which you belong.

Effective rights are the trustee rights' results after they have been filtered by the Maximum Rights Mask (MRM) in v2.2 or the Inherited Rights Mask (IRM) in v3.11. See Chapter 8 for more information on MRM, and Chapter 10 for more information on IRM.

File-Level Security

The status of individual files ultimately determines which functions you can perform. Earlier, you learned that if a directory enables the Erase right and a user has that right, files are subject to deletion. If a file is a read-only file, however, trustee rights and directory rights have no effect. Read-only files cannot be deleted, so the file's status takes precedence.

Files are secured by the use of *attributes*, conditions placed on the files. These conditions help to control what can be done to the files and how the files can be used on the network. Many combinations of attributes are attached to files and directories.

Attributes are handled differently in NetWare 2.2 and 3.11. NetWare 2.2 supports file attributes only; v3.11 supports directory attributes and file attributes.

The following sections discuss attributes common to both v2.2 and v3.11. For more information, please refer to Chapter 8 for v2.2 attributes and Chapter 10 for v3.11 attributes.

Archive Needed

NetWare uses the letter A to signify files that have been altered after the last backup. The Archive Needed attribute also is assigned to files that have been copied into another directory. Archive Needed looks for the DOS Archive Bit flag on a file.

Execute Only

Execute Only is designated with the letter X. After this attribute is placed on a file, it cannot be taken off. This attribute only affects files ending in COM or EXE and is the only attribute that you cannot reverse.

Only users with supervisor privileges can assign the Execute Only attribute.

Execute Only hinders application piracy by preventing files from being copied or downloaded.

Make sure that you have a copy of a file before you attach the Execute Only flag, because this attribute also prevents files from being backed up. In addition, many programs cannot operate when flagged with Execute Only.

Hidden File

The Hidden File attribute uses the letter H. Files hidden with this attribute do not show up when you use the DOS DIR command. If a user has the File Scan right, files hidden with this attribute appear after using NDIR.

Read Audit and Write Audit

NetWare still is in the process of perfecting a built-in audit trail on files. Currently, you can flag files with Ra for Read Audit and Wa for Write Audit, but they have no effect.

Read Only and Read/Write

You cannot write to, delete, or rename a read-only file. The Read Only attribute enables users to read and use files. Program files are most often flagged with Ro for read-only.

A Read/Write file attribute enables users to read from the file and write back to the file. This attribute is designated with Rw and is the default on newly created files. Flagging a file with Read Only deletes the Read/Write attribute. Data files are usually flagged with Read/Write.

When Read Only is used in v3.11, the attributes of Delete Inhibit and Rename Inhibit also are included.

Shareable and Nonshareable

NetWare uses the letter S to designate shareable files. This attribute enables several users to access a single file at the same time. This flag is used most often with read-only files and database files.

Nonshareable, or Normal, is the system default. If you flag a file with N, you set the attributes as Nonshareable Read/Write. Nonshareable files normally are assigned to program files that are single-user applications. This attribute ensures that only one person can use the file at any one time.

System File

System files, flagged with Sy, are not listed after you use the DOS DIR command. These files cannot be deleted or copied. If you have the File Scan right, you can see these files by using the NDIR command.

Transactional

Files marked with T can be tracked using the Transaction Tracking System (TTS). All database files that need to be tracked while being modified must have this attribute.

TTS is a method the file server uses to track the integrity of database files during database file updates. For more information about TTS, see Chapter 8, "NetWare 2.2 System Manager."

Using Command-Line Utilities

This section discusses the command-line utilities available in NetWare that administrators and managers can use to manipulate user accounts. Command-line utilities are used from the DOS prompt.

The RIGHTS Command

The RIGHTS command shows the user which rights they have in any given directory. If you seem to have more rights in one directory than you were granted originally, then rights have flowed down from a higher directory. This event is referred to as flow-through. *Flow-through* automatically occurs to all subdirectories beneath the directory in which rights have been granted.

The following syntax is used for the RIGHTS command:

    RIGHTS path

In the example shown in figure 4.2, the RIGHTS command is entered from the O prompt to see the available rights in that directory.

Figure 4.2
The RIGHTS command lists and explains each available right.

```
O:\OFFICE>rights
B386\SYS:OFFICE
Your Effective Rights for this directory are [SRWCEMFA]
        You have Supervisor Rights to Directory.    (S)
  * May Read from File.                             (R)
  * May Write to File.                              (W)
    May Create Subdirectories and Files.            (C)
    May Erase Directory.                            (E)
    May Modify Directory.                           (M)
    May Scan for Files.                             (F)
    May Change Access Control.                      (A)

* Has no effect on directory.

        Entries in Directory May Inherit [SRWCEMFA] rights.
        You have ALL RIGHTS to Directory Entry.

O:\OFFICE>
```

The TLIST Command

The TLIST command displays the users that have been given explicit rights in a specific directory. Flow-through does not occur in TLIST. The TLIST command is typed in the following manner:

    TLIST path

In figure 4.3, the TLIST command shows that the user DBATEMAN and the group TECHS have all rights except Supervisory.

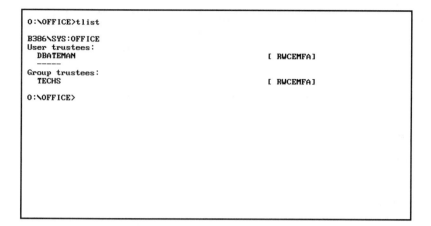

Figure 4.3
TLIST displays the rights granted to users and groups.

The GRANT Command

The GRANT command grants rights to users or groups. You also can use menu items in the User Information menu in SYSCON to grant rights. Any information changed by using the GRANT command is permanent and appears in the user's trustee information screens in SYSCON. The GRANT command is typed in the following manner:

    GRANT *rightslist* [FOR *path*] TO [USER¦GROUP] *name*

In figure 4.4, for example, the user DBATEMAN requests Read and File Scan rights in the SYS:SERVICE directory. The supervisor uses the GRANT command and a shortcut to give him the rights. Instead of spelling out the full path name, the system needs only the drive letter that points to the proper path. The TLIST command is used after GRANT to verify that the rights are granted.

The REVOKE Command

The REVOKE command takes away rights from a user in either directories or files. REVOKE uses the following syntax:

    REVOKE *rightslist* [FOR *path*] FROM [USER¦GROUP] *name*

Chapter 4: Understanding NetWare Security

Figure 4.5, for example, shows that the user DBATEMAN has more rights than necessary in the SYS:PUBLIC directory. The excess rights are removed by using the REVOKE command; the TLIST command is used to verify the process.

Figure 4.4
The GRANT command gives rights to a user for a specific directory.

```
O:\SERVICE>grant r f for o: to dbateman

B386/SYS:SERVICE
SERVICE                                        Rights set to [ R    F ]

O:\SERVICE>tlist

B386\SYS:SERVICE
User trustees:
  BACKUP                                                      [ R    F ]
  DBATEMAN                                                    [ R    F ]
  ─────
Group trustees:
  ACCOUNTING                                                  [ RWCEMFA ]

O:\SERVICE>
```

Figure 4.5
The REVOKE command is used to deny rights from a user for a specific directory.

```
O:\PUBLIC>revoke c e m a for o: from dbateman
B386/SYS:PUBLIC
Trustee's access rights set to [ RW   F ]
Rights for 1 directories were changed for DBATEMAN.

O:\PUBLIC>tlist

B386\SYS:PUBLIC
User trustees:
  DBATEMAN                                                    [ RW   F ]
  ─────
Group trustees:
  EVERYONE                                                    [ R    F ] Minimum rights ...

O:\PUBLIC>
```

The REMOVE Command

The REMOVE command removes the user from the trustee list. REMOVE uses the following syntax:

```
REMOVE [USER¦GROUP] name [FROM path]
```

In figure 4.6, the user DBATEMAN is removed from the O directory by using the REMOVE command. The TLIST command then confirms the results.

```
O:\PUBLIC>remove dbateman from o:
B386/SYS:PUBLIC
User "DBATEMAN" no longer a trustee to the specified directory.

Trustee "DBATEMAN" removed from 1 directories.

O:\PUBLIC>tlist
B386\SYS:PUBLIC
No user trustees.
Group trustees:
   EVERYONE                                  [ R    F ] Minimum rights ...

O:\PUBLIC>
```

Figure 4.6

The REMOVE command is used to remove a user from a trustee list.

Understanding NCP Packet Signature

The server and the client on a NetWare network communicate by sending packets back and forth between them. A *packet* contains the data or request for a network service as well as information that identifies such things as the following:

- Where the packet originated
- Where the packet is to be delivered
- Information that authenticates the user to the network

Identifying the client and its right to access the network services or information being requested is an important aspect of each packet. It provides a certain level of network security. In the fall of 1992, however, students working in a laboratory at Lieden University in the Netherlands discovered a way to defeat this security. Using a very complex procedure, they were able to forge a packet's identification, giving a client greater security privileges than originally authorized.

Chapter 4: Understanding NetWare Security

This problem, however, is not just a NetWare problem. All networking products have the same problem inherent in their design. To correct the problem in NetWare, Novell developed a security enhancement. This enhancement became an operating system component for NetWare 3.12, and was released as an update for NetWare 3.11 servers and clients shortly after the problem was discovered. The enhancement is called *NCP Packet Signature*.

The NCP Packet Signature Process

To remedy this security problem, Novell developed a process of identifying packets. If the set level of NCP packet signature requires it, when a client logs into a NetWare 3.12 server, the server and client agree upon a single, shared identification key called the *session key*. Each client that logs into the server has a unique session key.

After the client is logged into the server, the client adds its unique signature to the packet each time the client requests services. The server checks the packet signature to ensure its correctness for this client. Correctly signed packets are processed.

Packets without the correct signature, or with no signature at all, are discarded. The server console then reports the offending client by placing an alert message in the server error log and by reporting it to the server console.

The client is notified that an error occurred during server attachment, but is not warned or told the reason for or type of error. This distinction also provides a certain amount of security. If someone at the client is trying to gain greater security rights than he or she is permitted, the server does not tell the client that an illegal request is being made.

Figure 4.7 shows the NCP packet signature process from client to server.

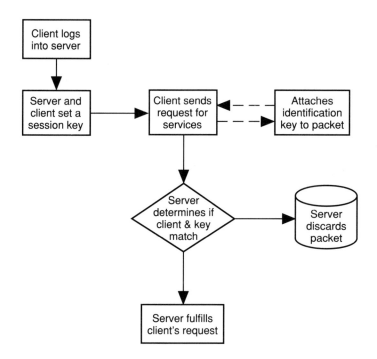

Figure 4.7
The NCP packet signature process.

NCP Packet Signature Security Levels

The NCP packet signature enables the network administrator to determine the level of security implementation on the network. Although many networking sites need the highest level of security provided by the NCP packet signature process, not all networks require as high a level of security. Because network performance is affected to a certain extent by the NCP packet signature process, network administrators might want to adjust the level of NCP packet signature used on their network.

Consider the following example. In a network on which a single server can contain highly sensitive information, such as patient health records in a medical facility, the NCP packet signature can be set at the highest level, level 3, at the server and at each client.

At server level 3, all packets sent from the server contain an NCP packet signature. This level requires that all packets received by the server from clients be correctly signed.

Chapter 4: Understanding NetWare Security

At client level 3, all packets are signed before they are sent to the server. This level requires that anything received by the client from the server be correctly signed.

Network administrators set the level of NCP packet signature security by choosing from one of four levels at both the server and the client. Each combination of client and server level settings affects the overall security of packets on the network.

Table 4.3 lists the security levels available for clients and servers and shows the net effect that each combination of server and client level settings has on the network's overall security. The default is marked with an asterisk (*).

Table 4.3
NCP Packet Signature Levels

Server Level	Effect on Server	+	Client Level	Effect on Client	=	Effective Level
0	Packets not signed		0	Packets not signed		No packet signature
0	Packets not signed		1	Signed if server asks		No packet signature
0	Packets not signed		2	Signs if server can sign		No packet signature
0	Packets not signed		3	Always signs and requires server to sign		Failed login
1	Signs only if client asks		0	Packets not signed		No packet signature
1	Signs only if client asks		1	Signed if server asks		No packet signature
1	Signs only if client asks		2	Signs if server can sign		Packet signature
1	Signs only if client asks		3	Always signs and requires server to sign		Packet signature

Understanding NCP Packet Signature

Server Level	Effect on Server	+	Client Level	Effect on Client	=	Effective Level
2	Signs if client can		0	Packets not signed		No packet signature
2*	Signs if client can		1*	Signed if server asks		Packet signature
2	Signs if client can		2	Signs if server can		Packet signature
2	Signs if client can		3	Always signs and requires server to sign		Packet signature
3	Always signs and requires client to sign		0	Packets not signed		No packet signature
3	Always signs and requires client to sign		1	Signed if server asks		Packet signature
3	Always signs and requires client to sign		2	Signs if server can sign		Packet signature
3	Always signs and requires client to sign		3	Always signs and requires server to sign		Packet Signature

After the network administrator has determined the level of packet security needed, she must then set that level on each affected server and client. If the default settings of level 2 for the server and level 1 for each client is sufficient, the network administrator does not need to change these levels. If changes are warranted, however, or if the network administrator decides that no packet signing is necessary, he or she can make changes to the appropriate server and client files.

Chapter 4: Understanding NetWare Security

Change or Disable Packet Signing

NCP packet signature levels are set at both the server and the client. As previously noted, level 2 is the default setting for the server, and level 1 is the default setting for each client. You can, however, modify both settings.

To change the server's default packet signature setting, type the following statement at the server console and press Enter, or edit the server's AUTOEXEC.NCF file to include the following statement:

SET NCP PACKET SIGNATURE OPTION = number

If you add the statement to the server's AUTOEXEC.NCF file, it does not take effect until the next time that the AUTOEXEC.NCF file is run, at server startup.

Figure 4.8 shows a server's AUTOEXEC.NCF file with the SET NCP PACKET SIGNATURE OPTION line included.

Figure 4.8
Server AUTOEXEC.NCF file with the NCP Packet option line.

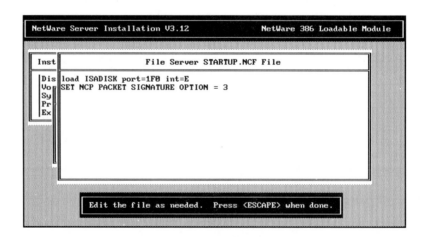

To change a client's default packet signature, modify the client's NET.CFG file to add the following statement as an indented line under the NetWare DOS Requester heading:

SIGNATURE LEVEL = number

Like the AUTOEXEC.NCF file, the change to the NET.CFG file does not take effect until the NET.CFG file is reloaded at client bootup.

Figure 4.9 shows a client's NET.CFG file with the SIGNATURE LEVEL line included.

```
[RUBY_1] C:\>TYPE NET.CFG
Link driver NE2000
    INT 5
    PORT 340
    MEM D0000
    FRAME Ethernet_802.3

Netware DOS Requester
    FIRST NETWORK DRIVE = F
    PREFERRED SERVER = JOHN
    SIGNATURE LEVEL = 1
    SHOW DOTS = ON
    VLM = NMR.VLM

Protocol IPX
    IPX SOCKETS 45
[RUBY_1] C:\>
```

Figure 4.9

Server AUTOEXEC.NCF file with the NCP Packet option line.

Review Questions

1. Who can change the supervisor's password?

    a. The supervisor

    b. Supervisor and all supervisor equivalents

    c. Supervisor, supervisor equivalents, and workgroup managers

    d. Supervisor and FCONSOLE operators

2. Can an account manager delete a user?

    a. Yes

    b. No

    c. Only if they manage that user

    d. Only if they created that user

Chapter 4: Understanding NetWare Security

3. Which of the following cannot be assigned to a group of users?

    a. Workgroup manager

    b. Account manager

    c. Print queue operator

    d. Supervisor equivalent

4. Who can create a workgroup manager?

    a. Supervisor only

    b. Supervisor and supervisor equivalents

    c. Supervisor, supervisor equivalents, and account managers

    d. Account managers

5. Which of the following is not a type of NetWare operator?

    a. Print queue operator

    b. Print server operator

    c. Console operator

    d. Account operator

6. Which user is most commonly found on an average network?

    a. The end user

    b. The supervisor equivalent

    c. The print server operator

    d. The FCONSOLE operator

7. Which is not a level of NetWare security?

    a. Rights

    b. File server console

    c. Menus

    d. Attributes

Review Questions

8. Which is the correct order of NetWare security from highest to lowest?
    a. File server, rights, attributes, password
    b. File server, attributes, rights, password
    c. Attributes, rights, password, file server
    d. Password, attributes, rights, file server

9. Which rights are necessary to use an executable file?
    a. Read, Write, and File Scan
    b. Read and File Scan
    c. Read
    d. Read and Access Control

10. Which right enables you to assign the Shareable attribute to a file?
    a. Access Control
    b. Access Control and Modify
    c. Modify
    d. File Scan and Modify

11. Effective rights include:
    a. All the rights you have plus the rights of any groups to which you belong
    b. All of the rights assigned to your user account
    c. The rights assigned to the supervisor
    d. All of your rights minus the rights of any group to which you belong

12. Which attribute enables you to change the contents of a file?
    a. Modify
    b. Access Control

Chapter 4: Understanding NetWare Security

   c. Read/Write

   d. Read Audit

13. Which command-line utility shows the effective rights of a user?

   a. RIGHTS

   b. TLIST

   c. GRANT

   d. ERIGHTS

14. Which statement takes the Access Control and Modify rights away from the user JOE for the file called DATA.FIL?

   a. REMOVE JOE FROM DATA.FIL

   b. REVOKE A M FOR JOE FROM DATA.FIL

   c. REMOVE A M FOR DATA.FIL FROM JOE

   d. REVOKE A M FOR DATA.FIL FROM JOE

15. Which of the following is the correct name for the NetWare security enhancement that prevents packet forgery?

   a. NCP Packet Signature

   b. NCP Packet Signing Process

   c. NCP Security Packet Process

   d. NCP Security Packet Signing Process

16. Where should security level be assigned in order to prevent packet forgery?

   a. At the file server only

   b. At the client only

   c. At all file servers and clients

   d. At only file servers and clients that need it

Review Questions

17. How many effective levels of security can the network administrator set?

    a. 1

    b. 4

    c. 8

    d. 16

    e. 17

18. What is the default setting for packet security?

    a. Server 1, Client 2

    b. Server 2, Client 1

    c. Server 2, Client 2

    d. No default setting exists

19. Which packet security levels should the network administrator set if the server contains sensitive information such as patient files?

    a. Server 1, Client 3

    b. Server 3, Client 1

    c. Server 2, Client 1

    d. Server 3, Client 3

20. What security levels should the network administrator set if the server contains some sensitive information, but users share clients for accessing that information?

    a. Server 1, Client 3

    b. Server 2, Client 2

    c. Server 3, Client 1

    d. Server 3, Client 3

Case Study

Refer back to the directory structure you created in Chapter 3. Assign security to the directory structure, keeping the following points in mind.

- BD and KMURPHY are the only users permitted into the accounting package.
- MYERS is the only supervisor equivalent, but wants GDALL and KMURPHY to be able to create and assign rights for future personnel.
- TERESA needs access to run all programs but not to modify the programs. She needs the ability to change data for all programs except payroll.
- GDALL only needs access to the Inventory and Name and Address databases.
- All users need to print, but MYERS needs to control the print server.

Program files need to be protected from deletion.

1. By using the preceding information, determine the user type for the following users. Decide who should be supervisor equivalent users, workgroup managers, or network users.

   BD, the owner
   MYERS, the system administrator
   KMURPHY, the controller
   GDALL, the quality control supervisor
   TERESA, the administrative assistant

2. Using the chart on the following page, determine the rights each user needs in each directory.

Case Study

	Directories	BD	MYERS	KMURPHY	GDALL	TERESA	Attributes
NetWare	SYS: Mail						
	SYS: Public						
	SYS: Mail \ Mail_ID						
Applications							

Utilities

In this chapter, you learn about the menu utilities NetWare offers to help you manage the network. The utilities covered in this chapter are common to NetWare 2.2 and 3.1x. These utilities include the following:

- SYSCON
- ATOTAL and PAUDIT
- FILER
- MAKEUSER
- USERDEF
- ROUTEGEN
- NBACKUP and SBACKUP

You need to become familiar with the screens shown in this chapter for certification testing. In this chapter, you learn about all the options in the menu utilities in the preceding list. You also learn to create a MAKEUSER script and to use USERDEF to make a script. You learn about the utilities associated with the Accounting option of SYSCON, and finally, you learn about backing up files by using the NBACKUP Utility.

Navigating the Menus

Before you learn the different menus and submenus of the utilities, you need to become familiar with the keys that enable you to navigate the various menus in the utilities. Following is a list of these keys:

- **Enter.** Moves you to the next level in the menu or accepts an item from the list.

- **Esc.** Takes you back to a previous level or stops the selecting process.

- **F1.** Shows you the definition of a highlighted item.

- **F1,F1.** Shows you a list of function key definitions.

- **F3.** Enables you to change the name of the object or path when the object or path is highlighted.

- **F5.** Enables you to select multiple items from a list, then press Enter to bring the selected item into the current list. When you select an item, the item blinks on-screen. To deselect an item, press F5 again.

- **F6.** Enables you to mark a pattern of items.

- **F7.** Enables you to unmark all marked items.

- **F8.** Enables you to unmark a pattern of items.

When you select or mark an item, NetWare places a marker on the object, causing it to blink. You then can delete or copy marked items. Some of these keys do not work in all menu items. F6, F7, and F8, for example, work best in FILER (discussed later in this chapter), but do not work in SYSCON (discussed in the next section).

Other ways to select an item in a list is to highlight the desired item by pressing the up or down arrow keys or by typing the name of the item. Repeat this process until the desired item is highlighted.

When you are in a menu that contains a list of many items, you can go directly to the item you want by typing in one letter at a time. If you want to go to a group called SUPERS, for example, simply type the letter **S**. If no other group exists with the letter S, you go directly to SUPERS. If, on the other hand, a group called SALES exists, you would jump to SALES. In this case, you need to type **SU** to go to SUPERS.

Exploring SYSCON

This section discusses the role of SYSCON. The SYSCON menu, which stands for SYStem CONfiguration, enables you to set up NetWare's accounting feature, check file server information, create users and groups, and perform administrative network functions. These functions are set up by using the options listed in the Available Topics menu, as shown in figure 5.1. Each option is described in more detail in the following sections.

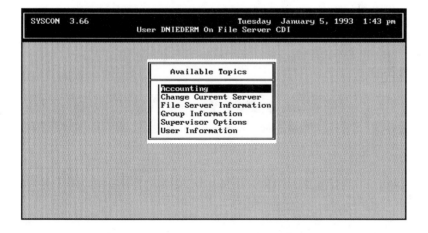

Figure 5.1
The Available Topics menu in SYSCON.

The SYSCON Accounting Option

The first option on the SYSCON menu is Accounting. The Accounting option enables you to charge users for use of the network based on the following five areas:

Chapter 5: Utilities

- Blocks read
- Blocks written
- Connect time
- Disk storage
- Service requests

Large installations can cover several departments. In many businesses that have networks, departments must pay for part of the network. NetWare's accounting feature enables the system administrator to charge each department for its portion of the total network usage. Users in each department then are charged only for what they do on the network.

To set up accounting on your network, you need to decide which charge rates you want to use and in what combinations. These areas, which appear on-screen on the Accounting menu (see fig. 5.2), can be joined in any combination to charge different users. NetWare automatically tracks user logins and logouts.

 The accounting information is stored in SYS:SYSTEM in a file named NET$ACCT.DAT.

Figure 5.2
Accounting options in the SYSCON menu.

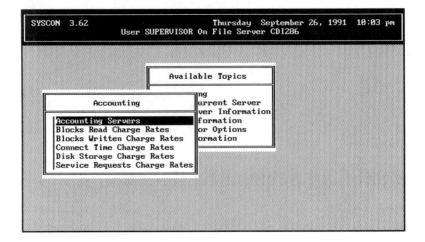

Each Accounting option is described in the following list:

- **Blocks Read Charge Rates.** Determines the amount of information users request from the file server. Users are charged for each block of information read from the file server. A *block* is the minimum size of a piece of information that NetWare can read and write. The default block size in NetWare is 4K. When you select this option, the Blocks Read Charge Rates screen appears (see fig. 5.3). This screen enables administrators to configure the accounting charge rates.

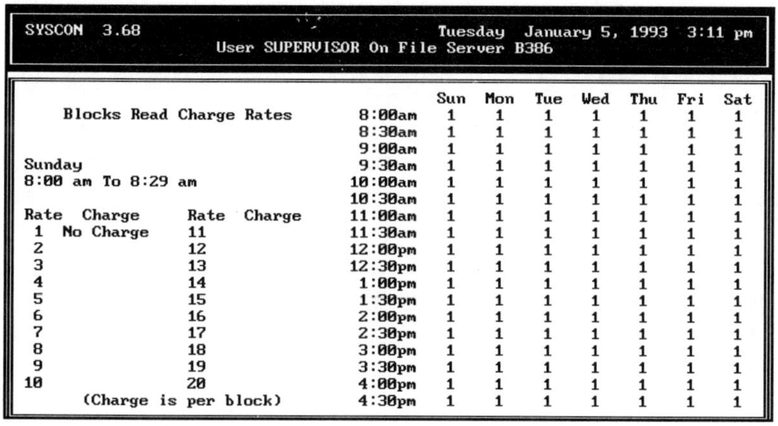

SYSCON 3.68 Tuesday January 5, 1993 3:11 pm
User SUPERVISOR On File Server B386

Blocks Read Charge Rates

Sunday
8:00 am To 8:29 am

Rate	Charge	Rate	Charge
1	No Charge	11	
2		12	
3		13	
4		14	
5		15	
6		16	
7		17	
8		18	
9		19	
10		20	

(Charge is per block)

	Sun	Mon	Tue	Wed	Thu	Fri	Sat
8:00am	1	1	1	1	1	1	1
8:30am	1	1	1	1	1	1	1
9:00am	1	1	1	1	1	1	1
9:30am	1	1	1	1	1	1	1
10:00am	1	1	1	1	1	1	1
10:30am	1	1	1	1	1	1	1
11:00am	1	1	1	1	1	1	1
11:30am	1	1	1	1	1	1	1
12:00pm	1	1	1	1	1	1	1
12:30pm	1	1	1	1	1	1	1
1:00pm	1	1	1	1	1	1	1
1:30pm	1	1	1	1	1	1	1
2:00pm	1	1	1	1	1	1	1
2:30pm	1	1	1	1	1	1	1
3:00pm	1	1	1	1	1	1	1
3:30pm	1	1	1	1	1	1	1
4:00pm	1	1	1	1	1	1	1
4:30pm	1	1	1	1	1	1	1

Figure 5.3
An example of the Blocks Read Charge Rates screen.

- **Blocks Written Charge Rates.** Determines the amount of information being written back to the file server. Users are charged for each full block of information written to the server.

- **Connect Time Charge Rates.** Determines the amount of time a user is logged in to the network. Users are charged for each minute that they are attached to the network.

- **Disk Storage Charge Rates.** Determines the amount of disk space each user takes up on the file server. Users are charged for space occupied by files they own.

If you plan to charge for disk storage in v2.2, make sure that the Limit Disk Space Option is selected. This option frees up the server if you charge during peak network usage times. This option needs to be run only once or twice a day, because users are charged for any files that they own each time this charge is assessed.

- **Service Requests Charge Rates.** Determines the amount of network traffic a user generates. Users are charged for each request they make to the file server.

Setting Up a Network Account

When you set up accounting on your network, the *charge rates* specify the amount each user's account is to be debited when using the network. A charge rate appears as a fractional number, such as 1/4. The *multiplier*, or top portion of the fraction, specifies the amount of monetary units debited against an account. The *divisor*, or lower portion of the fraction, determines the number of units that must accumulate before the charge is made. The most common unit of measure is one cent.

A charge of 1/4, for example, means that one cent is charged for every four units of measure. A unit of measure can equal one minute, one read, one write, one server request, or one block of disk storage.

Before you set the charge rates, you need to know the times during the week that you want to use those rates. You might, for example, want to charge different rates for different days of the week. NetWare enables you to set different rates for different times and different days. When you select a charge rate from the Accounting menu, a grid appears that divides each day, including Saturday and Sunday, into half-hour increments (see fig. 5.3). Each increment has a number that corresponds to the Rate column in the lower left corner of the screen. The numbers in the Rate column, in turn, correspond to the rate shown in the Charge column. Each half hour on the grid is set to charge rate number 1 (no-charge rate) by default. To see the times before 8:00 am and after 4:30 pm, use the up and down arrows and the PgUp and PgDn keys to scroll the screen.

To change the charge rate of a particular time, highlight the desired time or block of time and press Enter. To highlight a block of time, use the cursor arrows to move the cursor to the desired time and press F5. This action marks the upper left corner of the time you want to change. Next, use the right- and down-arrow keys to position the lower right corner of the highlight box. This action highlights the block of time that you want to set. Press Enter and a menu appears that enables you to define the charge rate. You can establish up to 20 charge rates by using this method of blocking time periods (see fig. 5.4 and fig. 5.5).

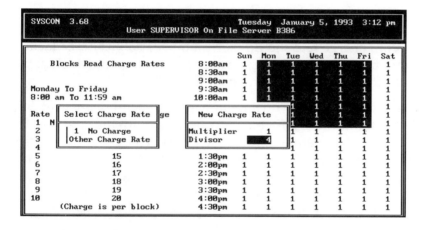

Figure 5.4

Creating a new charge rate.

Figure 5.5

Viewing multiple charge rates.

Chapter 5: Utilities

Figure 5.4 shows a block of time marked using F5 (from Monday 8:00 am to Friday 11:30 am). The Select Charge Rates screen appears. To choose another charge rate, select the Other Charge Rates option and press Enter. The New Charge Rate screen appears. NetWare prompts you for the multiplier and divisor. This formula becomes the charge rate. After you enter the charge rate, press Esc to save your entries. In the example shown in figure 5.4, the charge rate is set to one monetary unit for four network usage units used. Figure 5.5 shows that the time period marked in figure 5.4 is now set to a charge rate of two, which is set to 1/4.

Determining Charge Rates

The supervisor determines the costs of maintaining the system and decides how much to charge for system usage. To determine what your charge rate should be, you must establish three factors: the amount of dollars to be returned, the services for which you want to charge, and the average units used.

The services for which you should charge depend on the way you want to monitor users. If you are concerned with the amount of traffic a user is generating, then you should charge for the service by using the Service Requests Charge Rates option. To track the amount of time a user is logged in, use the Connect Time Charge Rates option. If you want to determine the amount of hard drive space a user occupies, use the Disk Storage Charge Rates option.

NetWare also enables you to charge for combinations of the five charge rates. The supervisor determines the amount each charge rate affects the total. If 40 percent of your charges stem from service requests, 35 percent from disk storage, and 25 percent from connect time, for example, then you should recoup that percentage of the total from these different areas.

You can determine the average units used by using the ATOTAL command-line utility. ATOTAL shows the total system usage per day and for the week (see fig. 5.6). You should run Accounting for three to four weeks after you set the ratios as 1:1 in the services for which you are planning to charge. The one-to-one ratio gives an accurate usage accounting.

```
       Blocks read:              0    Blocks written:          0
       Blocks days:              0
Totals for week:
       Connect time:           386    Server requests:       109
       Blocks read:              0    Blocks written:          0
       Blocks days:              0
01/04/1993:
       Connect time:           145    Server requests:      4625
       Blocks read:            423    Blocks written:          0
       Blocks days:              0
01/05/1993:
       Connect time:           400    Server requests:      2745
       Blocks read:            230    Blocks written:          0
       Blocks days:              0
Totals for week:
       Connect time:           545    Server requests:      7370
       Blocks read:            653    Blocks written:          0
       Blocks days:              0

F:\SYSTEM>
```

Figure 5.6

An example of ATOTAL results.

Run ATOTAL from the SYS:SYSTEM directory; ATOTAL does not require any command-line switches.

An ATOTAL report can be lengthy if Accounting has been installed for a long time. The output can be redirected to a printer or to a file to be printed at another time. Redirect the printout by means of the DOS > command. To redirect the output to a file called ACCT.RPT, for example, type the following statement at the SYS:SYSTEM directory:

    ATOTAL > ACCT.RPT.

Accounting information is kept in a file called NET$ACCT.DAT. This file grows automatically as data accumulates. NetWare enables you to delete the data in this file; however, as the accounting program gathers new information, this file is re-created.

continues

The second file associated with accounting in NetWare is NET$REC.DAT. This file translates the compressed binary information kept in the NET$ACCT.DAT file. Do not, however, delete this file.

After determining the factors for accounting and running the ATOTAL command for several weeks, replace the 1:1 ratio with a ratio that enables you to calculate accounting charges for each user. To determine what your new ratio should be, use the following formula:

$$\frac{\text{Amount to charge for total system use per week}}{\text{Estimated average amount of charge used per week}}$$

You might, for example, want to receive $600 per week for the time twenty users spend logged in to the network. All twenty users work 40 hours a week. In NetWare, the connect time is calculated in minutes that a user is logged in to the network. In this case, 40 hours is 2,400 minutes. Multiply the minutes by the number of users (2,400 x 20) to get the number of minutes on the network per week (48,000 minutes) for the twenty users.

You now need to calculate the amount of money you want to charge each user. In this case, the unit of measure is one cent. To recoup or get back the $600 per week for the use of the network, calculate the number of pennies in $600, which is 60,000. This makes the numerator 60,000, or the amount to be charged for total system use per week. The ratio before reducing is 60000/48000 (60000 for the charge rate and 48000 for the minutes used on the network). Reduced, this ratio is 5/4, or five cents charged for every four minutes a user is logged in to the network.

Establishing Account Balances

One more step is required before you can begin to charge users for use of the network. (Time is only one of five things to be tracked.) You must establish an account balance for each user. When you open a checking account at your local bank, for example, you

Exploring SYSCON

must give the bank a sum of money before you can debit the account. This banking procedure is the same for NetWare accounting. The beginning balance is arbitrary. The system uses the balance to establish an account that is depleted as the user works on the system. If the balance is not limited, the account acts as an odometer by tracking the amount of units used. The maximum number of units for an account balance is 99999999.

Limiting NetWare account balances is useful when you want users to be aware of the amount of time they spend on a network. When a user's account reaches the low balance limit, they are asked to log out of the system. Users must log out at this time. If they do not log out, the system does it for them. To prevent this inconvenience, set the Low Balance Limit to a negative number. If you set a user's balance to -1000, for example, the message You have exceeded your credit limit for this server warns the user of a low account balance when the account reaches zero. The user now has 1000 units to use to finish and exit the network properly. The system tracks the way the user consumes certain network resources. As the user's account reaches zero, the counter starts using negative numbers.

Every time the user logs out of the system, NetWare accounting updates the account. You can use the PAUDIT file, illustrated in figure 5.7, to view login, logout, and system usage information for every user.

```
      Logout from address 00000003:00000000000E.
1/5/93 10:16:10  File Server CDI286
      NOTE: about User CBT4 during File Server services.
      Login from address 00000CDC:00001B1EC81A.
1/5/93 10:16:21  File Server CDI286
      NOTE: about User CBT2 during File Server services.
      Login from address 00000CDC:00001B1ECA96.
1/5/93 13:36:18  File Server CDI286
      CHARGE: 200 to User CBT4 for File Server services.
      Connected 200 min.; 506 requests; 000000000237508  bytes read;
      000000000000000 bytes written.
1/5/93 13:36:18  File Server CDI286
      NOTE: about User CBT4 during File Server services.
      Logout from address 00000CDC:00001B1EC81A.
1/5/93 13:36:33  File Server CDI286
      CHARGE: 200 to User CBT2 for File Server services.
      Connected 200 min.; 2239 requests; 000000001152034  bytes read;
      000000000000000 bytes written.
1/5/93 13:36:33  File Server CDI286
      NOTE: about User CBT2 during File Server services.
      Logout from address 00000CDC:00001B1ECA96.
1/5/93 13:55:56  File Server CDI286
      NOTE: about User SUPERVISOR during File Server services.
      Login from address 00000005:00001B191D38.
F:\SYSTEM>
```

Figure 5.7

An example of using the PAUDIT command.

The Change Current Server Option

The Change Current Server option in the Available Topics menu lists options for attaching to and logging out of a server. If you select the SYSCON Change Current Servers option, a menu appears that lists the file servers you are currently logged in or attached to (see fig. 5.8). Press Ins at this menu to list available servers to which you can log in. NetWare asks you for a valid user name and a password before it attaches you to the new server.

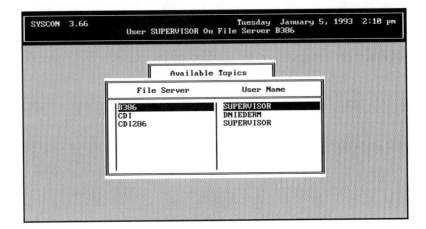

Figure 5.8
The Change Current Server screen.

The File Server Information Option

The File Server Information option in the SYSCON Available Topics menu enables you to view information about the operating system for each server on the network. To view information on a specific server, highlight the server name and press Enter in the Known NetWare Servers screen. This displays the File Server Information screen for the specified server (see fig. 5.9). You cannot change any information on this screen. If you are a supervisor or if you have supervisor privileges, the serial and application numbers for that server appear on this screen. Figure 5.9, for example, shows information about the file server named TSARINA that is important for the system administrator to know if it becomes necessary to contact an outside support person for assistance.

Exploring SYSCON

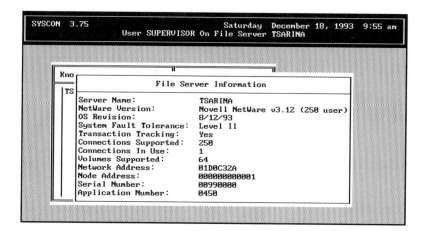

Figure 5.9

An example of the File Server Information screen.

The Group Information Option

In NetWare, groups are designed to save you time and work when privileges are granted to users. If you select the Group Information option in the SYSCON Available Topics menu, a list of existing groups appears in the Group Names Screen (see fig. 5.10). When NetWare is installed, the only group created by the system is the group EVERYONE. Every user added to the system is automatically added to this group so that global rights can be issued.

You can modify a group in several ways by using the Group Information menu. To access this menu, use the arrow keys to highlight a group, then press Enter (see fig. 5.11). The following sections discuss each option of the Group Information menu. To create a new group, press Ins, then name the group in the New Group Name screen (see fig. 5.12).

 In every NetWare version up to v3.11, the installation of the operating system creates the group EVERYONE and all users are automatically added to this group.

Chapter 5: Utilities

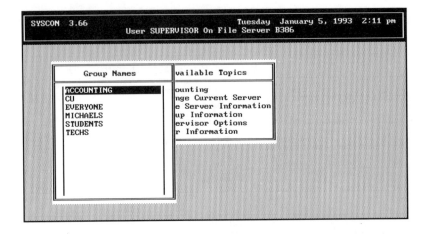

Figure 5.10
The Group Names screen.

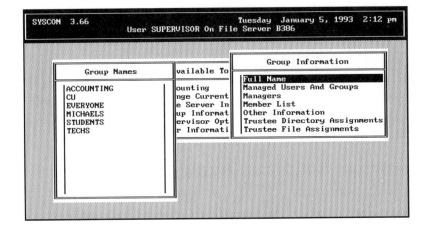

Figure 5.11
The Group Information menu.

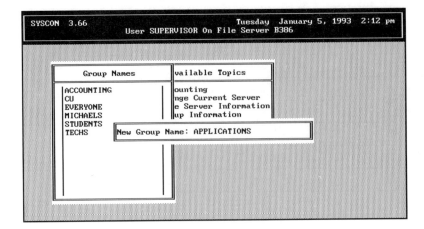

Figure 5.12
Adding a new group by using the New Group Name screen.

138

Full Name

If you select a group in the Group Names screen and press Enter, the Group Information menu appears. The Full Name option in this menu enables you to give a more descriptive name to the selected group.

Managed Users and Groups

This option lists users and groups for which the group selected in the Group Names screen can grant and revoke rights, assuming that your login name was chosen as a group manager or a workgroup manager. This option does not give you rights over the individual user accounts, but does enable you to modify member list and trustee assignments.

Managers

Select the Managers option in the Group Information menu to list the managers of the group you selected in the Group Names screen. You cannot modify this menu item unless you are a manager.

Member List

If you highlight this option and press Enter, members of the selected group are listed in the Group Members screen. When a group is created, it initially has no members (see fig. 5.13). To add users to a group, follow these steps:

1. Highlight the Member List option and press Enter.
2. Press Ins to list users who do not belong to the group.
3. For each user you want to add to the new group, highlight the user in the Not Group Members screen and press F5. Use F5 to mark each of the users you want to add to the group and press Enter.

Figure 5.13

Choosing from the Not Group Members list.

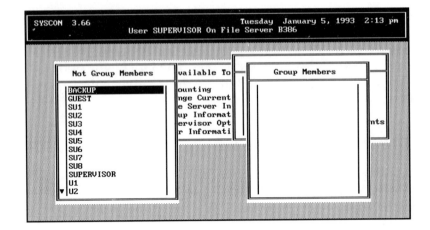

After you press Enter, the chosen user is added to the selected group.

Trustee Directory Assignments

Select this menu item to add rights to a group. If you highlight this item and press Enter, the currently assigned rights for the group are listed. As shown in figure 5.14, a new group has no assigned rights. To add rights, press Ins and enter the full path name.

Figure 5.14

Viewing the Trustee Directory Assignments menu.

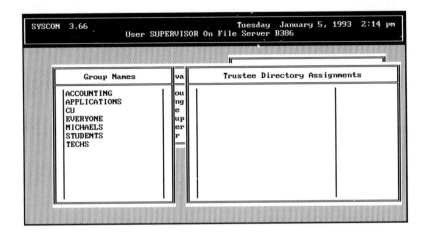

If you are not sure of the directory structure, press Ins a second time to have the network prompt you for information about the path. The File Servers menu appears. In this menu, NetWare prompts you to select the server for which you want to assign rights (see fig. 5.15). The server you select becomes the first part of the full path name.

After you select a server and press Enter, the Volumes menu prompts you for the volume (see fig. 5.16).

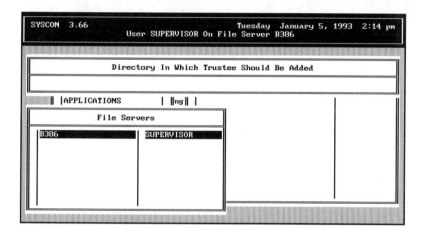

Figure 5.15

Choosing a file server for the path.

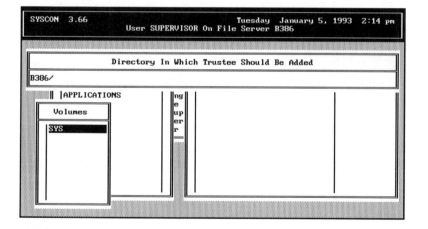

Figure 5.16

Choosing a volume for the path.

The last prompt asks for the directory for which you want to grant rights (see fig. 5.17). The Network Directories menu enables you

Chapter 5: Utilities

to go as deep into the directory structure as needed. The double dot (..) prompt at the top backs up one directory. The path you select appears at the top of the screen in the Directory In Which Trustee Should Be Added screen. Press Esc to stop the selection process and to return to the top window. At this point, you can press Enter to accept the path or press Esc to erase the path you have chosen.

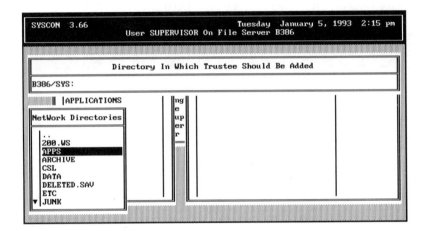

Figure 5.17

Choosing a directory for the path.

After you select a path, the Trustee Rights Granted screen appears. As shown in figure 5.18, File Scan and Read privileges are granted automatically to new groups.

To modify the rights assigned to a group, follow these steps:

1. Use the cursor keys to highlight the option that you want to change, then press Enter. A list of the full names of the rights.

Figure 5.18 shows that the File Scan and Read rights have been granted for the SYS:APPS directory.

2. Press Ins to list rights not granted in the Trustee Rights Not Granted screen. In figure 5.19, for example, a list of rights that have not been granted appears.

3. Use F5 to mark each right you want to grant to the group, then press Enter.

Exploring SYSCON

To delete rights in a group, mark the rights by using F5, then press Del.

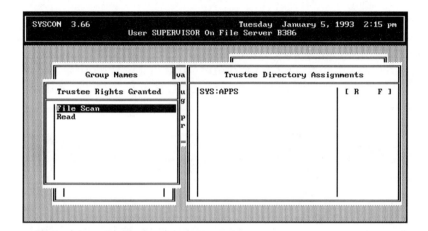

Figure 5.18
Assigning rights to a directory.

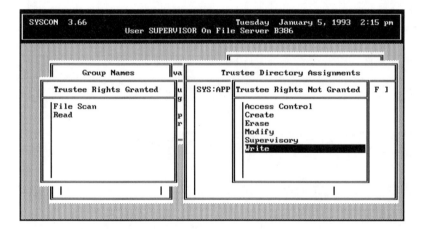

Figure 5.19
Modifying the rights assigned.

After you mark the rights you want to assign or delete, the new rights list is updated in the Trustee Directory Assignments screen (see fig. 5.20).

Chapter 5: Utilities

The Supervisor Options

The only users permitted to use the Supervisor Options menu of SYSCON are the supervisor and supervisor equivalents. In this menu, supervisors can specify system defaults, set up FCONSOLE operators, manage server-configuration files, initiate intruder detection, manage the system login scripts, view the error log, and create workgroup managers (see fig. 5.21). Each of these options is outlined in the following sections.

Figure 5.20
Viewing the modified rights.

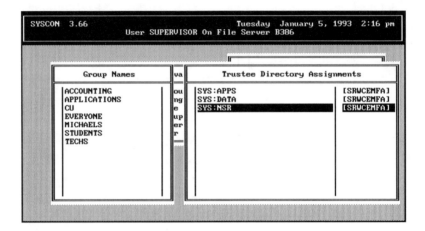

Figure 5.21
The Supervisor Options menu in SYSCON.

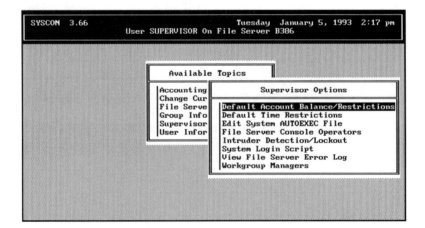

Default Account Balance/Restrictions and Default Time Restrictions

 The first two items in the Supervisor Options menu affect only future users added to the system:

- ◆ Default Account Balance/Restrictions
- ◆ Default Time Restrictions

These options are the same ones listed in individual user accounts. Default Account Balance/Restrictions and Default Time Restrictions have no effect on current users. As you add new users to the network, the parameters defined in these two options automatically are added to the new user's account.

Edit System AUTOEXEC File

The Edit System AUTOEXEC File option enables you to modify the file with which the file server boots up. Please see Chapters 8 and 10 for specific information about each operating system.

File Server Console Operators

In the File Server Console Operators Options menu, FCONSOLE operator status can be given to individual users or to groups. FCONSOLE is a menu utility used for monitoring the file server. Users who are supervisor equivalents can use all the options in FCONSOLE. Regular users whose names appear in this screen cannot clear connections or down the server from FCONSOLE. Users whose names do not appear in this list can use FCONSOLE, but are severely limited as to what information they can see. For more information on FCONSOLE, see Chapter 10.

Intruder Detection/Lockout

Intruder detection is designed to alert the network when someone tries to log in to the system using an invalid password. The Intruder Detection/Lockout option has several configurable parameters, because users often make a mistake when they enter a password.

The network enables you to track incorrect login attempts. An incorrect login attempt is considered to be the number of times in a specific number of minutes that a user can try to log in using an incorrect password. In figure 5.22, for example, users can attempt to log in to the network seven times in 59 minutes before intruder detection locks them out. The length of the lockout also is configurable. The Length Of Account Lockout line in figure 5.22 shows the maximum allowable lockout time—40 days, 23 hours, and 59 minutes.

To unlock an account, you must select the User Information option in the Available Topics menu, then select the Intruder Lockout Status option under the name of the user who has been disabled.

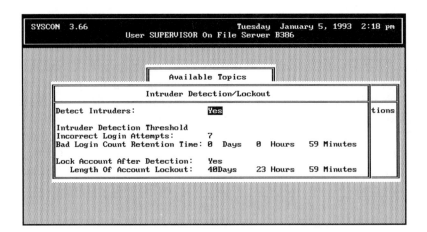

Figure 5.22

The Intruder Detection/Lockout option.

System Login Script

The System Login Script option is designed to configure the network environment for all users. This file is created and maintained by the system supervisor. For more information on the system login script, see Chapter 7.

View File Server Error Log

To view the File Server Error Log file, press Enter on the View File Server Error Log entry in the Supervisor Options menu. Then use the arrow, PgUp, and PgDn keys to move around the File Server Error Log screen (see fig. 5.23).

 The information shown in the error log is stored in a file called NET$LOG.ERR.

The *error log* contains system errors and other information not serious enough to crash a file server, but still important to the administrator. Press Esc to exit this screen. Before the error log exits, you are prompted with Clear Error Log. If you select Yes, NetWare deletes the current information. If you need to review this information in the future, save the error log to a file before deleting it.

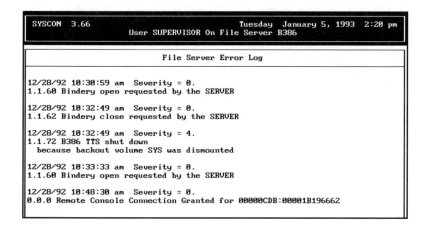

Figure 5.23

The File Server Error Log screen.

Workgroup Managers

The Workgroup Managers option in the Supervisor Options menu enables you to define workgroup managers. As you learned earlier in this chapter, *workgroup managers* are users or groups that can add, delete, and manage other user accounts. Workgroup managers, however, cannot make other workgroup managers or use the Supervisor Options in SYSCON. Press Enter to see the names of potential workgroup managers for users and groups on your network (see fig. 5.24). Press Ins to select other network users and groups to be workgroup managers.

Figure 5.24
The Workgroup Managers screen.

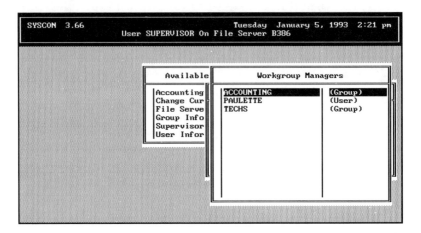

The User Information Option

The User Information option in the Available Topics menu enables you to set up individual user accounts. Highlight this option and press Enter to display every user who has an account on the network. Figure 5.25 shows the User Names screen that lists the names of users established on the network.

To create a new user, press Ins and use the User Name window to name the new user. Figure 5.26, for example, shows the user USERAM being added to the network.

Exploring SYSCON

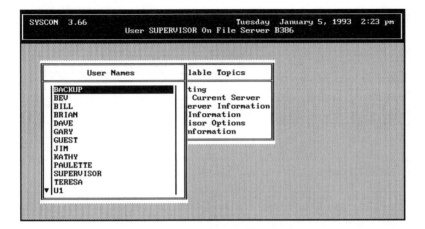

Figure 5.25
The User Names screen.

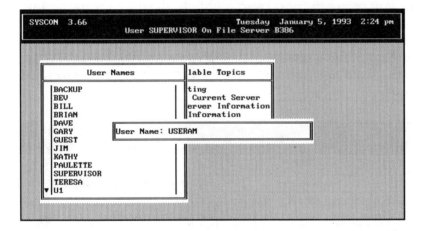

Figure 5.26
Adding a user to the network.

After you enter a name for a new user, the network prompts you to select whether you want a HOME directory created for the new user on volume SYS:. Press Esc if you do not want to create a HOME directory for the user. If you want to give the new user a HOME directory, you also can modify the path. After you finish, NetWare creates the directory and assigns all rights to it for the new user. Figure 5.27 shows the default path that the network creates for the user USERAM.

149

Chapter 5: Utilities

Figure 5.27
Creating a HOME directory.

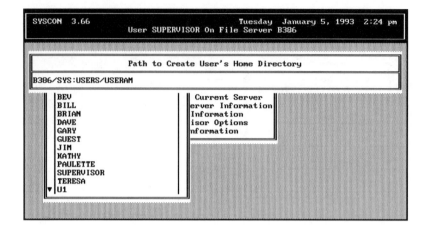

After you create the new user, highlight the user's name and press Enter. The User Information screen appears and enables you to modify the user's account (see fig. 5.28). This screen shows the information that a system manager can modify for a specific user's account. Each option in the User Information menu is described in the following sections.

Figure 5.28
The User Information screen.

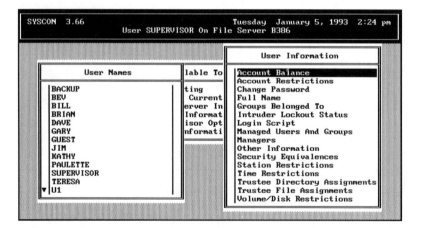

Account Balance

The Account Balance option enables supervisors to set up and monitor the user's account balance. When you select this option, the Account Balance For User screen appears on-screen. If the Accounting

150

option has not been installed on the network, the Account Balance option does not appear. In the example shown in figure 5.29, the user BRIAN has been given an account balance of 500,000. This amount decreases as BRIAN uses the accounting services.

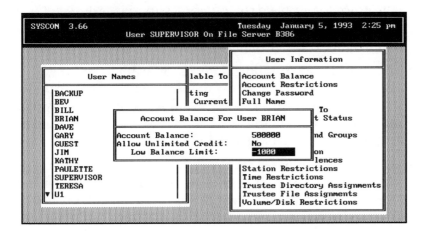

Figure 5.29
The Account Balance for User screen.

Account Restrictions

Supervisors can use the Account Restrictions option of the User Information menu to set up the password and connection parameters for a user. Figure 5.30 lists the account restrictions for the user BRIAN. Each parameter in this menu is discussed in the following list.

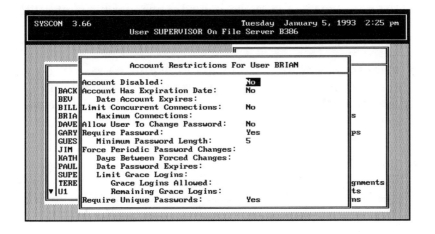

Figure 5.30
The Account Restrictions screen.

Chapter 5: Utilities

Supervisors can change the following items in the Account Restrictions screen to configure a new or existing user's account:

- **Account Disabled.** This line is set to Yes if any of the following conditions occur: the user's expiration date has passed; the grace logins have run out; or a supervisor does not want this user logging in to the network. If Account Disabled is set to No, the user can log in to the network.

- **Account Has Expiration Date.** If you want a new user to have only temporary access to the network, set an expiration date for his account. The user cannot log in to the network after the date set in this field. If you do not want to set an expiration date, set this line to No.

- **Limit Concurrent Connections.** The supervisor can use this field to specify the number of workstations a new user can log in to using the same login name. The default enables the user to log in from all nodes on the network simultaneously.

You might want to limit the number of allowable logins for supervisors and users with supervisor privileges. A limited number of connections prevents privileged users from leaving a trail of workstations logged in with supervisory rights.

- **Allow User To Change Password.** If this field is set to Yes, the user can change his password whenever he wants. If this field is set to No, only the system supervisor can change the user's password.

- **Require Password.** If you want to require a password, set this field to Yes. You also need to specify the minimum length for the password. If you set this field to No, the user is not required to have a password. Even if Require Password is set to No, the user still can have a password.

- **Force Periodic Password Changes.** If you set this parameter to Yes, specify the number of days between forced changes and the next date that the password expires. The network default is 40 days.

One of Murphy's laws states that whenever something must be done immediately, it is always the worst possible time to do it. This "law" also applies to network users. The morning a user logs in to the network to find that his password has expired, for example, probably will be the same morning that a record number of crises occur. This problem is the reason for *grace logins*. Grace logins tell the network that you are too busy at the moment to think of a new password, but to ask for a new password the next time you log in.

The default for grace logins is six. In other words, you can answer No to a new password request six times before the network locks your account.

Only a supervisor equivalent or workgroup manager can unlock the account after grace logins have run out.

◆ **Require Unique Passwords.** This option requires that you do not repeat the most recent passwords when your current password expires.

This option for v2.2 requires each user to create up to eight new passwords before he can repeat the first password. In v3.11, users must create ten new passwords before they can repeat the first password. In addition, these passwords must be in effect for 24 hours.

◆ **Limit Server Disk Space.** If this option is set to Yes, you must specify the maximum amount of disk space in kilobytes that the user is permitted. When you limit a user's disk space, make sure that the user knows that if he runs out of space while he saves or prints a file, he might lose the information. The network needs to store print files as temporary files on the network. If his memory space runs out while he prints a large job, the job is lost.

Change Password

The Change Password option in the User Information menu adds or changes passwords. The DOS command for this task is SETPASS.

Users cannot see the password, but are asked to repeat the new password to make sure that it is typed correctly. Supervisors do not need to know the old password, but regular users need to put in the old password before they can change it.

Full Name

The Full Name option in the User Information menu enables you to give a more descriptive name to the user. This requirement is optional and is used with the identifier variable FULL_NAME in login scripts.

Groups Belonged To

The Groups Belonged To option in the User Information menu provides an opposite view of the Group Information option in the Available Topics menu. In the Groups Belonged To option, you can view the groups to which the highlighted user belongs. Press Ins to view the groups to which the user does not belong (see fig. 5.31).

The system manager can pick from this list the groups to which he wants a user to belong. To add a user to a group, such as TECHS, highlight the group and press Enter. The Groups Belonged To screen then shows the updated groups list (see fig. 5.32).

Exploring SYSCON

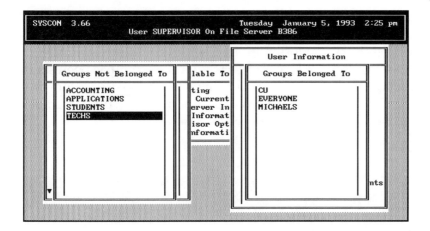

Figure 5.31
Choosing groups to belong to.

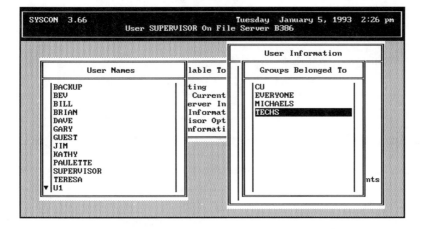

Figure 5.32
The modified groups list.

Intruder Lockout Status

Intruder Lockout Status displays the network and workstation address out of which a selected user is locked and the time remaining until the lockout is reset. When the user tries to log in and activates the Intruder Detection/Lockout feature, the following message appears:

    Intruder Detection/Lockout has disabled this account.

Chapter 5: Utilities

If the user is not currently locked out, you can view only the system. As a user with supervisor rights, you can see the Intruder Detection/Lockout option in the User Information list for the specific user, only if Intruder Detection/Lockout has been set for this server. If you are a system manager and the user is locked out, the border for this menu becomes a double line. You can unlock the account if you have supervisor rights.

Figure 5.33 shows an active lockout for user CHRIS.

Figure 5.33

Intruder Lockout Status screen.

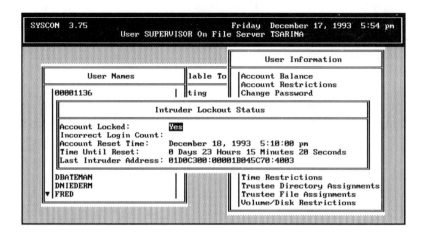

Under the address portion of the Intruder Lockout Status screen, the first portion of the address is the network address (shown as 01D0C300 in figure 5.33). The second part is the workstation address (shown as 00001B045C70), and the third number is a network socket number (shown as 4003).

Socket numbers provide a type of mail slot for processes that occur within a workstation. These mail slots exist so that each process can identify itself to IPX. Whenever a workstation needs to access the NetWare Core Protocol (NCP), which is the heart of the operating system, the workstation uses socket 45lh, for example.

Login Script

The Login Script option in the User Information menu enables the user or a system manager to add or manage the login script for a selected user. In addition, login scripts can be copied from other users, but only if no existing login script exists for the current user. If a login script exists, and you want to assign another user's login script, perform the following steps:

1. Highlight the existing login script by pressing F5 and using the arrow keys to mark it.
2. Press Del.
3. Press Esc to exit, then save the changes.
4. Press Enter to return to the login script screen. When you go back into this option, the system tells you that a login script does not exist. You now can read the login script from another user.
5. Replace the current user's name in the screen with the user's name from which a login script is copied. Figure 5.34, for example, shows that the user BRIAN does not have a login script. To copy one from the user JIM, use Backspace to delete BRIAN, then enter **JIM**.

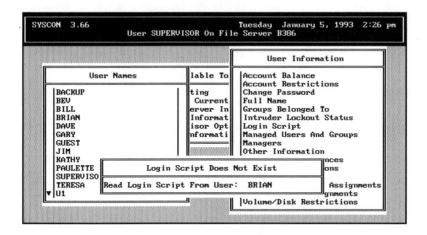

Figure 5.34
An example of copying login scripts in SYSCON.

Managed Users And Groups

The Managed Users And Groups option in the User Information menu lists the users and groups that can be granted rights and that can have rights revoked by the selected user. In addition, this category designates the users whose accounts are managed by the selected user. You can use this option to modify member lists and trustee assignments.

In figure 5.35, the classification Direct means that the selected user is assigned specific users and groups to manage. Indirect-managed users and groups are assigned by the network so that the manager can change rights to the group EVERYONE. Although EVERYONE is created by NetWare, the system managers can add and delete rights for this group.

Figure 5.35

Examples of managed users and groups.

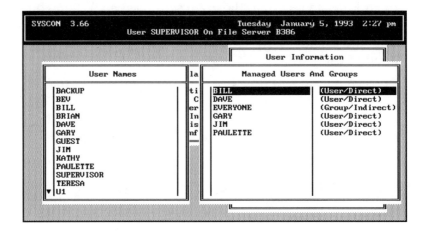

Managers

The Manager options in the User Information menu item lists the manager or manager of a selected user (see fig. 5.36). You can modify this option only if you are a manager.

Other Information

The Other Information option in the User Information menu shows you when a selected user last logged in to the network (see fig. 5.37). If this is a new user, the message Not known appears. This screen also shows if this user is an FCONSOLE operator. The Maximum Server Disk Usage setting in the Account Restrictions option also appears here, including information about the amount

Exploring SYSCON

of disk space the user currently is using on the network. The final field is the User ID, which is the same as the directory under SYS:MAIL that belongs to this user.

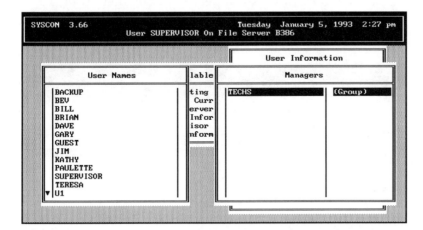

Figure 5.36
Account managers for the selected user.

Figure 5.37
The Other Information option.

Security Equivalences

The Security Equivalences option in the User Information menu assigns the security rights of one user to another user. When you assign a new user to a group, that user automatically receives the equivalent privileges of every other user in that group. Figure 5.38 shows that the user BRIAN belongs to the groups EVERYONE and TECHS and has the same security rights as the groups listed.

159

Chapter 5: Utilities

The following steps show you ways to assign supervisor privileges to a user. Figure 5.39 shows that SUPERVISOR has been added to the Security Equivalences option screen. This setting makes the new user BRIAN a supervisor equivalent user. To assign supervisor privileges, select Security Equivalences in the User Information menu and perform the following steps:

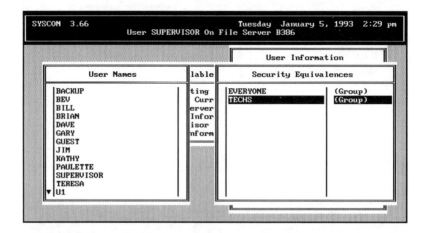

Figure 5.38
The Security Equivalences option screen.

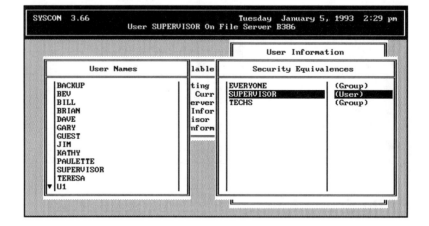

Figure 5.39
Creating a supervisor equivalent user.

1. Press Ins at the Security Equivalences menu to display a list of other users and groups.

2. From the list, find the heading SUPERVISOR (User).

Exploring SYSCON

3. Highlight SUPERVISOR and press Enter. The selected user now is a supervisor equivalent (see fig 5.38).

This process is the only way to make a supervisor equivalent user.

Station Restrictions

By default, NetWare enables a user to log in to any workstation attached to the network. Through the Station Restrictions option in the User Information menu, the system administrator can create a list of networks and workstations to which a user can log in. The user cannot log in to any network or workstation whose address does not appear on this list. Figure 5.40 shows the list of node addresses and network addresses of the workstations from which a selected user is permitted to log in.

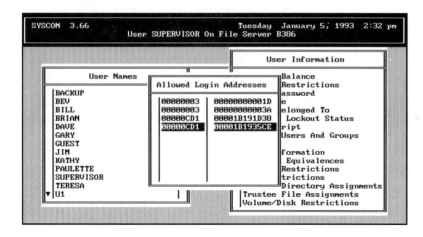

Figure 5.40
A list of login addresses.

Time Restrictions

The Time Restrictions option in the User Information menu enables you to restrict individual users to network use at specific times. In figure 5.41, asterisks denote half-hour time increments during which a user can be logged in to the network. Every empty space represents one half hour of time that a user is denied access. To set restrictions on times when users can log in, use the following steps:

161

Chapter 5: Utilities

1. Open the Allowed Login Times For User screen.
2. Use the arrow keys to move the cursor to the day and time when the time restriction is to start.
3. Press F5.
4. Use the arrow keys to move the cursor to the day and time when the time restriction is to end.
5. Press Enter.

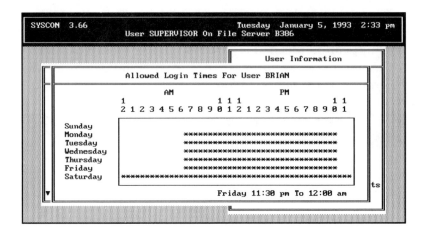

Figure 5.41
Setting time restrictions for a user.

Trustee Directory Assignments

Select the Trustee Directory Assignments option in the User Information menu to view the rights assigned to a user and to add rights that a user needs. A new user automatically has rights to his HOME directory and to his SYS:MAIL/USER_ID directory. To add rights, press Ins and enter the full path name, or press Ins again to select the path. See the section on adding rights to groups for more information about entering full path names.

NetWare grants the File Scan and Read privileges automatically. To modify the rights assignments on any directory, use the following steps:

Exploring SYSCON

1. Press Enter on the directory whose trustee rights you want to change.
2. When the list of trustee rights granted showing the full names appears, press Ins to see the list of trustee rights that have not been granted.
3. Press F5 to mark each right that you want to grant to the user, then press Enter. (To delete marked rights, press Del rather than Enter.)

Press Esc to return to the new rights. The list then is updated in the Trustee Directory Assignments window. Figure 5.42 shows the screens for modifying trustee directory rights.

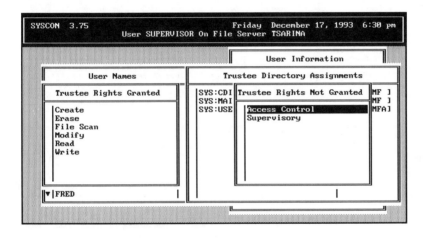

Figure 5.42
Screens for modifying trustee directory rights.

 In v3.1x, you also can grant rights to specific files. Please see Chapter 10 for more information on this option.

Volume/Disk Restrictions

The User Volume/Disk Restrictions option in the User Information menu enables you to limit the disk space available to the user. This option appears in v2.2 only if the Limit Server Disk Space option is selected during installation. Figure 5.43 shows that the

163

Chapter 5: Utilities

user can use 10240K, or about 10M of space. The administrator can check this number to see the amount of space a user has taken up on the system. The Volume Space In Use field shown in figure 5.43, for example, shows that the user currently has used 468K of disk space.

Figure 5.43
The User Volume/Disk Restrictions screen.

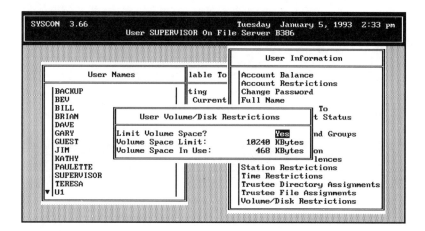

 The following command-line utilities also can be accomplished by using SYSCON:

   ATTACH

   GRANT

   REMOVE

   REVOKE

   RIGHTS

   SETPASS

   SLIST

   TLIST

Exploring the FILER Menu Utility

This section describes FILER, a menu utility that you can use to manipulate directories and files. The utilities discussed in this section are used differently, depending on your security status. System supervisors can use all the functions, but the typical end user might be limited to only certain functions. This section describes all the options for FILER.

FILER can be used as an alternative to DOS commands when you manage directories. The main screen in FILER enables you to view a specific directory or a directory's contents, specify search options, or look at volume information (see fig. 5.44).

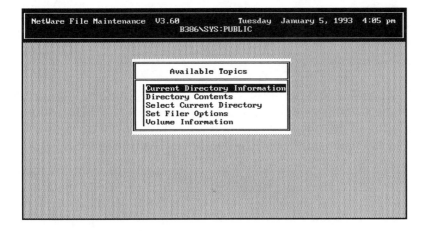

Figure 5.44
The FILER main menu.

Current Directory Information Menu

The first menu item in FILER, Current Directory Information, enables you to see and assign the following information (see fig. 5.45):

- Who created, or owns, a specific directory
- When a directory was created
- The setting of the directory attributes

Chapter 5: Utilities

- ◆ The setting of the Maximum Rights Mask in v2.2
- ◆ The setting of the Inherited Rights Mask in v3.11
- ◆ Who has specifically been granted rights to this directory

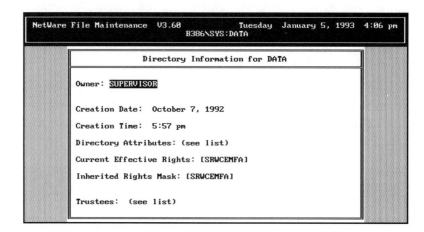

Figure 5.45
Current directory information.

The Current Effective Rights line shown in figure 5.45 lists current rights for the user; the Inherited Rights Mask line lists the allowable rights. The Inherited Rights field cannot be changed directly. It reflects what you are able to do currently in a directory.

At the DOS prompt, you can change directory attributes by using the FLAGDIR command. Inside FILER, you add attributes by pressing Ins, then choosing from the available list shown in figure 5.46. You can delete attributes just as easily by highlighting the attribute, then pressing Del.

Figure 5.46 shows directory information for the \DATA directory. The current attributes show that this directory was flagged by using the FLAG command to immediately purge any files deleted from the directory. By pressing Ins, another menu appears that displays all other available flags that can be assigned to this directory.

You can assign and manage trustees by choosing the Trustees option from Current Directory Information in FILER. At the DOS prompt, trustees are managed by using the GRANT, REMOVE, and REVOKE commands. Figure 5.47 shows that two groups are given rights to the directory SYS:DATA. Rights are discussed in depth in Chapter 7. By giving groups rights, you make them the directory's trustees.

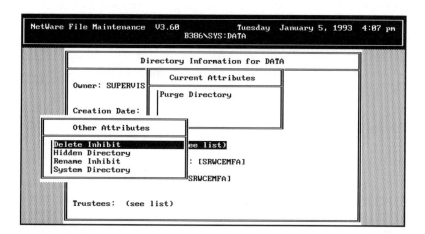

Figure 5.46

Choosing directory attributes.

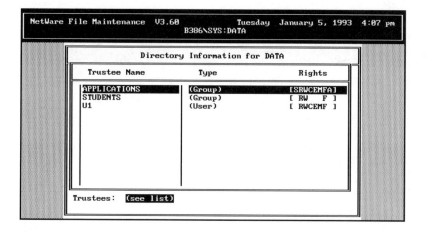

Figure 5.47

Viewing trustee assignments from FILER.

Directory Contents Menu

The next FILER main menu option, Directory Contents, enables you to perform the following tasks after choosing Directory Contents (see fig. 5.48):

Chapter 5: Utilities

- Create and delete subdirectories (press Ins).

- Copy subdirectory structures (press Enter on a subdirectory).

- Move file and subdirectory structures (press Enter on a file or subdirectory). This option applies to v3.1x only.

- Copy files (press Enter on a file or subdirectory).

- View and set directory information (press Enter on a subdirectory—see fig. 5.49).

- View and set file information (press Enter on a file—see fig. 5.50).

- Change directories (select a subdirectory, parent, or root).

Figure 5.46 shows two subdirectories and two files in the directory SYS:DATA. After you highlight a directory and press Enter, you see the menu options shown in figure 5.47. Highlighting a file and pressing Enter shows you the menu options displayed in figure 5.48.

Figure 5.48
Directory Contents with subdirectories and files.

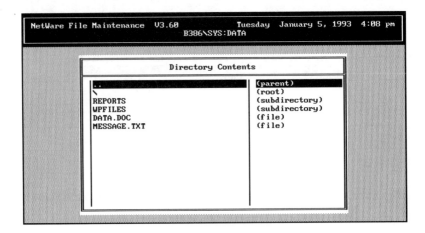

To create directories from the Directory Contents screen, press Ins. A box appears in which you type the new directory name, then press Enter. The MD (Make Directory) command at the DOS prompt is the same procedure.

Exploring the FILER Menu Utility

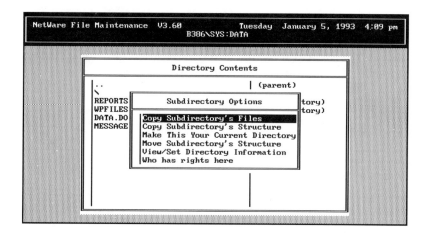

Figure 5.49

NetWare 3.1x Subdirectory Options in Directory Contents.

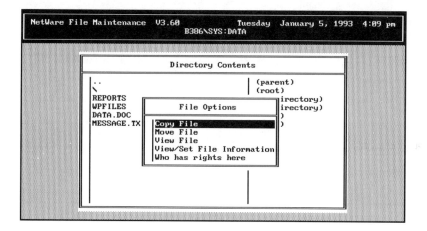

Figure 5.50

NetWare 3.1x File Options in Directory Contents.

To delete a directory, highlight the directory to be deleted and press Del. Another menu appears that enables you to select between deleting files only from this directory and any subdirectories under it, or deleting the complete directory structure beneath the highlighted directory.

Files also can be deleted by highlighting the file and pressing Del. Other function keys work to mark multiple files. See the beginning of this chapter for more information on function keys.

When you work in DOS, you often need to delete several directories at once. If you delete directories in DOS, you must specify the directory and the files you want to delete, which can be a tedious process—especially if the directories contain read-only or hidden files. If you use FILER instead, you can delete an entire directory structure, all files in a directory structure, or specific files.

Select Current Directory Menu

The third option in the main FILER menu, Select Current Directory, enables you to change the directory being viewed (see fig. 5.51). If you are not sure of the exact directory path, press Ins to call up a list of available file servers, volumes, and directories.

Figure 5.51
Setting a directory path for viewing.

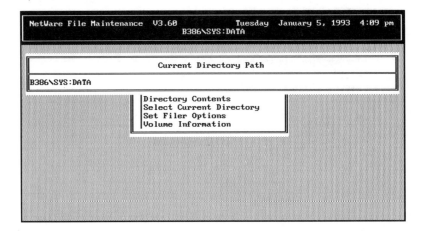

Set Filer Options Menu

The fourth FILER main menu option, Set Filer Options, enables you to set the parameters for viewing and manipulating the directory structure (see fig. 5.52). In FILER, under Set Filer Options, you can specify letter patterns to view directories or files. You also can search for hidden and system files and directories under the Search Attributes.

The Notify Extended Attributes/Long Name Lost line in the Filer Settings box applies to OS/2 attributes (see figs. 5.53 and 5.54).

Exploring the FILER Menu Utility

These two figures are examples of help screens that Novell provides in all the menu utilities and that can be accessed by pressing F1 whenever you need additional information about a current screen.

Any options set in FILER under Filer Settings apply only to that FILER session. (Figure 5.52 shows the default settings.) The settings have no effect at the DOS prompt.

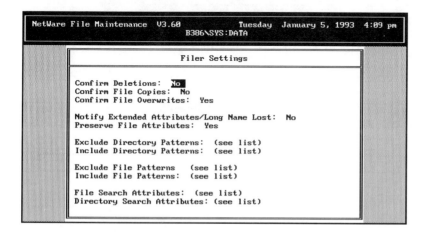

Figure 5.52
Filer Settings options.

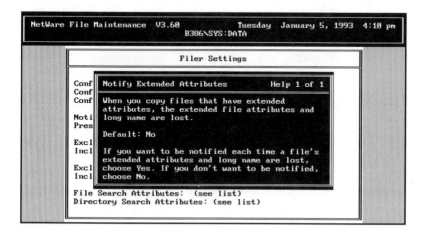

Figure 5.53
A Filer Settings sample Help screen.

Chapter 5: Utilities

Figure 5.54
Another Filer Settings sample Help screen.

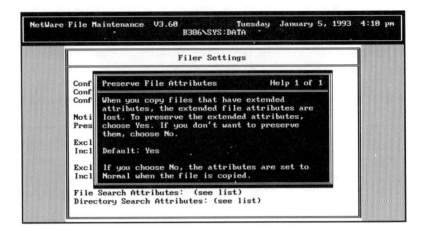

 The following command-line utilities also can be accomplished by using FILER:

    FLAG

    FLAGDIR (v3.*lx* only)

    LISTDIR

    NCOPY

    NDIR

    REMOVE

    REDIR

    REVOKE

    TLIST

The Volume Information Menu

The last option in FILER's Available Topics menu, Volume Information, displays information about network volumes (see fig. 5.55). A good reason for using FILER is to clean up cluttered directories for increased disk space. The Volume Information option enables you to view your progress in cleaning the system. To change the volume being viewed, change Select Current

Directory to the desired volume. Figure 5.55 shows information on the current volume SYS: on a file server called B386.

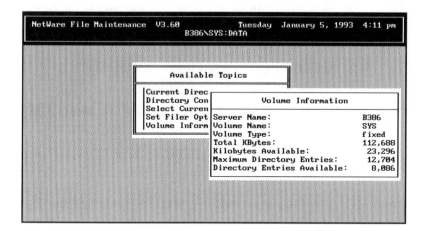

Figure 5.55
Viewing volume information.

Exploring the MAKEUSER Utility

MAKEUSER is a utility you can use to create, edit, and process a script that adds users to the network (see fig. 5.56).

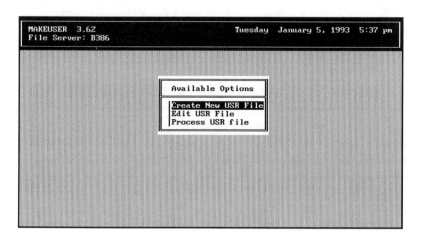

Figure 5.56
The MAKEUSER utility options.

Chapter 5: Utilities

The following rules help you develop a MAKEUSER script:

- ◆ All keywords must be uppercase and must be preceded with a pound sign (#).

- ◆ If you want to use any keywords concerned with passwords, you must type **#PASSWORD_REQUIRED**.

- ◆ The flow of events is always upward. #CREATE always refers to the commands preceding it to determine the user's parameters.

- ◆ MAKEUSER files are saved with a USR extension in the directory from which the MAKEUSER utility is accessed.

- ◆ After the file is processed, MAKEUSER leaves a report file with the same file name, but with an RPT extension. This file shows if the users have been created.

You can use a MAKEUSER file as computerized notes for adding users to the network. All that is necessary for reprocessing this file is to change the user's name on the CREATE statement.

Figure 5.57 shows an example of a MAKEUSER file. In this example, two users are added to the system. Each user has several unique restrictions and shared parameters. Because of the way MAKEUSER interprets keywords, the user DIANA is affected only by the keywords listed before the #CREATE DIANA statement. The user HENRY, on the other hand, is affected by all the keywords in this file.

After you fill in the Creating a New USR file and press Esc, NetWare prompts you to save and name the USR file. Do not give the file a dot extension. The extension is always USR. You name the file TEST.USR, for example, by typing **TEST**. The dot extension USR is added automatically.

Exploring the MAKEUSER Utility

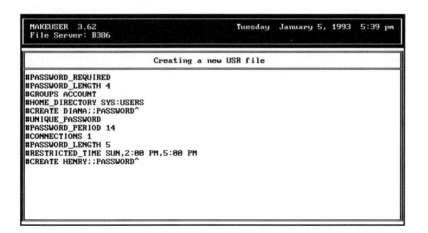

Figure 5.57
An example of a MAKEUSER script.

After you create a USR file, you must process it. Processing it tells you what syntax errors you have made. If there are no syntax errors, processing the file runs the file's commands. If errors appear, you must correct the errors, then reprocess the file to run the commands.

Edit the USR file by selecting the Edit USR File option. Figure 5.58 shows the error report that results from processing the TEST.USR file with errors.

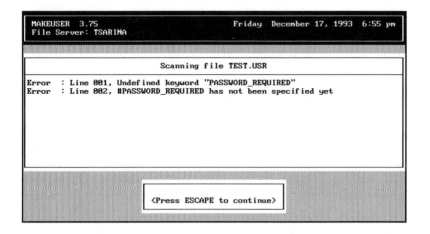

Figure 5.58
USR Error Report.

175

Chapter 5: Utilities

 Figure 5.58 shows two errors in this file. In truth, however, only one error exists. Because the line that contains the error must run correctly before the line that includes the second error, both lines display an error. Fix the errors in your USR file, therefore, from the top down. Fixing one error can correct several subsequent errors. You might, in fact, want to reprocess the file after you fix each error to see the number of other errors it cleared up.

MAKEUSER Keywords

The following list contains the available MAKEUSER commands and syntax:

- **#ACCOUNT_EXPIRATION** *month day, year.* The account no longer permits access after the date specified.

- **#ACCOUNTING** *balance, lowlimit.* The account is given an account balance with which to start and a low limit below which it cannot go. Both parameters are required.

- **#CLEAR** or **#RESET.** These commands act as stop markers. When the script is processed, a #CREATE or #DELETE statement processes all keywords until it encounters a #CLEAR or #RESET.

- **#CONNECTIONS** *number.* The account is limited as to the number of workstations it can log in to at one time.

- **#CREATE** *username;fullname;password;groups;rights.* Establishes a user ID. The only required field is *username*; if #PASSWORD_REQUIRED is used, the *password* field also is required. You must leave a blank space between semicolons if you do not intend to use a field. Use the carat (^) to end the #CREATE field if you do not plan to use all fields.

- **#DEFAULT_PROFILE** *profile.* If NetWare Name Service is used, this keyword enables the account to access a preassigned profile name.

Exploring the MAKEUSER Utility

- **#DELETE** *username*. If you use MAKEUSER to clean up user accounts no longer active, this keyword wipes out old accounts.

- **#GROUPS** *group*. This keyword adds to the listed groups any user defined by the #CREATE statement.

- **#HOME_DIRECTORY** *path*. MAKEUSER creates a HOME directory for each user defined by the #CREATE keyword. The default HOME directory is off the root of SYS:. This keyword enables you to redirect the HOME directory path.

- **#HOME_SERVER** *server*. NetWare Name Services utilizes this keyword, which enables you to specify the file server in which the HOME Directory is created. This keyword is used in conjunction with #HOME_DIRECTORY. If you use the #MAX_DISK_SPACE keyword, the #HOME_SERVER keyword must come first.

- **#LOGIN_SCRIPT** *path\filename*. This keyword copies the specified text file into the user account's MAIL_ID directory as the LOGIN file.

- **#MAX_DISK_SPACE** *vol:,number*. This keyword enables you to specify the maximum disk space allowed to the user for the volume specified.

- **#NO_HOME_DIRECTORY**. This keyword disables MAKEUSER's function of creating a HOME directory for the user.

- **#PASSWORD_LENGTH** *length*. This keyword defines the minimum length of a password.

- **#PASSWORD_PERIOD** *days*. This keyword specifies the number of days a password is valid.

- **#PASSWORD_REQUIRED**. Use this keyword if you require users to have passwords. This keyword must come before all other password-related keywords.

- **#PROFILES** *profile*. This keyword enables you to assign existing profiles to users. This keyword is new for NetWare Naming Services.

Chapter 5: Utilities

- **#PURGE_USER_DIRECTORY.** When using MAKEUSER to delete users, this keyword deletes all the files and subdirectories under the specified user's HOME directory. Use #HOME_DIRECTORY to specify where to find the user's HOME directory if it is not off SYS:.

- **#REM or REM.** These keywords enable you to keep notes in the MAKEUSER file. Anything typed on the same line as #REM or REM is not processed.

- **#RESTRICTED_TIME** *day,start,end.* Use this option to specify when a user cannot be logged in to the network.

- **#STATIONS** *network,station#,station#....* The #STATIONS keyword enables you to specify the network and node addresses to which the user can log in. The first number after #STATIONS is the network address followed by a comma; then a list follows of all the node addresses on that network to which the user can log in. Separate each node address with a comma.

- **#UNIQUE_PASSWORD.** This keyword requires that users cannot repeat the most recent passwords.

Exploring the USERDEF Utility

The USERDEF utility enables you to add, create, and edit templates, then use those templates to process users. Figure 5.59 shows the Available Options menu for USERDEF. Instead of creating and managing several files from MAKEUSER, you can use templates available in USERDEF by using different user parameters. Figure 5.60, for example, shows three templates created by the system administrator.

Each template enables you to create or edit login scripts and other parameters (see fig. 5.61). The parameters you can use include setting up default directories, copying PRINTCON jobs from other users, determining which groups to which users should belong, and creating account restrictions. Figure 5.62 shows all the available parameters for configuring a template.

Exploring the USERDEF Utility

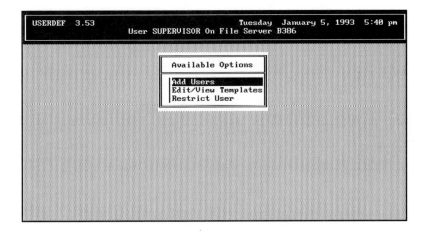

Figure 5.59

The Available Options menu in the USERDEF utility.

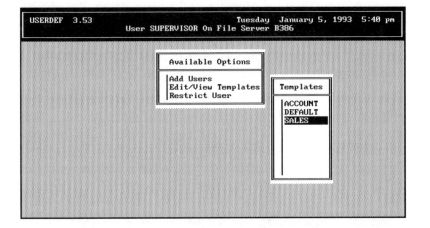

Figure 5.60

Examples of USERDEF templates.

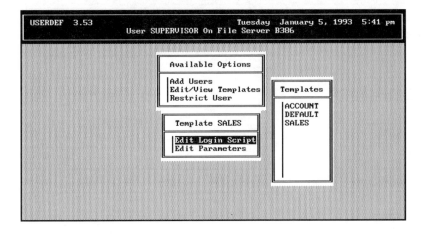

Figure 5.61

USERDEF template options.

Chapter 5: Utilities

Figure 5.62

USERDEF template parameters.

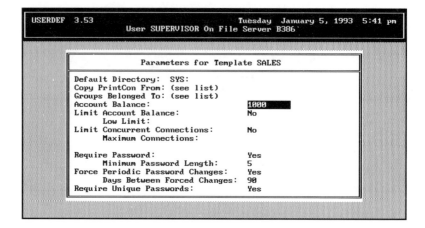

When you add users, a list appears that shows users that already exist on the network and those that have not yet been added. If you press Ins, the USERDEF utility asks for the user's full name. In figure 5.63, for example, a new user named PM - Afternoon Shift is added to the list of users by using the Account template.

After you add the user, USERDEF uses the first name as the login name. If you press Esc, USERDEF asks if you want to create the user by using the specified template. Figure 5.64 shows the confirmation menu for the Sales template when you add a new user to the sales list. After you confirm that you want to create a new user using that template, NetWare compiles and processes a USR file.

Figure 5.63

Adding a new user in the USERDEF Account template.

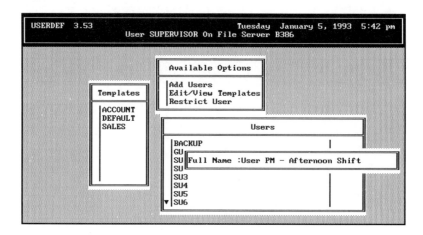

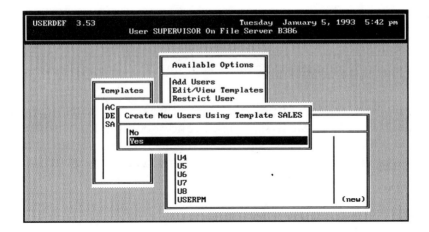

Figure 5.64
Confirming a new user in the Sales template.

Introducing ROUTEGEN

ROUTEGEN is NetWare's external routing generation menu. This utility used to be called BRGEN when Novell called their internetworking devices *bridges*. The correct term now being used is router. A *router* is an internetworking device capable of directing information to other internetworking devices. You use a router when you send packets of information from a workstation on one network cable type like ARCnet to another workstation on a different type of cable like Ethernet.

ROUTEGEN enables you to create three different types of routers:

- Nondedicated protected mode
- Dedicated real mode
- Dedicated protected mode

Nondedicated Protected Mode

A *nondedicated* router can function as both a workstation and a router. The computer that runs this type of router must meet the following requirements:

Chapter 5: Utilities

- ◆ 286 or better microprocessor
- ◆ Minimum of 1M RAM; maximum of 8M RAM

The router's workstation portion uses the 640K conventional memory to run programs.

This router is the most unreliable of the three types. Nondedicated routers are susceptible to locking up, and rebooting the workstation downs the router. This problem means that entire network segments can lose their connection to the server.

Dedicated Real Mode

A *dedicated* router can only be used as a router. The dedicated real mode router must have or emulate an 8086 or 8088 microprocessor. The computer running this type of router must have at least 640K of RAM and cannot access anything over 1M of RAM.

This type of router is more reliable than the nondedicated router, because it does not need to share its processing time between routing and acting as a workstation.

Dedicated Protected Mode

A router running in *dedicated protected mode* is the best solution for external routing, but the following hardware conditions must be met:

- ◆ 286 or better microprocessor
- ◆ Minimum of 1M RAM; maximum of 8M RAM

The dedicated protected mode router can place v2.2 value-added processes (VAPs) into extended memory. For more information on VAPs, please refer to Chapter 8.

Introducing ROUTEGEN

The following steps show you ways to create a ROUTER.EXE file to use on a dedicated protected mode router.

1. Copy all the files on the ROUTEGEN disk into a directory called ROUTEGEN. Copy the ROUTEGEN.EXE file into the parent directory of ROUTEGEN. From the parent directory, type **ROUTEGEN**.

NetWare utilities always look into a subdirectory for their files. If you try to run the EXE file from the same directory where all the OBJ files are kept, you are asked for unnecessary disks. Always copy the EXE file into the parent directory and use that file in the parent directory. This note is true for ROUTEGEN, SHGEN and WSGEN.

In figure 5.65, you see the welcome screen that appears after you type **ROUTEGEN**. ROUTEGEN is found on a disk labeled ROUTEGEN included with your NetWare disks.

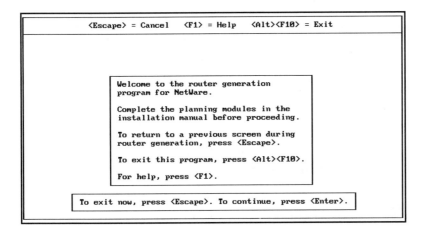

Figure 5.65
ROUTEGEN Welcome screen.

2. Press Enter on the space next to Operating mode. This option enables you to select the type of mode that this router will be. Figure 5.66 shows all your options. To select dedicated protected mode, make sure that your highlight bar is on that option, then press Enter.

Chapter 5: Utilities

Figure 5.66
Choosing mode options.

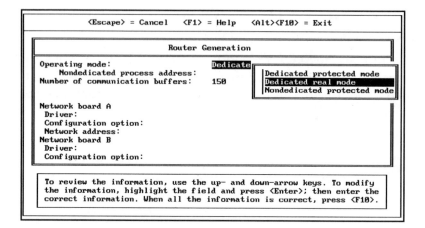

If you select nondedicated protected mode, you are asked for a nondedicated process address. This address is used to identify the computer when it is being used as a workstation. The address must be in hexadecimal digits and must be unique to all network addresses.

The next option is to set communication buffers. This setting is the number of buffers that the routing computer sets aside memory for so that it can hold incoming data packets until they can be processed. Each buffer uses approximately .5K of RAM. The default is 150; the minimum is 40 and the maximum is 1000 buffers.

3. Move to DRIVER under Network board A as shown in figure 5.67 and press Enter. This enables you to select your first network board type.

You can configure up to four network boards in an external router.

Introducing ROUTEGEN

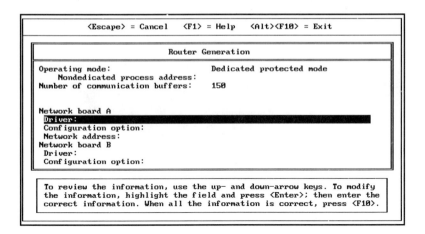

Figure 5.67
Configuring the first network board.

Use your arrow keys to move through the selections until you find the network board you want to configure. If you have a driver disk that contains a driver not found in this list, place the disk in the drive and press Enter. NetWare searches the disk for the driver. Figure 5.68 shows an RX-Net board chosen for this demonstration.

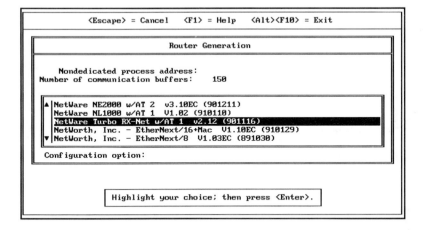

Figure 5.68
Choosing a network board driver.

Next, you are asked to select the hardware settings that match the board you are configuring. Figure 5.69 shows the default option 0 chosen for the first board configuration.

185

Chapter 5: Utilities

Figure 5.69
Choosing the network board hardware settings.

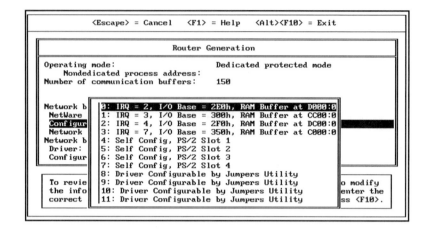

Finally, you need to enter the network address. This setting is the same cable address as set up on the file server for the same board. Figure 5.70 shows that the network address for Network board A is DEC1.

Repeat step 3 for each board in the router. Figure 5.71 shows two network boards configured for this router, an RX-Net board and a Novell NE2000.

Figure 5.70
Setting the network address.

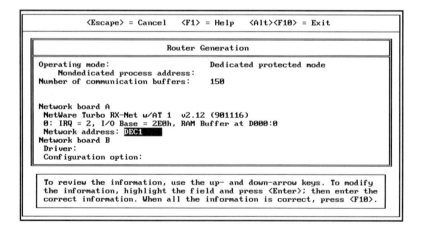

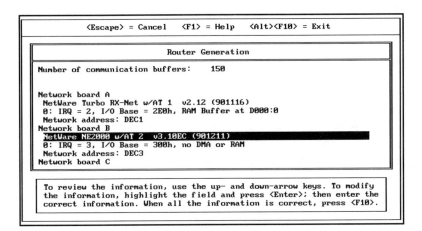

Figure 5.71
Viewing ROUTEGEN board configurations.

When you have completed configuring all boards, press F10. The message shown in figure 5.72 appears when everything has been successfully configured. Copy the ROUTER.EXE file from the ROUTEGEN directory onto a bootable floppy and reboot the router using that floppy.

Examining NBACKUP

The NetWare NBACKUP utility is used to back up and restore files on a NetWare file server and local hard drives.

 Storage Management Services (SMS) are included with NetWare 3.12 in the form of SBACKUP. SBACKUP is included with NetWare 3.12 to provide backup and restoration of data independent of the operating system or file system version. More information about SMS follows this section on NBACKUP.

A user does not require full or supervisory rights to properly back up files. Any user who has the minimum rights of File Scan and Read can use NBACKUP to back up personal files.

Chapter 5: Utilities

Figure 5.72
ROUTEGEN confirmation messages.

```
Creating NetWare Router:

Novell Linker, Version 2.1
Linking ROUTEGEN:ROUTER.EXE.

Configuring NetWare Router.


ROUTEGEN is complete.

You have created a Dedicated protected mode router.

Copy ROUTER.EXE from the ROUTEGEN diskette
(or from the ROUTEGEN directory on the network)
to a DOS bootable disk.

Using the DOS bootable disk, reboot the machine
that will serve as your router then type:

        ROUTER <Enter>.


G:\SERVICE\NOVELL\311SHELL>
```

NBACKUP enables the following devices to be used as backup media:

- Floppy drives
- Tape drives that use DOS device drivers
- Optical drives that use DOS device drivers
- Local hard drives
- Network drives
- Novell DIBI devices (Novell Wangtek Tape Drive)

To back up the complete file server, the user must have supervisor privileges to access the system security information. The first screen displayed enables the backup device type to be selected. Select the device required and continue.

If a non-DOS device is not available, you can remove this menu selection by deleting the DIBI$DRV.DAT file from the SYS:PUBLIC directory.

Select Backup Options from the NBACKUP main menu (see fig. 5.73). Next, select the Select Working Directory option. This directory is where the session and error log files are held. These files are important to determine the integrity of the backup session and to restore the session. Insert the path of the directory you want to use.

Examining NBACKUP

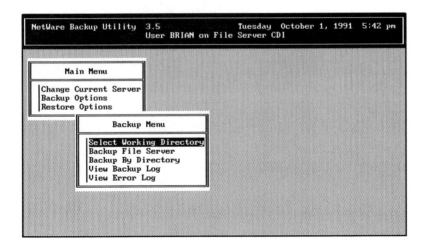

Figure 5.73
Backup menu.

After you select your working directory, choose the Backup File Server option. You then see a Backup Options window that enables you to customize the backup session. The session parameters are configured here (see fig. 5.74).

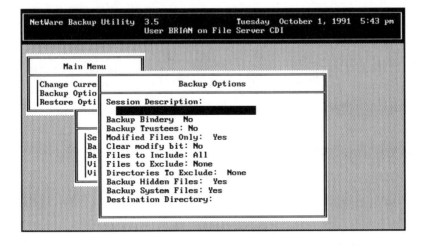

Figure 5.74
Session configuration.

 NBACKUP does not back up hidden and system files on a NetWare 2.x file server.

Chapter 5: Utilities

 Volumes that have additional name space support are not supported in NBACKUP.

You tell NBACKUP what task you want it to perform by responding to the following options:

- **Session Description.** Provides a means to place a label on each session, making it unique.

- **Backup Bindery.** Determines if the bindery is to be backed up.

- **Backup Trustees.** Determines if the trustees are to be included in the session.

- **Modified Files Only.** Checks the modify bit; if set to Yes, backs up the files that have been modified since the last backup.

- **Clear Modify Bit.** Enables you to select whether the Modify bit will be cleared.

- **Files to Include.** Enables you to back up selected files. The default is All.

- **Files to Exclude.** Used to prevent specific files from being backed up. The default is None.

- **Directories to Exclude.** Operates the same as the Files to Exclude option but at the directory level.

- **Backup Hidden Files.** Backs up hidden files.

- **Backup System Files.** Backs up system files.

- **Source Directory.** Locates where you have chosen to back up whether it is a file server, volume, or directory.

- **Destination Directory.** Locates the DOS device to which you want to archive data; can be any DOS device to which you have access and security privileges.

Examining NBACKUP

When you select from the Backup menu to back up a file server or a directory structure, the Backup Options window changes; options that do not pertain to that operation are disabled.

As with NetWare utilities, the data entry fields pertaining to volumes and directories provide a point-and-shoot menu choice when you press Ins, as figures 5.75 and 5.76 illustrate.

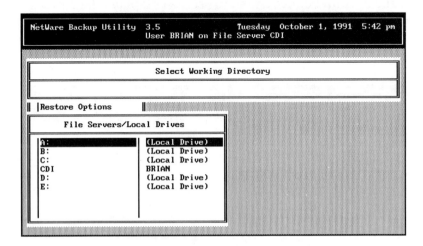

Figure 5.75
Select destination.

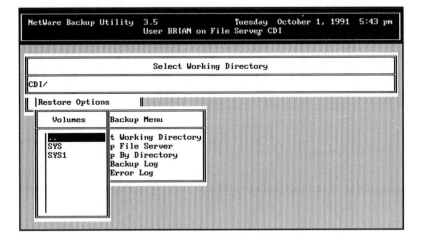

Figure 5.76
Select volume.

Chapter 5: Utilities

After completing the options window, the backup process is started by pressing Esc. You then are prompted to start the backup at that time or later. If you select to start it later, you must provide the start date and time. At this point, the workstation remains at that prompt until the desired time and date. The workstation can be interrupted simply by pressing the Esc key.

After the backup begins, the status screen displays the current activity, errors encountered, and total files and directories backed up. This screen remains active until the session is completed (see fig. 5.77).

Figure 5.77
The status screen.

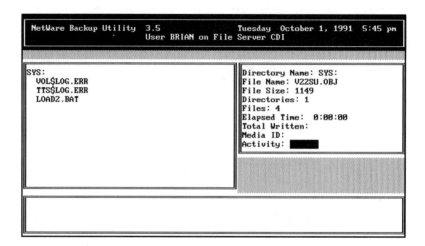

Always examine the error log after the session is complete. One of the most common problems encountered with backup systems is failure to check the log file. Most operators assume that everything is fine; when the backup is needed, they find out otherwise.

The error log is simple to inspect. After the backup or restore session is finished, simply highlight the View Error Log option of the Backup menu and select the current entry from the list that appears. A sample error log is shown in figure 5.78.

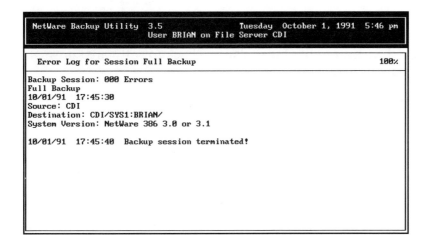

Figure 5.78
Session error log.

Enhanced Backup Using SBACKUP

NetWare 3.12 has eliminated the NBACKUP utility and replaced it with an improved version called SBACKUP. SBACKUP can be used to back up NetWare file systems and also lets Btrieve (SQL) databases, DOS workstations, and OS/2 workstations, take advantage of backup capabilities.

SBACKUP functions by using files called Target Service Agents (TSA). A TSA called TSA_DOS.NLM is loaded at the host server, along with the SBACKUP.NLM. (A *host server* is the one from which the backup capability is being run.)

A host server has the storage device and storage controller attached to it. All *targets* (devices being backed up) are backed up to the host.

Another TSA called TSA_SMS is loaded at the DOS client (target). When the TSAs are loaded with parameters correctly set, the client is able to specify drives to back up, the server to attach to in order to backup and restore, buffer size for faster access, and other options.

Chapter 5: Utilities

The backup software determines which files to back up based on the *modify bit*. Whenever a file is added or changed, the file is flagged with a modify bit so that the backup software knows it was added or changed.

SBACKUP provides four strategies (options) for backing up your server. These four options include the following:

- **Full backup.** Backs up all files on the target. It does not take into consideration whether these files were backed up previously and have not changed since. The modify bit is cleared when a full backup is performed.

- **Incremental backup.** Backs up all files that are new or that have been modified in some way since the last backup. The modify bit is cleared when an incremental backup is performed.

- **Differential backup.** Backs up all data that has changed since the last time a full backup was done, even if the changed files were previously backed up using an incremental backup. The modify bit is not cleared when a differential backup is performed. By not clearing this bit, the backup software knows to back up this file again during the incremental backup.

- **Custom backup.** Backs up what you specify. The status of the modify bit on changed or added files depends on what you decide to back up.

SMS provides these backup options so that you can reduce the amount of time spent doing a backup. If you perform a full backup on Friday, for example, then you can do an incremental backup on Monday through Thursday. Depending on the amount of work done during the week, each of your incremental backups should take just a few minutes.

If you have to restore your backup files at any time during the week, you will have to restore Friday's full backup as well as each day's incremental backup.

Assuming you performed a full backup on Friday, then performed a differential backup each day that week, restoring your

Enhanced Backup Using SBACKUP

files is much quicker. You only need to restore Friday's full backup as well as the differential backup for the day before you lost your files. The differential backup is cumulative, meaning that it backs up all files that were modified or added since the last full backup.

A differential backup takes longer than an incremental backup, but is quicker to restore—you only have to restore the full backup and the single differential backup. The incremental backup method requires that you restore the full backup and each of the incremental backups that have been run since the last full backup.

Using the HELP Utility

NetWare includes a utility to provide on-line help while you are logged in to the network. The utility that provides on-line help is called HELP.

 Note This help utility has been replaced in NetWare 3.12 by Novell's ElectroText. More information on ElectroText can be found in Chapter 10.

When you type **HELP** at any mapped drive, a menu screen similar to figure 5.79 appears. On this screen are several small downward-pointing triangles. By using your Tab key, you can move to each triangle.

After your cursor is on the triangle, press Enter to view more information about the selected topic. Figure 5.80 shows a screen full of topics from which you can select to view more information. Again, move your cursor by using the Tab key or your arrow keys until you arrive at the command you want to view, then press Enter.

195

Chapter 5: Utilities

Figure 5.79
HELP screen main menu.

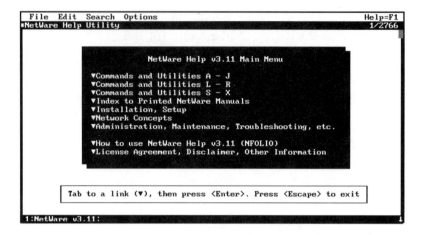

Figure 5.80
Command Utilities A-J in the HELP menu.

Figure 5.81 shows the information you see when you press Enter on COLORPAL. This screen defines the utility and gives you more triangles, which provide additional information about this utility.

 Another method that you can use to invoke the HELP utility is to enter the command you want to view immediately after the HELP command. To view figure 5.81, follow the steps listed in the preceding text, or type **HELP COLORPAL**.

Using the HELP Utility

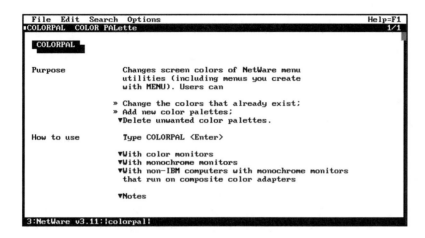

Figure 5.81
The result of pressing Enter on COLORPAL.

Understanding the SESSION Menu Utility

NetWare includes one utility used more for novice users than for system administrators. This utility is called SESSION. In the SESSION utility, you can map drives, send messages to users and groups, and view your effective rights.

Figure 5.82 shows the main SESSION menu screen. From this menu, you can perform the tasks discussed in the following sections.

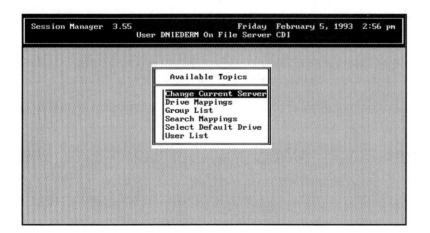

Figure 5.82
SESSION Main Menu.

197

Change Current Server

This option enables you to attach to another server and perform SESSION functions on another server.

Drive Mappings

From this option, you can add and delete regular drive mappings. Figure 5.83 shows a currently mapped drive. To add a drive mapping, press Ins, type an available drive letter, and press Enter. You then can enter the path or press Ins a second time and select the path through menus. Both methods were previously explained in the section on SYSCON.

Figure 5.83
Current Drive Mappings in SESSION.

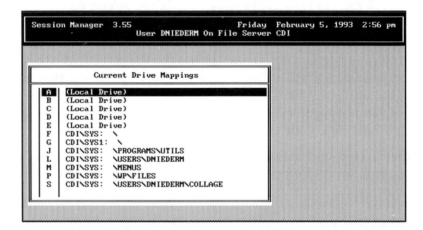

You also can view your effective rights in any of the mapped drives by highlighting the mapping and pressing Enter. Figure 5.84 shows a listing of Effective Rights for the \PROGRAMS\UTILS mapping.

 In figure 5.84, notice that the Current Drive Mappings menu has a double-line border. The Effective Rights menu has only a single-line border.

Understanding the SESSION Menu Utility

The double-line border is NetWare's notation that items from this menu can be chosen or changed. The single-line border means that the information can only be viewed, that there are no submenus, and the information cannot be changed from that location.

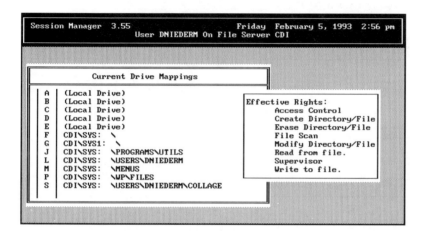

Figure 5.84

Viewing Effective Rights in SESSION.

Figure 5.85 reminds you that you cannot set Effective Rights for local drives.

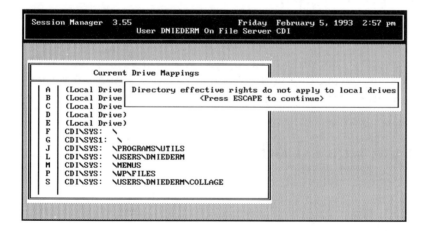

Figure 5.85

Reminder that you cannot assign rights to local drives.

Chapter 5: Utilities

Group List

This option displays all the groups that have been created in SYSCON. You can highlight a group and press Enter to send a message to any user who is logged in and also belongs to this group. Figure 5.86 shows a message sent to anyone belonging to the CASTELLE group.

Figure 5.86
Sending a message through SESSION.

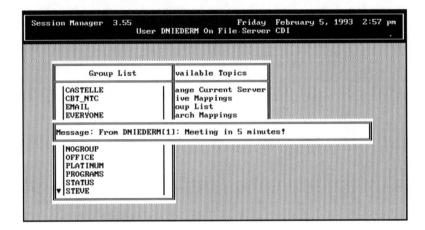

Search Mappings

The Search Mappings option enables you to view your current search drive mappings as shown in figure 5.87 and to create and delete search mappings. This option works the same way as Drive Mappings, except that you select a search drive number rather than a letter when creating a search drive mapping.

Select Default Drive

This option displays all your currently mapped drives. When you highlight a drive and press Enter, the SESSION menu sets the drive letter to which you exit when you leave SESSION.

Understanding the SESSION Menu Utility

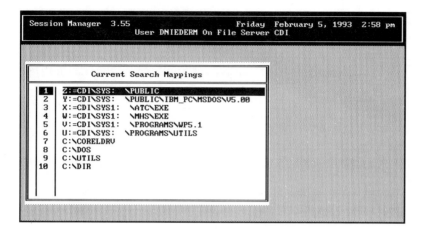

Figure 5.87
Viewing search mappings in SESSION.

User List

This option shows you all the users currently logged in to the network. After you highlight a user and press Enter, you see a menu with two options: View Information and Send Message.

 In NetWare 3.12, the View Information option is called Display User Information. The functionality, however, remains the same.

From this menu, you can view user information, as shown in figure 5.88, or you can send a menu.

Figure 5.88

Viewing information about a user in SESSION.

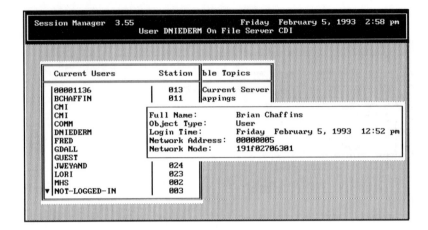

Using WSUPDATE

WSUPDATE is a command-line utility that enables you to update workstation files from newer files located on the file server. This utility is useful for updating shell files. By using the WSUPDATE utility, you can have the workstation compare the date stamp on a file located on the workstation's hard drive or floppy drive to a version of the file in a specified directory on the file server. If the version on the file server is newer than the one on the workstation, you can have the file on the workstation overwritten or copied to a file with an OLD extension and updated.

Use the following syntax for WSUPDATE:

    WSUPDATE source destination options

or

    WSUPDATE /F=scriptfile

In the preceding syntax, *source* is the location and name of the file on the network that other files are checked against, *destination* is the location and name of the file to be replaced or updated, and *scriptfile* is a file that you create that contains a list of source and destination pairs for automatic execution.

Using WSUPDATE

To update the workstation shells easily, copy the updated shells into one of the search drives on the network and type the following on a workstation using the regular memory shell:

WSUPDATE V:\UPDATE\NETX.COM C:\NETX.COM

You can update the workstation shells when the user logs on to the network, by creating a WSUPDATE configuration file for each user's workstation and executing the WSUPDATE program from the user's login script. If the user's WSUPDATE script is named WSUPD.CFG, for example, type the following into the login script:

IF DAY_OF_WEEK = 2 #WSUPDATE /F=WSUP.CFG

The script WSUPD.CFG resembles the following:

```
F:XMSNETX.COM C:XMSNETX.COM
F:CONFIG.SYS C:CONFIG.SYS
```

Be cautious about globally updating files using WSUPDATE, particularly IPX.COM or NET.CFG files. Not all workstations use the same configuration files; replacing a good configuration file with a generic file can cause the workstation to fail to connect to the network.

The WSUPDATE utility enables you to use the following options:

- **/I.** Prompts the user to input whether the file should be overwritten, renamed, or ignored (the default option).
- **/C.** Copies the new file over an existing one automatically.
- **/R.** Renames the old file with the OLD extension automatically.
- **/S.** Searches all subdirectories on the workstation for outdated files.
- **/O.** Updates read-only files.
- **/L=*path*/*filename*.** Creates a log file that tracks WSUPDATE activity.

203

Chapter 5: Utilities

The source path must be the full directory path including the file name.

The destination must be a specific drive; paths are not permitted. You also can use ALL or ALL_LOCAL in place of the drive letter. ALL searches *each* network drive.

Review Questions

1. Which function key shows you help screens?

    a. F1

    b. F3

    c. F5

    d. F6

2. Which function key enables you to change a file's name?

    a. F1

    b. F3

    c. F5

    d. F6

3. Which Accounting option requires you to activate the Limit Disk Space option in v2.2?

    a. Blocks Read and Written

    b. Connect Time

    c. Service Requests

    d. Disk Storage

Review Questions

4. What is the name and location of the file that stores accounting information?

   a. SYS:SYSTEM\NET$REC.DAT

   b. SYS:PUBLIC\NET$REC.DAT

   c. SYS:SYSTEM\NET$ACCT.DAT

   d. SYS:PUBLIC\NET$ACCT.DAT

5. The Accounting ratio 6/5 in Disk Storage means:

   a. Six cents is charged for every five files stored on the network.

   b. Six cents is charged for every five blocks of data stored.

   c. Five cents is charged for every six blocks of data stored.

   d. Five cents is charged for every six files stored on the network.

6. Where can you view the File Server Error log?

   a. SYSCON, SUPERVISOR OPTIONS

   b. FILER, FILE SERVER INFORMATION

   c. SYSCON, FILE SERVER INFORMATION

   d. FILER, VIEW ERROR LOG

7. What is a workgroup manager?

   a. Created in SYSCON under user information, these users can create and manage other users.

   b. Created in SYSCON under group information, these groups of users control the network administration.

   c. Created in SYSCON under supervisor options, these users cannot create users, but can manage existing users.

   d. Created in SYSCON under supervisor options, these users can create and manage other users.

8. Which key do you use to insert a new user in SYSCON?

    a. F3

    b. Ins

    c. F5

    d. Ctrl+Home

9. When does intruder detection protect the system?

    a. Whenever a user logs out of the network.

    b. Whenever the SECURITY program is run.

    c. Whenever someone uses a login name that does not exist on the network.

    d. Whenever a user does not use the correct password.

10. How can you create a supervisor equivalent user?

    a. SYSCON, user information, select user account, security equivalences, add supervisor

    b. SYSCON, user information, select supervisor, security equivalences, add user account

    c. SYSCON, supervisor options, security equivalences, add user account

    d. SYSCON, supervisor options, select supervisors, add user account

11. Which utility enables you to find out when a directory was created?

    a. SYSCON, Trustee Information

    b. FILER, Directory Contents

    c. SYSCON, User Information, Account Balance

    d. FILER, File Server Information

12. Which keyword is necessary in the MAKEUSER utility to enable you to set password parameters?

    a. #PASSWORD_REQUIRED

    b. #REQUIRE_PASSWORD

    c. #PASSWORD_PARAMETERS

    d. #PASSWORD_PERIOD

13. The MAKEUSER .RPT file is created:

    a. In SYS:PUBLIC

    b. In the directory in which MAKEUSER originally was executed

    c. In the user's HOME directory

    d. In SYS:SYSTEM

14. Which statement about USERDEF is correct?

    a. You can make someone a supervisor equivalent using USERDEF.

    b. You can create a PRINTCON job for the new user.

    c. When adding a user, you are asked for his full name, then for his login name.

    d. You can limit the user's volume space using a template.

15. Which of the following is not a router mode?

    a. Dedicated real mode

    b. Dedicated protected mode

    c. Nondedicated real mode

    d. Nondedicated protected mode

Chapter 5: Utilities

16. Which router mode can an XT computer run?

    a. Dedicated real mode

    b. Dedicated protected mode

    c. Nondedicated real mode

    d. Nondedicated protected mode

17. What can NBACKUP do?

    a. Back up to any tape drive

    b. Back up v2.2 hidden and system files

    c. Back up OS/2 files

    d. Back up to another network

18. Which SBACKUP option backs up only those files that have changed since the last backup, even if it was not a full backup?

    a. Full

    b. Incremental

    c. Differential

    d. Custom

19. Which SBACKUP option backs up only those files that have changed since the last full backup was performed?

    a. Full

    b. Incremental

    c. Differential

    d. Custom

Review Questions

20. Which of the following statements about Intruder Detection/Lockout is true?

    a. It is turned on by default during installation.

    b. It can be set for just one user.

    c. It always shows as an option in the User Information menu.

    d. It displays a message telling the user they have been locked out when it activates.

21. What rights are granted by default when you add a user as a trustee to a directory?

    a. F and R

    b. F, W, and R

    c. C, W, F, S

    d. No rights are granted by default

22. Which of the following tasks *cannot* be performed using the FILER utility?

    a. Create and delete subdirectories

    b. Copy files

    c. Assign trustee rights

    d. Change directories

23. Which utility has FLAG, NCOPY, NDIR, and REVOKE as command-line utility equivalents?

    a. FILER

    b. SESSION

    c. NBACKUP

    d. SYSCON

Chapter 5: Utilities

24. Which file name extension identifies a MAKEUSER file?

    a. TXT

    b. USR

    c. TST

    d. EXE

25. Which files must be loaded in order to run the SBACKUP utility?

    a. SBACKUP.EXE and SBACKUP.NLM

    b. SBACKUP.NLM and TSA_DOS.NLM

    c. SBACKUP.NLM, TSA_DOS.NLM, and TSA.EXE

    d. SBACKUP.NLM, TSA_DOS.NLM, and TSA_SMS

Case Study

1. Correct the following MAKEUSER file.

    The file is called NEWUSER.TXT

    ```
    #Account_Expiration December 31, 1994
    #CONNECTION 2
    #GROUPS ACCOUNT,TECHS
    #HOME_DIRECTORY SYS:USERS
    #LOGIN_SCRIPT SYS:SCRIPTS\LOGIN.NEW
    #NO_HOME_DIRECTORY
    #PASSWORD_LENGTH 6
    #PASSWORD_REQUIRED
    #UNIQUE_PASSWORD YES
    #CREATE TOM;TOM WEYAND;;TECHS
    ```

2. Several items must exist on the network before the corrected script will work. Please list them in the following spaces.

    a. _____

    b. _____

Case Study

      c. _____

      d. _____

3. Create a MAKEUSER script that does the following:

    a. Deletes the users Lori, Fred, and Marie.

    b. Deletes each user's HOME directory under SYS:USERS.

Printing on a Novell Network

Chapters 4 and 5 showed you ways to set up directory structures, add users and groups to the network, control and manage the system by using command-line utilities, and navigate the menu utilities. The next factor common to all current versions of NetWare is printing. Frequently, users need to print out hard copies of their work on a network, much as they do on stand-alone PCs. NetWare enables you to set up printing on your network so that any networked user can access the printer needed to get the job done.

In this chapter, you learn to do the following tasks:

- ◆ Define queues by using PCONSOLE
- ◆ Install print servers
- ◆ Direct the output
- ◆ Control the print server
- ◆ Customize the printers by using PRINTDEF
- ◆ Create print jobs by using PRINTCON
- ◆ Use related print commands
- ◆ Print from an OS/2 workstation

Keep in mind that this chapter explains the common features of printing. Core printing and the PSERVER VAP are explained in Chapter 8, and the PSERVER NetWare Loadable Module (NLM) is discussed in Chapter 11.

Chapter 6: Printing on a Novell Network

Understanding Network Printing

When you print from a stand-alone computer to an attached printer, the job goes through the cable to the printer's buffer. After the entire print job is in this buffer, the computer is free to perform other tasks.

When you print on a network, however, the job is sent from your workstation out through the network cable to the file server. The job then is directed into a queue, which is assigned a hexadecimally named directory under SYS:SYSTEM. A *queue* assigns printer jobs in the specific order in which they are printed. Queues can have English names to help you remember them and are created through the PCONSOLE menu utility.

In v2.2, you can create a queue at the file server console. You cannot create a queue at the v3.11 file server console.

All print jobs are kept in the queues until the designated printer is available. The file server is in charge of polling the printers and queues to make sure that jobs are getting to the printers.

Novell provides four basic methods of printing in the network environment:

- Core printing services
- VAP or NLM print servers
- Dedicated print servers
- Remote workstation printing

Understanding Network Printing

In this chapter, you learn about dedicated print servers and remote workstation printers as well as the command-line utilities involved with printing.

The printing methods discussed in this section require a dedicated workstation to be used as the print server. The PSERVER.EXE program supplies the same functionality as the PSERVER.VAP and the PSERVER.NLM that run on the file server, but adds the benefit of printer service dedication. This solution is best for heavy production printing. The capability to use computers as print servers—from the 8088 to the current 80486 series—enables you to tailor this configuration to your needs.

PSERVER.EXE runs on a workstation.
PSERVER.VAP runs on a v2.2 file server.
PSERVER.NLM runs on a v3.11 file server.

Older 8086 and 8088 PCs are considerably slower than the newer processors. For optimum performance, consider using an 80386 or 80486.

Novell also offers the capability to share a locally attached printer. To enable the RPRINTER.EXE command to function, you must set up a remote printer definition on a print server. The RPRINTER.EXE loads as a background task that uses approximately 5K to 9K of memory. Because of this background operation, do not use this method for heavy printing.

The NetWare RPRINTER.EXE command is selective regarding the hardware with which it works. If you experience problems with a particular computer port using this type of shared printing, use a different port.

215

Examining and Defining Queues Using PCONSOLE

The PCONSOLE menu utility enables system supervisors to create and define queues and print servers. Queue operators and print server operators can manage queues and print servers from this menu. Users can place jobs into queues and manage their own print jobs from this menu.

The first PCONSOLE menu, the Available Options menu (see fig. 6.1), enables you to select from the following three options: changing to another server, looking at print queue information, and looking at print server information.

Figure 6.1
PCONSOLE'S main menu.

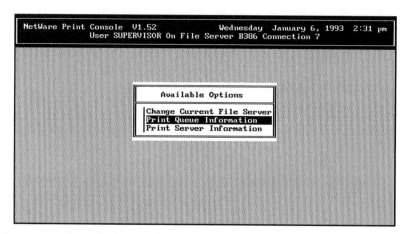

After you select the Print Queue Information option, a list of print queues appears on-screen (see fig 6.2). If you are a supervisor equivalent, you can create a new queue in this option by pressing Ins and entering the new queue.

After you press Enter on a queue, the Print Queue Information menu appears (see fig. 6.3). This menu has seven options, which are described in the following sections.

Examining and Defining Queues Using PCONSOLE

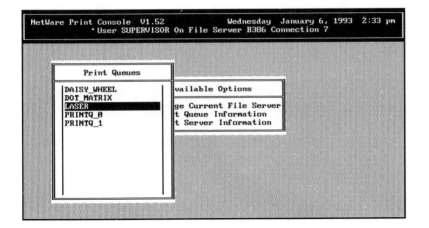

Figure 6.2
PCONSOLE'S print queue information.

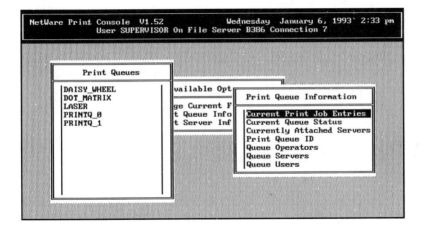

Figure 6.3
PCONSOLE'S specific queue information.

Current Print Job Entries

The Current Print Job Entries option in the Print Queue Information menu shows you all the jobs in a queue. The information is arranged, as illustrated in figure 6.4, in six columns. The first column, Seq, which stands for *Sequence*, shows the order in which the jobs will be printed. The second column, Banner Name, is the name of the user sending the print job. Description, the third column, lists the file names. If the job is sent through a DOS command such as PRINT, or a print screen, or is directed to a print device, this column shows the logical port from which the job was captured, and the word CATCH, as shown in the third job in figure 6.4. The Form column shows the form that has been mounted for this queue.

Figure 6.4

An example of PCONSOLE'S active jobs.

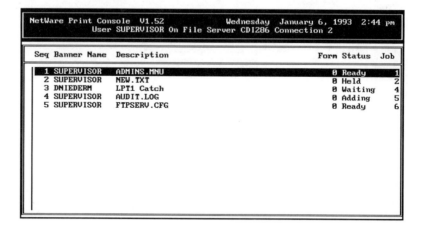

The fifth column, Status, displays one of five possible conditions: Active, Held, Adding, Waiting, and Ready.

 The Active condition designates the job currently printing. No parameters can be changed for this job.

The only thing you can do to a job marked Active is delete it. You must place the highlight bar on the desired print job and press Del. You also can use F5 to mark several jobs, then press Del. You are asked for confirmation if you attempt to delete the active job. The active job's deletion does not stop the printer. Before you can delete the active job and clear the job from the printer buffer, however, you must abort the job from the print server. Refer to the section on print servers later in this chapter.

Any jobs marked with the Held condition are not printed until the hold flag is removed. Two different hold flags can be placed on a job that has been queued to print. A User Hold can be placed on

Examining and Defining Queues Using PCONSOLE

the file by pressing Enter on the job and changing the User Hold to Yes. The job owner and the queue operators can place and remove this flag. The Operator Hold flag can be placed or removed only by the queue operator. To set this flag, press Enter on the job to be held and set the Operator Hold to Yes.

The Adding condition designates a job that is in the process of being sent by a user. If the user has exited an application and the job still says ADDING, the user should type **ENDCAP**, which forces the job into the Ready mode.

The Waiting condition is shown when a print job has been told to wait until a specific date and time before printing. To set deferred printing, press Enter on the queued job and set Deferred Printing to Yes. You can define the Target Date and Time for that file to be printed.

The Ready condition is put on any job available for printing.

The sixth column, Job, keeps track of the number of print jobs that have gone through the queue since it was created.

All v3.*x* copies of NetWare currently do not show a valid number in the Job field.

Highlight any queued job and press Enter to display additional information about print jobs. Figure 6.5, for example, shows the information you can obtain and the parameters you can set for each queued job after pressing Enter.

Table 6.1 explains what some of the terms stand for in the Print Queue Entry Information screen.

219

Chapter 6: Printing on a Novell Network

Figure 6.5
Job entry information in PCONSOLE.

```
NetWare Print Console  V1.52           Wednesday  January 6, 1993  2:45 pm
         User SUPERVISOR On File Server CDI286 Connection 2

                        Print Queue Entry Information
Print job:        4                    File size:         2052
Client:           SUPERVISOR[2]
Description:      LPT1 Catch
Status:           Waiting for Target Execution Date and Time

User Hold:        No                   Job Entry Date:    January 6, 1993
Operator Hold:    No                   Job Entry Time:    2:42:36 pm
Service Sequence: 3

Number of copies: 1                    Form:              LETTERHEAD
File contents:    Byte stream          Print banner:      No
Tab size:                              Name:
Suppress form feed: No                 Banner name:
Notify when done: No
                                       Defer printing:    Yes
Target server:    (Any Server)         Target date:       January 7, 1993
                                       Target time:       2:00:00 am
```

Table 6.1
Print Queue Entry Information

Item	Description
Print Job	Specifies the job number in the queue.
File Size	Specifies the size of the print job.
Client	Specifies who sent the print job.
Description	Specifies the name of the job.
Status	Denotes the condition of the job.
User Hold	Denotes the print jobs that are placed or removed by the job owner or queue operator. Held jobs are not printed.
Operator Hold	Denotes the print jobs that are placed or removed by the queue operator. Held jobs are not printed.
Service Sequence	Specifies the order in which the job is to be printed.
Job Entry Date	Shows the date that the queue received the print job. This field cannot be altered.

Examining and Defining Queues Using PCONSOLE

Item	Description
Job Entry Time	Shows the time that the queue received the print job. This field cannot be altered.
Number of Copies	Specifies the number of copies of the file to be printed. This number can be set from 1 to 65,000.
File Contents	Specifies text or byte stream print jobs. Text converts indents to spaces. Byte stream enables the application to determine the printer codes.
Tab Size	Specifies the number of spaces to convert indents if File contents line is set to Text.
Suppress Form Feed	Sets the form feed to On or Off.
Notify When Done	Turns on or off notification of job completion.
Form	Sets the form number to use for the print job.
Print Banner	Sets the banner to On or Off.
Name	Displays the name printed on the banner. The sender's login name is the default.
Banner Name	Displays the file name by default.
Target Server	Displays the print servers that can service the current print job.
Defer Printing	Enables you to defer printing. Set to Yes or No.
Target Date & Time	Enables you to set the time and day. Default is set to the following day at 2:00 am.

Chapter 6: Printing on a Novell Network

You can add jobs at the Current Print Job Entries screen. Press Ins to bring up the current directory. Change to the directory that contains the file to be printed and press Enter. The next screen is a list of all files in the directory (see fig 6.6).

Figure 6.6
Selecting a file to print in PCONSOLE.

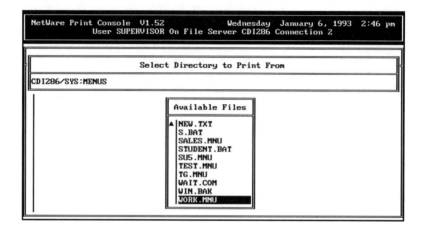

After you highlight the file in this list to be printed, press Enter. If you want to print several files, use F5 to mark each file, and then press Enter. The Print Job Configurations screen appears on-screen. This screen displays the list of printer configurations that you can use (see fig. 6.7). Highlight the desired configuration and press Enter.

Figure 6.7
The Print Job Configurations screen in PCONSOLE.

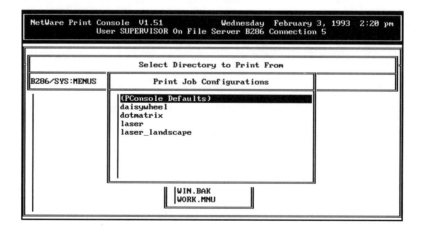

PCONSOLE then displays configuration options. After changing any necessary fields, press Esc and save the job. This job now appears in the queue to be printed.

Current Queue Status

The Current Queue Status option of the Print Queue Information menu has the following five items (see fig. 6.8):

- **Number of entries in queue.** Displays the number of print jobs currently in a queue.

- **Number of servers attached.** Displays the number of file servers that have this queue defined.

- **Users can place entries in queue.** Enables users to place jobs (Yes) or not place jobs (No) in this queue.

- **Servers can service entries in queue.** Enables you to have jobs printed (Yes) or not printed (No) in this queue.

- **New servers can attach to queue.** Enables users on other file servers to use this queue (Yes) or denies users on other file servers access to this queue (No).

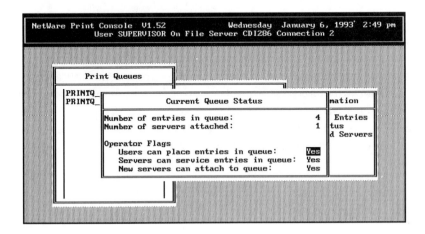

Figure 6.8

PCONSOLE'S Current Queue Status option.

Currently Attached Servers

The Currently Attached Servers option of the Print Queue Information menu shows a list of all servers using this queue. This option can be used to see which file servers currently are putting jobs into the queue.

 All PCONSOLE screens are viewed in *real time*. As jobs are added and deleted, servers attached, or print servers activated, you see the screens change.

Print Queue ID

The Print Queue ID option of the Print Queue Information menu indicates the name of the hexadecimally named subdirectory under SYS:SYSTEM with the QDR extension. Jobs printed to this queue are held in the subdirectory until printed.

Queue Operators

The Queue Operators option of the Print Queue Information menu lists all users who can manage the selected queue. *Queue operators* manage the queue and all jobs going through the queue. Supervisor equivalent users automatically are queue operators. Queue operators can rearrange the order in which jobs print. They also can mark print jobs as Held so that they do not print. To add users or groups to this list, press Ins and select the users or groups that you want to manage this queue. Press Enter to accept your choices.

Queue Servers

The Queue Servers option of the Print Queue Information menu lists all the print servers that can service the selected queue. To

Examining and Defining Queues Using PCONSOLE

add servers to this list, press Ins and select the desired servers. Press Enter to accept your choices. After a printer is defined and attached to the selected queue, the print server for which the printer was configured appears on this list.

Queue Users

The Queue Users option of the Print Queue Information menu lists all the users and groups that can add jobs to this queue.

 The group labeled EVERYONE automatically becomes a queue user.

To modify this list, delete the group EVERYONE. You then can add users or groups to this list by pressing Ins and choosing the users or groups that can use this queue. Press Enter to accept your choices.

Installing Print Servers

 Print servers can be file servers or dedicated PCs. PSERVER.VAP files are used on a router or v2.2 server; PSERVER.NLM files are used on a v3.11 server; and PSERVER.EXE files are loaded onto a PC designated as a dedicated print server.

A NetWare print server can manage up to 16 printers. Up to five of those printers can be attached to the print server, and the rest can be remote printers. A *remote printer* is any printer hooked up to a workstation that is attached to the network and that can share its printer with other network users.

The following procedure shows the way to set up a basic print server that has two printers—one local and one remote. This setup can be modified to fit your networking needs.

225

1. Type **PCONSOLE**.
2. Select the Print Queue Information option from the Available Options menu.
3. Press Ins and add the new queue name, then press Enter. Repeat this step for every queue.

One Printer Servicing Multiple Queues

Figure 6.9 shows an example of one printer serviced by three queues. Each queue in this example is set at a different priority. The DEFAULT queue is set at priority 3, RUSH is set at priority 2, and NOW is set at priority 1. By setting up system defaults, users print to the DEFAULT queue. If a rush job comes in, it goes to the RUSH queue. In the event of a super-high priority job coming in while jobs are in the RUSH queue, the print job is sent to the NOW queue. Jobs currently printing are allowed to finish before priority queues are serviced.

Figure 6.9
One printer serviced by multiple queues.

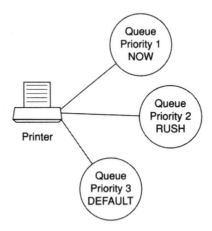

One Queue Using Identical Printers

In the example shown in figure 6.10, one queue is used to service three printers. This setup requires identical printers. When a job enters the queue, the queue polls the printers to find the next available one and sends the job there. Jobs are processed quickly using this arrangement.

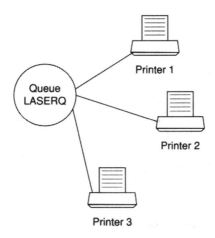

Figure 6.10

One printer queue servicing multiple printers.

1. Press Esc to return to the Available Options menu.

2. Select the Print Server Information option.

3. Press Ins to add the new print server name, type the new print server name, and press Enter (see fig. 6.11).

4. Select the Print Server Configuration option (see fig. 6.12).

5. Select the Printer Configuration option in the Print Server Configuration Menu (see fig. 6.13).

Chapter 6: Printing on a Novell Network

Figure 6.11
PCONSOLE'S Print Server Information option.

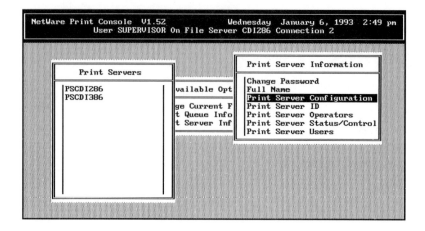

Figure 6.12
PCONSOLE'S Print Server Configuration Menu.

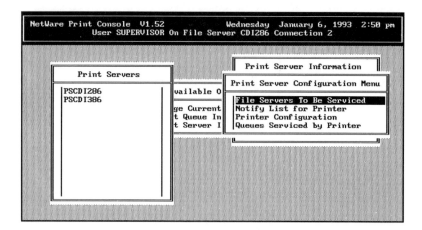

Figure 6.13
Choosing configured printers in PCONSOLE.

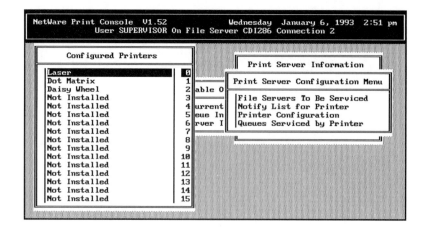

You now need to set up printers for local or remote ports. Select a printer number that you want to configure and press Enter. Add a logical name for the printer and press Enter. Next, press Enter on the Type field. This action displays the Printer types screen. The first seven options in this screen enable you to hook up a printer to the print server (see fig. 6.14). The next eight remote options in this screen are for remote printers.

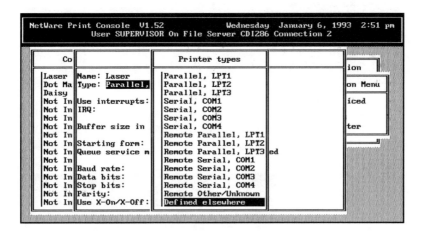

Figure 6.14

Selecting printer types in PCONSOLE.

Remote Other/Unknown has two functions in NetWare:

1. Enables printer setup for a workstation without definition of the printer port from PCONSOLE.

2. Enables you to attach printing devices that connect directly to the LAN, bypassing a workstation.

The last option on the Printer types screen, Defined elsewhere, assumes that another print server has this option defined.

When you select a printer type, NetWare displays several screens to modify the printer setup (see fig. 6.15). These screens present all the hardware configuration options for the printer. Defaults usually work fine. If your printer requires special consideration, however, use these screens to customize the printer. When you are finished defining the printer options, press Esc. Then select Yes from the Save Changes menu and press Esc.

229

Figure 6.15
PCONSOLE'S Printer Configuration menu.

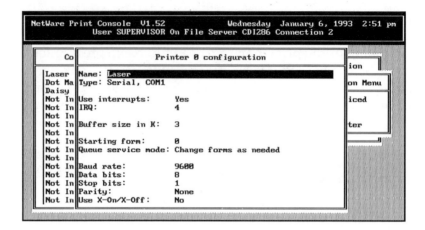

In the Print Server Configuration menu, select the Queues Serviced by Printer option. Next, select the defined printer name in the Defined Printers screen (see fig. 6.16).

Figure 6.16
Choosing a defined printer.

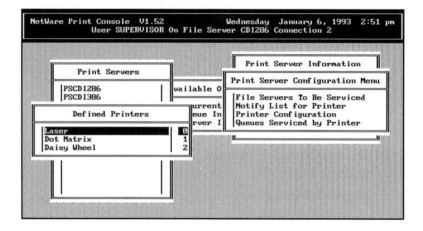

Press Ins to add a queue for each printer configured. Priority 1 is the highest queue priority that you can define, as shown in figure 6.17. Press Esc twice when finished.

 Queue priority enables a queue with higher priority to print all queued jobs before it looks to see if lower-priority queues have jobs waiting.

One Queue Using Identical Printers

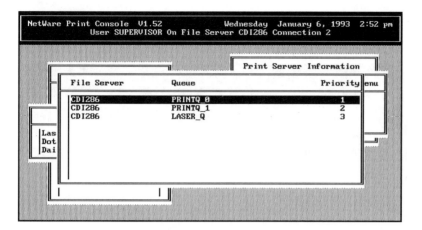

Figure 6.17
Adding a queue to a printer.

Next, select the Notify List for Printer option on the Print Server Configuration menu. Then press Ins to add users or groups who should be notified if problems arise, such as if the printer is off-line or out of paper. At the top of the list of potential users and groups (see fig. 6.18), the option labeled (Job Owner) (Unknown Type) appears. This option reports any messages back to the job originator.

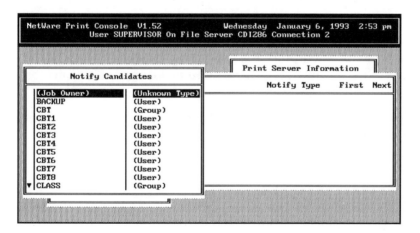

Figure 6.18
The Notify Candidates screen for printer problems.

After you select users or groups to be notified, the system prompts you for information about when they are to be notified and how often. By default, the persons in the notify list are first told of printer problems in 30 seconds and again every 60 seconds

231

Chapter 6: Printing on a Novell Network

until the problem is solved (see fig. 6.19). Press Esc three times when you are finished making your selections.

Figure 6.19
The list of users to be notified in case of a printer problem.

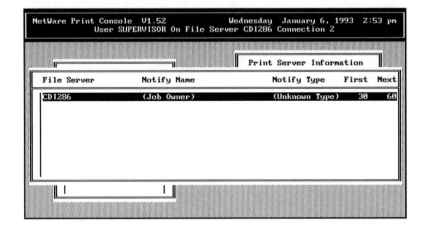

The default Queue Operator is the group EVERYONE.

The default Print Server Operator is the user SUPERVISOR.

Select the Print Server Operators option in the Print Server Information menu. Then press Ins to add any users or groups that need to support the print server. After you make your selections, press Alt+F10 to return to DOS.

At the file server, type the following to launch the print server. You should spool printer 0:

    S *nn* TO *queuename*

The S *nn* TO *queuename* command enables the administrator to accomplish the following:

- **Create a path for a default queue.** This procedure helps when a user issues a CAPTURE or NPRINT statement without any

One Queue Using Identical Printers

flags. If a default queue is not chosen with the spool statement, the user receives an error message.

- **Route jobs from applications that print to printer numbers.** Many older applications are hard-coded to print to printer numbers. NetWare no longer enables the user to specify a printer number. To ensure that the file prints, a spool statement also enables administrators to designate to which queue a job goes if the application sends it to a printer number.

- **Print on a v2.2 system.** NetWare 2.0a uses the SPOOL statement rather than the CAPTURE statement. This option enables v2.0a system users to print on both v2.0a and v2.2 operating systems.

At the workstation designated as the dedicated print server, log in as a user who has Read and File Scan rights to the SYS:PUBLIC directory. Type the following command to launch the print server:

PSERVER *printservername*

Any workstation used as a print server must have the number of its sequenced packet exchange (SPX) connections increased. Create a text file called NET.CFG. Older versions of NetWare had you create a SHELL.CFG file, which also can be used. Place the line **SPX=60** in this file. This file needs to be in the directory from which IPX.COM is called when attaching to the file server (see fig. 6.20).

No matter where the print server is activated—at a dedicated print server or at the file server—the print server screen looks the same. Figure 6.21 provides an example of a typical print server screen. When you press Spacebar, you can see the next group of printers—8 through 15.

Chapter 6: Printing on a Novell Network

Figure 6.20

The SHELL.CFG file and its contents.

```
A:\SHELLS>dir

 Volume in drive A is SYS
 Directory of  A:\SHELLS

SHELL    CFG        8  11-08-91   6:32p
TEMP     FIL        7   7-31-91   6:42p
IPX      COM    29919  10-10-91   6:38p
AUTOEXEC BAT       13   8-01-91   9:35a
NET3     COM    49198   2-06-91   4:44p
NET4     COM    49625   2-06-91   4:39p
NETBIOS  EXE    21506  11-15-90   3:48p
        7 File(s)   60473344 bytes free

A:\SHELLS>type shell.cfg
SPX=60

A:\SHELLS>
```

Figure 6.21

An example of the print server information screen.

```
              Novell NetWare Print Server V1.21
                  Server PSCDI386 Running

 0: Laser                         4: Not installed
    Printing
    Job #: 7, 080991.RPT
    Queue: CDI286/LASER

 1: Dot Matrix                    5: Not installed
    Not connected


 2: Daisy Wheel                   6: Not installed
    Not connected


 3: Not installed                 7: Not installed
```

The final step in installing a print server to host a remote printer is to type **RPRINTER** at each of the Remote Stations. A list of print servers then appears (see fig 6.22). After choosing the print server, all available remote printer setups appear (see fig 6.23). Select the workstation that you want, and NetWare displays a message telling you that a successful installation of the 9K TSR (see fig. 6.24) has occurred.

One Queue Using Identical Printers

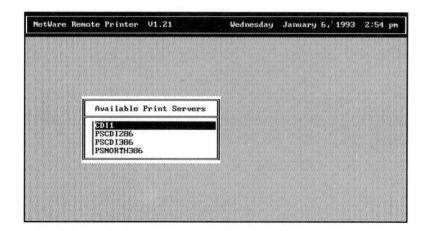

Figure 6.22
RPRINTER's main menu selections.

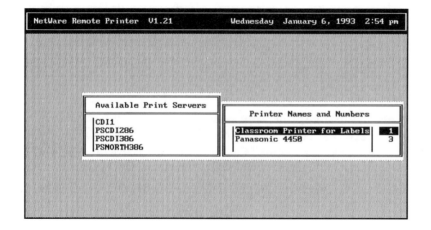

Figure 6.23
RPRINTER's remote printer choices.

```
*** Remote Printer "PRINTQ_1 printer" (printer 1) installed ***
F:\SHELLS>
```

Figure 6.24
RPRINTER's installation confirmation.

RPRINTER

The RPRINTER command has several options. The full syntax line for this command is as follows:

```
RPRINTER printservername printernumber flag
```

By placing the printer server name and printer number in the command line, you can avoid using the menu.

The -R flag removes the RPRINTER from the workstation's memory.

The -S flag displays the status of the RPRINTER.

After the print server is installed, workstations can send jobs to network printers by indicating the queue name attached to those printers. The next section describes this process.

Directing Printer Output

If you are using an application written to run on a Novell NetWare network, chances are that the program knows the way to "talk" to a network printer. Many newer programs enable you to define a queue name as a print device. In these instances, the user is not required to define the printing environment before entering the application.

A significant number of programs, however, still need help to print on a network. For these programs, the user must set up the printing environment before entering the program.

CAPTURE and NPRINT are two commands that enable you to print on the network. Figure 6.25 shows the way each command is filtered to the printer. CAPTURE sets up a printing environment for the user. This command dictates the way all print jobs sent by that user are directed and does not change unless the user reissues a CAPTURE command or logs out. NPRINT is used outside of an application to send a file to a printer. This command is intended specifically for a set of files and does not reset previous CAPTURE commands.

Directing Printer Output

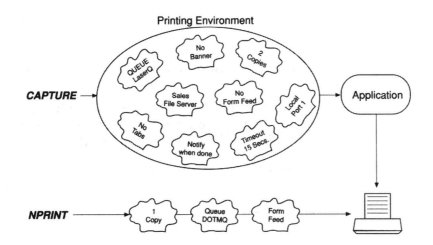

Figure 6.25
Directing printer output by using the CAPTURE and NPRINT commands.

 Remember that NPRINT *always* requires a file name. CAPTURE does not.

The CAPTURE Command

CAPTURE sets up the printing environment for a user. Before using a print screen, the user must first execute a CAPTURE statement.

Figure 6.26 shows an example of a CAPTURE statement directed to the queue called LASER, with no banners, no form feed, no tabs, and a timeout of 5 seconds.

```
F:\DATA>capture q=laser nb nff ti=5 nt
Device LPT1: re-routed to queue LASER on server CDI286.

F:\DATA>
```

Figure 6.26
An example of using the CAPTURE command.

237

Chapter 6: Printing on a Novell Network

The CAPTURE command is not used to print existing files; CAPTURE sets up the way in which a file is printed. The generic syntax when using CAPTURE is the following:

    CAPTURE flags

The ENDCAP Command

If the CAPTURE command is set up for No Autoendcap, then ENDCAP must be specified at the DOS prompt before anything is printed. When used by itself, the ENDCAP command ends the CAPTURE statement to LPT1.

You can also use ENDCAP to return the workstation ports to local use.

Table 6.2 lists the various flags that you can use to direct the ENDCAP statement.

Table 6.2
ENDCAP Flags

Flag	Description
ALL	Ends the CAPTURE statement on all ports, such as ENDCAP ALL.
L=*n*	Stops the CAPTURE statement to a specified port. Replace *n* with the logical port number, such as ENDCAP L=1.
C	Ends the CAPTURE statement to LPT1 and abandons any data without printing it, such as ENDCAP C.
CL=*n*	Ends the CAPTURE statement for a specific port and discards the data to be printed, such as ENDCAP CL=2.
C ALL	Ends the CAPTURE statement for all ports and abandons all data to be printed.

The NPRINT Command

The NPRINT command is used to print data files or files that have been formatted for a specific printer. The syntax for NPRINT is the following:

NPRINT *filenames flags*

 Wild cards are acceptable when indicating file names.

A file name must be specified directly after the NPRINT statement and before indicating which flags to use.

Figure 6.27 shows an NPRINT statement that prints all files that end in RPT and sends the job to the LASER queue.

```
F:\DATA>nprint *.rpt j=laser
Queuing data to Server CDI286, Queue LASER.
CDI286\SYS:DATA
        Queuing file 092491.RPT
        Queuing file 092691.RPT
        Queuing file 092791.RPT
        Queuing file 092591.RPT

F:\DATA>
```

Figure 6.27
An example of using the NPRINT command.

CAPTURE and NPRINT Flags

This section discusses each flag that you can use with the CAPTURE and NPRINT commands. See table 6.3 for a complete list and description of flags.

When you use the NOTI flag, NetWare notifies the user after the job is printed. When several jobs are *buffered* (temporarily stored

Chapter 6: Printing on a Novell Network

in memory) in the printer, you might want to know when the job is ready for the user to pick up. The normal default is not to notify the user when the job has been printed. Both NOTI and NNOTI work with CAPTURE and NPRINT. Use the following syntax lines for each flag:

```
CAPTURE NOTI
```

The preceding command requests notification.

```
CAPTURE NNOTI
```

The preceding command prevents notification.

You can designate exactly where the job is to be printed by using the Server and Queue flags to specify the queue name and file server. If neither of these is specified, the system relies on the SPOOL statement for printer 0 as the default. As mentioned earlier, you should spool printer 0. The S and Q flags work with both CAPTURE and NPRINT. Use the following syntax for these flags:

```
CAPTURE S=CDI386 Q=LASER
```

Table 6.3
CAPTURE and NPRINT Flags

Flag	Description
NOTI	NOTIfies when the job is done
NNOTI	Does Not NOTIfy when the job is done
S	Specifies the Server
Q	Specifies the Queue
J	Specifies the Job configuration
F	Specifies the Form name
C	Specifies the number of Copies to print
T	Specifies the Tabs (TEXT)
NT	Specifies when No Tabs (BYTE STREAM) are used
B	Specifies when the Banner name is printed

Directing Printer Output

Flag	Description
NB	Specifies when No Banner is printed
NAM	Specifies the NAMe
FF	Specifies the Form Feed from the printer
NFF	Specifies No Form Feed from the printer
D	Deletes the file after it is printed (NPRINT only)
The following flags work only with CAPTURE:	
TI	Specifies the TImeout period before printing
AU	Denotes AUtoendcap
NA	Denotes No Autoendcap
L	Specifies the Local port
CR	CReates a file
K	Keeps the received portion of the job in the file server and prints it
SH	SHows the current CAPTURE settings
?	Lists the available flags

The PRINTCON menu utility enables the system administrator or user to create print jobs with parameters similar to the CAPTURE flags. The Job flag enables the user to call on one of the jobs that have been created. The J flag works with both CAPTURE and NPRINT. Use the following syntax with this flag:

```
CAPTURE J=LASER_LANDSCAPE
```

By using the PRINTDEF menu utility, the system supervisor can create forms. *Forms* in NetWare force a user to verify that the proper form is in the printer before printing begins. At the command line, the user can specify which form to use for a particular job. The default is form 0. The Form flag works with both CAPTURE and NPRINT. Use the following syntax with this flag:

```
CAPTURE F=14
```

241

Chapter 6: Printing on a Novell Network

At the DOS prompt, you can specify between one and 999 copies of a particular job. The system default is one copy. The Copies flag works with both CAPTURE and NPRINT. Use the following syntax with this flag:

```
CAPTURE C=3
```

When sending a print job to the printer as a text file, the Tabs flag is the fastest method of printing. Formatting codes are interpreted by the printer and text is printed. NetWare enables you to set the number of spaces between tabs at the command line. The default is 8.

Remember that these sets of terms are often interchanged in NetWare menus and documentation:

Tabs and Text
No Tabs and Byte Stream

When you use the No Tabs flag, all control characters are interpreted by the sending application. This also is called *byte-stream printing*. This method is slightly slower than text.

If an application is sending simple text, such as a nongraphics spreadsheet, send the job as Tabs. If the application sends more complex text, such as text created by a desktop publisher, send the job as No Tabs.

If the printer adds miscellaneous characters on the page, switch printing methods. If you print the file by using the Tabs flag (text), then resend the print job and use the No Tabs flag (byte stream). The problem can occur when codes are being misinterpreted; the alternative method usually clears up any problems. No Tabs is a good default.

The T and NT flags work with both CAPTURE and NPRINT. Use the following syntax with these flags:

    CAPTURE T=5

The preceding command requests a tab of five characters. The following command requests printing in byte stream:

    CAPTURE NT

The network, by default, sets up a banner page before each job is printed. This page contains information about who sent the job, the name of the file, and when and where it was printed. The banner page is separated into three sections. The top section is information about the job and sender and cannot be modified. The second section is the name of the sender by default, and you can change it by using NAM=*n* (up to 12 characters). The third section, by default, is the name of the file; you can change it by using B=*n* (up to 12 characters).

If you do not have a need for a banner page, use the No Banner flag after the CAPTURE statement.

The Banner, No Banner, and NAMe flags work with both CAPTURE and NPRINT. Use the following syntax with these flags:

    CAPTURE NAM=GARY B=JUNERPT

The preceding command sets the top of the banner to read GARY and the bottom of the banner to read JUNERPT.

 Banners do not work with PostScript printers.

The following command does not print a banner:

    CAPTURE NB

Sometimes printers give you more or less paper than you really need. The Form Feed and No Form Feed flags help you tell the printer what you are expecting. Many laser printers kick out extra sheets of paper after printing a job. Use the NFF switch to tell the printer not to send out the extra sheet after the job is done.

Dot-matrix printers often stop and reset the Top of Form if you send only a half-page of data. To make sure that the printer returns to the true top of the page, use FF to issue a form feed after the print job.

The FF and NFF flags work with both CAPTURE and NPRINT. Use the following syntax with this flag:

```
CAPTURE NFF
```

The Delete flag only works with NPRINT. When the print job is finished, the file automatically is deleted from the system. Use the following syntax with this flag:

```
NPRINT SYS:DATA\*.RPT D
```

The system default requires you to exit, or *shell out*, to DOS before the job is printed. This requirement is considered Autoendcap. Nothing prints until the user exits the program.

Most of the time, a user wants the job to print before exiting an application. The Timeout flag helps the user print immediately, and you can set it from zero to 1,000 seconds. This feature tells the system the amount of time to wait for new information to be sent to the printer before considering the job closed and beginning to print. Fifteen seconds is an average timeout period, but some applications might require more time.

Occasionally, you might find that neither the Timeout flag nor the Autoendcap flag produces the desired results. Some printers that contain downloadable fonts in combination with graphical interfaces cannot work with an automatic endcap. In such cases, you can use the No Autoendcap flag to enable the printer to work.

 Before the job prints, the user first must type **ENDCAP** at the DOS prompt. LOGIN, LOGOUT, NPRINT, and CAPTURE also force an ENDCAP statement.

Directing Printer Output

The Autoendcap, No Autoendcap, and TImeout flags work only with CAPTURE. Use the following syntax with these flags:

```
CAPTURE TI=15
```

The preceding command requests a timeout of 15 seconds. The following command requires the capture statement to be terminated manually:

```
CAPTURE NA
```

NetWare enables the user to specify CAPTURE statements for up to three logical LPT ports. If you need two or three different CAPTURE statements, depending on the application you are using, the user can run CAPTURE each time he or she accesses the program. An alternative method is to issue different CAPTURE statements for each logical port and to tell the application which LPT port to use.

The Local Port flag works only with CAPTURE. Use the following syntax with this flag:

```
CAPTURE L=1 Q=LASER NFF
CAPTURE L=2 Q=LASER FF NT
CAPTURE L=3 Q=DOTMATRIX
```

You can capture print jobs to a file rather than a printer. This method imports screen captures to an editor or accumulates data from multiple programs. When using the Create flag, you must include the path and file name. By default, if you capture to a file that previously was used, the existing contents are overwritten with the new print job. To append information to a CAPTURE CR= file, use NA after the file name.

The CR flag works only with CAPTURE. Use the following syntax with this flag:

```
CAPTURE CR=SYS:DATA\SAVE.SCR NA
```

If there is a risk of your workstation hanging up or disconnecting during the printing process, use the Keep flag. This flag ensures that the server knows to accept as much of the job as possible and print it. The default environment permits the file server to discard print jobs if the sending workstation is disconnected during the print job.

The K flag works only with CAPTURE. Use the following syntax with this flag:

    CAPTURE K

NetWare displays the current CAPTURE settings for a user. Figure 6.28 shows the CAPTURE statement issued and the result shown by using the SHow flag.

Figure 6.28

Displaying current CAPTURE settings by using the SHow flag.

```
F:\DATA>capture q=laser nb nff ti=5 nt
Device LPT1: re-routed to queue LASER on server CDI286.

F:\DATA>capture sh

LPT1:   Capturing data to server CDI286 queue LASER.
        User will not be notified after the files are printed.
        Capture Defaults:Enabled       Automatic Endcap:Enabled
        Banner :(None)                 Form Feed       :No
        Copies :1                      Tabs            :No conversion
        Form   :0                      Timeout Count   :5 seconds

LPT2:   Capturing Is Not Currently Active.

LPT3:   Capturing Is Not Currently Active.

F:\DATA>
```

The ? flag lists all the available flags. SH and ? work only with CAPTURE. Use the following syntax with these flags:

    CAPTURE SH
    CAPTURE ?

Controlling the Print Server

After you get the print server up and running, a new option appears in the Print Server Information menu (see fig. 6.29). This option, Print Server Status/Control, enables a print server operator to manage the print server (see fig. 6.30).

Under Printer Status, a print server operator can view information about the job currently being serviced. Figure 6.31 shows a job that has just entered the queue.

Controlling the Print Server

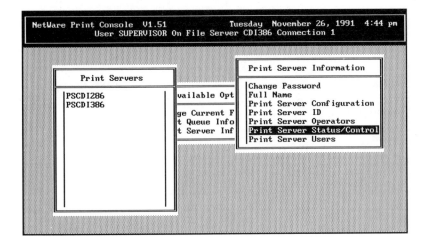

Figure 6.29
The Print Server Information menu.

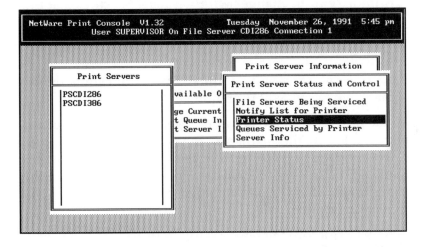

Figure 6.30
The Print Server Status and Control menu.

The Status line shows that this job is being sent to the printer. The following service modes are available:

- **Change forms as needed.** Prompts the user to change forms each time a different form is encountered.

- **Minimize form changes across queues.** Specifies that the printer print all jobs with the same form number before proceeding to the next highest form number. This procedure is done for all queues regardless of queue priorities.

247

Chapter 6: Printing on a Novell Network

Figure 6.31

An example of a print job status.

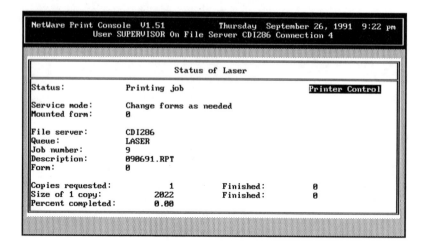

- **Minimize form changes within queue.** Specifies that the printer print all jobs within a high-priority queue that share similar form numbers before servicing lower-priority queues.

- **Service only currently mounted form.** Prints only the jobs that have the current form number.

When the printer status screen appears, the Printer Control field is highlighted. Press Enter to display the next options menu (see fig. 6.32). The following options enable you to modify the print job currently printing. These options are not available from the Print Queue options, which enable you to modify only those print jobs not currently printing.

- **Abort print job.** Enables the printer to abandon the current job. The job then is deleted from the queue. This method is the best way to stop a print job, because it clears the job from the print buffer.

- **Form feed.** Specifies that the printer advance to the top of the next page.

- **Mark top of form.** Prints a row of asterisks (*) across the top of the page to check for form alignment.

- **Pause printer.** Temporarily pauses the printer. To restart the printer, select the Start Printer option.

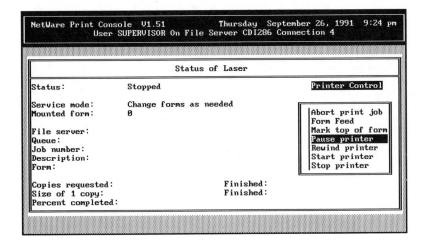

Figure 6.32
The Printer Control menu.

- **Rewind printer.** Enables the printer to rewind a specific number of bytes or advance a specific number of bytes. This line also enables you to specify which copy to print if multiple copies are specified at the time of printing.

- **Start printer.** Starts the printer if stopped or paused.

- **Stop printer.** Stops the printer and returns the print job to the queue. Printing is stopped until the printer is started again by using the Start Printer option.

You now can select the Server Info item of the Print Server Status and Control menu. The Print Server Info/Status screen (see fig. 6.33) then displays the following information about the print server:

- **Print server version.** Specifies that the print server version is 1.2.1.

- **Print server type.** Specifies that the print server is running on a dedicated DOS machine rather than on the file server.

- **Number of printers.** Specifies that the print server is hosting three printers.

- **Queue service modes.** Denotes the number of service modes available.

- **Current server status.** Specifies that the print server is currently running.

Figure 6.33

An example of the Print Server Info/Status screen.

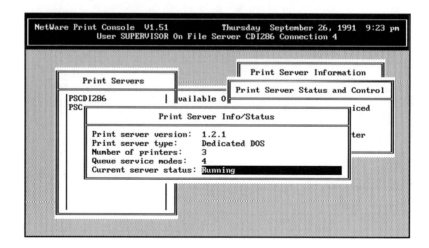

When you select the Current server status option, a screen appears (see fig. 6.34) that enables the server operator to do the following three things:

- ◆ Down the print server immediately.
- ◆ Down the print server after the last job is printed.
- ◆ Enable the server to continue running.

Figure 6.34

The Print Server Info/Status menu.

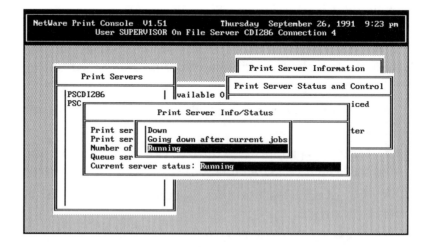

Customizing the Printers Using PRINTDEF

NetWare's PRINTDEF menu utility enables a system administrator to create forms and define printers (see fig. 6.35).

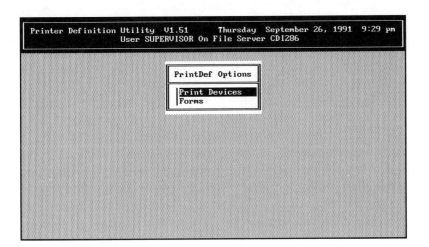

Figure 6.35
PRINTDEF's main menu.

Print Devices

If you have a printer capable of advanced features and fonts and you are using a program that does not know how to make full use of the printer's capabilities, you can solve this problem by using PRINTDEF. Perhaps you want to print a document sideways from a spreadsheet program using condensed print. This type of printing can be difficult to set up internally in the spreadsheet program. By using PRINTDEF, however, you can define a mode that has the functions necessary for the printer to print condensed and sideways.

To edit, import, or export print devices, select the Print Devices option in the PRINTDEF Options menu. The Print Device Options screen then appears (see fig. 6.36).

Chapter 6: Printing on a Novell Network

Figure 6.36
PRINTDEF's Print Device Options menu.

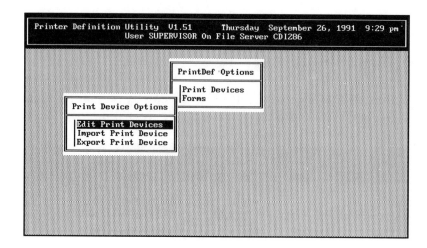

The PRINTDEF command contains a database of information about printers. Each printer has an entry in this database. If you create a print device and want it to be used on another network, you can select the Export Print Device option. This option enables you to create a file with a PDF (printer definition file) extension that you can copy and import into another network.

Importing is done when an administrator wants to use a PDF file that someone else has created. A large list of printer definition files are included with NetWare. These files are copied into the SYS:PUBLIC directory.

 By default, the Printer Definition Files (PDF) are kept in SYS:PUBLIC.

To see a list of PDF files in the SYS:PUBLIC directory (or whatever directory contains the files), select the Import Print Device option in the Print Device Options menu. Press Enter again and NetWare displays a list of PDF files (see fig. 6.37). To import a PDF file into the list of editable items, highlight the file and press Enter.

If you activate the Edit Print Devices option, a submenu appears that enables you to edit device modes or device functions (see fig. 6.38). A *device mode* is a list of functions that produce a desired output.

Customizing the Printers Using PRINTDEF

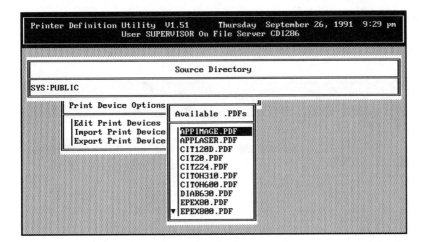

Figure 6.37
PRINTDEF's available files.

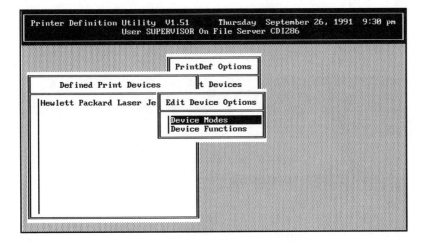

Figure 6.38
PRINTDEF's Edit Device Options menu.

You must begin this editing process by activating the Device Functions choice. When you press Enter after highlighting the Device Functions option, NetWare displays a screen that shows all the escape sequences necessary for a specific printer (see fig. 6.39). To add new functions, press Ins and input the escape codes. You can input the codes in ASCII or hexadecimal format.

The other Edit Device option, Device Modes, enables you to combine print functions to customize the printer output. As illustrated by figure 6.40, this example shows a Hewlett-Packard

Chapter 6: Printing on a Novell Network

LaserJet with the following possible settings: condensed, letter head, letter quality, spreadsheet, memo, CAD drawings, sideways, and reinitialize.

Figure 6.39
PRINTDEF's printer escape codes.

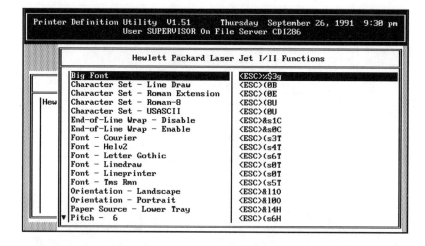

Figure 6.40
PRINTDEF's Device Modes screen.

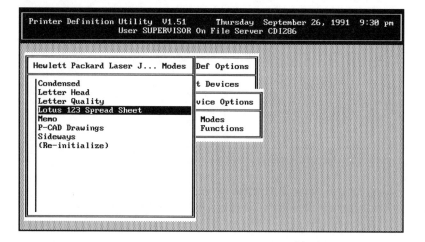

Figure 6.41 shows the suggested functions to print a Lotus 1-2-3 spreadsheet sideways.

To use the modes and devices defined here, you need to set up print job configurations in PRINTCON, discussed in the next section.

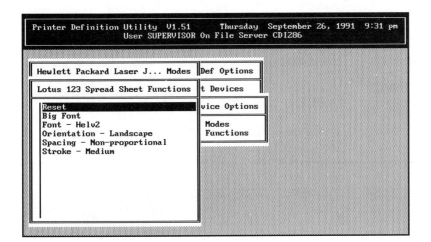

Figure 6.41
The device mode for a spreadsheet.

Forms

The second choice under the PRINTDEF Options menu is Forms. Some businesses need to share one printer for several different types of forms. By creating jobs that use different forms, you can control the printer's use. Each time the printer encounters a change of form, it waits until either a statement is typed at the file server (such as **PRINTER** *printernumber* **MOUNT** *formnumber*) or the Print Server Command is issued (such as **PSC PS=***printserver* **P=***printer* **MO=2**). You can replace *formnumber* with *formname* when mounting a form with PSC.

After you select the Forms option, NetWare displays the Forms and Form Definition screen. Table 6.4 describes the four items that you need to fill in to define a form, as shown in figure 6.42.

Table 6.4
Form Definitions

Item	Definition
Name	Specifies the form's name, up to 12 characters
Number	Specifies the form number, from 0 to 255

continues

Chapter 6: Printing on a Novell Network

Table 6.4, Continued
Form Definitions

Item	Definition
Length	Indicates the number of lines in the form, between 1 and 255
Width	Indicates the number of columns in the form, between 1 and 999

Figure 6.42
Defining a form in PRINTDEF.

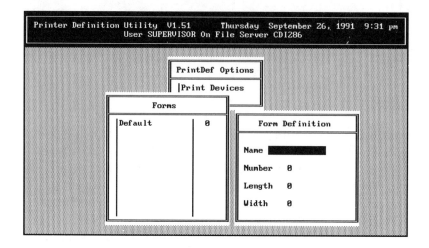

 The form's length and width are there to help the administrator keep track of the form's use. Neither the network nor the printer is affected by these numbers.

Creating Print Jobs Using PRINTCON

The PRINTCON command enables administrators and users to create print configurations. This capability means the difference between a user needing to know each of the CAPTURE flags or

Creating Print Jobs Using PRINTCON

learning the name of a print job that uses all the same flags. Jobs work as shortcuts. You usually can remember job names easier than you can all the flags that make up the job name.

The main menu in PRINTCON displays three options for supervisors (see fig. 6.43). Regular network users see only the first two options. Only supervisors can copy print job configurations.

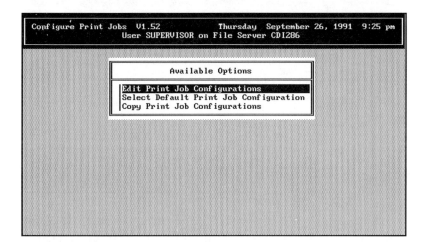

Figure 6.43

PRINTCON's main menu.

To display a list of jobs, select the Edit Print Job Configuration option in the Available Options menu (see fig. 6.44). You then can add a new job by pressing Ins or modify a current job by pressing Enter.

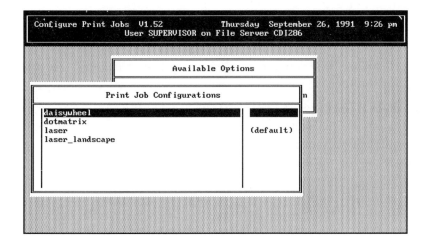

Figure 6.44

An example of PRINTCON's available jobs.

Chapter 6: Printing on a Novell Network

You can set up many of the CAPTURE and NPRINT flags in the Print Job Configuration screen, as shown in figure 6.45. The bottom half of the screen also enables you to use the Device and Modes set up in PRINTDEF.

Figure 6.45
PRINTCON's Edit Print Job Configuration menu.

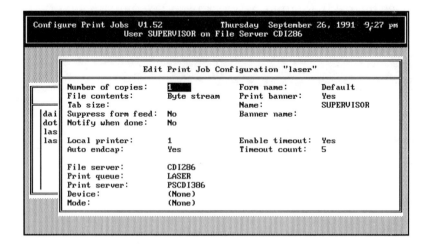

In the example shown in figure 6.45, the print job named "laser" sends the printout to the queue named LASER. Before she can use this job, the user needs only to type the following command:

```
CAPTURE J=LASER
```

If the user does not set up this printer job to include all the parameters in figure 6.45, she needs to type the following rather than the preceding syntax:

```
CAPTURE S=CDI386 Q=LASER C=1 NT F=0 FF NAM=SUPERVISOR NNOTI
↪L=1 AU TI=5
```

As you can see, it is much easier to set up the print job once, then type in the short job name.

The Select Default Print Job Configuration option in the Available Options menu enables you to select which job is the default. If you issue a CAPTURE or NPRINT command without specifying any commands, the parameters of the default job are used.

Creating Print Jobs Using PRINTCON

 Study Note The Copy Print Job Configurations option in the Available Options menu enables supervisors to copy PRINTCON jobs to other users. The personalized PRINTCON file is called PRINTCON.DAT and is kept in the user's ID directory under SYS:MAIL.

When you select the Copy Print Job Configurations option, NetWare displays the Source User prompt (see fig. 6.46). At this prompt, enter the name of the user (the *source user*) whose job you want to copy. NetWare then asks you for the name of the user, called the *target user*, to copy the selected file to (see fig. 6.47). The PRINTCON.DAT file then is copied from the source user to the target user. You must perform this procedure separately for each user who needs the selected file.

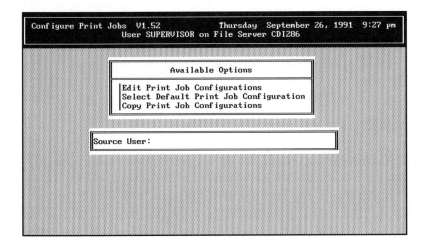

Figure 6.46
The Source User prompt.

The following steps enable you to make use of a common PRINTCON.DAT file that uses your files, if defined, or uses one kept in SYS:PUBLIC if undefined.

1. Copy the desired PRINTCON.DAT file into the SYS:PUBLIC directory.

2. Execute the following commands from the SYS:SYSTEM directory while logged in as a supervisor, and have drive Z mapped to SYS:PUBLIC.

259

Chapter 6: Printing on a Novell Network

```
SMODE Z:PCONSOLE.EXE 5
SMODE Z:CAPTURE.EXE 5
SMODE Z:NPRINT.EXE 5
```

Figure 6.47
The Target User prompt.

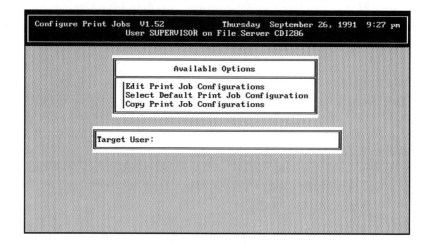

After you modify the search mode, the network uses this method to search for the specified file unless you issue another SMODE statement.

The PSC Command

The PSC command, which stands for *Print Server Command*, is used to control and view the status of print servers. Many of the functions that you can control with PSC you can also do from within PCONSOLE. Sometimes, though, you might find that issuing a command at the DOS prompt is quicker than accessing a menu utility. Table 6.5 lists the various flags available in the PSC command. The flags are discussed in more detail following the table.

Creating Print Jobs Using PRINTCON

Table 6.5
PSC Flags

Flag	Description
AB	ABorts the print job
CD	Cancels a Down server
FF	Advances (Form Feeds) the printer to the top of the next page
K	Keeps the received portion of the job in the file server and prints it
MA	MArks an asterisk (*) at the printer head
MO	Specifies a different MOunt form
PAU	PAUses the printer
PRI	Specifies that the printer is PRIvate
SH	Enables the printer to be SHared
STAR	STARts the print job
STAT	Shows the STATus of the connected printers
STO	STOps the print job

The ABort flag stops the current job from printing. The job is deleted from the queue. The following command tells print server PS1 to abort the job going to printer 2:

```
PSC PS=PS1 P=2 AB
```

The Cancel Down flag enables print server operators to override the PCONSOLE command after the Going down after current jobs option in PCONSOLE is selected to down the print server. Use the following syntax when issuing this flag:

```
PSC PS=PS1 CD
```

The Form Feed flag is used to advance the printer to the top of the next page. The user must stop or pause the printer before she can issue a form feed. Use the following syntax when issuing this flag:

    PSC PS=PS1 P=2 FF

The MArk flag is used to position the form in the printer. The MArk flag places an asterisk (*) at the position of the printer head. The user can use any character to mark the form by placing that character after the MArk flag. When issuing this flag, use the following syntax:

    PSC PS=PS1 P=1 MA ?

The MOunt Form flag is used if you select a form number different from the one currently mounted. The correct syntax is MO=*formnumber*. Use the following example when issuing this flag:

    PSC PS=PS1 P=0 MO=2

The PAUse flag temporarily pauses a printer. Use the following syntax when issuing the PAUse flag:

    PSC PS=PS1 P=3 PAU

Use the STARt flag to resume printing.

The PRIvate flag is used when you are at a remote printer and want to prevent others from using the attached printer. This flag removes the printer from the print server list. When issuing this flag, use the following syntax:

    PSC PS=PS1 P=2 PRI

The SHared flag is used after issuing the PRIvate flag. This flag enables the remote printer to be used as a network printer again. Use the following syntax when using this flag:

    PSC PS=PS1 P=2 SH

The STARt flag is used to resume printing if the STOp or PAUse flags are issued. The syntax for this flag is the following:

    PSC PS=PS1 P=2 STAR

Use the STATus flag to show the status of printers connected to a specific print server (see fig. 6.48).

Creating Print Jobs Using PRINTCON

```
F:\>psc ps=pscdi286 stat
Printer 0: PRINTQ_0 Printer
Printing job
Off-line

Printer 1: PRINTQ_1 printer
Not connected


F:\>
```

Figure 6.48
An example of a PSC status.

STAT can display the following messages:

```
In private mode
Mark/Form feed
Mount Form n
Not Connected
Not installed
Off-line
Out of paper
Paused
Printing Job
Ready to go down
Stopped
Waiting for a job
```

The STOp flag is used to stop the printer. If the print job needs to be resubmitted from the beginning, then the Keep flag also should be used. Otherwise, the job is deleted from the queue. When issuing this flag, use the following syntax:

```
PSC PS=PS1 P=3 STO K
```

263

Printing Under OS/2

The latest version of the NetWare 3.1x operating system, NetWare 3.12, provides enhanced support for printing from an OS/2 client.

The enhanced printing features of NetWare 3.12 support extended attributes for OS/2. The support changes come mostly from the updated client software. To take advantage of the increased OS/2 printing support, therefore, workstations running OS/2 need to be updated with the OS/2 Requester 2.01.

OS/2 remote printing also is supported. It uses NPRINTER.EXE rather than RPRINTER.EXE.

If you want more information on NPRINTER.EXE, you can refer to the OS/2 Requester 2.01 manual. You also can refer to the NetWare 4.0 manual set, because NPRINTER.EXE also ships with NetWare 4.0.

Review Questions

1. Where does a print job go after leaving the workstation that printed the job?

    a. To the print server

    b. To the printer

    c. To a network queue

    d. To RPRINTER

2. Which of the following is not a method of printing?

    a. File server

    b. Nondedicated print server

    c. Remote workstation

    d. Core printing

Review Questions

3. In which order do you use the following utilities?
    a. PRINTDEF, PRINTCON, NPRINT, PCONSOLE
    b. PCONSOLE, PRINTCON, PRINTDEF, NPRINT
    c. PRINTCON, PRINTDEF, NPRINT, PCONSOLE
    d. PCONSOLE, NPRINT, PRINTCON, PRINTDEF

4. How do you defer printing a file?
    a. Use PRINTDEF, DEVICE
    b. Use PRINTCON, QUEUE CONTENTS
    c. Use PSC HOLD
    d. Use PRINTCON, CURRENT PRINT JOB ENTRIES

5. Which entry in PCONSOLE do you use to stop a queue from printing but still enable users to place jobs in the queue?
    a. Servers can service entries in queue: Yes
    b. Servers can service entries in queue: No
    c. New servers can attach to queue: Yes
    d. New servers can attach to queue: No

6. Who can modify the Print Server by default?
    a. Supervisor
    b. Supervisor equivalent users
    c. Print queue operators
    d. The group EVERYONE

7. Who can modify a print queue by default?
    a. Supervisor
    b. Supervisor equivalent users
    c. Print queue operators
    d. The group EVERYONE

Chapter 6: Printing on a Novell Network

8. When running RPRINTER, what needs to be set in the configuration file?

    a. IPX=40

    b. IPX=60

    c. SPX=60

    d. SPX=40

9. Which CAPTURE statement produces an error?

    a. `CAPTURE NB NA CR=SYS:TEMP.PRN`

    b. `CAPTURE NB NFF TI=15 D NT`

    c. `CAPTURE /TI=15 /NB`

    d. `CAPTURE /C=5 /FF /NOTI`

10. Which NPRINT statement produces an error when printing the file SYS:\INFO\DATA.TXT to the queue LASER?

    a. `NPRINT SYS:\INFO\DATA.TXT Q=LASER`

    b. `NPRINT D SYS:\INFO\DATA.TXT Q=LASER`

    c. `NPRINT SYS:\INFO\DATA.TXT Q=LASER T=5`

    d. `NPRINT SYS:\INFO\DATA.TXT NB Q=LASER`

11. Which of the following commands do you use to stop a printer?

    a. PSC

    b. PSTAT

    c. PRINTDEF

    d. CAPTURE

12. Which of the following statements marks the top of a form with an asterisk (*)?

    a. `PSC PS=PSCDI386 P=1 MA`

    b. `PSC PS=PSCDI386 MA`

c. `PSC PS=PSCDI386 MARK`

d. `PSC PS=PSCDI386 P=1 MARK`

13. The main difference between printing on a stand-alone computer and printing on a network computer is:

    a. Hexadecimal names are used instead of English names for print jobs on the network.

    b. A stand-alone computer sends the print job to a printer buffer, but the print job on the network goes to a queue on the file server.

    c. File server queues must have a name the same as a printer or the print job cannot be stored in a print buffer.

    d. You can send only one print job at a time to be printed on the network, but you can send several jobs simultaneously to a stand-alone printer.

14. The PSERVER.EXE program runs:

    a. On the v2.2 file server

    b. On the v3.1*x* file server

    c. On a print server attached to the network

    d. On the workstation

15. Which of the following statements is most true regarding PCONSOLE?

    a. Queue operators can manage print servers from this menu.

    b. Only print queue managers can place jobs in queues using this utility.

    c. Users can place jobs into queues but cannot manage jobs from this menu.

    d. Users and print server operators must have supervisor-equivalent rights to add jobs to queues.

16. If you are the supervisor or a supervisor equivalent, you can insert a job into a print queue using the PCONSOLE menu utility from which Print Queue Information menu option?

    a. Current Print Job Entries
    b. Current Queue Status
    c. Queue Operator
    d. Queue Servers

17. Which of the following is not a PCONSOLE print job status condition?

    a. Active
    b. Adding
    c. OnHold
    d. Ready

18. Which of the following is the status for any job available for printing?

    a. Active
    b. Adding
    c. OnHold
    d. Ready

19. Which of the following PCONSOLE print job parameters can you use to print your documents after you leave the office?

    a. Status
    b. Target time
    c. Job entry time
    d. Suppress form feed

Review Questions

20. Which of the following tasks *cannot* be done by a print queue operator?

    a. Reorder print jobs

    b. Mark print jobs to be held

    c. Add users as print queue operators

    d. Delete print jobs

21. The _____ command is used to set up the printing environment for a user.

    a. ENDCAP

    b. CAPTURE

    c. NPRINT

    d. ENDPRINT

22. The _____ command is used to print files that have been formatted for a specific printer.

    a. ENDCAP

    b. CAPTURE

    c. NPRINT

    d. ENDPRINT

23. Which of the following statements about PRINTDEF is most true?

    a. You can use the forms option in this utility to control the printer so that different users with different types of documents to be printed can share one printer.

    b. The forms option lets you define a database of print devices.

    c. Print device definitions must be created from scratch using the forms option.

    d. By using the forms option to define a print device, you can easily print documents in the landscape mode.

24. Supervisors can copy print jobs to other users by choosing the _____ option from the PRINTCON menu.

    a. Edit Print Job Configurations
    b. Select Default Print Job Configurations
    c. Copy Print Job Configurations
    d. Import Print Devices

25. Which PSC flag advances the printer to the top of the next page?

    a. AB
    b. MA
    c. PRI
    d. FF

Case Study

1. List the steps, in order, that you must follow to create a print server.
2. Create a CAPTURE statement that captures to two ports on the same machine, each with different parameters.
3. Create CAPTURE statements that accomplish the same things as shown in the following PRINTCON screens.

Case Study

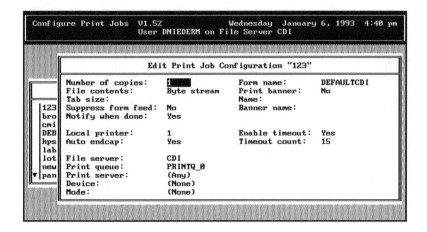

a. CAPTURE _____

```
Configure Print Jobs   V1.52           Wednesday  January 6, 1993  4:41 pm
                       User DNIEDERM on File Server CDI

                   ┌─────── Edit Print Job Configuration "new" ───────┐
                   │ Number of copies:     4           Form name:     DEFAULTCDI │
                   │ File contents:        Text        Print banner:  Yes        │
                   │ Tab size:             12          Name:          DEB        │
      123          │ Suppress form feed:   Yes         Banner name:              │
      bro          │ Notify when done:     No                                    │
      cmi          │                                                             │
      DEB          │ Local printer:        2           Enable timeout: No        │
      hps          │ Auto endcap:          No          Timeout count:            │
      lab          │                                                             │
      lot          │ File server:          CDI                                   │
      new          │ Print queue:          HP                                    │
    ▼ pan          │ Print server:         (Any)                                 │
                   │ Device:               (None)                                │
                   │ Mode:                 (None)                                │
                   └─────────────────────────────────────────────────────────────┘
```

b. CAPTURE _____

271

Chapter 6: Printing on a Novell Network

```
Configure Print Jobs   V1.52              Wednesday  January 6, 1993  4:42 pm
                         User DNIEDERM on File Server CDI

                        Edit Print Job Configuration "pana_12"

         Number of copies:     1             Form name:        default
         File contents:        Text          Print banner:     No
         Tab size:             8             Name:
   bro   Suppress form feed:   Yes           Banner name:
   cmi   Notify when done:     Yes
   DEB
   hps   Local printer:        1             Enable timeout:   Yes
   lab   Auto endcap:          Yes           Timeout count:    25
   lot
   new   File server:          B386
   pan   Print queue:          PRINTQ_0
   pan   Print server:         (Any)
         Device:               (None)
         Mode:                 (None)
```

    c. CAPTURE _____

Customizing the User's Environment

CHAPTER 7

This chapter is the final one that deals with the NetWare utilities common in all v2.1*x*, v2.2 and v3.*x* systems. In this chapter, you learn about the following topics:

- ◆ Choosing and installing application software
- ◆ Creating login scripts
- ◆ Creating menus
- ◆ Creating workstation files

In the first section of the chapter, you are introduced to the concepts involved in loading any software application. Included in this discussion are the steps you must take to enable a network user to have access to the new application.

Next, you learn to create and manage login scripts. These scripts are useful in streamlining the login process for all users. You learn all the commands that can be used in the login scripts.

Then you learn to create a menu. NetWare provides a convenient mechanism for automating the user's interface to the network through menus.

Finally, you learn to create the necessary files so that a user can gain access to the network. You learn about the older method of WSGEN as well as the newer Open Data-Link drivers method.

Choosing and Installing an Application

In this section, you learn what to look for when choosing an application for the network. You also learn some basic rules to help you install the programs and the methods available for securing the executable and data files.

Six essential steps are involved in choosing an application and installing it onto the network. You must do the following:

1. Verify network compatibility.
2. Ascertain if the software is meant for a single user or for multiple users.
3. Make a directory structure for the files.
4. Install the application.
5. Flag the files.
6. Grant access rights to the users.

Ascertaining Software Network Support

Four types of software packages are currently on the market: stand-alone, single-user, network-compatible, and NetWare-aware. These four types are discussed in the following sections.

Stand-Alone Applications

Stand-alone applications are written to run on computers not attached to a network. These applications can cause two types of problems:

- The application might not run properly while the user is logged in to the network. This problem can manifest itself in many different forms: the application might not load, might hang the workstation, might create garbage data, or might not print to a network queue.

- The application might be written to look for signs that the workstation is attached to a network and, if found, will not run. Most applications written in this way give error messages indicating that they do not run if the workstation has a network connection.

Stand-alone applications are not written to work on networks; and, as a result, these programs often are incapable of efficiently using NetWare resources.

Single-User Applications

A *single-user* application is an application that can run on a network, but is intended to be used by only one person at a time. The main problem with using a single-user application on the network is that everyone must share configuration files. Users cannot customize the program for their own needs without customizing the program identically for everyone.

Single-user applications are protected by law against multiple users using the program simultaneously. Although these programs might not give you problems, they are not the most desirable type of network applications. Site licensing, which calls for one entire software package per concurrent user, can become costly.

Network-Compatible Applications

Network-compatible applications are written specifically to run on a network. The problem is that you must determine whether the network it was written for was a NetWare network. Not all networks are the same. A product written for networks needs to provide information about whether it works with your version of NetWare.

Chapter 7: Customizing the User's Environment

Many applications that claim to be network-compatible require you to set rights to root directories and also need CAPTURE statements to run properly. You also might need special software to make the application function as you need it to.

NetWare-Aware Applications

A *NetWare-aware* application is guaranteed to run well on your NetWare network. Applications written to know about NetWare normally provide optimum use of NetWare resources.

Most vendors are proud of the fact that these applications were written with NetWare in mind and normally boast that fact. Look for applications that claim to run with the same versions of NetWare as you currently are running.

While you are looking at applications, also find out about telephone and on-site support. The more accessible the software-support people are, the easier it is to solve problems you might encounter. Find out also if the software company uses the same version of NetWare. This parallelism helps if they need to re-create any problems you are having.

You can obtain information about a program's NetWare compatibility from a variety of locations:

- Your local Novell office
- NetWire, Novell's electronic bulletin board
- The software vendor
- *Novell Support Encyclopedia*
- Most high-quality NetWare vendors

Creating a Directory Structure

At a minimum, you need to make a directory for the executable files and a directory for the data files. You might find that you

Choosing and Installing an Application

need to make even more directories. The basic concept to keep in mind is that the executable files and the data files should be kept in separate areas. This arrangement makes managing the files easier, because you do not have to sort through data files to find the application files. Keeping these files separate also helps prevent accidental deletion of program files.

Whenever possible, use directories to categorize specific groups of files. If, for example, you have word-processing files that everyone in the sales office shares, label a portion of the directory structure SYS:\WORDPROC\SALESDOCS.

Installing the Application

You can install an application in the following two ways:

- ◆ Use an installation option included with the application. This method is the preferred way to install a program; not all programs offer this option, however.
- ◆ Use NCOPY to copy the files from the floppy disks onto the network drives.

Flagging the Files

Application files, unless otherwise noted in the installation documentation, should be flagged as Shareable Read Only. To assign these flags, change to the directory that contains the files and issue the following command:

```
FLAG *.* SRO
```

This entry flags all files in the directory Shareable and Read Only. If you need to flag only some of the files, replace the wild cards with the correct file names.

277

The necessary attributes for all other application files should be documented in the application's installation guide.

Granting Access to Users

To grant users access to the files, you must map drives and assign rights to users or groups. Drive mapping can be done using login scripts, menus, or batch files.

Create search drive mappings to program directories and regular drive mappings to data directories.

Grant the users or groups rights to the application as specified in the installation manual. The rule of thumb in granting rights is that the user needs only Read and File Scan rights to the application files.

Remember these six steps in the following order:

1. Verify network compatibility.
2. Ascertain if the software is meant for a single user or for multiple users.
3. Make a directory structure for the files.
4. Install the application.
5. Flag the files.
6. Grant access rights to the users.

The final step, which is not required in all cases, involves updating CONFIG.SYS for each workstation to make use of environmental variables. Some programs require memory managers that must be loaded and configured in the CONFIG.SYS file.

Some programs also require you to load software at the file server.

In NetWare 2.x, you must copy any required VAP files into the SYS:SYSTEM directory and reboot the file server.

In v3.x, you need to copy any required NLM files into the SYS:SYSTEM directory, or any directory that the server searches for NLM files, and use the LOAD command from the server console to start the NLM.

Developing Login Scripts

Login scripts enable system managers and users to customize the network environment. *Map commands*, discussed in Chapter 3, are used in login scripts to establish paths to commonly used directories. This section discusses the three types of login scripts and the command options that can be placed in login scripts.

 The order of login script execution is as follows:

1. System login script
2. User login script
3. Default login script (only if a user login script does *not* exist)

System Login Scripts

The system login script is designed to service all users on the network. When a user logs in to the network, the system executes this login script. The system login script includes drive mappings intended for all system users, global DOS set variables, and

Chapter 7: Customizing the User's Environment

greeting messages (see fig. 7.1). System login scripts contain commands that all users need, such as a search mapping to SYS:PUBLIC. For more information on these commands, see the login script commands section later in this chapter.

 The system login script is a text file called NET$LOG.DAT stored in the SYS:PUBLIC directory. This file is created and maintained by the system supervisor in the SYSCON menu utility, under Supervisor options.

Figure 7.1
An example of a system login script.

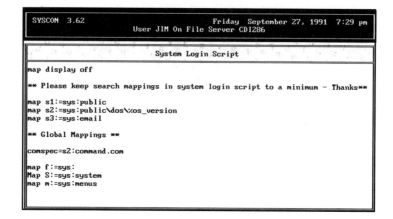

User Login Scripts

User login scripts are created and maintained by system administrators or by individual users for themselves.

 The user login script file, called LOGIN, is held in the user ID directory under SYS:MAIL.

User login scripts contain commands that personalize the network environment for the user. The section on login script commands discusses the commands that you can use with these scripts.

Default Login Scripts

Default login scripts set up basic mappings on the network if a valid user login script does not exist or if no readable characters are in the user login script.

The commands found in the default login script are established as part of the LOGIN.EXE file and cannot be altered.

For more information on default login scripts, see the v2.2 *Concepts Manual* or the v3.11 *Installation Manual*.

Script Parameters

NetWare offers a variety of script parameters. One parameter is called identifier variables. *Identifier variables* force the network to return information such as the time of day or a workstation address.

Identifier variables need to be presented in uppercase characters when enclosed in quotation marks.

Although many commands are not case-sensitive, less debugging is necessary if you present items in uppercase characters.

Each login script command requires its own line. The maximum is 150 characters per line, but 78 characters per line is recommended. Make sure that the line wraps naturally when it is longer than the width of the screen. Hard returns are interpreted as new lines. You also can use blank lines. Blank lines have no effect on the execution of the script, but help to break up its appearance.

Chapter 7: Customizing the User's Environment

 A cut-and-paste feature also is available in the login script screens. Use F5 to mark items and the arrow keys to highlight a block of data. By pressing Del, you can remove the block. You can return the information to the screen by pressing Ins; you can use Ins as many times as needed as long as you do not exit SYSCON. Each time you use the blocking-and-deleting process, you replace previous data.

Login Script Commands

You can use all the login script commands in system or user login scripts. Keep in mind that everyone needs to go through the system login script; personalization can be done through variables or user login scripts. The following commands show you a variety of ways to make a login script "personal."

The MAP Command

The MAP command can be placed in login scripts. In regular drive mappings, the syntax is as follows:

```
MAP options A-Z: = fileserver/volume:path
```

The options you can use are ROOT and *#:.

In search drive mappings, the syntax is as follows:

```
MAP options S1-16: = fileserver/volume:path
```

The options you can use are ROOT and INSERT.

NetWare also enables you to turn on and off what users see when they log in to the network. The DISPLAY statement functions like the DOS ECHO OFF command. MAP DISPLAY ON, which is the default, enables the user to see all commands as they are executed. MAP DISPLAY OFF does not display the login commands. The syntax for each switch follows:

```
MAP DISPLAY ON
MAP DISPLAY OFF
```

NetWare also provides many identifier variables, variables for which the file server automatically knows the values. You can use identifier variables in several ways in the login scripts. When you use them with the MAP command, a corresponding directory that matches the result of the variable must exist. See the section on identifier variables for a complete list of these variables.

When you use identifier variables in a MAP statement, the variables must be in uppercase characters and preceded by a percent sign (%).

To map a network drive letter to the next available drive letter in a login script, use %# in place of the drive letter. %1 maps to the first available network drive, %2 maps to the next available letter after %1.

The same function at the DOS prompt or in a menu uses MAP NEXT rather than MAP %#.

Some examples of the MAP command and identifier variables follow:

- When mapping a HOME directory that changes depending on who logs in, NetWare assumes that a directory that matches the user's login name is on the system. The following syntax shows you the way to map the H drive to a user's HOME directory:

    ```
    MAP H:=SYS:USERS\%LOGIN_NAME
    ```

This mapping requires a directory called SYS:USERS\TWEYAND for the user TWEYAND.

- If you want a mapping to a directory based on the current year and month, use the following map statement to check the file server for dates:

    ```
    MAP G:=SYS:%YEAR\%MONTH
    ```

This mapping requires a directory called SYS:1994\01 if you logged in during January, 1994.

Chapter 7: Customizing the User's Environment

- You should have a mapping for each different COMMAND.COM that your workstations use to boot. Depending on the number of different versions you have, the MAP statements that follow ensure that workstations find the appropriate files.

The following MAP statement assumes that the only differences are the DOS version numbers:

```
MAP S2:=SYS:PUBLIC\DOS\%OS_VERSION
```

This mapping requires a directory called SYS:PUBLIC\DOS\V3.30 for any users who have booted their PCs on DOS 3.3.

The following MAP statement assumes that you might have different DOS types, such as DR-DOS, MS-DOS, and PC-DOS, as well as different version numbers:

```
MAP S2:=SYS:PUBLIC\%OS\%OS_VERSION
```

This mapping requires a directory called SYS:PUBLIC\MSDOS\V500 for any users who have booted their PCs on MS-DOS 5.0.

Occasionally, DOS versions might be recognized as other types, due to similarities in size, dates, and signatures. In these cases, two different COMMAND.COMs might register as the same version, which means that some users might receive an `Invalid COMMAND.COM` or `COMMAND.COM Not Found` message. The following MAP statement solves this problem:

```
MAP S2:=SYS:PUBLIC\%MACHINE\%OS\%OS_VERSION
```

This mapping requires a directory called SYS:PUBLIC\XYZ\PCDOS\V330 for any users who have booted their PCs on PC-DOS 3.30 and have a statement in their SHELL.CFG or NET.CFG that says `LONG MACHINE TYPE = "XYZ"`. (See the section on required commands later in this chapter for more information on this procedure.)

The WRITE Command

The WRITE command enables you to print information to the screen. To use this statement, observe the following conditions:

- Enclose in quotation marks the text to be written to the screen.
- Type variables inside of quotation marks in uppercase characters.
- Precede the variables with a percent sign (%).

Figure 7.2 shows three statements in a user's login script. Figure 7.3 shows the results if the user, James Weyand, logs in to the network at 4:30 p.m. with the login name JIM.

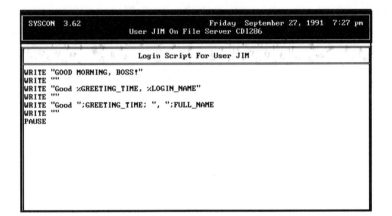

Figure 7.2

Examples of login script commands.

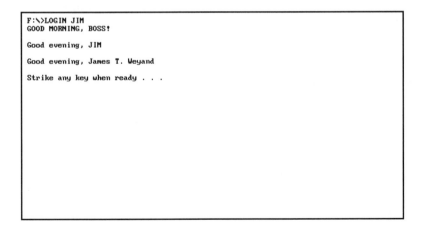

Figure 7.3

The results of the login script statements.

Chapter 7: Customizing the User's Environment

The PAUSE Command

The PAUSE command, when placed in a login script, issues the message Press any key when ready. The system waits until the user presses a key before continuing.

The FIRE PHASERS Command

The FIRE PHASERS command produces a "bloop" noise for every number placed after the command. The resultant noise is designed to draw attention to the screen without startling the user. This command is useful if you want to display a message to the user. Use the following syntax for FIRE PHASERS:

    FIRE nn

The IF-THEN-ELSE Statement

IF-THEN-ELSE statements are conditional statements that enable a parameter to be issued if a condition exists. In an IF-THEN-ELSE statement, the basic idea is "If the condition is true, then do something."

If you want the system to do only one thing, you can specify the command on one line. On the first line in figure 7.4, the system is checking whether today is Friday. If today is Friday, then the system writes TGIF!!!! on-screen. If today is any other day of the week, the system skips over this conditional statement.

If you need more than one thing to happen, BEGIN and END statements are necessary. Examples of these conditions are shown in figure 7.4. BEGIN appears before any executable statements, and END completes the entire statement.

You must always end an IF-THEN-ELSE statement with an END.

Developing Login Scripts

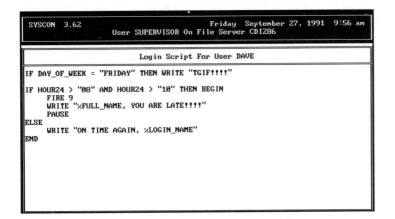

Figure 7.4

An example of an IF-THEN-ELSE statement.

In the second IF-THEN statement of in figure 7.4, the condition is true if the time is between 9:00 am and 9:59 am. If the file server time is in this range when a user logs in, then the workstation issues an attention-getting sound. The FIRE 9 command tells the user by name that he or she is late, and then pauses, as shown in figure 7.5. If the condition is false, then the ELSE statement is executed; in this example, the statement complements the user's timeliness (see fig. 7.6).

```
F:\>LOGIN CHRIS
TGIF!!!!
Christopher Winslow Bell, YOU ARE LATE!!!!
Strike any key when ready . . .
```

Figure 7.5

The result if both conditional statements are true.

Figure 7.6

The result if only the first conditional statement is true.

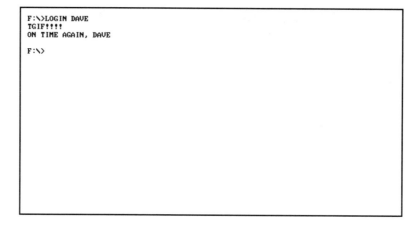

```
F:\>LOGIN DAVE
TGIF!!!!
ON TIME AGAIN, DAVE

F:\>
```

In this example, hours before or after 9:00 am, such as 8:00 am and 10:00 am, force the statement about being on time, which might not be the intended result. You cannot embed IF-THEN statements, so the best solution is to use two separate statements— one for hours before 9:00 am and one as shown in figure 7.4.

The BREAK ON/OFF Command

The BREAK ON/OFF command determines whether you can interrupt the login script by using Ctrl+Break or Ctrl+C.

The DISPLAY and FDISPLAY Commands

The DISPLAY and FDISPLAY commands enable you to display a text file on the user's screen as she logs in. If the file is an ASCII file, the DISPLAY command presents the file's contents. If the file was created using another program and extra characters appear, FDISPLAY filters out all control characters and displays only text. Use the following syntax for the DISPLAY command:

```
DISPLAY volume:path/filename
```

In figure 7.7, the system is looking for the date to be July 4. If the date is July 4, the screen shown in figure 7.8 is displayed.

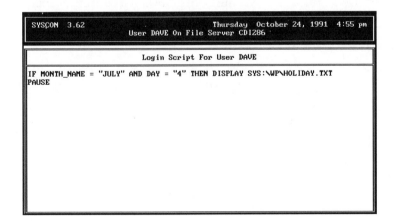

Figure 7.7
A DISPLAY command in a login script.

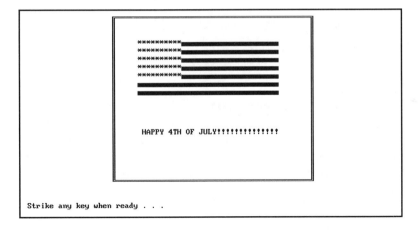

Figure 7.8
The result if the date is July 4.

The INCLUDE Command

The INCLUDE command enables the system administrator to control changes to the login scripts from a common text file.

INCLUDE works like a subroutine in a login script. This text file can be created by any text editor and should contain only valid login script commands. All the commands listed in this section qualify. INCLUDE's syntax is as follows:

```
INCLUDE volume:path/filename
```

If you have several users who share common scripts, placing an INCLUDE statement in their existing login scripts is convenient. Then any changes can be made to the text file.

DOS Commands

DOS BREAK determines whether you can use Ctrl+Break or Ctrl+C at the DOS prompt to interrupt programs.

DOS SET enables you to set DOS variables to a specified value. The syntax is as follows:

```
DOS SET variable name = "value"
```

DOS VERIFY enables you to verify that files are copied correctly to a local drive.

The COMSPEC Command

COMSPEC stands for *COMmand SPECifier*. You can use this command to specify the search drive that a workstation is to use to find the appropriate COMMAND.COM. The syntax is as follows:

```
COMSPEC = search drive:COMMAND.COM
```

The *search drive* variable should be replaced with the search drive assigned to the DOS directory.

The DRIVE Command

The DRIVE command specifies exiting to a previously mapped drive letter from a login script. The syntax is as follows:

```
DRIVE drive letter:
```

The GOTO Command

You use the GOTO command in the same way as you do in a DOS batch file. Do not use GOTO within a BEGIN-END conditional statement. For easy debugging, you also should use the BREAK ON command. For more information on the GOTO command, see your DOS manuals.

Exit Commands

This section discusses the various ways in which you can exit a login script. When you use the EXIT command by itself in the system login script, NetWare exits to DOS without going to the user login script.

In a user login script, EXIT takes the user to the DOS prompt, which usually is the default drive. To execute a DOS command, use the following syntax:

    EXIT *filename*

The file name in the EXIT statement can be any file ending in EXE, COM, or BAT.

When you use the EXIT *filename* command, the system takes you to DOS, closes the login script, and executes the command.

You are limited to 14 characters inside the quotation marks.

If no EXIT statement is called in the system login script, the user login script is executed. If no EXIT statement is called in the user login script, the user is taken to the default directory DOS prompt.

Using the # With a Command

If you type the following syntax, for example, you can execute a command at the DOS prompt, then return to the login script to complete further commands.

#filename

 This command only works with EXE or COM files.

If you have an internal DOS command, such as CLS, or you want to execute a batch file, you must use the following syntax:

#COMMAND /C command

This command loads an additional DOS environment to execute the command. If you want to clear a screen from the login script, for example, type the following:

#COMMAND /C CLS

If workstations frequently run out of memory with the programs you use, using # in login scripts is not advisable. The memory needed to execute the command at the workstation is not released back to the workstation until it is rebooted.

Remark Statements

Remark statements are used to leave notes for the administrator. Remark statements enable you to document, or make notes, on what you have done in a login script; these remarks are not executed. Three parameters are available for creating a remark statement in a login script.

 REM, *, and ; all are valid remark parameters. They must be the first characters on a line.

Command-Line Parameters

NetWare also enables you to use parameters in the login statement to customize your login even further. The available parameters are %0 through %9. %2 through %9 are user-definable.

%0 is the file server name
%1 is the user's login name

The example that follows enables a user named DIANA to exit to DOS, thereby skipping any additional login script commands, if she types **OUT** after her name on the login line.

First, the following line must be placed in the login script:

```
IF "%2" = "OUT" THEN EXIT
```

Then, at the DOS prompt, Diana can type the following to exit to DOS:

```
LOGIN DIANA OUT
```

In the preceding syntax, OUT is considered to be the %2 variable.

ATTACH Command

By using the ATTACH command, users can attach to other file servers from within the login script. The syntax is as follows:

```
ATTACH fileserver/username;password
```

A password placed in the login script file can be a security breach. NetWare prompts you for all information if you choose not to include the password, user name, or file server.

Chapter 7: Customizing the User's Environment

The PCCOMPATIBLE or COMPATIBLE Commands

Use the PCCOMPATIBLE or the shorthand COMPATIBLE command if you have set the LONG MACHINE TYPE variable. These commands tell the network that your machine is an IBM-compatible PC. This command uses no variables.

Required Commands

Novell requires the following three statements in the system login script:

```
MAP S1:=SYS:PUBLIC
MAP S2:=SYS:PUBLIC\%MACHINE\%OS\%OS_VERSION
COMSPEC=S2:COMMAND.COM
```

By placing the search mapping to PUBLIC first, you ensure that all commands kept there are executed with priority. You can alter the mapping to the DOS path to match your directory structure. In figure 7.9, you see a small network with five workstations that all use a different COMMAND.COM.

Figure 7.9
An example of automatic mapping to the proper COMMAND.COM.

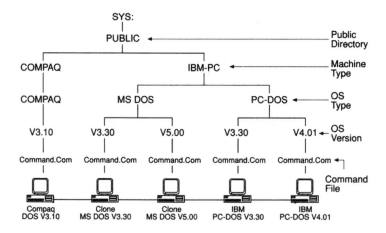

Novell uses the phrases *essential environmental components* and *essential system login script commands* to describe the following three statements:

```
MAP S1:=SYS:PUBLIC
MAP S2:=SYS:PUBLIC\%MACHINE\%OS\%OS_VERSION
COMSPEC=S2:COMMAND.COM
```

Developing Login Scripts

The network queries the workstation at bootup to fill in the variable values. By default, NetWare recognizes all workstations as IBM PCs. If you need to use another directory at this level, you must create a SHELL.CFG or NET.CFG text file wherever you call your IPX.COM. In that file is one line that should read as follows:

```
LONG MACHINE TYPE = directoryname
```

Standards help you to regulate the way systems are set up. They also help you to avoid conflicts. The previous three statements attempt to standardize the operating system environment. You can use other options, but these lines guarantee that you do not get Invalid or Missing COMMAND.COM messages that lock workstations when you are exiting programs.

Identifier Variables

Table 7.1 lists the identifier variables and their definitions. You can use these variables in login scripts.

Table 7.1
Identifier Variables

Conditional Items	Screen Display
ACCESS_SERVER	Displays TRUE if access server is functional; displays FALSE if not functional
ERROR_LEVEL	Displays the number of errors; if no errors are found
MEMBER OF group	Displays TRUE if the user is a member of a specified group; displays FALSE if the user is not a member of a specified group

Date	Screen Display
DAY	Displays the day from 01 to 31
DAY_OF_WEEK	Displays the day of the week

continues

Chapter 7: Customizing the User's Environment

Table 7.1, Continued
Identifier Variables

Date	Screen Display
MONTH	Displays the month from 01 to 12
MONTH_NAME	Displays the name of the month
NDAY_OF_WEEK	Displays the number of the weekday
SHORT_YEAR	Displays the year in short format, such as 92, 93, and so on
YEAR	Displays the year in full format, such as 1992, 1993, and so on
DOS Environment	Uses any DOS environment variable as a string

Network	Screen Display
NETWORK_ADDRESS	Displays the network number of the cabling system in eight hex digits
FILE_SERVER	Displays the name of the file server

Time	Screen Display
AM_PM	Displays the time as day or night, by using am or pm
GREETING_TIME	Displays the time of day as morning, afternoon, or evening
HOUR	Displays the time of day in hours, from 1 to 12
HOUR24	Displays the hour in 24-hour time, from 00 to 23
MINUTE	Displays the minutes from 00 to 59
SECOND	Displays the seconds from 00 to 59

User	Screen Display
FULL_NAME	Displays the full name of the user by using SYSCON information
LOGIN_NAME	Displays the user's login name
USER_ID	Displays the ID number of each user

Workstation	Screen Display
MACHINE	Displays the machine for which the shell was written, such as IBM PC
OS	Displays the workstation's operating system, such as MS-DOS
OS_VERSION	Displays the DOS version of the workstation
P_STATION	Displays the station address or node address in 12 hex digits
SMACHINE	Displays the name of the machine in short format, such as IBM
STATION	Displays the connection number

Creating Custom Menus

Menus make access to applications easy for end users. By using menus, users never have to learn what drives a program. Instead, they can focus their efforts in more productive areas. Many third-party menu programs are available, but few have the simplicity and network compatibility that the menus in NetWare offer. One of the most appealing features of NetWare menus is the cost: they are free with the NetWare operating system.

If you can write DOS batch files, you have an excellent background for writing a menu in NetWare. Almost anything that you

Chapter 7: Customizing the User's Environment

can accomplish using a batch file you also can do—with the same syntax—using a menu script.

 Menu files are DOS text files with the extension MNU. All the files displayed in figure 7.10 are menus.

Figure 7.10
Examples of menu files.

```
F:\MENUS>dir *.mnu

 Volume in drive F is SYS
 Directory of  F:\MENUS

12-2      MNU       557   7-31-91   2:40p
ADMINS    MNU       494  10-04-90   6:23p
SALES     MNU      1314   8-07-89   4:44p
BACKUP    MNU       425   8-13-90   1:21p
ACCOUNT   MNU      5171   4-15-91   1:05p
WORK      MNU      2072   7-25-90   1:36p
        6 File(s)   32436224 bytes free

F:\MENUS>
```

By calling a batch file from within a menu, you might experience unreliable results. You should replicate all commands within a batch file in the menu script for smooth execution.

Menu Format

This section discusses the format that you can use to create a menu. In NetWare, you can create menus by using any text editor. The following list outlines the format of a menu file:

- Precede menu and submenu names with a percent sign (%) and line them up with the left margin.

- Left-align the options you want to use as items that users can choose from a menu.

Creating Custom Menus

- Make sure that all executable statements appear on their own lines and are indented at least one space.

- Indent and use a percent sign (%) when calling a submenu.

- Make sure that no spaces exist between the percent sign (%) and a menu name.

- When defining a submenu, make sure that the menu name is identical to the way it is called. If you call a submenu %UTILITIES, for example, you must match the name when you later define it.

You can place menus and submenus anywhere on-screen and use one of eight colors as defined in NetWare's COLORPAL utility. After you name the menu, you must define three fields, which are separated with commas.

The syntax used for defining a menu's placement on the screen and which color palette it should use is as follows:

%MENUNAME,ROW#,COLUMN#,COLOR#

The order is row (from 1-24), column (from 1-80), and color. The row and column fields make up the size of the computer screen.

Do not use any spaces on this line.

In NetWare, the on-screen coordinates 12,40 are the default coordinates of menus. This point is the middle of a typical screen. You can place menus at any location on-screen; they do not wrap if you do not give the menu enough room. The coordinates 1,1 place the menu in the upper left corner, 1,80 in the upper right corner, 24,1 in the lower left corner, and 24,80 in the lower right corner.

To determine where you want to place your menu on-screen, you need to plan on a screen that has coordinates of 24 rows and 80

Chapter 7: Customizing the User's Environment

columns. You calculate menu positions by specifying the point at which the center of the menu should be placed.

You then need to determine the size of the menu. Figure the number of lines you want above the menu by making a rough sketch of the menu on lined paper. Your menu should be large enough to accommodate the desired text for the menu. The size of the menu is determined by the length of the menu text and the number of options in the menu. You need to determine where the middle of the menu needs to be placed.

You now need to decide the number of blank lines on the monitor you want above the menu. Next, count the number of lines you want in the menu and divide that number by two. This step locates the starting point of the menu at the middle of the screen. Add these two numbers together to determine the placement of the menu on the vertical axis, known as the *vertical placement*, as follows:

> # of lines above menu + (# of menu lines / 2) = row

If you want a menu that has six lines above the menu and six lines in the menu, for example, the vertical placement is 9.

Next, determine the number of columns you want before a menu. Count the number of characters in the longest menu item and divide by two. Add these two numbers together to determine the placement of the menu on the horizontal axis, known as the *horizontal placement*, as follows:

> # of columns before menu + (# of columns in longest menu option / 2) = column

The following is the syntax of a menu in NetWare:

```
%main menu name,row,column,color
option
   %submenu
option
     executable
%submenu,row,column,color
option
     executable
```

Creating Custom Menus

In the preceding syntax, the %main menu name,row,column,color line specifies the name of the menu. It also specifies the placement of the menu on-screen and the color of the menu. The option line specifies the names of the available options that you want to display on the menu. The %submenu line calls a submenu option, where an additional menu is defined. The executable line specifies the commands that can call the menu option.

Menu Requirements

NetWare requires you to have Read and File Scan rights in the directory that holds the menu (MNU) files. In addition, you need Read, Write, Create, Erase, Modify, and File Scan rights in the directory in which you call a menu.

In the optimum condition, MNU files are flagged as Read Only, and Read, Write, Create, Erase, Modify, and File Scan are the user's trustee rights in that directory.

Two sets of files are created when you use the NetWare MENU utility: GO*.BAT and RESTART*.BAT. These pointer files are used to call programs from a menu. The system creates one of each of these files for each user running the menu. These files tell the system where you are when you call a program and the way to get back when you are finished.

These files are *recyclable*—you never have more on your system than you have users using the menus. When a user exits the menu properly by pressing Esc and selecting Yes, or by selecting the logout option, these files are erased.

301

Chapter 7: Customizing the User's Environment

Limiting where a user can call a menu is a good idea; otherwise, you might find these files scattered throughout the network. To limit a user to one directory for calling menus, make sure that the user is aware of the acceptable location (directory) if the user calls a menu from a DOS prompt. Another way to make sure that a user is in the proper directory is to place him there in a login script and call the menu from the login script. This method is discussed in the section on menu-calling procedures.

NetWare enables you to exit from a menu by using the LOGOUT command. The network knows the way to close all open files, including the GO*.BAT and RESTART*.BAT files. When you exit in this manner, however, you are disconnecting yourself from the place where these files are kept. As a result, the menu program that was brought into the workstation's memory gives two error messages. The message Batch File Missing displays twice. The program is searching for the GO*.BAT and RESTART*.BAT files, but now you are logged out of the network.

Because users often are frightened by error messages, NetWare enables you to use the !LOGOUT command from a menu. The exclamation point (!) simply blocks the error messages from the screen.

Menu-Calling Procedures

Now that the menu is created and the rights are established, you need to bring the menu up on-screen. This step enables you to use the menu on your workstation. To call a menu from the DOS prompt, use the MENU command and type the name of the menu file name, as follows:

    MENU *filename*

The MNU extension is optional, because MENU knows to look for a file with an MNU extension. In figure 7.11, for example, the menu SALES is called from the menu subdirectory.

Creating Custom Menus

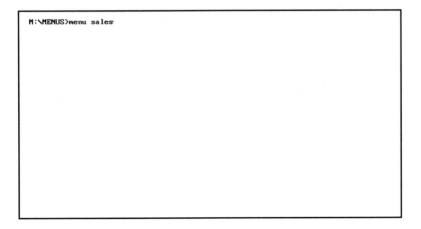

Figure 7.11
Calling a menu from the DOS prompt.

NetWare offers several ways to call a menu from a login script. The best method is to create a batch file that calls the menu. You then should call the batch file from the EXIT statement, as follows:

    EXIT NETMENU

In this example, the file NETMENU.BAT is in a directory mapped earlier in the menu. It contains the following command:

    MENU NETMENU

Another method to call a menu is to use the # call. This method enables you to return to the login script when you exit from the menu. The following is an example of calling up a menu by using the # call:

    #MENU NETMENU

This method does require more workstation memory, however. For more information, see the earlier section on login commands.

303

Chapter 7: Customizing the User's Environment

Techniques for Setting Up Menus

Many methods are available for setting up menu options. In this section, you examine a menu and learn a few hints for creating a clean, smooth-working menu environment. The following example is a menu created for the Sales department. The following file is called SALES.MNU:

```
%Sales Dept Main Menu
Applications
    %Application Menu
Utilities
    %Utilities Menu
Logout
    !LOGOUT
%Application Menu,1,1,3
Data Base
    map insert s3:=sys:apps\db
    map f:=sys:data\sales\db
    f:
    datab
    m:
    map del s3:
    map del f:
Spread Sheet
    map insert s3:=sys:apps\s2
    map f:=sys:data\sales\ss
    f:
    ssheet
    m:
   map del s3:
    map del f:
%Utilities Menu,24,80,5
Send a Message
    Send " @1"Type a message" " @2"Send it to?"
Capture Settings
    Capture q=@1"Type Queue Name" c=@2"# of Copies?" @3"FF or NFF?"
Ncopy a File
    NCOPY @1"Source path/file" @2"Destination"
```

After you create this menu as a text file, type **MENU SALES** at the DOS prompt. The screen that appears is shown in figure 7.12. Notice that NetWare puts the options in alphabetical order. If you

Creating Custom Menus

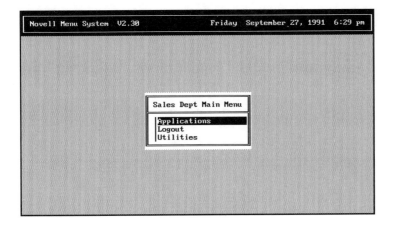

Figure 7.12
The Sales Dept Main Menu screen.

want options listed in a different order, you must place numbers in front of the options, then MENU displays the items in numerical order.

 If you number the menu options, you need to remember the way a computer counts. Numbering the options 1, 2, 3, and so on, works fine as long as you do not use the number 10. When a computer reads the number 10, 10 falls between 1 and 2. Use two-digit numbers, such as 01, 02, 03, and so on, if you need more options. A more conventional method is to use letters instead of numbers.

When you press Enter while the Applications option is highlighted, NetWare calls up the Application menu (see fig. 7.13). In this menu, two options are available—Data Base and Spread Sheet. You now can choose one of these options by highlighting it and pressing Enter. This action executes the commands contained under the option you select.

The idea behind the mappings in this example is to keep the system as lean as possible. Search mappings take up file server memory. By leaving drives mapped, users can get at them from DOS more easily. Keeping the mappings in menus instead of the login script works well.

305

Chapter 7: Customizing the User's Environment

Figure 7.13

The Application menu.

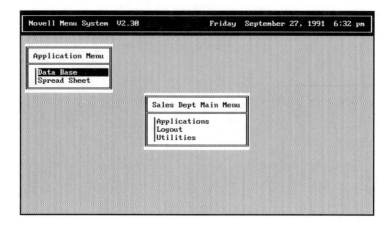

In figure 7.14, the system maps a search drive and a data drive. Then the system changes to the data drive and calls the program. At this point, the application, such as the Spread Sheet option, starts. You then exit the spreadsheet program after you finish working in it. As figure 7.15 shows, when you exit from the application, the system returns to the default directory. This ensures that GO*.BAT and RESTART*.BAT are deleted properly. The network then deletes the search drive and the data drive. The last step takes the user back to the menu.

Press Esc to close the option menu and to return to the Sales Dept Main Menu. The next choice is the Utilities option (see fig. 7.16). Under this option, several commands have been added that need user input. To get the user to answer questions, the menu utility allows input variables designated as @1 through @9.

Creating Custom Menus

```
M:\MENUS>map insert s3:=sys:apps\ss
SEARCH3:  = X:. [CDI286\SYS:  \APPS\SS]
M:\MENUS>map f:=sys:data\sales\ss
Drive  F: = CDI286\SYS:  \DATA\SALES\SS
M:\MENUS>f:
```

Figure 7.14

Choosing the Spread Sheet option.

```
F:\DATA\SALES\SS>m:
M:\MENUS>map del s3:
The search mapping for drive X: was deleted
M:\MENUS>map del f:
The mapping for drive F: has been deleted.
M:\MENUS>
```

Figure 7.15

Exiting the application to display the remaining executables.

Chapter 7: Customizing the User's Environment

Figure 7.16

The Utilities menu.

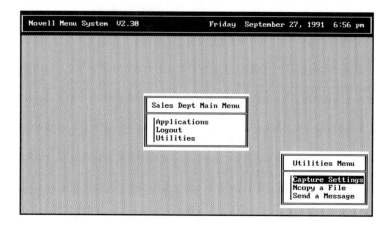

Input Variables

Input variables enable the user to type information into a window from the menu. This information is sent to the DOS prompt for execution. This feature is helpful if users have different needs for calling programs. A good example is printing by using the CAPTURE command. Different users might need to print to different queue names. The following option enables the users to input the appropriate queue name:

    CAPTURE Q=@1"ENTER QUEUENAME"

 You can use up to nine windows for each command, such as @1, @2, ..., @9. Enter the prompt that the user sees on-screen between the quotation marks in the preceding syntax.

The next item that you can choose is the Capture Settings option, which enables you to see the Type Queue Name prompt (see fig. 7.17). This prompt asks you for the name of the printer queue you want to use. When you created the menu, you placed the input question within quotation marks. No space exists between the input variable and the quotation marks. For the prompt to work, make sure that you do not insert spaces between the input question and the quotation marks. Spaces cause the window to fail to appear, and the command will be issued with an error.

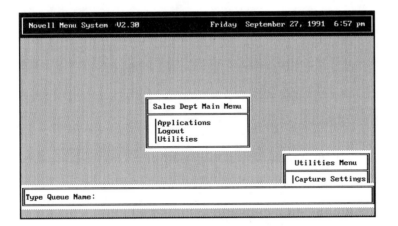

Figure 7.17
The Type Queue Name input box.

As you answer each prompt that appears on-screen, NetWare stores the information until you answer all the questions. Then, NetWare sends the information to the DOS prompt.

In figures 7.18 through 7.21, for example, NetWare prompts you for the printer queue name, number of copies, and whether you want form feed. After you answer the last question, NetWare returns you to the DOS prompt. You now can print by using the CAPTURE options.

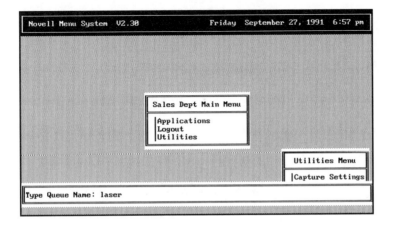

Figure 7.18
Inputting the name of the queue.

Chapter 7: Customizing the User's Environment

Figure 7.19

Inputting the number of copies for the printer.

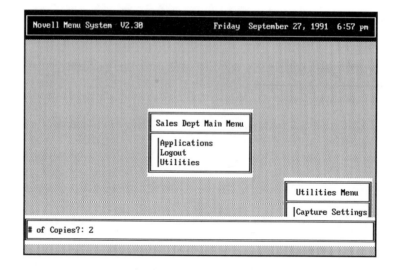

Figure 7.20

Selecting form feed or no form feed.

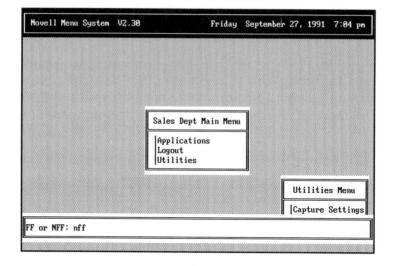

Creating Custom Menus

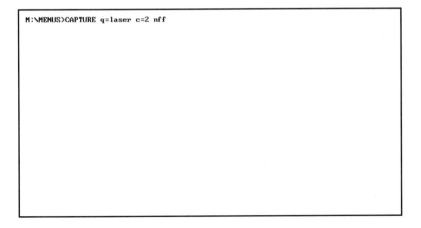

Figure 7.21
The result of the CAPTURE statement.

The user can answer the questions as they appear. The information is stored temporarily until all questions are answered; the input information then is sent to the DOS prompt and executed (see figs. 7.18 through 7.21).

This example shows you the way to create a menu that enables you to set up a CAPTURE statement. This type of statement helps you automate NetWare for yourself as well as all end users on the network. To take full advantage of NetWare's utilities, look for ways to automate every repetitious or time-consuming task. Be creative with menus. The interface truly helps users become comfortable with using network utilities.

NetWare 3.12 Menuing System

NetWare 3.12 includes a new menuing system. It is a scaled-down version of the Saber menu system. The biggest advantage that this new NetWare menu utility has over the menuing system used in earlier versions of NetWare is that it does not remain resident in RAM while it is executing applications. Thus, more RAM is available for the application itself.

Chapter 7: Customizing the User's Environment

Three primary files are used with the new menuing system. These files include the following:

- **NMENU.BAT.** Runs a menu. To start a menu, type **NMEMU.BAT**, then type the name of the menu and press Enter.

- **MENUCNVT.EXE.** Converts menus created in the older menuing system into menus that run under the new menuing system. To convert an older menu, type **MENUCNVT.EXE** followed by the menu file name, then press Enter.

- **MENUMAKE.EXE.** Compiles the menu you create following the conventions required by the new menuing system into a file that can be run. To compile the menu, type **MENUMAKE.EXE** followed by the name of the menu and press Enter.

Creating a Menu

The new menuing system, like the older version, has a title on every menu. It also uses Options (the menu item that the user can choose) that are set to the left margin. Under each option is a command that will execute or a submenu title that opens another menu window.

Unlike the old menuing system, when you create a menu using this new system, you cannot specify where the menu window displays. The modified Saber menuing system uses a series of sideways-cascading menu windows that are controlled by the program itself.

The modified Saber menuing system uses two types of commands. They are called organizational commands and control commands. *Organizational commands* determine what the menu program looks like when it appears on the screen. *Control commands* tell the NMENU.BAT program how to run the menu, processing information and executing commands.

The menuing system includes two organizational commands (MENU and ITEM) and six control commands (EXEC, LOAD,

Creating Custom Menus

SHOW, GETO, GETR, and GETP). Table 7.2 shows these commands, as well as the commands that you can use with them. (These commands are indented under each of the organizational and control commands.)

 Commands shown with braces ({}) are commands that are put into the menu with the braces around them, as shown in the examples included in the table. The BATCH command, for example, is shown as {BATCH}. Type it into the menu *with* the braces around it.

Also note in the table that sometimes a number is shown with a karat (^) in front of it. The karat is entered to cause the menu to display the number that follows it as part of the menu option. The entry **^1 Utilities**, for example, appears as option 1 Utilities on the menu that appears on the screen. This format enables the user to choose this option by choosing the number 1 instead of the letter U.

Table 7.2
New Menuing System Commands

Command	Purpose/Use	Example of its use in a menu
MENU	Starts menu	MENU *menunumber, menuname* MENU 1,Utilities
ITEM	Defines options	ITEM *itemname option option* ITEM ^2NetWare Utilities
BATCH	Remove menu from memory while running	MENU 1 Utilities {BATCH} memory

continues

Chapter 7: Customizing the User's Environment

Table 7.2, Continued
New Menuing System Commands

Command	Purpose/Use	Example of its use in a menu
CHDIR	Return to default menu. (Automatic when BATCH is used. Can use without BATCH)	MENU 1 Utilities {BATCH} MENU 1 Utilities {CHDIR}
PAUSE	Like DOS Pause, shows a Press any key message	MENU 1 Utilities {PAUSE}
SHOW	Shows DOS command if one is being run	MENU 1 Utilities {Pause}
EXEC	Runs executable or DOS commands	EXEC *executable* or *command* EXEC WP.EXE or EXEC LOGOUT
LOAD	Loads a separate submenu, by name	LOAD *menu_name* LOAD *Batch_files*
SHOW	Loads a separate submenu, by number	LOAD *menu_number* LOAD 2
GET*x*	Prompts for user input, then F10	GETx *command_format/parameters*
GETO	Input from user is optional	GETO Enter path: { }40,,P{}
GETR	Input from user is required	GETR Type name: { }25,,{}
GETP	Input from user is stored	GETP Enter source: {}40,,{} GETP Enter target: {}40,,{}

Table 7.2 shows the available options for the menu utility. One of the options it shows is the GET*x* option. You can use three parameters in place of the *x* in this menu entry. In addition, you must follow this specific command format:

```
GETx instruction{prepend}length,prefill,SECURE{append}
```

Replace each of the above format options according to these explanations:

instruction	Enter the message you want the user to see.
{prepend}	Enter information you want to be attached before the user types in their information. You *must* use the braces even if you have no information typed in between them.
length	Specify the maximum number of characters the user can enter in response to the instruction.
prefill	Enter any default response you want to appear.
SECURE	Use this option to make the user's response to appear as only asterisks. This feature is helpful for protecting passwords and other security-related input.
append	Enter information you want to be attached to the end of the response typed by the user.

Compiling a Menu

After you create a menu, you must save it as a file with a dot extension name of **SRC**. You also must compile the menu before it can be used. Compiling a menu is easy. Simply type the command for compiling a menu (**MENUMAKE**), followed by the path and name of the menu file. To compile a menu called MAINMENU.SRC saved to the MISC directory on drive C, for example, type the following at the system prompt, then press Enter:

```
MENUMAKE C:\MISC\MAINMENU.SRC
```

After you compile the menu, it is saved as a file with a dot extension of DAT. In the above example, the compiled menu name is *not* MAINMENU.DAT—the DAT version is run to start the menu.

To start the MAINMENU, type **NMAKE C:\MISC\MAINMENU**.

For more information on this new menuing system, refer to the ElectroText documentation that comes with NetWare 3.12.

Logging In to the Network

This section teaches you to log in to the network from a DOS workstation. In this section, you get hands-on practice with the following tasks:

- Running WSGEN to generate IPX
- Logging in through IPX and NETX
- Logging in through ODI drivers

In the following section, you learn to use the workstation generation program (WSGEN) to generate the required IPX driver.

Running WSGEN To Generate IPX

WSGEN is not available in NetWare 3.12.

The WSGEN utility configures a file that DOS workstations must use to gain access to the network. When you use WSGEN, you generate a file called IPX.COM. IPX stands for *Internetwork Packet Exchange*.

The WSGEN program and the NetWare 2.2 install program are actually menu-driven linkers. These

Logging In to the Network

programs enable you to select the program modules and link them into the customized executable files needed to log in to the network. In the case of WSGEN, you are linking the network board drivers with a file named IPX.OBJ to form IPX.COM.

You can run the WSGEN program from a floppy drive or hard disk. If you run the program from a floppy drive, you first must create a copy of the original disk. The original Novell disk is write-protected, and WSGEN must create a new IPX.COM file for you. Novell supplies a number of network card drivers with the WSGEN program. If the driver you need is not included with the Novell disks, you also need a driver disk from the hardware manufacturer. Network card drivers generally are found on a disk shipped with the interface card and must be placed on a floppy disk with the electronic label LAN_DRV_*xxx*, in which *xxx* is a three-digit number designated by the manufacturer.

The syntax for the DOS LABEL command is LABEL A:LAN_DRV_*xxx*. Refer to your DOS reference manual for more information.

When WSGEN runs, it searches all floppy drives for disks with these labels and includes the appropriate drivers in the lists presented to you for selection.

System administrators can set up a directory on their local hard drive or on the network to provide a fast method for creating network shells when needed. To set up the required directories, you need a main directory. The examples in this section assume you name this directory SHELLS.

After you use the DOS MD command to create a SHELLS directory, create a subdirectory named WSGEN. Then copy the contents of the Novell WSGEN disk into the \SHELLS\WSGEN directory. If any optional LAN drivers are required, you must copy them into directories that have the same name as the floppy

317

Chapter 7: Customizing the User's Environment

disk that contains the drivers. To allow for a floppy name with more than eight characters, place a period (.) before the last three characters or numbers, as in the following example:

```
\SHELLS\WSGEN\
         |
         |-LAN_DRV_.001
         |
         |-LAN_DRV_.002
```

Novell's WSGEN program looks for this label to locate the driver files.

Next, copy the WSGEN.EXE file into the SHELLS directory. You then can execute the WSGEN program from this directory by typing **WSGEN** and pressing Enter. NetWare displays a screen like the one shown in figure 7.22.

Figure 7.22
The WSGEN opening screen.

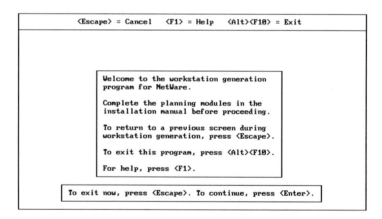

When this screen appears, press Enter to continue.

If WSGEN appears to lock up while searching the floppy drives, reboot the computer and check your directory structures. This problem is common when you try to run the WSGEN program from the wrong directory.

Logging In to the Network

The next screen that appears is the driver-selection screen (see fig. 7.23). At this screen, select the appropriate network board driver required by your network interface card. Simply use the arrow keys to scroll up or down until you find the correct driver.

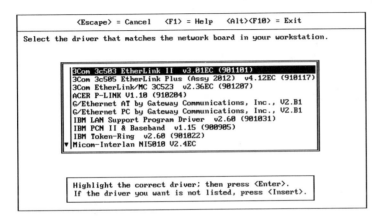

Figure 7.23
The driver-selection screen.

If the driver you need does not appear in the selection window, the driver might not be included with NetWare or the driver disk might not be installed correctly. If you install a LAN_DRV_.*xxx* directory, make sure that the underscores (_) and the period (.) are correct. If you create a LAN_DRV_.*xxx* directory, make sure that you do not confuse the underscore character (_) with the dash character (–).

Another way to handle the addition of new drivers is to press Ins while the driver selection screen is visible. NetWare then prompts you to insert the disk that contains the additional drivers. The new drivers then are added to the list of available drivers.

When you locate the desired driver, press Enter. The screen shown in figure 7.24 appears.

You need to know a few things about the particular workstation on which you are working. This screen provides you with the hardware options supplied by the interface manufacturer. These options include interrupts, base memory address, I/O address, and DMA channels. The default option, 0, is usually a good choice for a standard workstation configuration. If your workstation has

Chapter 7: Customizing the User's Environment

a modem, terminal emulator, or other special hardware, you need to have all the equipment settings available. When selecting a configuration option, you need to be aware of all the additional interface card settings in the computer.

Figure 7.24
The hardware configuration screen.

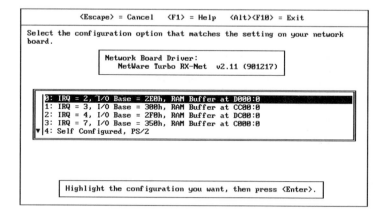

 Note You should make a list of all card settings. This list can help you locate unused hardware settings, which your network interface can use.

If none of the available choices appears to provide all the settings, select option 0. From here, you should be able to install a customized configuration with the JUMPERS utility, which is discussed in *NetWare Training Guide: Networking Technologies* and in *Inside Novell NetWare*, both from New Riders Publishing.

Use table 7.3 to determine the standard PC hardware settings. The table includes I/O addresses, memory addresses, interrupts, and DMA channels used by common equipment.

Table 7.3
Common Hardware Configurations

Device	INT	I/O Decode (h)	MEM Decode	DMA
Com1	4	3F8-3FF	-	-
Com2	3	2F8-2FF	-	-

Device	INT	I/O Decode (h)	MEM Decode	DMA
LPT1	7	378-37F	-	-
LPT2 (cannot be used with XT controller)	5	278-27F	-	-
If LPT3 exists, LPT1	7	3BC-3BE	-	-
LPT2	5	378-37A	-	-
LPT3	-	278-27A	-	-
XT controller	5	320-32F	C800:0000-3FFF	3
AT controller	14	1F0-1F8 170-177	- -	- -
Floppy controller	6	1F0-1F8 3F0-3F7	-	2
Tape controller	5	280-28F	-	3
Novell disk coprocessor	11.10, 12, or 13	#1 340-347 #2 348-34F	-	-
Novell SCSI adapter	2, 3, or 5	340-343 (enhanced only)	D000:0000-7FFF	1, 3, or none
EGA	2	3C0-3CF	A000:0000-1FFFE or B000:0000-7FFF or B800:0000-7FFF	0
Monochrome adapter	-	3B0-3BF	B000:0000-7FFF	0

continues

Chapter 7: Customizing the User's Environment

Table 7.3, Continued
Common Hardware Configurations

Device	INT	I/O Decode (h)	MEM Decode	DMA
Color graphics adapter	-	3D0-3DF	B800:0000-7FFF	0
Hercules monochrome (286A server)	-	3B4-3BF	B000:0000-7FFF B800:0000-7FFF	- -

After you select a configuration option, press Enter to begin the linking process. After you select the hardware option, NetWare displays your choice and prompts you for confirmation. Select Yes to confirm your selection or No to abort (see fig. 7.25).

Figure 7.25

Confirming your selection.

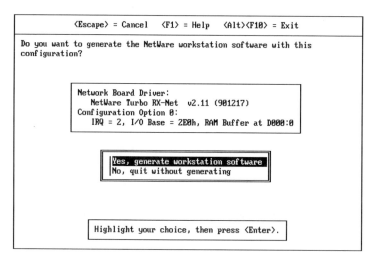

If the link process runs without error, NetWare displays a screen that informs you when workstation software generation is complete. At this time, you can copy the IPX.COM file from the \SHELLS\WSGEN directory to your workstation boot disk along with the appropriate shell: NETX.COM, XMSNETX.EXE, or EMSNETX.EXE, discussed in a following section.

Logging In through DOS

After you successfully generate your workstation files and copy them to your boot disk, you are ready to attach to the NetWare file server.

You can issue the following commands manually or place them in a batch file in the order listed (you can replace NETX with the optional XMSNETX or EMSNETX):

```
IPX
NETX
F:
LOGIN fileserver name/username
```

The drive letter F might not be available on some workstations; the number of drive letters available depends on the number of locally attached hard drives or on the CONFIG.SYS file's LASTDRIVE setting. The login drive is the first available unused drive letter.

When you issue the IPX and NETX commands, NetWare displays the information shown in figure 7.26.

```
[DR DOS] C:\SH386>ipx
Novell IPX/SPX v3.04 (910703)
(C) Copyright 1985, 1991 Novell Inc.  All Rights Reserved.

LAN Option: NetWare Turbo RX-Net   v2.11 (901217)
Hardware Configuration: IO: 350; MEM: D800; IRQ: 5 (Jumpers Config)

[DR DOS] C:\SH386>netx

NetWare V3.22 - Workstation Shell (910731)
(C) Copyright 1991 Novell, Inc.  All Rights Reserved.

Running on DOS V3.31

Using configuration file SHELL.CFG
SHOW DOTS ON

Attached to server CDI
09-30-91    5:06:13 pm

[DR DOS] C:\SH386>
```

Figure 7.26

A sample screen that appears after you successfully attach to the file server.

Chapter 7: Customizing the User's Environment

First, examine the NetWare LOGIN command. The LOGIN command is located in the SYS:\LOGIN directory, and you can issue the command from that directory to access the file server's resources.

After your workstation loads the NetWare shell, it transparently attaches to the nearest file server. After moving to the LOGIN drive (which usually is drive F), issue the LOGIN command. At the F:\LOGIN\> prompt, for example, enter the following:

LOGIN

NetWare prompts for your login name and password. After you successfully enter the requested information, you have access to the other services for which you have privileges. If your system utilizes more than one file server, you can prefix your login name with the file server's name. You can, for example, enter the following at the F:\LOGIN\> prompt:

LOGIN SALES\TOM

After the preceding information is entered, the program prompts Tom to enter his password. After Tom enters his password, NetWare processes the request for access to the SALES file server.

If your login script attaches you to more than one file server, LOGIN determines whether all passwords are valid. If a password has expired, you are prompted to change it. If you change your password, LOGIN asks if you want to synchronize all passwords on all servers. If you answer Yes, the password becomes the same on all attached servers.

The IPX, NETX, XMSNETX, and EMSNETX programs each have optional command-line switches that can simplify the network administrator's job.

IPX

IPX.COM provides four options, as shown in figure 7.27:

- **-I or /I.** Displays an informational screen. This option is handy for determining the version and hardware setting of the IPX you are using (see fig. 7.28).

- **-D or /D.** Displays all available options.

- **-O or /O***x*. Use this option to set IPX to use a hardware setting displayed with the D option.

- **-C or /C.** Enables advanced users to use a special configuration file rather than the Novell default SHELL.CFG or NET.CFG.

- **-? or /?.** Displays all available options (see fig. 7.28).

```
C:\SH386>ipx ?
Novell IPX/SPX v3.04 (910703)
(C) Copyright 1985, 1991 Novell Inc.  All Rights Reserved.

LAN Option: NetWare Turbo RX-Net  v2.11 (901217)
Hardware Configuration: IO: 350; MEM: D800; IRQ: 5 (Jumpers Config)


Usage: IPX [options]
valid options:
        -I or /I                  Display version information
        -D or /D                  Display hardware options
        -O or /O<num>             Load using hardware option <num>
        -C or /C=[path]<filename> Use an alternate configuration file

        -? or /?                  Display this help screen

C:\SH386>
```

Figure 7.27
The IPX options.

Figure 7.28

Displaying version information.

```
C:\SH386>ipx i
Novell IPX/SPX v3.04 (910703)
(C) Copyright 1985, 1991 Novell Inc.  All Rights Reserved.

LAN Option: NetWare Turbo RX-Net  v2.11 (901217)
Hardware Configuration: IO: 350; MEM: D800; IRQ: 5 (Jumpers Config)

C:\SH386>
```

The /D and /Ox command-line switches are handy when you need to test a shell or when a shell is included in the batch file. These switches enable you to use any standard configuration without relinking the IPX program.

Permanently configuring the IPX program for normal use is still a good idea. Doing so saves confusion if the user attempts to load IPX without the batch file.

NETX, XMSNETX, and EMSNETX

NETX, XMSNETX, and EMSNETX provide the following three options:

- **-I or /I.** Displays an informational screen (see fig. 7.29).
- **-U or /U.** Uninstalls or removes the shell from memory.
- **-PS or /PS (Preferred Server).** Specifies the server from which you get the LOGIN command.

```
C:\SH386>netx i

NetWare V3.22 - Workstation Shell (910731)
(C) Copyright 1991 Novell, Inc.  All Rights Reserved.

C:\SH386>
```

Figure 7.29

Displaying version information.

NetBIOS

NetBIOS provides the following two options:

- **-I or /I.** Displays an informational screen.
- **-U or /U.** Uninstalls or removes NetBIOS from memory.

When using the /U command-line switch, make sure that the programs are removed in the opposite order from which they were installed. You might receive unpredictable results if you unload any memory-resident program that might have another program loaded in after it.

Logging In through ODI Drivers

Implementing ODI drivers requires no generation or linking process. You can control the ODI files' custom configuration by creating a NET.CFG file. Loading the ODI files is a simple process when you understand what each file supplies.

Chapter 7: Customizing the User's Environment

The ODI drivers are configured in layers that correspond somewhat to the lower layers of the OSI reference model. A comparison of the ODI drivers to the OSI reference model is shown in figure 7.30.

Figure 7.30

Relationship of the ODI drivers to the OSI reference model.

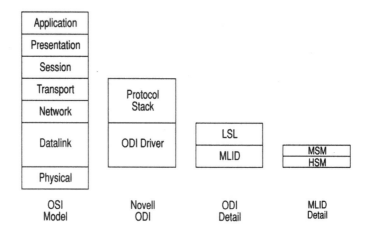

The Link Support Layer (LSL) is the first program loaded (see fig. 7.31). This program acts as a switchboard between the network interface driver and the protocol stack. LSL also handles traffic between multiple stacks when they are present.

Figure 7.31

The Link Support Layer (LSL) driver.

```
[DR DOS] C:\NET>lsl
NetWare Link Support Layer  v1.10 (910625)
(C) Copyright 1991 Novell, Inc.  All Rights Reserved.

[DR DOS] C:\NET>
```

Logging In to the Network

Study Note: A *protocol stack* is the process that controls the type of communication taking place. If your PC workstation requires access to both the NetWare file server and your SUN UNIX server, for example, you need to install a Novell IPX and TCP/IP protocol stack.

After the LSL.COM program is loaded, the network interface driver, or MLID (Multiple Link Interface Driver), is loaded (see fig. 7.32). This program, provided by the manufacturer, supplies the hardware support for the individual interface cards. ODI drivers are available for the vast majority of network interface cards intended for use with NetWare.

```
[DR DOS] C:\NET>ne2000
Novell NE2000 Ethernet MLID  v1.34 (910603)
(C) Copyright 1991 Novell, Inc.  All Rights Reserved.

Int 5, Port 320, Node Address 1B34C5BE
Max Frame 1514 bytes, Line Speed 10 Mbps
Board 1, Frame ETHERNET_802.3

[DR DOS] C:\NET>
```

Figure 7.32
The Multiple Link Interface Driver (MLID).

After the MLID is loaded, the protocol stack and shell are loaded to complete the attachment to a NetWare file server. A typical ODI driver loading sequence uses the following files in this order:

- LSL
- NE2000
- IPXODI
- NETX or VLM

Here, ODI drivers have the advantage over the standard IPX drivers. At this point, you might have loaded a TCP protocol stack if your company uses UNIX hosts. With ODI drivers, however, you can load the IPX and the TCP stacks to provide both protocols at the same time.

The preceding list of commands loads the LSL file and then the MLID required for a Novell NE2000 Ethernet card. Next, the standard IPX protocol stack is loaded (see fig. 7.33). Finally, a shell or requester must be loaded. Figure 7.34 illustrates the loading of a normal shell, NETX.

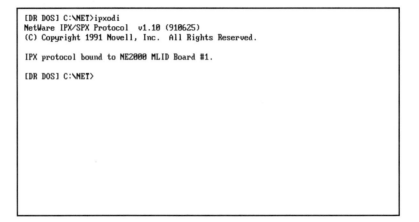

Figure 7.33

The IPX protocol stack.

If any nonstandard hardware settings are required, the NE2000 module reads them from the NET.CFG file. A simple example of a NET.CFG file follows:

```
Link Driver NE2000
    INT 5
    PORT 300
```

```
[DR DOS] C:\NET>netx

NetWare V3.22 - Workstation Shell (910731)
(C) Copyright 1991 Novell, Inc.  All Rights Reserved.

Running on DOS V3.31

Attached to server CDI
11-21-91    12:39:24 pm

[DR DOS] C:\NET>
```

Figure 7.34
The NETX shell.

The NET.CFG file enables many configuration options for each layer of the ODI drivers. At this time, you only need to be concerned with changing the network interface hardware settings. Further instructions usually are provided with hardware that might need special settings.

Any statements used in a SHELL.CFG file simply can be added to the front of NET.CFG in a left-justified manner.

You must follow a few simple rules when creating the NET.CFG file. The heading statement must be left-justified, and the configuration entries must be tabbed at least one space. If any commands were used previously in a SHELL.CFG file, add them to the beginning of the NET.CFG file.

Each ODI module provides command-line switches for unloading and for memory-saving loads.

Use /U to unload LSL, MLID, IPXODI, and NETX or (VLM) in reverse order of the way in which they originally were loaded. Figure 7.35 shows the screen display as the NETX shell program is being unloaded.

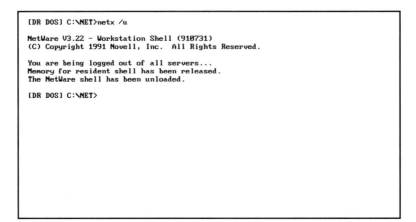

Figure 7.35
Successfully unloading NETX.

The IPXODI module provides two extra switches that enable memory savings if full functionality is not needed. Use /D to load IPX/SPX protocols only without any diagnostic capability; this switch provides a memory savings of 4K. Use /A to load the IPX protocol only; this switch provides a memory savings of 8K. Use /? to display information about any ODI module.

Novell has approved all ODI modules to operate in high memory.

Figure 7.36 shows the display during an unload in which the program module is being unloaded in the wrong order; this type of error results in a *fatal unload*.

ODI drivers might appear overly complicated when compared with IPX and NETX. When you understand the flow of the modules, however, you should find that changing a driver's configuration by editing a text file is remarkably convenient and much simpler than relinking IPX.COM with WSGEN.

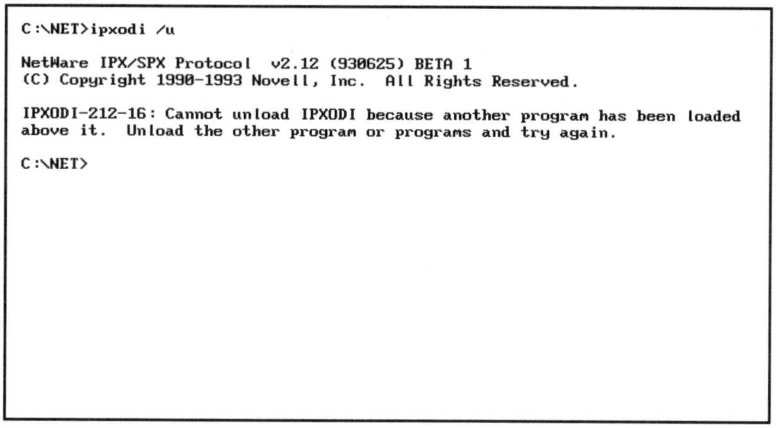

```
C:\NET>ipxodi /u

NetWare IPX/SPX Protocol  v2.12 (930625) BETA 1
(C) Copyright 1990-1993 Novell, Inc.  All Rights Reserved.

IPXODI-212-16: Cannot unload IPXODI because another program has been loaded
above it.  Unload the other program or programs and try again.

C:\NET>
```

Figure 7.36
An unsuccessful unload of IPXODI.

Using the NetWare VLMs

Newer versions of Novell's NetWare Shell (called the *DOS Requester*) use files called *Virtual Loadable Modules* (*VLMs*) to provide advanced functionality and support in a modular fashion.

VLMs are a series of files that are loaded in place of the NETX file. Several VLMs are loaded when the VLM command is entered in the following example:

```
LSL
NE2000
IPXODI
VLM
```

When VLM is run, it starts a program called VLM.EXE. This program is a manager for the other files (all with dot extensions of VLM) that load into memory and control the workstation environment and its ability to access network resources.

Running the DOS Requester in place of the old NETX command provides many advantages:

Chapter 7: Customizing the User's Environment

- It takes advantage of memory swapping and DOS redirection capabilities to handle requests

- It includes Packet Burst and LIP (described later)

- It provides backward compatibility with applications that still require the functions of the NETX shell

- It supports Microsoft Windows drivers that are included with the client software but do not work with the NETX shell

When the DOS Requester loads, a series of items appears on your workstation's screen. That screen should look similar to the one shown in figure 7.37.

Figure 7.37
Display of DOS Requester loading.

```
(C) Copyright 1990-1993 Novell, Inc.  All Rights Reserved.

Configuration File "C:\NWCLIENT\NET.CFG" used.

Max Boards 4, Max Stacks 4

Novell NE2000 Ethernet MLID   v1.53 (930730)
(C) Copyright 1991 - 1993 Novell, Inc.  All Rights Reserved.

Int 5, Port 340, Mem D0000, Node Address 1B1ED82D L
Max Frame 1514 bytes, Line Speed 10 Mbps
Board 1, Frame ETHERNET_802.2, LSB Mode

NetWare IPX/SPX Protocol   v2.12 (931007)
(C) Copyright 1990-1993 Novell, Inc.  All Rights Reserved.

IPX SOCKETS 45
Bound to logical board 1 (NE2000) : Protocol ID E0
VLM.EXE        - NetWare virtual loadable module manager   v1.10 (931209)
(C) Copyright 1993 Novell, Inc.  All Rights Reserved.
Patent pending.

The VLM.EXE file is pre-initializing the VLMs...............
The VLM.EXE file is using extended memory (XMS).
```

Three of the VLMs are of particular importance in a mixed networking NetWare environment. If you are running versions NetWare 2.*x*, NetWare 3.*x*, or NetWare 4.*x* in a network environment, these three VLMs enable you to access all three types of NetWare networks without conflict. These VLMs include the following:

Logging In to the Network

- **NDS.VLM.** Enables you to access NetWare 4 NetWare Directory Services.
- **BIND.VLM.** Enables you to access NetWare bindery service (NetWare 2*x* and 3*x* servers provide bindery services).
- **LITE.VLM.** Enables you to access services provided by NetWare Lite servers.

VLMs fall into three categories, depending on the service they perform:

- **DOS redirection.** Responsible for requesting file and print services from a server.
- **Service protocols.** Handle requests for several specific services including establishing connection with servers, sending broadcast messages across the network, servicing file reads and writes, and redirecting printing requests.
- **Transport protocols.** Responsible for two very important functions: maintaining connections to servers and providing various services related to the transport of network packets.

If you upgrade your client (workstation) to run the new DOS Requester, be sure to remove any calls to the NETX.EXE file. This file conflicts with the REDIR.VLM. Both the NETX.EXE file and the REDIR.VLM work with DOS to handle redirection tasks. Both must not be loaded.

To prevent any conflicts, delete the NETX.EXE line from your workstation's NET.CFG file and replace it with the VLM.EXE command.

You should consider some other reasons to upgrade to the DOS Requester in addition to those already mentioned.

- The NetWare 3.*x* shell only supports eight connections to the network, but the DOS Requester supports from 2 to 50 connections.

Chapter 7: Customizing the User's Environment

- The DOS Requester supports DOS 3.1 and above; the NetWare 3.*x* shell supports DOS 2.*x* and above. You do not need to continue to support DOS 2.*x* if you are not using it on your network.

- The DOS Requester supports nine LPT ports; the shell supports only three LPT ports.

- The DOS Requester helps to overcome some of the memory limitations of the NetWare 3.*x* shell. The shell is subject to a memory limitation of 64K; the DOS Requester requires memory for background processing and can have a large portion of itself loaded into extended or expanded memory as well as conventional memory.

If you upgrade to the DOS Requester, your configuration files are updated by the client installation as follows:

- **CONFIG.SYS.** The following line is added:

  ```
  LASTDRIVE=Z
  ```

- **AUTOEXEC.BAT.** A call to another file that is created during the installation of the client:

  ```
  @CALL C:\NWCLIENT\STARTNET
  ```

- **STARTNET.BAT.** This file is added and includes the following lines:

  ```
  @ECHO OFF
  C:
  CD\ NWCLIENT
  SET NWLANGUAGE=ENGLISH
  LSL
  NE2000
  IPXODI
  VLM
  ```

- **NET.CFG.** A new heading and a line are added to this file if the heading did not exist before. It is added after the Link Driver commands.

  ```
  NetWare DOS Requester
  FIRST NETWORK DRIVE = F
  ```

The NET.CFG file can have other modifications as well. Because the default frame type for the client is now Ethernet_802.3, the Link Driver section of your NET.CFG file needs to have the following line added to it:

```
FRAME Ethernet_802.3
```

If your NET.CFG file currently has a line that says `FRAME Ethernet_802.2`, change this line to 802.3. Because a new feature called Packet Burst is available with NetWare 3.12, if you are running NetWare 3.12, the following line can be added to your NET.CFG file under the (left-justified) heading of `NETWARE DOS REQUESTER`:

```
PB BUFFERS = number
```

In this syntax, `number` represents either Packet Burst off, if set to 0, or specifies the number of buffers set aside for Packet Burst, with 1 through 10 being available.

If you are running Windows as well as the DOS Requester, add the following line to your NET.CFG file as well:

```
SHOW DOTS = ON
```

This entry enables you to see dots appear across the screen as the VLM modules load into your workstation's memory.

NetWare 3.12 Environment Enhancements

As mentioned earlier, Packet Burst has been added as an enhancement to the NetWare 3.12 environment. One additional enhancement has been added as well, LIP (*Large Internet Packet*). These features are discussed in the following section.

Packet Burst

Packet Burst is a communication protocol that enables clients and servers to communicate more efficiently. It speeds up the transfer of multiple *NetWare Core Protocol (NCP)* packets across the network connection. This protocol is built into the NetWare 3.12 operating system code as well as the client-connection software.

Conceptually, Packet Burst is quite simple. Whenever you need a file or request a service on the network, a packet is sent across the network connection. This packet then is accepted by the server and an acknowledgment of its receipt is sent back across the network connection. Each packet sent receives an acknowledgment. Although this procedure helps ensure that packets are received and processed, it increases the traffic across the network connection.

Packet Burst enables the responding server to hold its acknowledgment of a packet until it receives several packets. It then sends a "burst" across the network connection that contains acknowledgment of all packets it received. Instead of a one-to-one relationship of request to acknowledgment, the server now can operate under a one-to-many relationship. This process substantially reduces network traffic.

For Packet Burst to function, it must be enabled at the server and the client.

Packet Burst increases the speed of packets distributed on the network. It also supports high transmission speeds such as those provided by T1 (fast links). In addition, Packet Burst allows a packet to travel over many routes if the network is using X.25. These packets also can make several hops over routers and bridges. A *router* is a workstation or file server running software that allows information exchange between different network cabling systems, and sends it the most efficient possible route. A *bridge* is also a router, but it does not have the ability to determine the most efficient route to send the packet.

Packet Burst also is included with NetWare 3.11, but it is loaded as an NLM (PBURST.NLM) at the 3.11 server and as a COM file

(BNETX.COM) at the workstation. In NetWare 3.12, Packet Burst is enabled at the server and workstation by default.

Large Internet Packet (LIP)

NetWare 3.12 also supports LIP. A router has limitations on the size of a packet it can handle. In NetWare 3.11, whenever a router exists between the server and the client, the maximum packet size that can be sent is 512 bytes, including 64 bytes of packet header information. This limitation can have a substantial effect on the performance of your network.

To get around that limitation, LIP was added to NetWare 3.12 at the server and in the client-connection software. LIP allows the server and the client to negotiate the size of the packet when it has to be sent through a router. If the router is capable of handling it (some are not; LIP is not effective for those routers), a packet size as large as 4202 bytes can be sent through the router.

In NetWare 3.12, LIP is part of the server and client code. In NetWare 3.11, LIP is supported through the BNETX shell at the client.

Using the ATTACH Command

The ATTACH command enables users to attach to additional file servers while they are logged in to the default server. ATTACH accepts two command-line parameters: *fileserver* and *loginname*. At the F:\> prompt, for example, type the following:

    ATTACH ACCOUNTING\TOM

If no parameters are specified, the user is prompted for each one. ATTACH does not provide drive mapping, because the system login script is not executed. To map network drives, simply use the MAP command after a successful server attachment.

Using the LOGOUT Command

Use the LOGOUT command to log out of all file servers. LOGOUT terminates your access privileges and removes all drive mapping that was set up while you were logged in.

You can log out of a specific file server by typing the name of the file server after the LOGOUT command. At the prompt, enter the following, for example:

LOGOUT SALES

This command terminates the access privileges and removes drive mapping to the SALES file server, but maintains all other file-server connections.

 Logging out of all file servers before shutting down for the day is important. If you do not log out of a workstation, some files might not be backed up properly, because most tape drives cannot back up open data files.

Review Questions

1. Which of the following statements is false?

    You can find out about an application's compatibility with NetWare by contacting:

    a. NetWire, Novell's electronic bulletin board

    b. NetWare Buyers Guide

    c. Your Local Novell office

    d. The software vendor

2. What needs to be done to enable multi-user access to an application?

   a. Flag executable file SRO, grant rights to users, map drives to application files

   b. Flag data files RO, grant rights to groups, map drives to data files

   c. Flag executable files RO, flag data files N

   d. Grant rights to users and groups

3. Which of the following statements is false?

   a. Application files need to be in a directory that is separate from data files.

   b. Multi-user applications require that the application files be flagged as Shareable.

   c. The Fake Root feature of the MAP command works to fool unruly applications that require the program to execute from a root directory.

   d. All network applications run on NetWare networks.

4. Which login script is used after the system login script?

   a. The user's login script

   b. The default login script if the user's login script does not exist

   c. The default login script

   d. The system login script is loaded last

Chapter 7: Customizing the User's Environment

5. What is an identifier variable?

    a. A variable used in creating menus that enables the user to answer questions.

    b. A variable that returns known information about NLMs.

    c. A variable that returns known information about network objects such as time of day and login name.

    d. A variable used in NET.CFG files.

6. Which of the following statements about login scripts is true?

    a. 80 characters per line is recommended.

    b. Identifier variables always are preceded with a %.

    c. Blank lines and remark statements are not a good idea.

    d. Putting all commands in uppercase cuts down on debugging.

7. If the following statement is in the system login script, which directory must exist for a user whose workstation booted with MS-DOS 5.0?

    MAP S2:=SYS:PUBLIC\%MACHINE\%OS\%OS_VERSION

    a. SYS:PUBLIC\IBMPC\MSDOS\V5.00

    b. SYS:PUBLIC\IBM_PC\MSDOS\V5.0

    c. SYS:PUBLIC\IBM_PC\MSDOS\V5.00

    d. SYS:PUBLIC\IBM_PC\MS_DOS\V5.00

8. Which of the following statements is false?

    a. The INCLUDE command enables you to display a text file.

    b. The DRIVE command is the same as typing in a drive letter and a colon at the DOS prompt.

c. If you put an EXIT command into the system login script, the user login script will not be executed.

d. Use the command #COMMAND /C CLS to clear the screen for the user from the login script.

9. What would the following login script lines accomplish?

```
IF "%2" = "EXIT" THEN BEGIN
   #COMMAND /C CLS
        EXIT
END
```

a. If the user issues the command **ATTACH EXIT**, the screen clears and he exits the login script.

b. If the user BMYERS issues the command **LOGIN BMYERS EXIT**, the screen clears, all other script commands are skipped, and the user proceeds directly to his user login script.

c. If the user issues the command **LOGIN %2 EXIT**, his screen clears and a batch file called EXIT.BAT starts.

d. If the user BMYERS issues the command **LOGIN BMYERS EXIT**, his screen clears and he quits the login script.

10. Which statement about menus is false?

a. All items to be chosen from one menu must be left-aligned.

b. All executable statements must be on their own line.

c. A space is necessary between the % and the menu name.

d. Submenu names must match identically where they are defined and then called for use.

Chapter 7: Customizing the User's Environment

11. The program used to change the colors for menus is called:
    a. COLORPAL
    b. PALETTE
    c. COLORMNU
    d. COLORS

12. The default position for a menu is:
    a. 12,40
    b. 24,80
    c. 1,24
    d. 40,12

13. Which of the following is not a valid way to call the menu CDI.MNU from a login script?
    a. `#MENU CDI.MNU`
    b. `MENU CDI`
    c. `EXIT "MENU CDI"`
    d. `EXIT "CALLMENU"`, where `CALLMENU` is a batch file that contains the command MENU CDI

14. Which of the following are valid switches for IPX.COM?
    a. /X, /D, /?, /C
    b. -I, -D, -?, -U
    c. /I, /D, /O, /C
    d. -I, -D, -O, -U

15. Which of the following is the correct order to load the following files to log in to the network?
    a. IPX, NETX, F:, LOGIN
    b. NETX, IPX, F:, LOGIN

Review Questions

    c. IPX, F:, NETX, LOGIN

    d. NETX, F:, IPX, LOGIN

16. Which of the following is the correct order to load the following files to log in to the network?

    a. LSL, IPXODI, NE2000, NETX, F:, LOGIN

    b. NE2000, LSL, IPXODI, NETX, F:, LOGIN

    c. LSL, NE2000, IPXODI, NETX, F:, LOGIN

    d. NE2000, IPXODI, LSL, NETX, F:, LOGIN

17. Which of the following is *not* one of the primary files used with the NetWare 3.12 primary files?

    a. NMENU.BAT

    b. CREATMNU.EXE

    c. MENUCNVT.EXE

    d. MENUMAKE.EXE

18. The two types of commands used by the Saber menuing system are:

    a. Organizational and Control

    b. Edit and Create

    c. Control and Create

    d. Organizational and Edit

19. Which character must be placed in front of the Saber menu option in order to make it possible for the user to choose a number to select a menu option?

    a. @

    b. #

    c. *

    d. ^

345

Chapter 7: Customizing the User's Environment

20. The Saber menu command {BATCH} has what effect when used?

    a. Executes a separate batch file

    b. Lists other files in a BATCH directory

    c. Automatically executes the PAUSE command

    d. Removes the menu from memory while running

21. Which of the following Saber menu commands runs a DOS command?

    a. BATCH

    b. CHDIR

    c. EXEC

    d. SHOW

22. Which of the following Saber menu commands executes a separate submenu?

    a. SHOW

    b. GET*x*

    c. CHDIR

    d. EXEC

23. Which dot extension must you use on your Saber menu file before you can compile it?

    a. .DAT

    b. .EXE

    c. .SRC

    d. .MNU

24. Which file replaces the NETX file in the NetWare 3.12 client?

    a. LSL.COM

    b. VLM.EXE

Review Questions

    c. IPXODI.COM

    d. EMSNETX.EXE

25. The NetWare DOS Requester includes Packet Burst and _____.

    a. Large Internet Packet
    b. NETX Shell
    c. drivers that work with MS Windows and NETX
    d. added memory

26. Which of the following VLMs, when loaded, supports NetWare Directory Services?

    a. BIND.VLM
    b. VLM.EXE
    c. LITE.VLM
    d. NDS.VLM

27. The VLM.EXE file is primarily responsible for:

    a. Swapping memory
    b. Managing the other VLMs
    c. Accessing NetWare Directory Services
    d. Preventing conflicts with NETX

28. Which protocol is responsible for establishing connections with servers?

    a. Service
    b. Transport
    c. Redirection
    d. Connections

Chapter 7: Customizing the User's Environment

29. Which startup file loads the DOS Requester if you do not specify otherwise?

    a. CONFIG.SYS

    b. AUTOEXEC.BAT

    c. NET.CFG

    d. STARTNET.BAT

30. Which NET.CFG command accurately specifies a number of Packet Burst buffers?

    a. PB = 3

    b. Packet Burst = 3

    c. PB Buffers = 3

    d. Packet Buffers = 3

31. The main benefit of LIP is:

    a. That it is part of the OS in NetWare 3.12

    b. That it improves performance across routers

    c. That it limits the size of packets going across bridges

    d. That it lets networks communicate without routers

32. LIP stands for:

    a. Large Internetwork Packet

    b. Large Interrouter Packet

    c. Listening International Packet

    d. Listening Interrupt Packet

Case Study

1. Debug the following system login script:

   ```
   COMSPEC = S2:COMMAND COM
   MAP NEXT SYS:USERS\THASSELL\REPORTS93
   IF %LOGIN_NAME <> "SUPERVISOR" THEN
   DOS SET USERNAME = "%LOGIN_NAME"
   DRIVE K:
   STOP
   IF MEMBER_OF_TECHS THEN BEGIN WRITE "CHECK YOUR
   EMAIL"
   ```

2. Create a user login script that accomplishes the following items:

   - Checks for the day of week and, if it is Tuesday, has a message telling the user about a meeting the next day at 10 am.

   - Maps a drive to a spreadsheet application and has the user change to that drive letter when he or she exits.

   - Maps a drive to a data directory that corresponds to the current month and year.

   - Checks for the user named BACKUP and has him exit to a batch file that starts the nightly backup. (This user can only log in between 7:00 pm and 11:00 pm)

   - Makes sure that only people belonging to the group ACCOUNTING can log in to the workstation whose address is 7E.

Chapter 7: Customizing the User's Environment

3. Create a menu with the following parameters:
   - ◆ Provides access to three applications—one for spreadsheets, one for accounting, and one for word processing. Use applications with which you are familiar.
   - ◆ Has a submenu with several NetWare menu utilities.
   - ◆ Has a submenu with SEND, NCOPY, and NDIR. Use input variables.
   - ◆ Places submenus in different positions on the screens and makes them in different colors.

PART 3

NetWare 2.2

Chapter 8

NetWare 2.2 System Manager

Chapter 9

NetWare 2.2 Advanced System Manager

NetWare 2.2 System Manager

This chapter focuses on the v2.2 System Manager objectives. In this chapter, you learn about the following items:

- ◆ File server requirements
- ◆ Security
- ◆ Printing

If your server is equipped with a 286 processor, NetWare 2.2 is the only version of NetWare that will work on your equipment. Version 2.2 also can be used on 386- and 486-based servers but will not take full advantage of the features offered by those more advanced processors. Four different configurations of NetWare 2.2 are available depending on the number of connections supported.

Connections, as defined by Novell, are taken up by print servers, communications, and specialized processes. Value-added processes (VAPs) take up most of the connections. *VAPs* are programs that increase the functionality of the server.

Common VAPs include print servers and file server keyboard software locks. You learn more about VAPs later in this chapter.

Chapter 8: NetWare 2.2 System Manager

Depending on the functionality of the VAP, it can take up several connections. The following list outlines the different versions of v2.2 and the number of connections provided with each version.

- The five-user version provides up to 32 connections
- The 10-user version provides up to 32 connections
- The 50-user version provides up to 64 connections
- The 100-user version provides up to 116 connections

Early NetWare versions, called *entry-level solutions* (ELSs), limited the functionality of the operating system. The newer versions limit only the number of users and none of the other features.

The only real limitation of features occurs when a file server runs in a nondedicated mode rather than a dedicated mode. Dedicated file servers are SFT Level II and provide transaction tracking system services. Nondedicated file servers do not provide the capability for disk duplexing. Disk duplexing is discussed later in this chapter.

NetWare 2.2 includes Macintosh 2.0 VAPs. Version 2.2 supports AppleTalk Phase II and TokenTalk. Novell allows several Macintosh file attributes to be carried over into the NetWare environment for compatibility.

File server requirements for v2.2 are as follows:

- 80286-, 80386-, or 80486-compatible computer
- 2.5M of RAM (more for hard drives larger than 80M)

- 10M hard disk (minimum)
- 1.2M floppy disk drive

Workstations need to be 8086-compatible computers or better. The faster the workstation, the faster the network operates because of distributed processing. The workstation processes a large amount of information for programs, so an 80386 system always outperforms an 8086 computer.

When the workstation loads an application from the file server into its memory and downloads files from the file server to use with the application, *distributed processing* has taken place. In distributed processing, the workstation can process information without requiring the file server's processing power. This capability enables the workstation to calculate, sort, and format information, leaving the file server free to service other requests.

NetWare 2.2 is intended to be a workgroup solution to fit the simple needs of small departments. This version works well as a specialized node in 386-based networks when a workgroup does not need connectivity to other systems.

Exploring the NetWare 2.2 File Server

You can create two different types of NetWare 2.2 file servers: dedicated and nondedicated.

The difference between these two types is in what the file server is asked to do. A *dedicated* file server operates solely as a file server. A *nondedicated* file server runs as both a file server and a workstation.

The following list explains the benefits that the dedicated server has over the nondedicated file server:

- ◆ The dedicated file server is faster than a nondedicated server, because the dedicated server does not have to split its time between servicing all network users and servicing the DOS process being used by the local user.

- ◆ The dedicated file server is more secure and reliable than a nondedicated server. If an application running on the workstation portion of the nondedicated server locks up, the entire network is affected. Rebooting the workstation also reboots the file server.

File Server Memory

The slowest function for any file server is accessing the hard drive. To improve the file server's performance, NetWare uses the RAM installed in the file server to store information accessed often.

A more detailed discussion of NetWare 2.2 file server memory is included in Chapter 9.

Value-Added Processes

NetWare 2.2 uses *value-added processes*—programs the file server runs to add features that the core operating system uses to customize the network.

Novell recommends a minimum of 2.5M RAM for the file server and 8 to 10M as the maximum amount of RAM.

A VAP must be placed in the SYS:SYSTEM directory. All VAPs have a VAP file extension.

To load a VAP, follow these steps:

1. Place the file with the VAP extension in the SYS:SYSTEM directory.
2. Down the file server and reboot.
3. When the file server comes up, NetWare asks if you want to load the VAP. Answer any questions specific to the VAP being loaded.

To unload a VAP, follow these steps:

1. Down the file server and reboot.
2. When asked to load the VAP, answer no.

NetWare 2.2 Disk Storage

NetWare 2.2 enables you to put up to two gigabytes (G) of storage onto the network. This storage capability enables you to use combinations of hard drives, CD-ROM drives, and optical disks.

You can create up to 32 volumes, each no larger than 255M.

System Fault Tolerance

NetWare 2.2 provides the following methods of system reliability:

- **Read-After-Write Verification and Hot Fix.** These features ensure that data is not written to bad blocks and tracks statistics when bad blocks are found. When you install NetWare, a portion of the disk—two percent by default—is set aside for dynamic bad block remapping. Every time a block of data is written to the hard drive, the server compares what was written to disk to what is in memory. If these things match, the server goes on to the next task. If any discrepancy exists, the server writes the block again to the area set aside during installation. This area is tracked as *hot fix*. The block to which the data is originally written is marked as a bad block so that it is not reused. Using FCONSOLE, you can view the number of hot fix blocks used. Each used hot fix block represents a server-detected bad block.

- **Duplicate File Allocation Tables (FAT) and Directory Entry Tables (DET).** These tables store information that the server uses to save and retrieve data on the hard disk. If the original tables become corrupt, NetWare can retrieve and use the backup copies, because they are stored on separate areas of the disk.

- **Disk Mirroring and Disk Duplexing.** NetWare allows certain pieces of equipment to be duplicated so that if the original piece fails, the secondary device can be used. *Disk mirroring* enables you to attach two drives on the same controller. *Disk duplexing* requires that you duplicate the disk interface board, the cable connection, the drive controllers, and the hard disks. This method is more secure than disk mirroring.

- **Transaction Tracking System (TTS).** Transaction Tracking System is used with databases. TTS is provided to application developers so that database files can be rolled back to their original state if a failure occurs during processing. This protection must be built into the application for you to take advantage of this feature. NetWare 2.2 uses TTS for some of its system files.

◆ **Uninterruptible Power Supply (UPS).** Uninterruptible Power Supply protection prevents power loss from causing the server to crash. The UPS contains a battery capable of maintaining power to the file server for a short period of time. By using a configuration file, the UPS can be configured to tell the server to issue the DOWN command after a specified time.

The file you use to configure the UPS is called CONFIG.UPS and needs to be placed into the SYS:SYSTEM directory.

In this file, you can set the following parameters:

- ◆ Type of hardware
- ◆ I/O address
- ◆ UPS down time
- ◆ UPS wait time

File Server Console Commands

The following is a list of commands that you can use on the NetWare 2.2 file server:

- ◆ **BROADCAST** *message.* Sends a message to all network users currently logged in to or attached to the network.

- ◆ **CLEAR MESSAGE.** Clears any messages that appear on the screen under the Monitor display.

Chapter 8: NetWare 2.2 System Manager

- **CLEAR STATION** *number*. Clears a workstation that has problems. This command should be issued before you press Ctrl-Alt-Del at the workstation.

 You can learn a user's station number by typing **USERLIST/A** at a workstation.

- **DISK.** Checks the status of each network drive.
- **DOWN.** Writes cache buffers to the file server hard drives and shuts down the operating system. This command must be used before you turn off power to the server.
- **MONITOR** *number*. Brings up a grid of six boxes, each containing information about a network connection.
- **SPOOL.** Lists spooled queues. See the following section on printing for other SPOOL options.
- **VAP.** Lists currently loaded VAPs.
- **WATCHDOG.** Enables monitoring of all network connections for inactivity.

Exploring Network Security

Trustee rights are the rights users or groups have in a directory. These rights also are referred to as *privileges*. Seven trustee rights exist in v2.2. Trustee rights are the "keys" each user has for a directory. These seven rights are listed and defined in table 8.1.

Table 8.1
Trustee Rights

Right	Function
Read	Enables the user to see the contents of a file and to use the file.

Right	Function
Write	Enables the user to alter the contents of a file.
Create	Enables the user to make new files and directories.
Erase	Enables the user to delete existing files and directories.
File Scan	Enables the user to view files and subdirectories in a directory. Without this right, you cannot see files. In v2.2, you still can see subdirectories, even if you are denied rights.
Modify	Enables the user to change the attributes of a file in v2.2. With this right, the user can change a file from Read/Write to Read Only or from Nonshareable to Shareable. In v3.11, this right also enables the user to change the attributes for directories.
Access Control	Enables the user to give any of the preceding rights to other users on the network.

Directory Rights

Directory rights, also known as the *maximum rights mask*, are the same as trustee rights, but directory rights belong to the system—not the users. Directory rights override trustee rights.

Suppose, for example, that a user has the Erase trustee right to a directory, and the directory enables the Erase right. The user then can erase files. If the directory does not enable the Erase right, however, no user can erase files in that directory—even if he or she has the Erase trustee right.

Effective Rights

You can think of directory rights as "locks" that you can put on your system. NetWare gives each directory a full set of locks by default. The trustee rights are the "keys" that fit the directory locks. Each user can have his or her own set of unique keys. As an example, think of your own key ring. You have your own house key, car key, and so on. Chances are that no one has the same keys as you. Everyone has different locks that need to be opened. The same concept applies to networks. You have specific needs in directories. Some users have the same needs, and others have different needs. Each user can have his or her own set of keys, or rights.

Effective rights are the trustee rights (keys) that actually match available directory rights (locks). If a lock exists and you do not have a key, you cannot perform the function. Likewise, if you have a key and no lock exists, you cannot perform the function. The only way you can use a right is to have matching locks and keys.

 Anyone who has the Access Control right in a directory can change the Maximum Rights Mask.

Each newly created directory automatically has all seven rights available through the Maximum Rights Mask.

Use table 8.2 as a guideline to determine which rights are required to perform common operations to files.

Table 8.2
Required Rights for Common Operations

Action	Required Rights
Read a closed file	R
Write to a closed file	W

Action	Required Rights
Create and write to a file	C & W
Delete a file flagged Read/Write	E
Rename a file	M or C & W
Change a file's attributes	F & M
See files using DIR	F
Create a directory	C
Change the Maximum Rights Mask	A
Change trustee rights	A

Examining Network Printing

Core printing service is the oldest method of network printing and was, at one time, the only method supplied by Novell. *Core printing* services enable you to connect printers directly to the file server. Thus, printer jobs are handled directly by the operating system. This method is supported only on NetWare 286 and has both advantages and disadvantages. If your system simply requires one or two printers in a central location, then core printing might be all that you need.

NetWare 2.2 uses the following files for printing and print services:

CAPTURE.EXE

NPRINT.EXE

END CAP.EXE

continues

continued

> PSC.EXE
> PCONSOLE.EXE
> PRINTDEF.EXE
> PRINTCON.EXE
> RPRINTER.EXE
> PSERVER.VAP
> PSERVER.EXE

Although basic, core printing can burden the file server with printing tasks that reduce file service performance. Core printing also requires downing the file server to make changes to printer port configurations. This method of printing usually must be scheduled after normal working hours to minimize any downtime inconvenience to other users. Reserve core printing for smaller, low-traffic situations that do not require extended control.

Setting Up Core Printing in a v2.2 Server

Core printing in a v2.2 server requires that you choose this option when you install NetWare. If you choose Basic Installation, core printing is initialized automatically for LPT1. Core printing enables you to attach up to five printers directly to the file server. To use these printers, the administrator must be aware of the following commands:

- **P *n* CREATE *port*.** Assigns a printer number to a port on the file server. If you want LPT1 assigned as printer 0 and COM1 assigned as printer 2, type the following:

    ```
    P 0 CREATE LPT1
    P 1 CREATE COM1
    ```

If you need to set a COM port for anything other than the parameters listed here, use this command to reset parameters for the port:

```
P n CONFIG BAUD=a WORDSIZE=b STOPBIT=c PARITY=d
XONXOFF=e
```

Options	Values
BAUD	300, 1200, 4800, 9600
WORDSIZE	7, 8
STOPBIT	1, 2
PARITY	Even, Odd, NONE
XONXOFF	Yes/No

- **Q *name* CREATE line.** Enables the administrator to make a queue on the network. If you want to create a queue for a laser printer, for example, type **Q LASERQ CREATE**. A hexidecimally named subdirectory is created automatically on the network for storing print jobs.

- **P *n* ADD *queuename* AT PRIORITY *x*.** Hooks up the queue with the appropriate printer. Type the following command to attach printer 0 with the LASERQ queue:

    P 0 ADD LASERQ

    Normally, each printer has one queue. Other configurations are available, depending on the needs of the users on your network. Queues also can have priorities. Priority 1 is the highest. No other queues are serviced until the queue with priority 1 is empty. Then the queue with priority 2 is serviced. To add a queue called DRAFTMODE to PrinterQ at priority 2, for example, use the following command:

    ```
    Q ADD DRAFTMODE AT PRIORITY 2
    ```

All the preceding commands can be entered into the file server at the DOS prompt. The best place for these commands, however, is the AUTOEXEC.SYS file, which you can edit in the SYSCON Supervisor Options. When entered at the prompt, these commands are valid only while the file server remains running. Downing the file server loses all the command's information except queue names. Placing these commands in the AUTOEXEC.SYS file ensures that they are executed whenever the file server is rebooted.

Review Questions

1. Which of the following is not a correct NetWare 2.2 system requirement?

    a. 10M hard disk

    b. Minimum 2.5M memory, 10M maximum

    c. XT or better PC

    d. 1.2M floppy

2. VAP stands for:

    a. Value-Added Process

    b. Variable-Added Process

    c. Value-Aided Process

    d. Value-Added Procedure

Review Questions

3. Which of the following statements is true?
    a. VAPs are stored in the SYS:PUBLIC directory.
    b. VAPs can be loaded only while the server is booting.
    c. VAPs can be unloaded while the file server is up and running.
    d. VAPs are necessary if you want to print.

4. Which of the following statements is false?
    a. NetWare 2.2 creates duplicate DET and FAT tables in separate disk partitions.
    b. The CONFIG.UPS file is used to configure the length of time that the file server waits to see if the power returns.
    c. Only files written for TTS can use it.
    d. Nondedicated file servers can do disk duplexing.

5. Which command is the most appropriate to use on the workstation at connection 3 that has crashed?
    a. Ctrl-Alt-Del at workstation
    b. CLEAR STATION 3 at file server
    c. CLEAR CONNECTION 3 at file server
    d. MONITOR 3 at file server

6. Which rights would you need to create a file in the SYS:PROGRAM\DATA?
    a. C, W
    b. C
    c. W
    d. C, F, W

7. Which rights would you need to change the attributes of a file from Read/Write to Read Only?

    a. F, M
    b. M
    c. C, M
    d. A, M

8. Which statement is *not* necessary to fully enable a printer using core printing?

    a. P 0 CREATE LPT1
    b. Q 0 ADD DOTMAXQ
    c. S 0 TO DOTMAXQ
    d. CAPTURE Q=DOTMAXQ

9. Which *two* of the following are supported in NetWare 2.2?

    a. TokenTalk
    b. AppleTalk Phase I
    c. AppleTalk Phase II
    d. EtherTalk

10. What is the maximum number of network connections supported by NetWare 2.2?

    a. 32
    b. 64
    c. 116
    d. 128

Review Questions

11. Which of the following statements about NetWare 2.2 is true?

    a. No SFT Level II support is available.

    b. It runs in dedicated or nondedicated mode.

    c. TTS is not available in this version.

    d. Disk duplexing works in dedicated and nondedicated modes.

12. Loading applications and files from the server into workstation memory is called:

    a. Data processing

    b. File server processing

    c. TTS

    d. Distributed processing

13. Which server type can run as both a file server and a workstation?

    a. Dedicated

    b. Nondedicated

    c. Either dedicated or nondedicated

    d. NetWare 2.2 servers can run only as nondedicated

14. Programs that the file server runs to add features for the core operating system to use in customizing the network are called:

    a. NLMs

    b. NNSs

    c. VLMs

    d. VAPs

Chapter 8: NetWare 2.2 System Manager

15. Programs that the NetWare 2.2 file server runs to add customizing operating system features always have the extension:

    a. NLM

    b. APP

    c. VAP

    d. VLM

16. The maximum storage space available on a NetWare 2.2 server is:

    a. 3G

    b. 2G

    c. 255M

    d. Unlimited

17. The largest volume that a NetWare 2.2 server can address is:

    a. 3G

    b. 2G

    c. 255M

    d. Unlimited

18. Which of the following is *not* a method of system reliability provided by NetWare 2.2?

    a. Bad block reuse

    b. Duplicate FAT and DET

    c. TTS

    d. UPS

Review Questions

19. Which of the following is *not* true regarding Read-After-Write verification?

    a. Two percent of the disk is set aside at installation for Read-After-Write verification.

    b. It lets the server reuse bad blocks, because it repairs them first.

    c. You can see the number of bad blocks used by running FCONSOLE.

    d. Server compares what is written to the disk with what is still in memory each time the server writes a block of data.

20. Which of the following must be set when configuring the UPS?

    a. File server name

    b. UPS start time

    c. UPS name

    d. UPS down time

21. Before downing the NetWare 2.2 server, which console command should you issue?

    a. CLEAR MESSAGE

    b. CLEAR *station*

    c. USERLIST/A

    d. BROADCAST

22. Which command enables you to find out a user's workstation number?

    a. BROADCAST

    b. WATCHDOG

    c. CLEAR *station*

    d. USERLIST/A

23. Which command enables monitoring of all network connections for inactivity?

    a. BROADCAST

    b. WATCHDOG

    c. CLEAR *station*

    d. USERLIST/A

24. To rename a file, the user must have which of the following rights?

    a. M or C & W

    b. R, W, & C

    c. M, C, W, & A

    d. C, E, & W

25. Which of the following commands adds a queue called ACCOUNTING to the network?

    a. CREATE Q ACCOUNTING

    b. ADD Q ACCOUNTING

    c. Q ACCOUNTING CREATE

    d. Q ADD ACCOUNTING

Case Study

1. Why would you want to use a dedicated server rather than a nondedicated server?

2. List the steps necessary to add a VAP.

3. Describe the process of removing a VAP.

Case Study

4. List and describe SFT options.
5. Set up an AUTOEXEC.SYS that allows core printing to use two parallel printers and one serial printer. Use one queue per printer and make one of the parallel printers the default printer.

NetWare 2.2 Advanced System Manager

CHAPTER 9

This chapter focuses on NetWare 2.2 Advanced System Manager issues. The topics covered in this chapter are as follows:

- NetWare 2.2 installation
- Network management using FCONSOLE
- NetWare 2.2 memory

Installing NetWare 2.2

You can install NetWare 2.2 from floppy disks, a hard disk, or a network drive.

When you install from floppies, first make disk copies of the following disks: SYSTEM-1, SYSTEM-2, OSOBJ, and OSEXE. Program files are written to these four disks as they are created by the installation program.

When installing from a local hard drive or a network drive, you must copy the appropriate floppies into the directories with the same name as the floppies. This procedure can be done manually, but NetWare 2.2 has a utility that does this for you automatically. This utility is called UPLOAD and is found on the SYSTEM-1 disk.

Chapter 9: NetWare 2.2 Advanced System Manager

 When you finish generating the operating system and want to put the changed files onto the appropriate disk, you must run the DOWNLOAD program on the SYSTEM-1 disk.

The installation program for NetWare 2.2 is broken into four modules, each having a specific function. These modules are as follows:

- Module 1: Operating System Generation
- Module 2: Linking and Configuring
- Module 3: Track Zero Test (ZTEST)
- Module 4: File Server Definition

Module 1: Operating System Generation

This module enables you to do the following:

- Select Dedicated or Nondedicated mode for the file server
- Select the number of communications buffers (discussed later in this chapter)
- Select and configure the network boards
- Select and configure the disk controllers

Module 2: Linking and Configuring

This module creates executable files from the configuration information set up in Module 1. The linked and configured files include the following:

- **ZTEST.EXE.** This file performs the ZTEST in Module 3.
- **INSTOVL.EXE.** This file is the INSTallation OVerLay used when you install NetWare 2.2.
- **COMPSURF.EXE.** This file performs a COMPrehensive SURFace analysis. Many hard drives are *NetWare-ready*,

which means that they have been tested thoroughly and do not require another exhaustive surface test. Older drives and drives not known to be NetWare-ready should be tested to ensure integrity. COMPSURF tests the entire disk for bad blocks.

- **VREPAIR.EXE.** VREPAIR is used to repair problem volumes. In NetWare 2.2, VREPAIR is configured for the hardware options you choose when you generate the operating system.
- **NET$OS.EXE.** This file is the NetWare 2.2 Operating System.

Module 3: Track Zero Test

This module performs the ZTEST, which is used to check the integrity of Track Zero on the hard drive. *Track Zero* is the boot track on a hard drive and must be clear of defects for NetWare to load.

Module 4: File Server Definition

This module is used to fine-tune file server parameters. With Module 4, you can perform the following tasks:

- Name the file server
- Limit hard drive space
- Assign volumes
- Set up the drives for mirroring
- Set a flag to prompt for loading the Macintosh VAP

Starting the INSTALL Program

The modules described in the preceding section are accessed through the INSTALL menu or command-line variables.

The following list explains each installation option and which modules they execute.

-E: Expert—Advanced Installation

Use this option to install a new system. This option completes modules 1 through 4 if you answer Yes to the question, "Will this machine be the server?"

This question appears in the first input screen of the install option. Figure 9.1 shows an example of this screen.

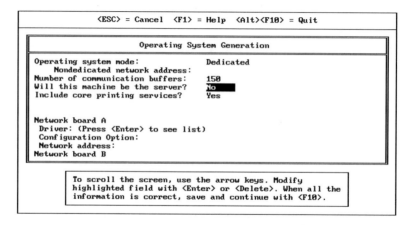

Figure 9.1
First input screen of Advanced Installation.

The -E option completes modules 1 and 2 if you answer No to the question, "Will this machine be the server?"

-L: Linked or Linking Complete

This option is used when you answer No to "Will this machine be the server?" with another option, and you are attempting to complete the installation. Variables that -L can follow include -M and -U. Make sure that -L follows another letter; do not use this option alone. If you put -L first, it automatically performs the ZTEST on the drive. This option completes modules 3 and 4.

Starting the INSTALL Program

-N: No Linking

Use this option if you are configuring an operating system for someone else and they will complete the installation. This option completes module 1. Follow this up with INSTALL -C.

-C: Configuration Complete

Use -C to finish an INSTALL -N. This completes modules 2 through 4.

-M: Maintenance

Use the -M option to change an existing system. This option completes modules 1 through 4 if you answer Yes to the question "Will this machine be the server?" It completes modules 1 and 2 if you answer No to "Will this machine be the server?"

-F: File Server Definition

Use this option to change volumes, server names, and mirroring. The -F option completes module 4 only.

-U: Upgrade

Use this option to upgrade from a v2.x system.

No version of NetWare earlier than v2.0a can be upgraded by using the UPGRADE option of INSTALL.

Changing from v3.x to v2.x is not considered an upgrade. No utility facilitates going backward from v3.x.

379

Chapter 9: NetWare 2.2 Advanced System Manager

The -U option completes modules 1 through 4 if you answer Yes to "Will this machine be the server?"; it completes modules 1 and 2 if you answer No to this question.

Investigating the INSTALL Options

In the main menu of the INSTALL program, as shown in figure 9.2, you see four options: Basic Installation, Advanced Installation, Maintain existing system, and Upgrade from NetWare 2.x.

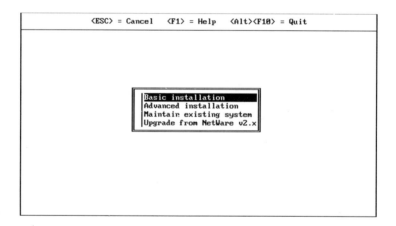

Figure 9.2
The INSTALL menu.

Basic Installation

You are asked only three questions when you install by using the Basic Installation option. These questions ask for the following information:

- File server type: Dedicated or Nondedicated
- File server name
- Network board type

Investigating the INSTALL Options

This method is the easiest and most restricted method of installation. When using Basic Installation, the INSTALL program assumes that the following points are true:

- Only one file server is on the network. INSTALL sets the network number to 1.
- The file server has only one network board. (Each network board needs a unique number, and Basic Installation does not give you the option to change the network number.)
- The file server has only one hard disk controller.
- The file server has one parallel printer attached.

Basic Installation sets up everything needed for printing to one parallel printer attached to the file server.

- Basic Installation expects all workstations on the network to run DOS. With the Basic Installation option, you cannot load the Macintosh VAPs.
- The file server does not use internal routers (multiple network boards) or an external disk subsystem.

If any of the preceding statements are not true of your network, you will need to run Advanced Installation.

The Basic Installation interrogates the CMOS in the file server to discover the disk controller type. Basic Installation defaults to Option 0, or factory default settings.

Filling in the Blanks

This section guides you through both a basic and an advanced installation of a new file server. Complete your hardware installation and resolve any conflicts before proceeding.

381

Chapter 9: NetWare 2.2 Advanced System Manager

Basic Installation Demonstration

After you prepare your installation method, whether it is the floppy-drive, hard-drive, or network-disk method, you can start the install programs. The main INSTALL menu appears, as you saw in figure 9.2.

After you select the Basic Installation option, you see the introduction screen, as shown in figure 9.3. This screen has a welcome and a warning message that confirms your choice.

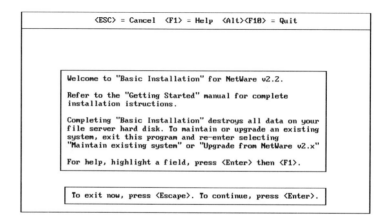

Figure 9.3
Introduction screen.

After confirming that you want to continue (by pressing Enter), you are asked to select the file server mode (see fig. 9.4), either dedicated or nondedicated. A *dedicated* file server is dedicated to the task of being a file server. Unless the system you are installing is small (up to five users) and has lightly used disk access, you should install in the dedicated mode. The option of using the file server as a workstation can sometimes be a problem rather than an advantage. To choose an option, simply highlight your choice and press Enter.

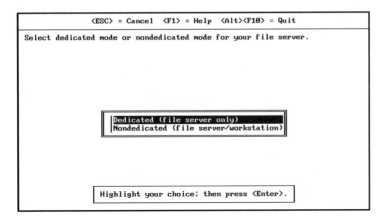

Figure 9.4
File server mode menu.

Many system administrators do not realize the critical liability of operating a nondedicated file server. A nondedicated file server's processing power as a file server is greatly reduced by switching between the workstation and file server modes.

With a nondedicated file server, the system runs a much higher risk of system failure and data corruption. The single workstation user who operates programs on the file server has the ability to disrupt all other users if a program crashes or "hangs."

After you select the file server mode of operation, you must name the file server. Each file server located on the LAN must have a unique name. If you have only a single file server, the name is simply a label and is not used by the users (as in a multiserver environment).

The file server name screen, as shown in figure 9.5, is self-explanatory. The name given to your file server is not limited to any particular words. The name can be as simple as your company's name or the name of a department the file server is servicing. You can use any name containing two to 45 characters. No spaces or periods are permitted as part of the server name.

Chapter 9: NetWare 2.2 Advanced System Manager

Figure 9.5
File server name screen.

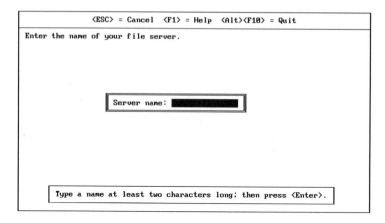

Next, you need to select the network interface card installed in your file server. The NetWare install program presents you with a list of drivers supplied with NetWare, as in figure 9.6. If the driver you need is not shown, press Ins and provide the required driver from the disk supplied by the manufacturer or Novell.

Figure 9.6
Network card driver selection.

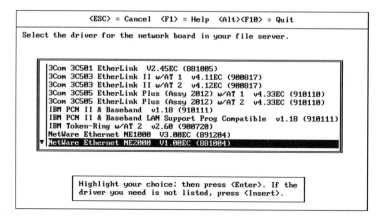

After you complete the network card selection, the linking and configuration information appears on the screen as each process is performed.

After module 2 or the Link and Configure processes finish, you are prompted, as illustrated by figure 9.7 with the ZTEST screen. This screen warns you about data loss that occurs if you proceed.

384

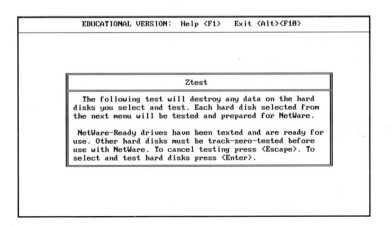

Figure 9.7
ZTEST warning screen.

At this point, you have completed modules 1 through 3, and you are ready for the module 4 installation process. By using the Basic option, the file server definition screen defaults to a generic configuration, and the loading of all files begins automatically.

Advanced Installation Demonstration

The Advanced installation method is the most commonly used of the installation options. You must understand file server hardware and your system requirements to complete the information on-screen.

To begin, run the install program again and select the Advanced installation option, as shown in figure 9.8.

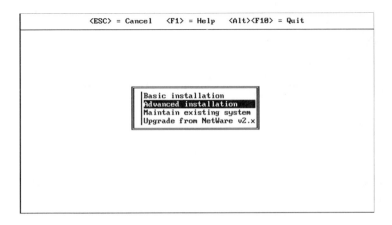

Figure 9.8
Advanced installation screen.

Chapter 9: NetWare 2.2 Advanced System Manager

After you select this option, the familiar welcome screen appears and informs you of your choice. After you press Enter, the welcome screen clears and the main Operating System Generation screen appears. This screen, as shown in figure 9.9, offers hardware configuration options.

Figure 9.9
Operating System Generation windows.

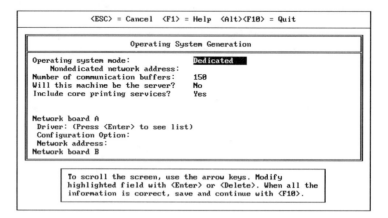

The Operating System Generation screen contains the following options:

- Operating system mode: Dedicated or Nondedicated
- Nondedicated network address
- Number of communication buffers
- Will this machine be the server?
- Include core printing services?

This screen also has options for disk controllers, network card drivers, addresses, and hardware. Note the set of instructions at the bottom of the screen.

First, select the operating system mode (as with the Basic option, discussed previously). If you choose a nondedicated server, you also must supply a network address for this process. This address must be different from any other you use.

Next, configure the communication buffers. The required number of buffers varies, depending on the equipment used and the number of users and their work load.

To ensure the integrity of your data, you must have sufficient communications buffers. If your system runs out of buffers during normal operation, data will be lost. The default of 150 buffers is sufficient for most installations.

You can estimate the number of required buffers by using two buffers for each user and ten buffers for each file server network card. If this number is fewer than 150, use the default.

NetWare 2.2 gives you the option of generating the operating system on a machine other than the file server and then transferring the linked and configured files to the server. If you have chosen this method of OS generation, answer No when prompted as to whether this machine will be the server. If you are performing the installation on the server itself, respond Yes to this question.

Next, NetWare asks if you want to include core printing. If you only need a couple of printers connected to a file server, core printing might be the best solution. If your printing requirements are more involved, and you need printers distributed throughout the office, you can use the server VAP rather than core printing.

You should know the hardware configuration of your network and disk controllers, because you must insert a network-interface driver for each of the four LAN cards you might have installed. To select a network driver, highlight the Network board A field and press Enter. The driver option window appears (see fig. 9.10).

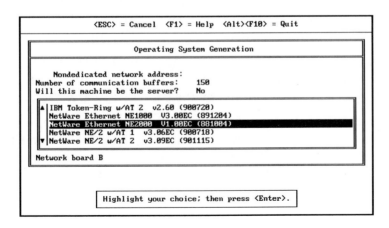

Figure 9.10
Network board driver selection windows.

Chapter 9: NetWare 2.2 Advanced System Manager

This window enables you to scan through the Novell-supplied drivers and choose the one required. If your driver is not listed in this window, you can press Ins and supply the INSTALL program with the appropriate disk.

In this example, the Novell NetWare Ethernet NE2000 driver (see fig. 9.10) and the first configuration option (0) are chosen (see fig. 9.11).

Figure 9.11
Hardware options.

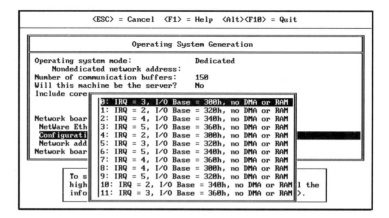

In the Network address field, enter an address different from any other network segments to which your system might be connected. This process is repeated for network boards B, C, and D, if needed.

Next, enter configuration information for disk channels 0 through 4. Because you are selecting an ISA standard disk controller in this instance, choose channel 0.

Novell provides support for four concurrent disk channels. Channel 0 generally is reserved for an ISA disk controller, but other devices can use it if permitted by the driver software.

Channels 1 through 4 are designed for high-performance controllers. These controllers normally are not intended for use on DOS-based computers. The Novell DCB (Disk Coprocessor Board) was the first to make use of channels 1 through 4 and does not support channel 0.

Filling in the Blanks

Press Enter and the disk driver selection window appears. For this example, select the Industry Standard ISA controller choice, as shown in figure 9.12.

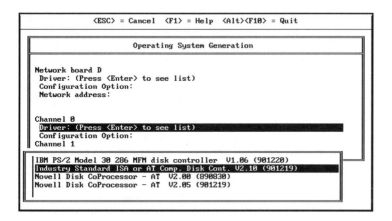

Figure 9.12

Disk driver selection window.

After selecting your disk controller type, you need to configure hardware options. For an ISA disk controller, the selected option is 0, as shown in figure 9.13.

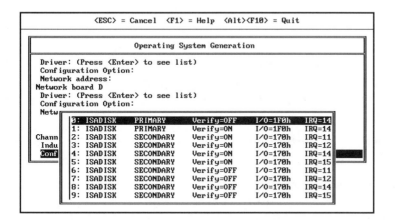

Figure 9.13

Disk driver options.

The ISA controller also provides options 1 through 9, but these options might not be supported on all controllers. Currently, the only ISA disk controller certified to use all options is the standard Compaq controller.

389

After you complete the disk controller information fields, press F10 to save the selections and continue with module 2. You see the link and configuration information scroll as the different steps take place. If you selected the option that identifies the machine you are working on as the file server, you see the same ZTEST screen that appeared in the Basic Installation method.

Figure 9.14 shows the screen that appears as each drive is tested. If you selected the option that your machine is not the file server, Advanced Installation is almost complete.

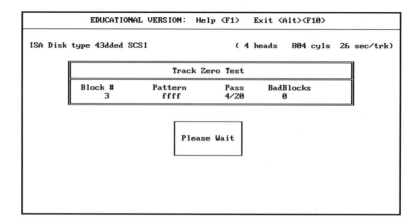

Figure 9.14
ZTEST testing screen.

The next step is to set up the hardware on the machine that will be a server. Boot the server under DOS and put in the SYSTEM-1 disk. Type **INSTALL -M-L** to complete the steps in creating the server.

The last step is performed in module 4 and is the actual file server definition screen. It is used in both maintenance and installation.

Figure 9.15 shows the first part of the form in module 4. In this screen, you are asked for the file server name, the maximum number of open and indexed files, Transaction Tracking information, and information on limiting disk space and setting the flag to install NetWare for Macintosh.

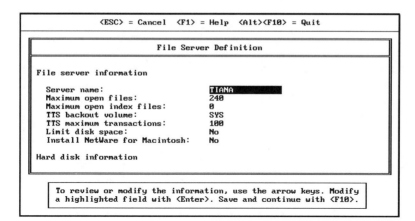

Figure 9.15
Module 4 Part 1.

Figure 9.16 shows you the default information that the INSTALL program filled in for the demonstration. Much of this information can be modified. Other entries provide information about the drives. The important information you should notice in figure 9.16 is the size, type, and current status of the drives, which channel they are on, if they are mirrored, and the amount of space set aside for Hot Fix.

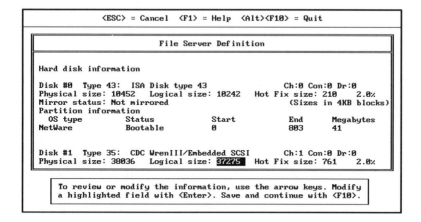

Figure 9.16
Module 4 Part 2.

Figure 9.17 shows the final input portion of module 4. Here you can modify the volume information. You can view and modify the volume names and size and determine if they should be cached and how many directory entries are allowed. Each volume also shows which drive it is on.

Figure 9.17
Module 4 Part 3.

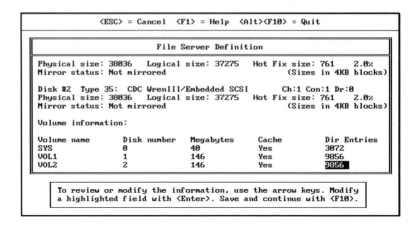

After all the screens are completed, you see messages similar to those shown in figure 9.18. In this figure, you see that the cold boot loader was successfully installed on the hard drive. This procedure allows NetWare 2.2 to boot up without a bootable floppy disk.

Figure 9.18
Successful load of files.

```
Installing NetWare v2.2 operating system files:

Installing the Cold Boot Loader.

Cold boot loader successfully installed.

Copying NET$OS.EXE to SYS:SYSTEM

Copying Files to SYS:LOGIN
        LOGIN.EXE
        WHOAMI.EXE

Copying Files to SYS:PUBLIC
        LOGIN.EXE
        WHOAMI.EXE
        MAP.EXE
        VOLINFO.EXE
        FCONSOLE.EXE
        LOGOUT.EXE
        SYSCON.EXE
```

Next, you see the files as they are copied to their appropriate directories.

The following events take place during a successful installation:

- NET$OS.EXE is copied to SYS:SYSTEM
- The appropriate files are copied into the SYS:LOGIN, SYS:PUBLIC, and SYS:SYSTEM directories.

Managing NetWare 2.2 Using FCONSOLE

In this section, you learn to use some simple tools and methods that help you monitor your file server. Careful monitoring and knowledge of your file server enables you to prevent many problems before they happen. Except for hardware failures, most file server problems are visible through monitoring utilities long before the critical stage.

The network administrator's main responsibility is to monitor and record any file server problems. In most cases, if the administrator does not watch out for these problems, no one will. System monitoring and troubleshooting is enhanced by a wide range of Novell NetWare diagnostic and monitoring utilities. These utilities can give both users and system administrators the data required to maintain a file server efficiently. By monitoring a few of the system's resource statistics, you can make adjustments to the file server that can prevent system failure and increase performance.

The administrator easily can monitor and change NetWare's active parameters to maintain a properly operating file server. With a simple understanding of the following parameters, many system problems can be prevented:

- File service processes
- Disk cache performance

- File server utilization
- Communications buffers
- Dynamic memory pools

Using FCONSOLE for Management Operations

The File Server Console, or FCONSOLE menu utility, enables the system administrator to maintain and fine-tune the file server. This command finds all file servers and places them in a list. FCONSOLE enables you to view user connections, memory management statistics, and LAN I/O statistics. FCONSOLE also can provide advanced diagnostic information that can assist debugging procedures.

User limitations depend on the user's security level. All functions and submenus are open for use by the system supervisor or equivalent. Selected functions and submenus are locked and not functional if you are a normal system user. Users designated as FCONSOLE operators in the SYSCON supervisor options have limited use of FCONSOLE, but more options than the normal end user.

Being aware of FCONSOLE's specific tools for management operations should help you filter out the screens of detailed technical information that are of reduced importance in day-to-day administrative concerns. After executing the FCONSOLE command, you are presented with the opening menu (see fig. 9.19).

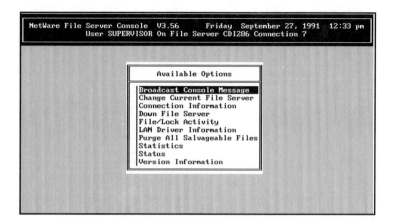

Figure 9.19
FCONSOLE's main menu.

The first menu option, Broadcast Console Message, enables you to send a message to every user currently logged in to the file server. This feature is useful when you need to inform users of scheduled downtime or other global announcements.

The second option is used in a multiserver environment. It enables the FCONSOLE user to attach to other file servers from within the FCONSOLE utility. This option enables you to use FCONSOLE to examine multiple file servers. The interface follows the NetWare utility standard by making use of Ins to add other file servers to the pick list. After choosing a file server from the list, you then are required to supply both a login name and password.

The Connection Information option provides a submenu that enables operations on that particular connection. The Connections Information Menu, shown in figure 9.20, shows the Current Connections submenu, which lists the options provided.

When entering this menu, the Current Connections window displays all users currently logged in to the file server. After selecting a user by highlighting that user's name, press Enter. The Connection Information window appears.

The options listed here are useful when attempting to inspect connections on the system. From here, you can broadcast messages, clear connections, and inspect a user's open files.

Chapter 9: NetWare 2.2 Advanced System Manager

Figure 9.20
The Connection Information menu.

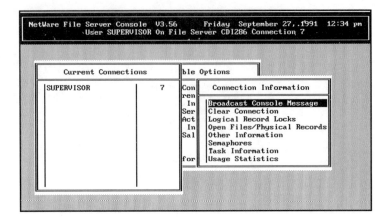

The most commonly used options of FCONSOLE are Broadcast Console Message, Clear Connection, and Open Files/Physical Records. These options are often used while requesting users to log off the system for maintenance. You can, for example, broadcast a message that asks users to please log off the system. After a reasonable period of time, you then can check the Open Files option to determine if they are still in an application. You can decide whether their connections should be cleared by using the Clear Connection option.

If a user does not log out properly, files might be left open on the system. If a user's workstation is turned off, that person's workstation continues to show on the FCONSOLE and an improper logout procedure has probably occurred. In this case, clearing the connection is the proper solution to the problem.

Not all applications show up as an open file on the system. Due to the nature of the program, a user can use Lotus 1-2-3, for example, and show no files open. This fact should be considered when deciding to clear a connection.

Some older technology application programs might be more sensitive to clearing a connection than others. You always should test or confirm this process with the software developers to prevent having to rebuild data files if damaged.

The other Connection Information options are used by advanced system developers when troubleshooting problems related to file sharing and the proper operation on a network. This specialized information is generally useful to programmers and applications development people. A brief description of these other options follows.

The Logical Record Locks option displays the logical record locks that the connection has logged to the file server. This information can be useful when debugging a network application sharing data files.

The Open Files/Physical Records option displays the connection's open files. This option also displays tasks and file status information. By highlighting a particular file and pressing Enter, various status messages appear, depending on the file's open state. More detailed information about this option can be found in the NetWare manuals.

The Other Information option shows additional information about the connection, including login name, full name, login time, and network address.

The Semaphores option enables you to get a list of semaphores that might be used. A *semaphore* is used by system tasks to limit the number of tasks that can use a resource at one time and to limit the number of workstations that can run a program at the same time.

The Task Information option shows which tasks are active at the selected workstation.

The Usage Statistics option shows the total disk usage and packet requests since the selected user logged in. This option can determine the activity of a workstation.

The Statistics option in FCONSOLE's main menu calls up the File Server Statistics menu (see fig. 9.21). This menu has several useful choices for getting information about network performance and system integrity. In particular, the Cache Statistics, Disk Statistics, and Summary options are important monitoring and diagnostic tools.

Chapter 9: NetWare 2.2 Advanced System Manager

Figure 9.21
FCONSOLE's Server Statistics menu.

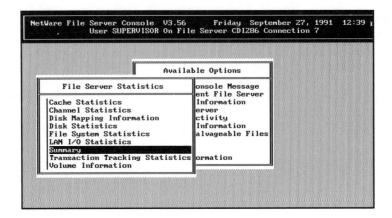

Cache Statistics

The Cache Statistics screen deals almost exclusively with memory usage. This screen tells you about NetWare file caching in the current server. Several of the screen parameters help you determine if enough memory is available in your file server. An example of the Cache Statistics screen is shown in figure 9.22.

Figure 9.22
A typical Cache Statistics screen.

```
NetWare File Server Console  V3.56    Friday September 27, 1991  12:40 pm
                User SUPERVISOR On File Server CDI286 Connection 7

                              Cache Statistics

File Server Up Time:   17 Days 19 Hours  9 Minutes 41 Seconds
Number Of Cache Buffers:              534   Cache Buffer Size:         4,096
Dirty Cache Buffers:                    0
Cache Read Requests:              594,411   Cache Write Requests:     65,236
Cache Hits:                       636,325   Cache Misses:             27,482
Physical Read Requests:            16,564   Physical Write Requests:  22,436
Physical Read Errors:                   0   Physical Write Errors:         0
Cache Get Requests:               619,256
Full Write Requests:               40,391   Partial Write Requests:   24,845
Background Dirty Writes:            9,715   Background Aged Writes:   12,479
Total Cache Writes:                22,224   Cache Allocations:        27,462
Thrashing Count:                        0   LRU Block Was Dirty:          20
Read Beyond Write:                    201   Fragmented Writes:           212
Hit On Unavailable Block:             623   Cache Blocks Scrapped:         0
```

The Cache Hits and Cache Misses parameters show you the number of times a memory cache handled a read-write request and the number of times the hard disk had to be accessed instead. In other words, a *cache hit* occurs when the requested information is found in memory, and a *cache miss* occurs when the information has to be taken from the hard disk. Because the minimum requirement for the network is 80 percent or more of requests serviced from cache, the amount of misses should never be more than 20 percent of the total. Make sure that you have allotted enough memory for cache buffers in the server.

The Physical Read Errors and Physical Write Errors parameter values always should be low, if not zero. An increase in these numbers indicates a communication problem with the hard disk when cache is requesting a read or write.

Physical Read and Write Errors, along with Hot Fix blocks (discussed in the next section), should be zero in a healthy system.

An occasional error or Hot Fix block might occur with normal equipment wear, but continual errors or Hot Fix blocks used weekly and daily indicate possible future failure. Errors can occur over a period of time and then stop. This problem generally indicates a media failure that NetWare handled properly. When errors continue and do not stop, however, you should be concerned.

The Thrashing Count parameter number also should always be near zero. *Thrashing* occurs when a cache block is needed but is not available. File server performance is seriously degraded when this problem occurs. Adding memory until this number goes to zero is the first strategy. If the problem does not go away at 12M of memory, the only alternative is to upgrade to v3.11 to take advantage of dynamic memory allocation.

NetWare 2.2 allocates memory in a static manner. All memory must be allocated upon startup and cannot be changed during operation. NetWare 2.2 memory is explained later in this chapter.

Disk Statistics

Two important parameters in the Disk Statistics screen are IO Error Count and Hot Fix Table Size/Hot Fix Remaining. Figure 9.23 shows the information available for a typical physical disk.

Figure 9.23
FCONSOLE's Physical Disk 0.

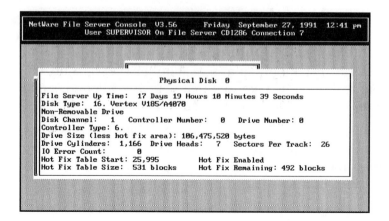

The IO Error Count parameter figure indicates the number of problems encountered when trying to read or write to the hard disk. A separate information screen appears for each drive.

The Hot Fix Table Size parameter tells you exactly how many Hot Fix blocks were allocated when the system was generated. The Hot Fix Remaining parameter tells you how many of those blocks are left. Every time a bad block is encountered on the hard disk, the Hot Fix Remaining parameter decreases.

As part of a normal maintenance schedule, system administrators should check Hot Fix Remaining once a month. If the number goes down by more than five blocks, check the Hot Fix numbers once a week. The nature of hard disks is that they will accrue an occasional bad block, but if a problem exists, they usually accumulate bad blocks quickly. If you see a steady decrease in the number of blocks remaining, be prepared to repair or replace the drive.

File Server Statistics Summary

Choose the Summary option from the File Server Statistics menu to get to the File Server Statistics Summary screen. As figure 9.24 illustrates, this summary screen provides the technical summary data gathered since the file server has been up. This tool is helpful when monitoring the operation and reliability of your server.

```
NetWare File Server Console  V3.56      Friday  September 27, 1991  12:39 pm
             User SUPERVISOR On File Server CDI286 Connection 7

                        File Server Statistics Summary

File Server Up Time:  17 Days 19 Hours  8 Minutes 59 Seconds
Number Of File Service Processes:      6   Current Server Utilization:      6%
Disk Requests Serviced From Cache:   96%   Packets Routed:                   0
Total Packets Received:          527,763   File Service Packets:             6
Total Number Of Cache Buffers:       534   Dirty Cache Buffers:              0
Total Server Memory:           4,194,304   Unused Server Memory:         3,072

                             Maximum     Peak Used    Currently In Use
Communication Buffers            150            13                   0
Open Files:                      240            41                  21
Indexed Files:                     5             0                   0
Bindery Objects:                 500            69                  41
Connections:                     116            10                   1
Dynamic Memory 1:             12,232         2,374                 994
Dynamic Memory 2:             26,576         6,124               5,264
Dynamic Memory 3:             59,500         1,130                 694
Dynamic Memory 4:             63,646           944                 144
```

Figure 9.24

The File Server Statistics Summary screen.

The File Server Up Time parameter shows the amount of time the file server has been running. This time resets if the server is downed or shut off.

The Number of File Service Processes parameter, also known as FSP, tells you the number of processes the file server has. A file server should have at least three processes, but four is recommended and is the average. NetWare 2.2 has a maximum of ten FSPs. Although three processes enable your file server to operate, a slow CPU, a single heavily used disk controller, or a low amount of cache memory might require more. This number can be manipulated by adjusting devices that used memory from Dynamic Memory Pool 1, described later in this chapter.

If your file server appears to have a problem with File Service Processes, a system reconfiguration generally is required. Consult a Novell engineer who is familiar with this problem if reconfiguring the system does not correct the situation.

The following factors can decrease the number of FSPs available on a network:

- Network board packet size is too large
- Network boards using DMA
- An overabundance of directory entries

Note Be cautious about reducing directory entries. You can lose files, directories, and trustee rights if this number is reduced drastically.

The most complete reference about all the factors that affect FSPs is the September 1991 *NetWare Application Notes*. The *Notes* can be purchased from the Novell Research Order Desk. For more information, call 800/453-1267, extension 5380.

The Disk Request Serviced from the Cache parameter is the disk cache performance indicator. This number shows the number of requests received at the file server that are taken from the cache memory. The remainder of the requests received go to the hard disk. Accessing information from cache is 100 times faster than going to the hard disk. The more the file server can get from memory, the faster the network functions. If disk cache performance drops below 93 percent, you should add more memory. According to Novell recommendations, this number should never fall below 80 percent. The actual number of cache buffers your system needs depends on your applications and the load created by the users. If users request more data than their cache buffers can handle, file server performance suffers.

A good rule of thumb is to have between 800 and 1000 cache buffers. You might need to adjust this number after monitoring system statistics.

 Study Note In some cases, you can have too much memory. In a NetWare 2.2 file server, more than 10M of memory can be almost as slow as direct disk I/O, but normally is not a problem.

The Current Server Utilization parameter shows the percentage of use of the file server processor. A utilization that continually reaches a high percentage might require making hardware changes or splitting the network load.

The Communication Buffers parameter also is an important area to watch. These numbers tell how many buffer areas have been set aside to hold incoming packets while currently held packets are being processed. These buffers are necessary to handle both incoming and outgoing packets. If no buffer is available, that packet is lost and a retransmit is required, which can greatly decrease performance.

You should have at least 100 communication buffers, plus one for each workstation. If the Peak Used is equal to the maximum, increase the number of buffers. An overabundance of these buffers is a waste of cache memory.

The Open Files parameter tells you how many open files the server can track. As the Peak Used reaches the maximum, users are not able to run applications.

Four dynamic memory pools are at the bottom of the File Server Statistics Summary screen. The dynamic memory pools are important to monitor, but in most cases difficult to adjust. Make sure that the Peak Used number is always at least 2K below the Maximum number.

Dynamic memory pools are 64K memory segments defined by NetWare 2.2. These segments hold information such as drive pointers, file handles, print queue pointers, and other system housekeeping information.

Dynamic Memory Pool 1, the all-purpose memory pool, is used for global allocated data, process stacks, packet buffers, volume tables, and general purpose workspace. This number is not user-configurable.

Dynamic Memory Pool 2 is used for file and record locking. You can modify this number by reducing the maximum number of open files.

Dynamic Memory Pool 3 contains Router and Server tables. It is not user-configurable.

Dynamic Memory pool 4 is used for drive handles. Each mapping you create uses 16 bytes of memory. This number is not user-configurable, but if you decrease the number of mappings you keep, you can reduce this number.

Exploring File Server Memory

The personal computer has gone through many changes since its introduction. With each class of microprocessor released by Intel came a new way of handling memory. The 8086, 8088, and 80*x*86 series of Intel microprocessors each brought a higher level of functionality. Conventional memory, extended memory, and high memory areas all are available to the applications programmer depending on the Intel microprocessor being implemented.

The original IBM PC design, based on the Intel 8086 and 8088, allowed a total memory capability of 1M. This original design reserved the upper 384K of this 1M for items like system BIOS (Basic Input/Output System), video memory, and adapter cards such as network adapters. This configuration left the 640K with which you already are familiar. Although the Intel 80286 can access 16M of memory and the 80386 4G, the 640K limit still is present for many DOS applications that remain compatible to all previous versions of the Intel microprocessor.

The Intel 80486 microprocessor is a highly optimized version of the 80386 machine that owes most of its performance to a faster instruction execution and integrated math coprocessor. The 80486SX version provides the increased instruction speed without the math coprocessor benefit.

Before you can understand NetWare's memory usage, you need a basic understanding of memory itself.

Conventional memory is the memory you use every time you run your PC—the memory area up to 640K. This area is used by the real-mode operating system DOS and also is the area that presents the common problem of application memory shortage. This 640K must be shared by programs such as DOS itself, disk drivers, LAN card drivers, and many others you might require to run your applications. All applications load into this memory area by default. This configuration sometimes presents a problem, because it does not leave enough free memory to properly run the desired application.

The *upper memory*, or *UMB (upper memory blocks)*, is the area between 640K and 1M. This area is accessible by DOS, but reserved for special functions. This memory area starts at hexadecimal A000 through FFFF and is used by many common PC hardware interfaces. Many common VGA adapters, for instance, use from A000h to CBFFh. The BIOS, which every PC has, normally is located at F000h to FFFFh, although IBM uses a larger area of E000h to FFFFh.

Anyone who uses computers runs into hexadecimal numbers sooner or later. They are easy to recognize, because they usually mix the letters A through F with digits 0 through 9.

Hexadecimal number notation represents numbers in base 16, in contrast to base 10, which we use in most everyday numeric activities. Base 16 requires digits with values ranging from 0 to 15, and the letters A through F are used to represent values from 10 through 15 (A equals 10, B equals 11, and so forth).

Hexadecimal or *hex* notation is popular, because it is easier for humans to read than binary. You probably will agree that CBFF is easier to scan than its binary equivalent, 1100101111111111.

The other areas can be used for other interface cards such as LAN adapters, which might require a memory address; this varies depending on the manufacturer. This UMB area also can be used to load drivers and TSR (terminate-and-stay resident) programs. This feature is supported by DOS 5.0, DR-DOS 6.0, and many third-party memory managers. Figure 9.25 illustrates some of the resources that utilize the UMB.

Figure 9.25

UMB memory utilization.

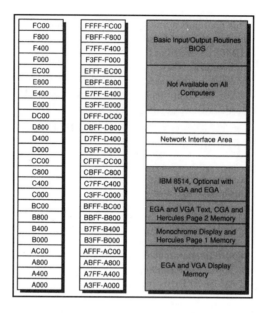

Extended memory is the area above 1M and is not directly addressable to DOS while running in real mode. This memory area is available directly to applications written by using DOS extenders and to memory manager programs that provide access through special driver software. Extended memory, however, is directly accessible when operating in protected mode. This extended memory is what Novell's NetWare products require to supply the performance and functionality for which they are known.

 Comparison Note

The term *real mode* came about when the 80286 processor was developed to operate like *real* 8088/8086 processors, which could utilize a maximum of 1M of memory. DOS is a real-mode operating system, and the old 640K memory limit is a holdover from the oldest IBM PCs and the oldest versions of DOS.

Protected mode was introduced when the 80286 processor was given the capability to manage 16M of memory as a continuous memory block. The 80386 and 80486 processors also offer protected mode and can manage even more memory—up to 4G in the case of the 80486. DOS programs cannot work with this mode, but more advanced operating systems such as NetWare require far more memory than DOS and utilize protected mode.

Expanded memory, used by many applications, is not actually part of the directly addressable memory, but is accessed through a "page frame" setup in the UMB area. This page frame allows applications to access the expanded memory area by mapping in 64K pages. This memory standard is used by many popular applications such as Lotus 1-2-3 and Ventura Publisher. Expanded memory is not used in any of the NetWare operating systems, but can be used on the workstation.

NetWare 2.2 Memory Model

Currently, NetWare 2.2 is the workgroup solution provided by Novell. This product offers many high-performance features and is intended for the smaller workgroup in which multiple communications protocols and large amounts of disk storage are not required.

The minimum amount of memory required for NetWare 2.2 is 2.5M.

Memory usage in NetWare 2.2 has been modified from earlier NetWare 2.*x* products to improve performance and prevent running out of file server processes (FSPs).

To properly calculate the amount of memory needed to operate, a NetWare 2.2 file server requires the information discussed in the following sections.

Directory Entries

Each directory entry is made up of a 32-byte entry stored in the *directory entry table (DET)* and located on the drive itself. This DET is loaded into cache memory. The number of total directory entries is determined during installation.

 The number of directory entries refers to the total number of directories, subdirectories, and files that can be created on a particular volume.

Directory Hashing

The *hashing table* is a simple index stored in memory to the directory entry table. This table requires 8 bytes of memory for each directory entry.

Directory Caching

This feature requires 32 bytes for each directory entry and improves the disk file access time. This option is not implemented if the file server does not have enough memory.

Volume Bit Maps

The *volume bit map* is created for each volume on the file server. This table increases performance by informing the server if a particular disk block is free.

Hot Fix Tables

The *Hot Fix tables* store information pertaining to data redirected because of a bad disk block.

Exploring File Server Memory

By default, two percent of the hard drive is set aside for Hot Fix.

Hot Fix is also known as *dynamic bad block remapping*.

File Caching

File caching is the process that stores often-used file blocks in memory for quicker access. This process also attempts to bring the next most likely accessed data block into memory in case it is needed.

Disk Cache Buffers

After all memory is allocated, the remaining memory is used as disk cache buffers to service file caching. This number should be between 800 and 1000.

Limited memory results in poor performance because of insufficient file cache; too much memory can result in poor performance because of increased system overhead. You can adjust this balance by increasing communication buffers or directory entries if needed.

Cache Memory Work Area

This area is a general work area used to manage disk cache buffers. The size of this area can be determined by multiplying the number of disk cache buffers by 32 and adding 4.7K.

File Allocation Table (FAT)

The *File Allocation Table (FAT)* is an index or link to the disk storage locations. Each FAT entry contains a sequence number and a pointer to the corresponding block for the file. This table requires 1K of memory for each megabyte of disk space.

File Handles (Dynamic Memory Pool 2)

File handles are used to track open files on the file server. Each file handle requires 56 bytes of memory. The maximum number of open files supported by NetWare 2.2 is 1000.

Workstation Tables

This area maintains information pertaining to users and connections to value-added processes (VAPs). This area is not configurable. Approximately 170 bytes is allocated per possible connection.

Index File Tables

This area is used to maintain Turbo Indexes or Turbo FATs. These indexes are built into RAM to speed disk access to large files. When a file larger than 262,144K (64 blocks) is marked with the I file attribute, NetWare maintains a Turbo FAT for the file.

 Note Specifying more indexed files than you need wastes memory.

Operating System

When calculating memory requirements, be sure to include the memory requirements for the operating system files.

The following worksheet can help you to calculate server memory requirements:

Exploring File Server Memory

Server Resource Memory Requirements	Your Server Requirements
Directory Entries (KB) = directory entries x 32 / 1024	KB
Directory Hashing (KB) = directory entries x 8 / 1024	KB
Directory Caching (KB) = directory entries x32 / 1024	KB
Volume Bitmaps (KB) = 32 x volume size (MB) / 1024	KB
Hot Fix Tables (KB) = 14.5 KB x # of drives /1024 + 32 x volume size + 4096	KB
File Caching (KB) = Minimum of 40 cache blocks or 160KB	KB
Cache Memory Work Area (KB) = Minimum of (40 cache buffers x 32) / 1024 + 4.7 KB	KB
Caching FAT (KB) = 1 KB memory per MB disk space	KB
File Handles (File Control Blocks) (KB) = 7 KB file control workarea + # of open files x 56 /1024 *(default is 240, maximum is 1000)*	KB
File Locking (KB) = 2.5KB *(support for 100 WS)* + # open files x 100 /1024	KB
Workstation Tables (KB) = 174 bytes per possible service connection *5 user OS (32 x 174 = 5568) / 1024* *10 user OS (32 x 174 = 5568) / 1024* *50 User OS (60 x 174 = 10440) / 1024* *100 user OS (110 x 174 = 19140) / 1024*	KB
Index File Tables (KB) = (1040 x # indexed files) / 1024	KB
Operating System (KB) = size varies between 460 - 560 KB *(obtain size from SYS:SYSTEM\NET$OS.EXE file size)*	KB
Additional OS Memory (KB) = *To include the following:* Interrupt and Segment table: 35.25KB Dynamic Memory 1: 64KB Dynamic Memory 3 and 4 *(96KB for 5-10 user system* *128KB for 50-100 user system)*	KB
Non-Dedicated Workstation (KB) = If using Non-Dedicated WS 640KB	KB
VAP (KB) = *Depends on VAP requirements*	KB
Communications Buffers (KB) = Three buffers per WS and 50 per network interface *1 buffer = 64 + 42 + (maximum packet size)* *(# WS x 3 buffers) + (# NIC x 50 buffers) =* *Communications Buffers / 1024*	KB
Total Server Memory Required	KB

VAP Requirements

VAPs require memory and sometimes buffer space. When determining the total memory to be used, consult the software developer to determine the actual requirements.

Communication Buffers (Routing Buffers)

This memory area is used as a temporary storage area for data arriving from the network. It ensures that data is not lost during file server busy times. The actual number of buffers to be configured varies with each installation, but you should start with three for each user and 50 for each network interface.

 The optimum amount of communication buffers is to have 25 percent more than the peak used.

File Service Process

In NetWare, a *File Service Process (FSP)* is used to service a file service packet. This process normally is an NCP (NetWare Core Protocol) request from a workstation. An FSP is the only process that can service an NCP request. If an FSP is not available to service the request, then the request is stored in an FSP buffer until it can be serviced. If these buffers fill up, all NCP requests are ignored and requests are lost. This problem was common with previous versions of NetWare 2.*x* and resulted in the restructuring of NetWare 2.2's memory.

NetWare 2.2 memory is allocated into *dynamic memory pools*. Because of limitations imposed by the Intel 80286 microprocessor, these pools are limited to 64K in size. NetWare 2.2 contains four separate dynamic memory pools; earlier versions of NetWare contained only three. The fourth pool was added to solve a problem that caused file servers to run out of FSPs when supporting many resources.

Dynamic Memory Pools

These dynamic memory areas are used for many functions. The following sections briefly describe each pool. These areas are not directly configurable, but when troubleshooting, you should understand what each group affects.

Dynamic Memory Pool 1

Dynamic Memory Pool 1 is considered a general purpose workspace. It is used for global static data, process stack information, volume information, and packet buffers. Because of the limitations of the Intel 80286 processor, this memory pool is limited to 64K. The memory in this pool is collectively referred to as the DGROUP.

Dynamic Memory Pool 2

This memory pool is used to maintain the file and record locking features of NetWare. Dynamic Memory Pool 2 also is used for the workstation tables. This memory pool can be as large as 64K.

Dynamic Memory Pool 3

Dynamic Memory Pool 3 contains the router and file server tables. This table lists the other file servers that might be on the network and the different routes available. This memory pool is fixed in size and can present a problem if connected to a large internetwork that contains many servers and routers.

Dynamic Memory Pool 4

Dynamic Memory Pool 4 was previously part of Dynamic Memory Pool 1. With the growth of networks, the size of disk drives available became a problem that resulted in file servers with too few FSPs. In NetWare 2.2, this memory pool handles user drive mappings. Thus, Dynamic Memory Pool 1 has more memory to allocate to packet buffers, resulting in more FSPs and higher performance. The size of this dynamic memory pool is fixed and determined by the number of users your version supports.

Review Questions

1. Which of the following is the correct order for the installation modules?

    a. Operating System Generation, ZTEST, Linking and Configuring, File Server Definition

    b. Operating System Generation, Linking and Configuring, ZTEST, File Server Definition

    c. File Server Definition, Linking and Configuring, ZTEST, Operating System Configuration

    d. File Server Definition, ZTEST, Linking and Configuring, Operating System Configuration

2. Which of the following is not a valid INSTALL command-line parameter?

    a. INSTALL -U

    b. INSTALL -N

    c. INSTALL -L-M

    d. INSTALL -F

3. Which INSTALL command-line parameter takes you straight to Module 4?

    a. INSTALL -M

    b. INSTALL -M4

    c. INSTALL -F

    d. INSTALL -L

Review Questions

4. Which of the following questions is not asked during a Basic Installation?
    a. What is the name of the file server?
    b. What type of network adapter is in the file server?
    c. Will the file server be dedicated or nondedicated?
    d. Will this machine be the file server?

5. Which item on the Install Main Menu is incorrect?
    a. Basic Installation
    b. Expert Installation
    c. Maintain existing system
    d. Upgrade from NetWare 2.x

6. In which module are you asked to load the Macintosh VAP?
    a. MODULE 1
    b. MODULE 2
    c. MODULE 3
    d. MODULE 4

7. What can you *not* do from FCONSOLE?
    a. Load a VAP
    b. Down the file server
    c. Clear a connection
    d. View Hot Fix statistics

Chapter 9: NetWare 2.2 Advanced System Manager

8. Which function of FCONSOLE can be performed only by a supervisor equivalent?

    a. Clear a connection

    b. Down the file server

    c. Reset the file server time

    d. All of the above

    e. A & B

9. In which FCONSOLE screen can you find Hot Fix information?

    a. CACHE STATISTICS

    b. SUMMARY

    c. DISK STATISTICS

    d. LAN I/O STATISTICS

10. In which FCONSOLE screen can you best see memory performance?

    a. CACHE STATISTICS

    b. SUMMARY

    c. DISK STATISTICS

    d. LAN I/O STATISTICS

11. In which FCONSOLE screen can you see Dynamic Memory Pool Maximums and Peak Used?

    a. CACHE STATISTICS

    b. SUMMARY

    c. DISK STATISTICS

    d. LAN I/O STATISTICS

Review Questions

12. Which Dynamic Memory Pool is responsible for File Handles?

    a. Dynamic Memory Pool 1

    b. Dynamic Memory Pool 2

    c. Dynamic Memory Pool 3

    d. Dynamic Memory Pool 4

13. Communication buffers also are known as:

    a. Routing buffers

    b. Communication cache

    c. Cache buffers

    d. Routing cache

14. Which dynamic memory pool can be decreased by limiting the number of drive mappings a user has?

    a. Dynamic Memory Pool 1

    b. Dynamic Memory Pool 2

    c. Dynamic Memory Pool 3

    d. Dynamic Memory Pool 4

15. Which dynamic memory pool is most affected by a large number of servers and routers?

    a. Dynamic Memory Pool 1

    b. Dynamic Memory Pool 2

    c. Dynamic Memory Pool 3

    d. Dynamic Memory Pool 4

Chapter 9: NetWare 2.2 Advanced System Manager

16. Which dynamic memory pool is responsible for file and record locks?

    a. Dynamic Memory Pool 1

    b. Dynamic Memory Pool 2

    c. Dynamic Memory Pool 3

    d. Dynamic Memory Pool 4

17. Which utility automatically copies the installation files from the disks to the network?

    a. UTILCOPY

    b. XCOPY/SUB

    c. UPDATE

    d. UPLOAD

18. Which module requires you to choose between Dedicated and Nondedicated mode for the file server?

    a. Operating System Generation

    b. Linking and Configuring

    c. Track Zero Test (ZTEST)

    d. File Server Definition

19. Which of the following is a true statement regarding VREPAIR.EXE?

    a. Two percent of the disk is set aside at installation to save files that have been repaired by running VREPAIR.

    b. VREPAIR is configured for the server's hardware options during the installation of NetWare 2.

    c. VREPAIR can be used to repair a single directory on a local disk.

    d. COMPSURF can be run in place of VREPAIR after a disk drive has been readied for NetWare installation.

Review Questions

20. Which of the following install options should you use if you are updating an existing NetWare 2.2 server?

    a. -C

    b. -M

    c. -F

    d. -U

21. Which of the install options should you use if you are updating an existing NetWare 2.x server to a 2.2 server?

    a. -C

    b. -M

    c. -F

    d. -U

22. Which of the following is *not* assumed when running the Basic Installation?

    a. Only one file server exists on this network.

    b. The file server has one parallel printer attached.

    c. The file server will be duplexed.

    d Only one network board is installed in this file server.

23. When is installing a nondedicated file server considered an advantage rather than a problem? (Mark only the two best answers.)

    a. When the system has five or fewer users

    b. When the file server disk will be accessed very little

    c. When the file server does not need to also be run as a workstation

    d. When only one person will be using this particular workstation as a workstation, even though the network has 20 or more users

Chapter 9: NetWare 2.2 Advanced System Manager

24. Which of the following tasks *cannot* be done using the FCONSOLE utility?

    a. Broadcast console messages

    b. Restart the install program to update the file server

    c. Purge all salvageable files

    d. Change from one file server to another

25. How can you determine if the hard disk on a network file server might be going bad and needs to be replaced?

    a. By checking the thrashing count parameter to see if it is near or above zero

    b. By looking at the number of Hot Fix blocks allocated when the system was generated

    c. If you see a steady decrease in the number of Hot Fix blocks remaining

    d. If users begin to complain about lack of disk storage space

Case Study

1. Figure out the memory requirements for the following scenarios by using the memory worksheet in this chapter. Determine if the file servers have enough memory. If you determine a need for more memory, state how much more is adequate.

Case Study

A. File Server #1
   OS: Nondedicated 50-user NetWare 2.2
   Hard Drive: One 300M hard disk
   Volumes: SYS: 255M and SYS1:45M
   SYS: 5,000 directory entries
   SYS1: 1,000 directory entries
   20 users
   20 open files per user
   NET$OS.EXE is 500K
   1 Ethernet Network Board

B. File Server #2
   OS: Dedicated 100-user NetWare 2.2
   Hard Drives: Two 300M hard disks
   Volumes: SYS: 255M, SYS1: 45M, SYS2: 255M, SYS3: 45M
   SYS: and SYS2: 4,000 directory entries each
   SYS1: and SYS3: 1,000 directory entries each
   40 users
   35 open files per user
   NET$OS.EXE is 500K
   6 indexed files
   One VAP using 100K
   2 Ethernet Network Boards

PART 4

NetWare 3.1x

Chapter 10
NetWare 3.1x Administration

Chapter 11
NetWare 3.1x Advanced System Manager

NetWare 3.1x Administration

Chapter 10 focuses on information specific to the basic NetWare 3.1x operating system. This chapter provides information about NetWare 3.1x from the perspective of the system administrator. The following items are discussed in this chapter:

- Hardware and software features
- Security
- File and directory attributes
- Workstation utilities
- Console commands
- NetWare loadable modules

Exploring NetWare 3.1x

File server requirements for NetWare 3.1x include the following:

- 80386- or 80486-compatible computer
- 4M of RAM (more for drives larger than 80M)
- 20M hard disk (minimum)
- 1.2M floppy drive

NetWare 3.1x offers the following five different user quantities:

- 5-user version
- 10-user version
- 20-user version (in NetWare 3.11)
- 25-user version (in NetWare 3.12)
- 50-user version
- 100-user version
- 250-user version
- 500-user version (NetWare 3.11 only)
- 1000-user version (NetWare 3.11 only)

The only difference in functionality between the user versions of v3.1x is the number of users that can access the file server at one time. This number is different from v2.15, in which connections such as VAPs stole available connections.

NetWare 3.1x enables you to use any 8086-compatible or better PC as a workstation. Keep in mind that 486 and 386 systems currently are the best for local processing, upon which NetWare relies heavily.

One major advantage to networking with v3.1x is the capability to communicate with multivendor computers.

TCP/IP and NFS connections are not possible with v2.2. This means that the v2.2 system is severely limited in the methods available to communicate with other computer systems.

NetWare 3.1x provides the means to communicate with diverse single- and multiple-user systems. V3.1x is a corporate solution;

its networking features work for the entire company as opposed to a single workgroup within the company.

NetWare 3.1x su pports the following operating systems and environments:

- DOS
- OS/2
- Windows
- Macintosh
- UNIX
- OSI

NetWare 3.1x is far more advanced than v2.2 in its maximum limitations for hardware and services. Table 10.1 is a list of specifications.

Several of these numbers are theoretical, because you reach hardware limitations before NetWare limitations. As soon as hardware vendors catch up and can provide more slots, more unique hardware addresses, and more storage capabilities, these maximums will become practical instead of theoretical.

Table 10.1
NetWare 3.1x Specification List

Specification	Maximum
User connections per server depending on version	Up to 1,000
Simultaneous open files per server	100,000

continues

Chapter 10: NetWare 3.1*x* Administration

Table 10.1, Continued
NetWare 3.1x Specification List

Specification	Maximum
Simultaneous TTS transactions	10,000
Hard drives per server	2,048
Maximum disk storage	32T
Hard drives per volume	32
Volumes per file server	64
Largest volume	32T
Directory entries per volume	2,097,152
Largest file	4G
Maximum RAM on file server	4G

In Chapter 8, you learned the way in which NetWare uses System Fault Tolerance features. These features are offered in v3.1*x* as well as v2.2. Each of these processes, however, has been improved. NetWare 3.1*x* uses directory caching and hashing. *Directory caching* can reduce the response time of disk I/O by 30 percent. *File caching* can be up to 100 times faster than accessing a file on hard disk.

 In NetWare 3.12, file access speed has been increased by the addition of a feature called *cache read ahead*, which reads more information into memory at a single time than could be read in with NetWare 3.11.

Elevator seeking has been improved for performance. UPS monitoring is done by loading an NLM and is configured by using the LOAD UPS and UPS TIME console commands.

Elevator seeking is used because data is not stored sequentially on a hard drive. *Elevator seeking* is an algorithm that eliminates disk thrashing and excessive seeks.

An additional enhancement is the capability for the server to dynamically configure memory. NetWare 3.1*x* does not require the installer to allocate memory for different services. The NetWare operating system can allocate memory for a process and, in many cases, release it back to the server when the memory is no longer needed. This process is covered in greater detail in Chapter 11.

Understanding NetWare 3.1*x* Security

NetWare 3.1*x* adds several features to the security concepts you learned about in the preceding chapters. The most obvious changes are found when you compare the trustee rights and attributes of v2.2 and v3.1*x*.

NetWare 3.1*x* has improved the way passwords are handled. Passwords now are encrypted at the workstation before they go onto the cable. This procedure prevents anyone from tapping into the cable, extracting a packet, and viewing an unencrypted password.

NetWare Core Protocol (NCP) Packet Signature also has been added to NetWare 3.1*x*. *NCP Packet Signature* is a security enhancement for NetWare 3.1*x* servers and clients that prevents people from forging packet identifications. NCP Packet Signature is built into the NetWare 3.12 operating system and client software, and can be added to NetWare 3.11 systems. Chapter 7 discusses NCP Packet Signature in more detail.

NetWare 3.1*x* adds the following features:

- ◆ Trustee rights can be granted to files as well as to directories.
- ◆ Attributes can be added to directories as well as to files.

User Rights

The rights a user or group has in a directory or on a file are called *trustee rights*. Eight trustee rights exist in v3.1*x*. Trustee rights are the keys each user has for a directory or file.

NetWare 3.1*x* also has replaced the concept of v2.2's Maximum Rights Mask with the *Inherited Rights Mask (IRM)*. The IRM is a filter. Each directory has an IRM that allows all rights to flow through to subdirectories. The system administrator can change the IRM to allow only certain rights to flow down to subsequent subdirectories. This change can be made by using the ALLOW command or the FILER menu utility, which are discussed later in this chapter.

You must remember the following rules when figuring the results of setting up an IRM:

1. IRMs only affect the rights that flow down from the directory above. If you are granted rights specifically through the GRANT command, FILER, or SYSCON, the IRM has no effect, because these rights do not flow down.

2. *Effective rights* equal trustee rights when the user has been given the rights in a directory explicitly. In other words, when you give the user rights in a directory, those rights become her effective rights, and the IRM has no effect.

3. When the user has the Supervisory right, the IRM has no effect. The *Supervisory* right, described in the next section, gives the user all rights to all subdirectories under the directory in which it was granted.

4. Every directory has a full set of rights in its IRM by default. When you change a directory's IRM, you do not affect the IRMs of any of that directory's subdirectories.

5. IRMs cannot add rights back for the user; the IRM can state only what rights are not allowed to flow from a parent directory.

NetWare security measures, from lowest to highest security, include the following:

- Login name
- Password
- Directory rights
- File rights
- Directory attributes
- File attributes

If a file is flagged Read Only and the directory or the file has the Erase right, the file cannot be deleted until the Read Only file attribute is changed to Read/Write.

The following rights are available to users:

- **Read.** When assigned to a directory, Read enables the user to see the contents of the files in the directory. The user can use or execute files in the directory.

    When assigned to a file, Read enables the user to see the contents of a closed file and to use or execute the file even if the directory does not allow the Read privilege.

- **Write.** When assigned to a directory, Write enables the user to alter the contents of files in the directory.

    When assigned to a file, Write enables the user to alter the contents of the file even when the Write privilege is not given to the directory.

Chapter 10: NetWare 3.1x Administration

In either case, the file must be flagged Read/Write for the Write privilege to have any effect.

- **Create.** When assigned to a directory, Create enables the user to make new files and directories.

  When assigned to a file, Create enables the user to salvage the file if it has been deleted.

- **Erase.** When assigned to a directory, Erase enables the user to delete existing files and directories.

  When assigned to a file, Erase allows the file to be deleted even if the directory does not have the Erase right.

  Files flagged as Read Only cannot be erased until they are flagged Read/Write.

- **File Scan.** When assigned to the directory, File Scan enables the user to view files and subdirectories in a directory. Without this right, you cannot see files.

  NetWare 3.1x hides subdirectories from the user when he does not possess this right.

  When assigned to a file, File Scan enables the user to view the file by using DIR. If the user does not have File Scan rights to other files, these files do not appear when the DIR command is issued.

If you grant the File Scan right to a file, users can see subdirectories all the way back to the root directory. They cannot see any files in these directories, however, unless they have rights to them.

- **Modify.** When assigned to the directory, Modify enables the user to change the attributes and names of subdirectories.

  When assigned to a file, Modify enables the user to change the attributes and the name of a file. This right enables the user to change a file from Read/Write to Read Only or from Nonshareable to Shareable.

- **Access Control.** When assigned to the directory, Access Control enables the user to give any of the preceding rights to other users on the network.

Access Control does not enable you to assign the Supervisory right. You must be the Supervisor, a supervisor equivalent, or a workgroup manager with the Supervisory right to the directory in which rights are assigned.

When assigned to a file, Access Control enables the user to give any of the preceding rights to another network user.

- **Supervisory.** When assigned to a directory, Supervisory gives all the other rights to the user or group. This right makes the user a *directory supervisor*, someone who has control over what happens to a branch of the directory structure.

    When assigned to a file, Supervisory enables the user to have all rights to that file.

Combining IRMs and Trustee Rights

Now that you understand what Trustee rights can accomplish and how the IRM affects the outcome of flow through, the next step is to take a look at combining trustee rights and IRMs.

The following example uses this directory structure:

Chapter 10: NetWare 3.1x Administration

The following IRMs and rights have been assigned:

IRMs:

SYS:	[SRWCEMFA]
SYS:APPS	[SR F]
SYS:APPS\ACCT	[SRWCEMFA]
SYS:DOCS	[SRWC F]
SYS:DOCS\JUNE	[SRWCE F]

DAVE has the following rights:

SYS:APPS\ACCT	[RWCE F]
SYS:DOCS	[S]

BEV has the following rights:

SYS:	[R F]
SYS:DOCS	[RWCEMFA]

PAULETTE has the following rights:

SYS:	[S]

The following is a list of rights each user has based on the rules stated in the preceding section on IRMs.

DAVE

SYS:	[ ] Rule #1
SYS:APPS	[ ] Rule #1
SYS:APPS\ACCT	[RWCE F] Rule #2
SYS:DOCS	[SRWCEMFA] Rule #3
SYS:DOCS\JUNE	[SRWCEMFA] Rule #3

BEV

    SYS: [R   F]
                                 Rule #2

    SYS:APPS   [R   F]
                                 Rule #1

    SYS:APPS\ACCT   [R   F]
                               Rule #5

    SYS:DOCS   [RWCEMFA]
                               Rule #2

    SYS:DOCS\JUNE   [RWCE F]
                             Rule #1

PAULETTE

    SYS: [SRWCEMFA]
                               Rule #3

    SYS:APPS   [SRWCEMFA]
                             Rule #3

    SYS:APPS\ACCT   [SRWCEMFA]
                             Rule #3

    SYS:DOCS   [SRWCEMFA]
                             Rule #3

    SYS:DOCS\JUNE   [SRWCEMFA]
                             Rule #3

Understanding Attributes

On the network, files are secured by the use of *attributes*, conditions placed on the files. These conditions help to control what can be done to the files and the ways in which the files can be used on the network. Many combinations of attributes are attached to files and directories. This section discusses NetWare attributes and how you can use them on your network.

Archive Needed

NetWare uses the letter A to signify files that have been altered since the last backup. The Archive Needed attribute also is assigned to files that have been copied into another directory. Archive Needed looks for the DOS Archive Bit flag on a file.

Execute Only

Execute Only is designated with the letter X. After this attribute is placed on a file, it cannot be removed. This attribute affects only files ending in COM or EXE and is the only attribute that you cannot reverse.

 Only users with Supervisor privileges can assign the Execute Only attribute.

Execute Only prevents files from being copied or downloaded to prevent application piracy.

Make sure that you have a copy of a file before you attach the Execute Only flag, because this attribute also prevents files from being backed up. In addition, many programs cannot run when flagged with Execute Only.

Hidden File

The Hidden File attribute uses the letter H. Files hidden with this attribute do not show up when you use the DOS DIR command. If a user has the File Scan right, files hidden with this attribute appear.

Read Audit and Write Audit

NetWare still is in the process of perfecting a built-in audit trail on files. Currently, you can flag files with Ra for Read Audit and Wa for Write Audit, but they have no effect.

Read Only and Read/Write

You cannot write to, delete, or rename a read-only file. The Read Only attribute enables users to read and use files. Program files usually are flagged with Ro for Read Only.

A Read/Write file enables users to read from the file and write back to the file. This attribute is designated with Rw and is the default on newly created files. If you flag a file with Read Only, the Read/Write attribute is deleted. Data files usually are flagged with Read/Write.

Read Only includes the attributes of Delete Inhibit and Rename Inhibit.

Shareable and Nonshareable

NetWare uses the letter S to show shareable files. This attribute enables several users to access a single file at the same time. This flag is used most often with Read Only files and database files.

Nonshareable, or Normal, is the system default. If you flag a file with N, you set the attributes as Nonshareable Read/Write. Nonshareable files are assigned normally to program files that are single-user applications. This attribute ensures that only one person can use the file at any one time.

System File

System files, flagged with Sy, are not listed when you use the DOS DIR command. These files cannot be deleted or copied. If you have the File Scan right, you can see these files by using the NDIR command.

Transactional

Files marked with T can be tracked with the Transaction Tracking System (TTS). All database files that need to be tracked while being modified should have this attribute.

The Indexed attribute is used in v2.2 only.

In v3.1*x*, data files that use more than 64 regular *File Allocation Table blocks* (FAT blocks) are automatically assigned the Indexed attribute, which increases the access time for the file. The attribute can be assigned to smaller files, but it has no real effect.

Copy Inhibit

Marked as a C, Copy Inhibit prevents files from being copied to another directory. This attribute is used only with Macintosh files.

Delete Inhibit

The Delete Inhibit attribute is one half of the Read Only file designation. Rename Inhibit represents the other half of Read Only. The Delete Inhibit flag, marked as a D, prevents files from being deleted.

Rename Inhibit

Along with Delete Inhibit, Rename Inhibit is the second Read Only attribute. Marked as an R, Rename Inhibit prevents users from renaming files.

Purge

Purge uses the letter P to show files considered purged when deleted. If you mark a file with the P flag, you ensure that it cannot be restored after it is deleted.

Using Directory Attributes

You also can use attributes on directories. The attributes discussed in the following sections can be used on directories in NetWare.

Hidden Directory

The Hidden Directory attribute uses the letter H. Directories hidden with this attribute do not show up when you use the DOS DIR command. If a user has the File Scan right, files hidden with this attribute appear.

System Directory

System directories, designated with Sy, are hidden from the DOS DIR command. These directories cannot be deleted or copied. If a user has the File Scan right, these directories appear when using the NDIR utility.

Purge Directory

This attribute uses the letter P to show directories in which all files are considered purged when deleted. This flag ensures that after the directory is deleted, any files in the directory cannot be restored.

Using NetWare 3.1*x* Documentation

As a system administrator, you need to know where to find information about the NetWare 3.1*x* operating system. Novell provides many manuals with NetWare 3.1*x*. You should be familiar with five books and with Novell's ElectroText. The five books include the following:

- *NetWare Concepts.* This book is the most interesting of all the manuals. In the *Concepts* manual, you find definitions and examples of the key features in NetWare 3.1*x*.

- *Utilities Reference.* This book contains information about the NetWare 3.1*x* command-line utilities and menu utilities provided with the operating system.

- *Installation.* This book describes the process of installing and upgrading to a NetWare 3.1*x* network. You also find information about setting up the network for users and login script commands.

- *System Administration.* This book contains information about file server utilities, troubleshooting, and maintenance.

- *Print Server.* This book covers network printing utilities, setting up a print server, and troubleshooting network printing.

Novell ElectroText is an electronic method of distributing Novell's documentation. ElectroText is available with NetWare 3.12, and is distributed on CD-ROM. ElectroText is graphical-based and runs only on MS Windows clients. During installation, a file called ET.INI is copied to the Windows client directory in order to support ElectroText.

ElectroText consists of a *search engine* that enables you to search for and find information and an electronic set of manuals called a "bookshelf."

Novell's NetWare 3.12 ElectroText includes three components:

- **Library Window**. This window enables you to choose the book that you want to read.
- **Book Window**. This window shows you the table of contents and text for the book you chose.
- **Search Window**. This window enables you to select a word or phrase to search for within the book.

To install the ElectroText, you need a minimum of 30M of extra disk space. The program that runs ElectroText, ET.EXT, is installed to the SYS:PUBLIC directory, and the books are installed into a directory called DOC.

Understanding Workstation Utilities

NetWare 3.1*x* does not use some utilities found in many previous versions of NetWare. Several new utilities were added, but the bulk of the utilities remain the same in NetWare 3.1*x*.

The following utilities (defined in Chapter 9) can be found in earlier versions of NetWare, but are not included in NetWare 3.1*x*:

    HIDEFILE, SHOWFILE

    HOLDON, HOLDOFF

Chapter 10:   NetWare 3.1x Administration

> LARCHIVE, LRESTORE
>
> NARCHIVE, NRESTORE
>
> MACBACK
>
> MAIL
>
> NSNIPES
>
> PSTAT

The following sections outline the utilities added to NetWare 3.1x:

ACONSOLE

This command is part of the remote management provided by NetWare 3.1x. ACONSOLE is used for an asynchronous link to a remote server. You learn more about this feature in Chapter 11.

ADMIN

The ADMIN utility is used to add and manage mail user accounts and to maintain mail distribution lists. This utility is part of the Basic MHS (Message Handling Service) that Novell has added to NetWare 3.12 to provide an entry-level mail solution for small (single-server) networks.

> **Note** Before running ADMIN.EXE at the workstation, run the Btrieve Requester (BREQUEST.EXE). The Btrieve Requester is an important requirement for running ADMIN.

If your network has 25 or fewer users, Basic MHS is an effective way to establish communication among users across the network. As your network grows, Basic MHS can be upgraded to Global MHS.

Understanding Workstation Utilities

When you start ADMIN.EXE, the first screen that appears is the Admin Functions screen. The ADMIN utility enables you to accomplish the following tasks:

- Create new users. If you use the ADMIN utility to create new users, however, a HOME data directory is not created for them.
- Modify or delete existing user accounts.
- Create, modify, or delete mail distribution lists.
- Register electronic mail applications that are allowed to use Basic MHS.
- Modify the Basic MHS system configuration.

Although Basic MHS provides the background functionality of mail services in a small network environment, the actual interface is called First Mail. To start First Mail, type **MAIL** at a DOS prompt, and press Enter. First Mail enables you to do the following:

- Send messages to users
- Send messages to a list for distribution
- Add an attachment to the message you are sending
- Read your messages

ALLOW

The ALLOW command enables the system administrator to modify an IRM. The following example illustrates the way in which this command is used:

```
ALLOW path\filename rightslist
```

The *rightslist* is a list of the first initials of each right. If, for example, you want to set the IRM to allow only Read and File Scan for the directory SYS:APPS\ACCT, you type the following:

```
F:>ALLOW SYS:APPS\ACCT R F
```

You also can use the parameters ALL or N for No rights in place of the *rightslist*.

 Remember that you cannot add the Supervisory right with the ALL command, nor can you deny the Supervisory command by using the N flag. The Supervisory right always is in place.

CHKDIR

CHKDIR is used to view information about a volume or directory. CHKDIR displays space limitations for the file server, volume, and directory you are checking.

This command displays the maximum storage capacity of a volume or directory if a space limitation has been placed on it. CHKDIR is a useful utility for determining the amount of free space available in a directory.

If space limitations are placed on users, the CHKDIR utility enables them to keep track of the amount of space they have left. To use CHKDIR, simply enter the command by itself or enter the command and the path of the directory you want to check.

DSPACE

NetWare's DSPACE utility enables system administrators to place limits on the amount of disk space a particular user can use. DSPACE is designed to limit a user's personal use of disk space. Many network users assume that the file server has unlimited storage capacity. A knowledgeable computer user easily can use a large amount of disk space. When used properly, DSPACE can limit a user's available space without jeopardizing normal network operations. Figure 10.1 shows the opening screen of the DSPACE utility.

Understanding Workstation Utilities

The DSPACE utility provides the following options:

- Limit users' disk space
- Limit disk and directory space
- Change current file server

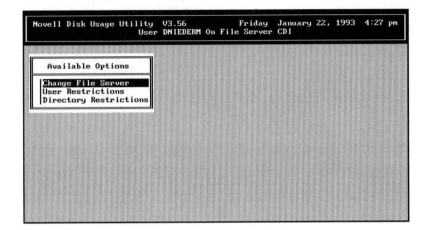

Figure 10.1
The DSPACE utility's opening screen.

To limit disk space in a volume directory, select the Directory Restrictions option from the menu. Then select a directory and modify the field presented in the Directory Disk Space Limitation Information data entry box (see fig. 10.2). If you do not have rights to modify this directory area, the DSPACE utility does not provide you with modifiable fields.

To limit a user's space on a disk drive, select the User Restrictions option from the DSPACE main menu (see fig. 10.1). After selecting a user, a list of available volumes appears. You are presented with the User Disk Space Limitation Information screen (see fig. 10.3) if you have the proper rights.

In figures 10.2 and 10.3, the user SUPERVISOR has no restrictions. To limit disk space, you must answer Yes to Limit Space, then fill in the memory limit.

445

Chapter 10: NetWare 3.1x Administration

Figure 10.2
Directory Disk Space Limitation Information data entry box.

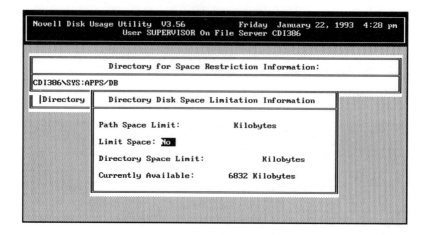

Figure 10.3
User Disk Space Limitation screen.

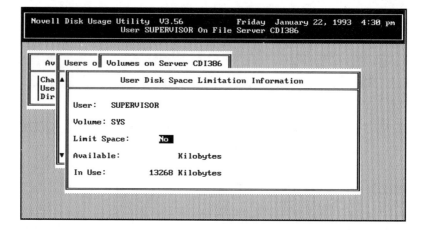

MIGRATE

NetWare 3.12 includes the MIGRATE.EXE utility, which enables you to upgrade an existing NetWare network to NetWare 3.12. It is run from a client attached to a network.

By using the MIGRATE utility, you can perform an *across-the-wire* migration (which upgrades a NetWare server running an earlier version of NetWare from another NetWare server running NetWare 3.12) or a *same-server* migration (which updates the existing pre-NetWare 3.12 server to a NetWare 3.12 server).

Understanding Workstation Utilities

If you run the across-the-wire version of the MIGRATE utility, you must have an existing NetWare 3.12 server (called the source server). An across-the-wire migration follows these general steps:

1. The old bindery information on the *source* server (the server running the previous version of NetWare) is copied to a DOS client.

2. At the DOS client, the old bindery information is updated to v3.12.

3. NetWare 3.12 is installed on another server (the *destination* server).

4. The updated bindery information is migrated from the DOS client to the NetWare 3.12 server.

With an across-the-wire migration, users' trustee assignments also can be migrated to the new NetWare 3.12 server.

If you run the same-server version of the MIGRATE utility, you upgrade the bindery and related files. A same-server migration follows these general steps:

1. A backup is performed on the server running the older version of NetWare.

2. MIGRATE.EXE is run to migrate the bindery information to a working directory on a network client.

3. NetWare 3.12 then is installed on the server running the older version of NetWare.

4. The backup is restored to the server that now is a NetWare 3.12 server.

5. The MIGRATE utility is run and the bindery information that was restored to the new NetWare 3.12 server is migrated.

NMENU

NMENU.BAT is the file that executes the menu program that is new to NetWare 3.12. This utility is a modified version of the

Saber menuing utility. As such, it provides many enhancements in menu design and creation. One of the best reasons for using this newer menu utility, however, is its capability to be unloaded from memory while it is executing a menu option, thus leaving more memory for application execution.

More information about the new NetWare 3.12 menuing system is provided in Chapter 7, "Customizing the User's Environment."

RCONSOLE

Although many of the familiar FCONSOLE functions are no longer available when used on the 3.1x file server, Novell provides a workstation connection through RCONSOLE that enables system administrators to access the MONITOR and other console utilities. RCONSOLE enables system utilities and CONSOLE operations that normally require direct console access from the workstation.

The RCONSOLE utility requires two NLMs to be loaded at the file server. Both REMOTE.NLM and RSPX.NLM must be loaded on any 3.1x file server that requires access by the RCONSOLE utility. After selecting the file server from the list provided and typing in your password, you are presented with a connection to the file server console. You learn more about RCONSOLE in Chapter 11.

UPGRADE

The UPGRADE utility enables the installer to upgrade versions of NetWare from v2.0a to v2.2 to v3.1x.

In NetWare 3.12, an in-place upgrade is provided that upgrades a NetWare 3.x server to a NetWare 3.12 server. The *in-place upgrade* upgrades the current file system, then installs the new operating system. VAPs, core printing services, and volume and disk restrictions, however, are not upgraded to NetWare 3.12 with the in-place upgrade.

Understanding Workstation Utilities

Modified Utilities

The following utilities exist in previous NetWare versions, but have changed noticeably in NetWare 3.1x.

SALVAGE

In v3.1x, SALVAGE is much more sophisticated than in previous versions. From the main menu, users can view or recover files, choose a directory, or set the viewing options (see fig. 10.4). Users must have the Create right before they can retrieve a file by using SALVAGE.

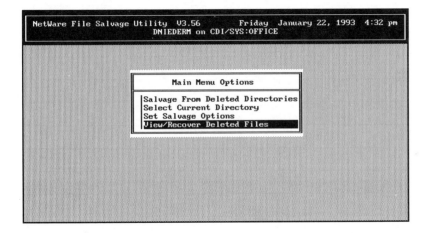

Figure 10.4
The v3.1x SALVAGE Main Menu Options screen.

Files retrieved using SALVAGE are placed back into the directory from which they were deleted. If a file with the same name already exists, the system prompts you to rename the file being salvaged. Files are tracked by date and time, so several versions of the same file name can accumulate. NetWare does not keep track of deleted directories, but the program does track the files in deleted directories. When you are salvaging files from a deleted directory, the files are restored to a hidden directory called DELETED.SAV. Although you do not see this directory, one exists on every volume. Supervisors can use the DOS CD command to make DELETED.SAV the current directory.

449

Chapter 10: NetWare 3.1x Administration

SALVAGE also enables the user to choose specific file names to view (see fig. 10.5). Each file shown in the resulting list has been deleted, but the directories still exist. The directories display so that you can change directories from this screen. If you press Enter with a file highlighted, you are shown when the file was deleted, when it was modified prior to deletion, who owned it, and who deleted it. At this time, you can restore the file by answering Yes at the Recover This File menu (see fig. 10.6).

Figure 10.5
Specifying the files to view.

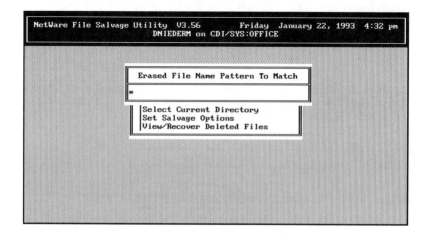

Figure 10.6
Preparing to restore a deleted file.

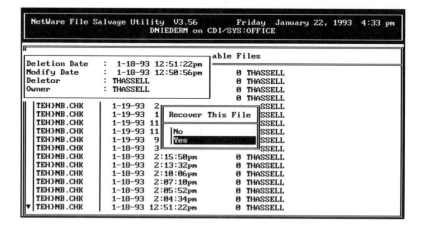

Understanding Workstation Utilities

You can use F5, F6, F7, and F8 to mark and unmark patterns of files for restoring or purging. When you press Del with a file highlighted, NetWare purges the file from the list (see fig. 10.7). When you purge a file, it cannot be retrieved under any circumstances.

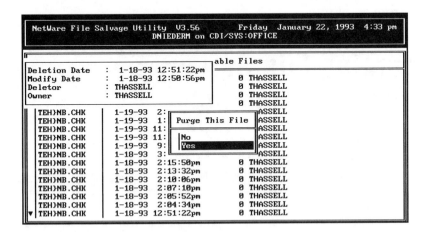

Figure 10.7
Purging a deleted file.

When preparing to view a list of files that can be salvaged, you can sort by deletion date, deletor, file size, or file name (the default). These options are on the Salvage Options menu (see fig. 10.8).

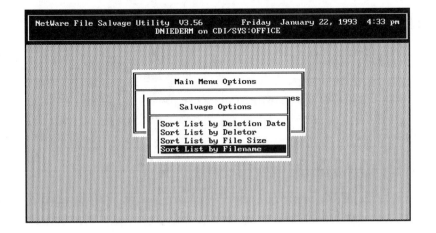

Figure 10.8
The Salvage Options menu.

451

Files can be salvaged as long as the files and the directory are not marked with a P (for Purge) and the system has enough room. As room is needed on the server's hard drive, the oldest files are removed from SALVAGE.

The DOS PURGE /ALL command also clears out all salvageable files from a volume.

Learning File Server Console Commands

NetWare 3.1x has more console commands than v2.2. In this section, you are introduced to several commands that work at the file server's prompt, which is the colon (:). Many of these commands are explored in depth in Chapter 11.

ABORT REMIRROR

This NetWare 3.12 console command enables you to stop the remirroring of a logical disk partition.

ADD NAME SPACE *name* TO VOLUME *volume*

This command enables you to store non-DOS files on a NetWare volume. The following name spaces are available: MAC, OS2, NFS, and FTAM.

BIND, UNBIND

The BIND command attaches the desired protocol to the network board through which it is expected to communicate. The protocol is usually IPX for pure Novell Networks, but other protocols, such as IP, can be bound to the board. The parameters are used to tell the network about the hardware and configuration settings for each board. If you do not state the driver or protocol parameters when binding the board, you are prompted for the necessary information.

The UNBIND statement releases the protocol from the board, and memory used by this process is returned to the server.

Use the following syntax for these commands:

BIND *protocol* **TO** *board_name parameters*
BIND *protocol* TO *LAN_driver* [*driver_parameters*] *protocol parameters*
UNBIND *protocol* **FROM** *LAN_driver* **or** *board_name*

CLS

This command, as well as OFF, clears the screen of any accrued messages.

ENABLE TTS, DISABLE TTS

These commands tell the network to start or stop using the Transaction Tracking System.

DISPLAY NETWORKS

This command shows all known network numbers, including cable numbers, as well as v3.*x* internal IPX numbers.

Internal IPX numbers are used only with NetWare 3.*x*. This number is set when installing NetWare and should be unique for all file servers. The internal IPX number allows multiple NLMs to communicate within a single server.

Chapter 10: NetWare 3.1x Administration

You also see a fractional number displayed after the network address. This number signifies the number of hops and ticks necessary to reach that board.

Hops are the number of network boards that must be crossed to reach the destination from the server where the command was issued.

Ticks are the amount of time it takes a packet to reach the destination. One tick is equal to 1/18th of a second.

Figure 10.9 shows 21 unique network addresses on the internetwork. The addresses CDB, CDBA, and BAC all have a hop and tick count of 0/1. These addresses are for the server on which DISPLAY NETWORKS was executed. This server is running NetWare 3.1x, so you can deduce that this server is displaying numbers for two network boards and an internal IPX number.

Figure 10.9

Viewing the effects of DISPLAY SERVERS and DISPLAY NETWORKS.

```
:display servers
    A386           0    A386           1    A386           1    A40            1
    A40            1    B386           1    B386           2    B386           2
    B40            1    B40            1    BART           1    BART           1
    BART           1    CBT            2    CBT            3    CDADS          1
    CDADS          1    CDADS          1    CDBF           2    CDBF           2
    CDI            2    CDI            3    CDI            3    CDI1           3
    CDI_ACCESS     1    CDI_NACS       1    CPNETAV_8295   2    CPNETAV_8295   3
    CPNETAV_8295   2    CPNETAV_8295   2    CPNETAV_8295   2    CRIS           2
    CRIS           2    D386           1    D386           2    D386           2
    FAX1           2    MASTER_CPNET   2    MERLIN         1    MERLIN         2
    MERLIN         2    MHS            3    NORTH386       1    NORTH386       2
    NORTH386       2    PS-B40         1    PSB386         2    PSD386         2
    PSNORTH386     2    merlin         2
There are 50 known servers
:display networks
    00000003   2/3    00000005   1/2    00000020   2/3    00000022   2/3
    000000AB   1/2    000000FE   2/3    00000100   2/3    000000ACE  2/3
    00000BAC   0/1    00000CDA   0/1    00000CDC   1/2    00000CDD   1/2
    00002EE2   1/2    0000CDBA   1/2    0000CDDA   1/2    00BAC802   1/2
    00CDA386   0/1    00CDB802   1/2    00CDC802   1/2    00CDDB02   1/2
    2BEE6B8C   1/2    2C7D2AFB   1/2    A1100001   1/2    FEFEFEFE   1/2
There are 24 known networks
:
```

DISPLAY SERVERS

This command displays the names of any file server processes that the network is aware of, as well as a hop count. File server processes are services that various file servers on the network have to offer. Print servers show up as server processes, as do some third-party NLMs.

 If volume SYS: is not mounted, the file server does not appear in the DISPLAY NETWORKS list.

EXIT

The EXIT command takes the file server back to the DOS prompt after the DOWN command has been issued.

DOWN

The DOWN command ensures that all files have been properly closed and everything stored in memory is written to the hard drive. When the server is rebooted, FAT and DET tables are replaced in memory.

LIST DEVICES

This NetWare 3.12 console command displays information about devices loaded on the server.

LOAD *path* NLM *parameter*

This command is used to initiate an NLM. The *path* is necessary only if the NLM does not appear in the SYS:SYSTEM directory and you have not used the SEARCH command to direct the system to look in the directory where the NLM resides.

UNLOAD releases the NLM, and memory used by the NLM is returned to the server.

MAGAZINE

This NetWare 3.12 console command is used to verify that magazine requests from the server have been satisfied or to see that they have not been satisfied, if that is the case.

MEDIA

This NetWare 3.12 console command is used to verify whether media requests made by the server have been met.

MEMORY

This command displays the total amount of memory in the file server.

MIRROR STATUS

This NetWare 3.12 console command is used to display all mirrored logical partitions and to see the status of each of these partitions.

MODULES

This command displays all the currently active NLMs that have been loaded onto the file server.

PROTOCOL

This command lists each protocol loaded onto the server along with the packet frame type the protocol uses.

REGISTER MEMORY

This command is used on ISA machine architectures that have more than 16M of RAM in the file server. Microchannel and EISA computers do this automatically.

REMIRROR PARTITION

This NetWare 3.12 command starts the remirroring of a logical partition that has been stopped with the ABORT REMIRROR command.

REMOVE DOS

This command prevents the file server from returning to the DOS prompt after the DOWN command is typed. A small amount of memory is returned back to the file server. This command also forces a reboot after DOWN is issued.

RESET ROUTER

This command forces the internal routing table to be updated in the file server.

SCAN FOR NEW DEVICES

This NetWare 3.12 command checks for hardware that has been added since the server was last booted. Running this command lets the server recognize any newly added disk hardware without having to reboot the server. Rebooting the server automatically performs a scan for devices.

SEARCH

The SEARCH ADD *number path* and the SEARCH DEL *number* commands add and delete paths that the file server uses when looking for NLMs. The number is used to set priority levels for searching. Search #1 is the first path searched, #2 is the second path searched, and so on. The path must include the volume name.

SECURE CONSOLE

This command is used to protect your file server from sabotage. Five security measures are taken when SECURE CONSOLE is used at the file server. These measures include the following:

1. REMOVE DOS is executed so that when the file server is downed, the DOS prompt is not available, which protects the DOS partition.

2. All users except FCONSOLE operators are prevented from changing the time and date on the file server, which protects the integrity of Intruder Detection Lockout.

3. Entry into the OS debugger is prevented. The OS debugger is useful if the server crashes. It enables you to dump the contents of the memory registers for evaluation of what was happening when the server crashed.

4. The SEARCH command is disabled so that NLMs only run from the SYS:SYSTEM directory.

5. The copying of NLMs into the SYS:SYSTEM directory is limited only to those who have rights to the SYS:SYSEM directory.

The only way to remove the effects of SECURE CONSOLE is to down the file server and reboot. Make sure that SECURE CONSOLE is not in the AUTOEXEC.NCF configuration file. This file is explored further in Chapter 11.

SET

This command is used to display and change tunable file server parameters. In Chapter 11, you learn about several of the SET variables.

SET TIME ZONE

This parameter is used to synchronize internetworked servers that reside in different time zones.

SPEED

This parameter represents the relative speed of the file server. This number is useful only when comparing servers running the same version of NetWare.

VERSION

This command tells you what version of NetWare the file server is using and the copyright information.

VOLUMES

This command displays all mounted volumes on the file server.

Understanding NetWare Loadable Modules

Four different types of NetWare Loadable Modules (NLMs) are used. These modules, listed by their extensions, include the following:

- **NLM**. These modules usually are menu utilities and services that can be added to the file server. MONITOR.NLM, VREPAIR.NLM, and INSTALL.NLM are examples.

- **DSK**. These NLMs are disk drivers; they provide communication with the disk drives. DCB.DSK, ISADISK.DKS, and PS2ESDI.DSK are a few examples.

- **LAN**. These NLMs are LAN drivers. Loading one of these NLMs provides communication with the network boards. NE2000.LAN, TOKEN.LAN, and TRXNET.LAN are examples of LAN Driver NLMs.

- **NAM**. These NLMs add name space to a volume. There are four of these NLMs: MAC.NAM, OS2.NAM, NFS.NAM, and FTAM.NAM.

Review Questions

1. Which statement about NetWare 3.1x is false?

    a. NetWare 3.1x requires a minimum of 4M memory on the file server.

    b. NetWare 3.1x can run on an 80286 or better computer.

    c. You can have a hard drive as small as 20M for volume SYS.

    d. Workstations can be XTs.

2. Which workstation operating system is not available on NetWare 3.1x?

    a. UNIX

    b. OS/2

    c. CTOS

    d. Macintosh

Review Questions

3. Which statement about NetWare 3.1x maximums is true?

    a. NetWare 3.1x allows hard disk storage of up to 32T.

    b. The maximum amount of RAM on the file server is 16M.

    c. The maximum amount of open files is 1,000,000.

    d. The largest file allowed is 2.2G.

4. Which of the following is not a feature of NetWare 3.1x Security?

    a. Trustee rights

    b. File rights

    c. Directory attributes

    d. Maximum Rights Mask

5. Which statement about rights is incorrect?

    a. The C right enables you to create files and directories.

    b. The C right enables you to salvage a file.

    c. The M right enables you to rename a directory.

    d. The A right enables you to change a file from Ro to Rw.

6. Which of the following is the only attribute that cannot be revoked after it is granted?

    a. X

    b. H

    c. E

    d. SY

Chapter 10: NetWare 3.1x Administration

7. Which statement about attributes is false?

    a. The A attribute is assigned to files that are new or have just been copied to a new directory.

    b. Ra and Wa are not currently being used.

    c. Workgroup managers can assign the X attribute if they have the S right.

    d. C is used only with Macintosh.

8. To make sure that files are removed from the file server's memory when they are deleted, place this flag on the file or directory.

    a. P

    b. C

    c. M

    d. X

9. Which command displays the maximum storage capacity of a volume?

    a. CHKDIR

    b. CHKVOL

    c. DIRCHK

    d. VOLCHK

10. Which console command do you use to get the cable addresses of all known networks?

    a. DISPLAY ADDRESSES

    b. DISPLAY SERVERS

    c. DISPLAY NETWORKS

    d. DISPLAY NETNUMBER

Review Questions

11. Which console command prevents access into the OS debugger?

    a. REMOVE DOS

    b. REMOVE SERVER

    c. SECURE SERVER

    d. SECURE CONSOLE

12. Which of the following is not a type of NLM?

    a. DSK

    b. NAM

    c. NIC

    d. NLM

13. What feature of NetWare 3.12 increases access speed?

    a. Cache read ahead

    b. File buffers

    c. Disk hashing

    d. Maximum Rights Mask

14. The feature added to NetWare 3.1x that prevents people from forging packets is called:

    a. Inherited Rights Filter

    b. Internetwork Security Exchange

    c. NetWare Core Protocol

    d. Protocol Packet Protection

Chapter 10: NetWare 3.1x Administration

15. Which of the following utilities registers electronic mail applications for use with Basic MHS?

    a. BREQUEST

    b. ADMIN

    c. MAIL

    d. EMAIL

16. Which of the following is *not* one of the ElectroText windows:

    a. SEARCH

    b. BOOK

    c. BOOKCASE

    d. LIBRARY

17. If your network has 25 or fewer users, which of the following mail packages is recommended?

    a. ADMIN.EXE

    b. GLOBAL MHS

    c. ADMIN EMAIL

    d. BASIC MHS

18. Which of the following *cannot* be done using ADMIN.EXE?

    a. Modify Basic MHS configuration

    b. Delete user accounts

    c. Register electronic mail applications

    d. Send electronic mail messages

Review Questions

19. Which of the following programs enables you to send messages to other users?

    a. First Mail

    b. ADMIN.EXE

    c. BASICMHS.EXE

    d. GLOBLMHS.EXE

20. Which program enables you to upgrade an existing NetWare network to NetWare 3.1*x*?

    a. INSTALL.NLM

    b. MIGRATE.EXE

    c. BINDUPD.EXE

    d. UPGRADE.NLM

21. What is the main benefit of updating your existing NetWare menus to the new Saber-based menuing system?

    a. Menus have a better look.

    b. Menus can have more options.

    c. Menus can be unloaded from memory when running other menus.

    d. Menus can be limited to a single user.

22. Which of the following statements is *not* true about the inplace upgrade?

    a. Volume disk restrictions are upgraded.

    b. Printing services are not upgraded.

    c. The current file system is upgraded.

    d. A new version of the operating system is installed.

Chapter 10: NetWare 3.1x Administration

23. Which console command enables you to interrupt remirroring?

    a. REMIRROR INTERRUPT

    b. ABORT REMIRROR

    c. REMIRROR STOP

    d. STOP REMIRROR

24. Which console command enables you to restart remirroring?

    a. MIRROR STATUS

    b. REMIRROR PARTITION

    c. RESTART REMIRROR

    d. SET REMIRROR RESTART

Case Study

Using the directory structure described here, IRM assignments, rights assignments, and attribute assignments, answer the following questions.

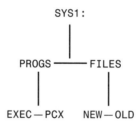

IRM Assignments:

```
SYS1:                      [ S      ]
SYS1:PROGS                 [ SR    F ]
SYS1:FILES                 [ SRWC  F ]
SYS1:FILES\NEW             [ SRWCE F ]
SYS1:FILES\OLD             [ SR    F ]
```

Case Study

TRUSTEE Assignments:

CHRIS

    SYS1:   [S   ]

JOE

    SYS1:FILES   [R   F]

    SYS1:PROGS   [RWCEMFA]

TERESA

    SYS1:FILES   [RWCEMFA]

    SYS1:FILES\OLD   [R   E F]

ATTRIBUTE Assignments:

SYS1:PROGS has been flagged DI and RI

1. Fill in the following form listing each user's effective rights in each directory.

	Sys1:	Sys1:Prog	Sys1:Prog/Exec	Sys1:Prog/PCX	Sys1:Files	Sys1:Files/New	Sys1:Files/Old
Chris							
Joe							
Teresa							

2. Who can delete files from the SYS1:PROGS directory? The SYS1:PROGS\PCX directory? The SYS1:FILES\OLD directory?

NetWare 3.1x Advanced System Manager

CHAPTER 11

This chapter focuses on advanced NetWare 3.1x features. In this chapter, you learn about the following topics:

- Protocol support
- ODI configuration files
- SBACKUP
- VREPAIR
- Memory management
- Remote capabilities
- NetWare Name Service
- NetWare 3.12 server and client installation and upgrade

Providing Protocol Support in NetWare 3.1x

Chapter 7 introduced you to the Open Data Link Interface (ODI), which provides a flexible, multiprotocol interface between the workstation and the Novell network. The Open Data Link puzzle has five pieces. These five pieces make up the capability to support multiple protocols, because you can change the pieces to fit your system's unique requirements.

- LAN adapter (Network Interface Board)
- LAN driver (Software driver for LAN Adapter)
- Link support layer (LSL)
- Protocol stack layer
- Protocol-independent services

In Chapter 7's discussion on loading the workstation ODI files, you learned that the first file loaded is LSL.COM. This file allows the network board to communicate with the desired protocol.

The next file loaded is a LAN driver or Multiple Link Interface Driver (MLID). The MLID reads the NET.CFG for configuration information. This step takes care of pieces one and two.

Next, load the protocol stack files such as IPXODI.COM or TCPIP.EXE. This step is piece number four.

Piece number five is the most diverse and represents utilities that can speak to the network boards regardless of which protocols are used. Examples of protocol-independent services are NETX for IPX networks, Apple FileTalk Protocol (AFP) for AppleTalk networks, or File Transport Protocol (FTP) for TCP/IP networks. NetWare 3.1x is considered a protocol-independent service.

Discovering Other Protocol Options

NetWare provides the capability to communicate with many protocols other than IPX. The following section discusses supported protocols and the methods used to implement them.

NetWare Requester for OS/2

OS/2 uses the High-Performance File System (HPFS) rather than FAT tables. OS/2 also uses long file names of up to 255 bytes and extended attributes that describe file names and values. NetWare Requester provides the support for OS/2 files on the NetWare network.

Transport Control Protocol/Internet Protocol (TCP/IP) and Network File System (NFS)

NetWare includes the capability to bind the Internet Protocol (IP) to network boards to communicate with UNIX client-host machines. Support files for TCP/IP are kept in the SYS:ETC directory. NetWare also includes Transport Control Protocol/Internet Protocol (TCP/IP) Network Loadable Modules (NLM). NetWare supports TCP/IP through these NLMs.

The Network File System (NFS) is another protocol used in conjunction with TCP/IP. Novell's NFS product allows full implementation of Sun Microsystems' NFS.

NetWare for Macintosh

NetWare 3.1*x* supports Macintosh workstations through NLMs that support AppleTalk Filing Protocol. This support allows Macintosh workstations to print, save files, and route through a NetWare 3.1*x* server.

Exploring the ODI Configuration Files

With standard NetWare protocols, two files are used to control the configurations of network software that runs on the PC. NET.CFG is the primary ODI configuration file.

SHELL.CFG is used to configure non-ODI drivers, but many of the SHELL.CFG parameters are applicable to ODI workstations as well. You can leave these parameters in the SHELL.CFG file or move them to NET.CFG.

These files are created by a text editor and must be located in the current directory when the network drivers are started.

NET.CFG Driver Configuration Options

When using ODI drivers, the driver configurations are controlled by entries in the NET.CFG file. This section outlines the LAN Driver parameters and their options in the NET.CFG file.

The NET.CFG file contains three major sections:

- The Link Driver section is used to configure the drivers associated with the network interface cards in the workstation. Some of these parameters control hardware functions; others control software functions.

- The Link Support section configures the link support layer of the network protocols. This layer is controlled by the ODI LSL program.

- The Protocol section determines which protocols are associated with each network interface card.

In addition, NET.CFG can contain any parameters that earlier driver versions placed in SHELL.CFG.

Table 11.1 shows the Link Driver hardware parameters. Each option is explained in detail after the table.

Table 11.1
Link Driver Hardware Options

Option
Link Driver *drivername*
CONNECTOR DIX
DMA *channel number*

Exploring the ODI Configuration Files

Option
INT *interrupt request number*
MEM *hex starting address [hex length]*
PORT *hex starting address [hex number of ports]*
NODE ADDRESS *hex address*
SLOT *number*

Link Driver *drivername*. This heading should start at the left margin in the NET.CFG file. The *drivername* is the name of the driver you are using. If you are using the NE2000.COM driver, for example, then your drivername is NE2000 and the Link Driver section looks like the following:

```
Link Driver NE2000
```

The following list defines the hardware options that you can use to configure the shell to the hardware settings on the network board. These options must be indented underneath the Link Driver statement.

- **CONNECTOR DIX.** This option is used only with 3Com's 3C503 network board for 3Com EtherLink Series II to change the connector type from thinnet BNC to thicknet DIX. The following example demonstrates the way to set a 3C503 board to use the DIX connector.

   ```
   Link Driver 3C503
        CONNECTOR DIX
   ```

- **DMA** *channel number*. If the network board you are using needs to be configured for Direct Memory Access (DMA), use this option. In the following example, a 3Com 3C505 card is configured to use channel 3.

   ```
   Link Driver 3C505
        DMA 3
   ```

- **INT** *interrupt request number.* This option is used to state the interrupt—often seen stated as IRQ or INT—that the network board uses. The following example shows the way to set an ARCnet board to interrupt 5 using the TRXNET driver.

  ```
  Link Driver TRXNET
       INT 5
  ```

- **MEM** *hex starting address.* This option is used to specify the memory range that the network board is configured to use. This number should be entered as a hex value. The following example demonstrates the way to set an ARCnet board to use the hex memory address of D000.

  ```
  Link Driver TRXNET
       MEM D000
  ```

- **PORT** *hex starting address.* This option is used to specify the I/O port address that the network board is configured to use. This number should be entered as a hex value. The following example shows the way to set an Ethernet board to use the hex port address of 300.

  ```
  Link Driver NE1000
       PORT 300
  ```

- **NODE ADDRESS** *hex address.* Some network boards allow the hardware address to be set in the NET.CFG file. The NODE ADDRESS option enables you to define the hex address. The following example shows the way to set a Novell Ethernet NE2100 board to use the address of 22A31.

  ```
  Link Driver NE2100
       NODE ADDRESS 22A31
  ```

- **SLOT** *number.* When using a network board in a slot-based machine, the driver attempts to locate boards by scanning the slots from the lowest to highest. This option speeds up the process by telling the driver in which slot to look for the board. In the following example, you learn to set a Novell Ethernet NE/2 board to use slot 3.

  ```
  Link Driver NE2
       SLOT 3
  ```

Exploring the ODI Configuration Files

Table 11.2 shows the Link Driver software parameters and the default options. These options are used to configure the shell to the hardware settings on the network board. Each option is explained in detail after the chart. These options must be indented beneath the Link Driver statement.

Table 11.2
Link Driver Software Options

Option	Defaults
ALTERNATE	
FRAME *frame type*	
LINK STATIONS *number*	1
MAX FRAME SIZE *number*	
PROTOCOL *name hex protocol ID frame type*	
SAPS *number*	1

- **ALTERNATE.** This option is used only with the LANSUP driver for IBM LAN Support, the TOKEN driver for IBM Token-Ring, or the PCN2L driver for the IBM PC Network II and II/A. It is used when you want the driver to use a network board other than the primary network board. The following example shows the PCN2L driver configured to use the secondary board.

```
Link Driver PCN2l
     ALTERNATE
```

- **FRAME *frame type*.** This option is used to enable multiple frame types for network boards. This option works only if the network board supports multiple frame types. Ethernet drivers default to ETHERNET_802.3 frames. Other options include: ETHERNET_802.2, ETHERNET_II, and ETHERNET_SNAP. Token-Ring drivers default to TOKEN-RING frames, but can support TOKEN-RING_SNAP as well. ARCnet supports only one frame type, NOVELL_RX-NET.

The following example shows the way to use both the ETHERNET_II and the ETHERNET_802.3 frames with an NE2000 driver.

```
Link Driver NE2000
     FRAME ETHERNET_II
     FRAME ETHERNET_802.3
```

- **LINK STATIONS** *number*. This option is only used with the LANSUP driver for IBM LAN support. Set LINK STATIONS to allow for all applications using the IBM LAN Support Program.

- **MAX FRAME SIZE** *number*. This option enables you to set the maximum number of bytes that the LAN driver can put onto the network cable at one time. This option is used only with the LANSUP driver for IBM LAN Support or the TOKEN driver for IBM Token-Ring. The default size for TOKEN is 4216 bytes; however, if the board has 8K of shared RAM available, the default size is 2168. Use the following formula to figure the number:

    number of bytes for the data packet (1, 2, 4, or 8K)
    plus 6 bytes for adapter overhead
    plus the largest possible header (currently 114 bytes)

  This number needs to be a multiple of eight. If 4K packets are used, this number is 4096+6+114, or 4216. To set the maximum size to 4216 using the TOKEN Link Driver, place the following lines in your NET.CFG.

```
Link Driver TOKEN
     MAX FRAME SIZE 4216
```

  If you are using TBMI2 or TASKID, this option is not available.

- **PROTOCOL** *name hexprotocol frametype*. This option is used to allow existing LAN drivers to handle network protocols. The name of the new protocol is *name*; the protocol ID stated in hex is *hexprotocol*; and *frametype* is the name of the frame that the protocol uses.

Exploring the ODI Configuration Files

- **SAPS** *number*. This option is used only with the LANSUP driver for IBM LAN Support. This option enables you to define the number of Service Access Points (SAPs) needed. Set this number to allow for all applications using the IBM LAN Support Program.

Table 11.3 shows the Link Support options and their defaults in NET.CFG. Each option is explained in detail after the chart.

Table 11.3
Link Support Options

Option	Default
Link Support	
BUFFERS *number [size]*	0 [1130]
MAX BOARDS *number*	4
MAX STACKS *number*	4
MEMPOOL *number*	

Link Support. This heading should be placed at the left margin in the NET.CFG file. The following are the definitions for the Link Support options that you can use to configure the shell. These options must be indented beneath the Link Support statement:

- **BUFFERS** *number [size]*. This option enables you to configure the number and size of the receive buffers. This number must take into account enough room to hold all headers as well as the maximum data size. Using the *size* parameter is optional. The minimum is 618 bytes, and the total buffer space must fit into 59K.

- **MAX BOARDS** *number*. This option enables you to specify the maximum number of logical boards the LSL can handle. The range is from 1 to 16, and the default is 4. If you load all possible frame types for Ethernet, you would load four frames. Your MAX BOARDS number must be set for at least four protocols.

- **MAX STACKS** *number*. Because each protocol stack uses one or more resources, you need to define a sufficient amount of stacks or you receive Out of resource errors. The range is from 1 to 16, and the default is 4.

- **MEMPOOL** *number*. The IPXODI protocol stack does not use this option; however, other protocol stacks might require the size of the memory pool buffers to be adjusted. See the documentation supplied with the protocol for recommended settings.

Table 11.4 lists the Protocol Selection parameters and their options in NET.CFG. Each option is explained in detail after the table.

Table 11.4
Protocol Selection Options

Option
Protocol *protocol name*
BIND *board name*

Protocol *protocol name*. This heading should start at the left margin in the NET.CFG file. The *protocol name* is the actual protocol you choose for the LAN board.

The following is the definition for the Protocol Selection option that you can use to configure the shell. This option must be indented beneath the Protocol Selection statement.

- **BIND** *board name*. This option binds the protocol to the appropriate LAN board. In the following example, the IPXODI protocol is bound to a Novell Ethernet NE2000 board.

```
Protocol IPXODI
     BIND NE2000
```

The file used before NET.CFG is SHELL.CFG. You can use the options listed in table 11.5 in SHELL.CFG as well as NET.CFG. If they are used in NET.CFG, they should come before any parameters used in tables 11.1 through 11.4.

SHELL.CFG Parameters

SHELL.CFG is used to configure non-ODI drivers. Many of these parameters are applicable to ODI and might be included in NET.CFG. ODI drivers, however, look for configuration parameters in the SHELL.CFG and the NET.CFG files.

 If a SHELL.CFG exists, you might choose to leave it alone and place only new information into the NET.CFG. Alternatively, you can add the SHELL.CFG information to the beginning of the NET.CFG file.

If neither file exists, create only the NET.CFG file.

Table 11.5 contains the definitions for the options that you can use to configure the shell. These options must be placed at the left margin in NET.CFG. The options are discussed in detail after the table.

Table 11.5
Shell Options

Option	Default
INT64=on/off	ON
INT7A=on/off	ON
IPX RETRY COUNT=n	20 retries
SPX ABORT TIMEOUT=n	540 ticks
SPX CONNECTIONS=n	15 connections
CACHE BUFFERS=n	5 cache blocks
FILE HANDLES=n	40 open files

continues

Table 11.5, Continued
Shell Options

Option	Default
LOCAL PRINTERS=*n*	# of ports
LONG MACHINE TYPE=*name*	IBM_PC
MAX TASKS=*n*	31
PREFERRED SERVER=*name*	
PRINT HEADER=*n*	64 bytes
PRINT TAIL=*n*	16 bytes
SHOW DOTS=on/off	OFF

- **INT64.** Certain applications, including earlier versions of NetWare, use this interrupt to access IPX services. Set this option to OFF if an application requests interrupt 64h, or if you have an application that works with NetWare 2.0a but locks up the workstation when using v3.*x*. The default is ON.

- **INT7A.** Certain applications, including earlier versions of NetWare, used this interrupt to access IPX services. Set this option to OFF if an application requests interrupt 7Ah or if you have an application that works with NetWare 2.0a but locks up the workstation with v3.*x*. The default is ON.

- **IPX RETRY COUNT.** This option enables you to specify the number of times a packet can be resent. Use this option if you are losing many packets. The default is 20 retries.

Increase IPX RETRY COUNT when users need to cross a router to access a printer on a remote workstation running RPRINTER. Increase it also if the network supports heavy traffic and long distances.

Exploring the ODI Configuration Files

- **SPX CONNECTIONS.** This option sets the maximum number of SPX connections a workstation can use at one time. If the workstation uses RPRINTER, set this number to 60. The default is 15 connections.

- **SPX ABORT TIMEOUT.** This option sets the amount of time in ticks that SPX waits for a response before ending the session. The default is 540 ticks.

- **CACHE BUFFERS.** You can use this option to speed up the processing of sequential reads/writes. The option enables you to set the number of 512 byte buffers available for local caching of non-TTS, nonshared files. The default is five cache buffers.

- **FILE HANDLES.** This option indicates the number of files the workstation is allowed to have opened on the network at one time. Set the number of open local files in CONFIG.SYS. The default is 40 open files on the network.

CACHE BUFFERS in NET.CFG corresponds to BUFFERS in CONFIG.SYS.

FILE HANDLES in NET.CFG corresponds to FILES in CONFIG.SYS.

- **LOCAL PRINTERS.** This option is used to override the number of local printer ports on the workstation. If you set this option to 0, the workstation does not hang when Shift+PrntScrn is pressed and the workstation does not have a local printer or a CAPTURE statement was not issued.

- **LONG MACHINE TYPE.** This option tells the network what type of machine is being used. This option works in conjunction with the %MACHINE login script variable. Because the default for all machines is IBM_PC, this option is used to correctly identify the machine type.

- **MAX TASKS.** This option sets the maximum number of active tasks. Programs like Microsoft Windows or DESQview allow

481

multiple active tasks. Increase this number if you are unable to open additional tasks.

- **PREFERRED SERVER.** Use this option to force a connection to a specific server. The shell polls up to five servers for available connections.

- **PRINT HEADER.** This option enables you to set the buffer size for the print header. The information held in this buffer is used to initialize a printer. Increase this buffer if the printer is not receiving all the requested attributes. The default is 64 bytes, and the range is from 0 to 255.

- **PRINT TAIL.** This option enables you to set the buffer size for the print tail. The information held in this buffer is used to reset the printer after issuing a print job. If the printer fails to reset, increase this buffer. The default is 16 bytes, and the range is from 0 to 255.

- **SHOW DOTS.** The NetWare file server does not have directory entries for . and .. as DOS does. If you are using an application that requires the use of . and .., such as Windows, you must set this option to ON. The default is OFF.

Protecting Your Network

When it comes to protecting your network data, most companies feel that an occasional backup is all they need. After all, the system runs fine—why should it crash? You might be surprised by the number of companies, large and small, that do not own a reliable backup device or maintain a reliable backup schedule. If the same data was located on a minicomputer or a mainframe, a reliable system of backing up data would be a requirement.

To effectively determine a data-protection system, you first need to evaluate the importance of your data in relation to the impact of losing it. Can your company or department operate without your system data for one hour, four hours, eight hours, 24 hours, or longer? Can you continue to operate with the total loss of your system data? Most companies cannot afford to experience these losses. A study performed by the University of Texas reports some alarming statistics: 43 percent of all companies that did not plan for a total system failure never reopened after the failure occurred. And 90 percent of those unprepared companies that did reopen after a total system failure went out of business within two years.

Data backup on a shared data-storage device is critical. Yet this area seems to be the first place the budget is cut. Data can be lost or damaged in many ways. A user can cause accidental damage, and although this type of data loss can be controlled by system security, it is still one of the most common occurrences. Software bugs or improper setups can cause data loss. Hardware failures vary from drive or controller failure to a workstation hanging or the file server itself failing. The computer virus is becoming more common in the workplace and also should be a concern when designing a protection plan. Sooner or later, all computer equipment fails. Data loss or data corruption might require files to be restored from an earlier copy. Investing in an adequate and reliable backup system minimizes the inconvenience and cost of downtime.

You might find it difficult to choose the backup device right for you from among all the backup devices on the market today. Both hardware and software are required to create a complete backup system, but also a motivated individual is required to make the backup system work.

SBACKUP

The SBACKUP utility is actually a v3.1x NetWare Loadable Module (NLM) that enables a tape drive to be attached directly to the file server. The SBACKUP system implements a technology that uses a host and a target. The target technology allows multiple file servers located on the LAN to be selected for backup as long as the target file server is running the TSA.NLM.

Chapter 11: NetWare 3.1x Advanced System Manager

A *host* is a file server that has a backup device attached. A *target* is a file server being backed up. A *parent* is anything backed up that has a subordinate data set. A directory, for example, has a subordinate data set of subdirectories and files. A *child* has no subordinates—a file.

Remember four terms dealing with the SBACKUP utility:

- **HOST.** Where the backup device is attached
- **TARGET.** Each server that is backed up
- **PARENT.** Directories, subdirectories, and binderies
- **CHILD.** Files

The SBACKUP system is made up of five modules—three host modules and two target modules. These modules are provided by Novell and are included with NetWare 3.1x.

The host modules include the following:

- **SBACKUP.NLM.** The main user interface.
- **SIDR.NLM.** The data requester. This module passes data to and from the host and target NLM by using Novell's Storage Management Services Protocol (SMSP).
- *driver*.**NLM.** The actual device driver required for interface. The module name varies for different interface cards.

The target modules include the following:

- **TSA.NLM.** The link between the data requester and the target.
- **TSA-311.NLM.** The target module for NetWare 3.1x.

In addition to the minimum memory needed to operate NetWare, the host file server requires approximately 3M to operate the backup device properly.

Protecting Your Network

Together the five SBACKUP modules make a system that enables you to back up data from any target on the network to the host. Figure 11.1 depicts a network of four file servers, all using the SBACKUP system with one acting as host and three acting as targets.

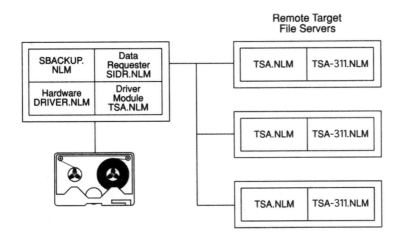

Figure 11.1

Host/target communications.

Novell has licensed the use of ArcServe from Cheyenne Software to enable SBACKUP to support a reasonable range of devices. This support is only at the hardware device driver level—SBACKUP and Cheyenne's ArcServe product are not the same.

Novell supplies drivers that support approximately 50 tape drives currently being sold by various manufacturers. These drives, along with a SCSI controller, enable you to back up the complete file server at speeds generally not possible on the workstation.

The SBACKUP system is made up of a hardware NLM, a target NLM, and the SBACKUP NLM itself. The Adaptec driver pictured in figure 11.2 is included with NetWare 3.1*x*. This driver supports the common 16-bit 154*x* series SCSI controller that supports many popular SCSI tape drives.

485

Figure 11.2

Adaptec driver.

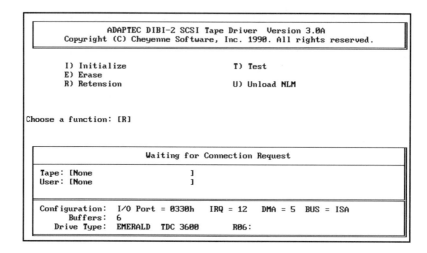

The Adaptec 154x controller also is a popular NetWare SCSI disk controller but cannot be used for both disk drives and tape drives simultaneously. Only a Certified NetWare Engineer should configure the Adaptec controller, because an incorrectly installed interface can cause problems with other installed devices.

Because the tape drive is installed directly in the file server, the data transfer rate is determined by the throughput rate of the file server's bus and the tape and hard drive interface cards. This arrangement provides high performance when backing up the locally attached server. When backing up a remote target file server located on the LAN, however, the data throughput drops drastically due to performance limits of the network cable and possible bridge hops required to reach the data.

The operation of SBACKUP is similar to NetWare's NBACKUP. After loading the hardware driver with the console LOAD command, you can check your hardware operation directly with the driver, which provides the erase, initialize, and retention options. At this point, you can load the TSA.NLM and SBACKUP. Because you are not normally logged in at the file server, SBACKUP prompts for a login name and password as figure 11.3 illustrates.

Protecting Your Network

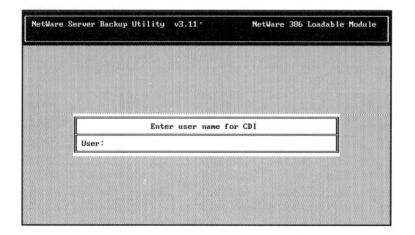

Figure 11.3
SBACKUP user login prompt.

The main menu option Select Target to Backup/Restore displays a menu of all file servers currently running the TSA target NLM. After selecting a target, you are prompted again to log in to the selected file server. After your target selection, you return to the main menu to select the Backup or Restore option. At this time, you see a Backup menu similar to the one in the NBACKUP utility. The screens in SBACKUP have been altered slightly from those in NBACKUP, but still provide the necessary session configuration options. Figures 11.4 and 11.5 show the additional submenus that make up the SBACKUP configuration screens.

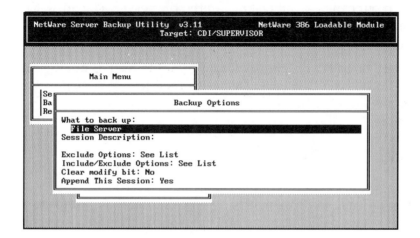

Figure 11.4
Backup Options main menu.

487

Figure 11.5
Exclude Options submenu.

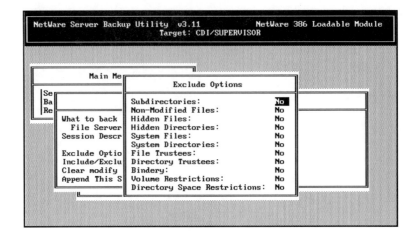

In figure 11.4, you are presented with a menu that asks what you want to back up and if any special configuration options are to be used. The first item asks what to back up—the file server, a directory, or a list of files. By making use of the available options under the exclude and include selections, as shown in figure 11.5, you can customize the backup session. These options generally default to the most commonly used settings. Changing these parameters requires you to understand the way in which your system is structured and, in most cases, which defaults are safe to use.

The SBACKUP utility provides a high-speed solution to data backup but can be cumbersome on the file server. The SBACKUP system is a limited version of some of the full backup systems available.

The tape cartridge data format used by SBACKUP is not the same as that used by NBACKUP. Data sets, therefore, cannot be read from one utility to the other.

Backup Hardware

The only thing constant in the computer industry is change. Hardware and software evolve so quickly that most companies cannot keep up with the constant changes. Rather than keeping up with technology, however, you should be taking advantage of it. Not all new products are right for everyone. As technology makes advances, it provides the user with a wider range of products. If selected carefully, new products can provide efficient and economical solutions for your computer needs.

The most commonly used backup devices use floppy disks, hard drives, tapes, and optical drives. Floppy drives do not provide an efficient means to back up a file server because of their size. Some systems use nonremovable disk drives as the backup media. These devices should only be considered as temporary or secondary backup devices, because they are susceptible to the same defects as the original hard drive. Likewise, because hard drives generally are not kept off-site to protect against hazards such as fire, they are a poor choice as a primary backup device. This section discusses the technology available in tape and optical drives.

Interface Adapters

Any backup device, whether a tape drive or a disk drive, requires an interface card. Currently, three popular interface standards are available: the floppy controller, SCSI Host Adapter, and QIC (Quarter-Inch Cartridge) interfaces. All these interfaces can provide adequate data throughput in the right environment.

The floppy interface is used by many popular personal tape systems and provides an acceptable level of data transfer on small systems and personal computers. This interface, however, generally cannot handle the data transfer of a larger company's file server. The floppy controller can supply throughput from 250kbps on an XT class computer to 500kbps on the AT class computer. The floppy controller also is limited to a single tape drive and is not expandable beyond the initial installation.

The Quarter-Inch Cartridge (QIC) interface was developed primarily for the DC6*xxx* tape systems providing a capacity of 60M and larger. This interface provides backup rates of up to 5 megabytes-per-minute in a properly designed system. This standard, although early technology, still can provide an adequate backup system with a properly designed software system. The QIC standard at this time consists of many variations that provide standards for the DC6*xxx* and DC2*xxx* series of data cartridges.

For any corporation with a wide variety of computer equipment and needs, standards might be the key to a successful future. When multivendor communication is important, following standards is almost a requirement. Without standards in a complex system, you cannot ensure functionality and support in the future.

Although support of industry standards always should be a concern when you design a system, many good networking solutions are not necessarily standards. Most network hardware manufacturers support Novell NetWare, and many manufacturers provide small companies with low-cost, highly reliable solutions that might not follow a standard.

Using standards is not always the best approach when you implement a system. In cases that require connectivity to larger systems, standards might offer the highest degree of reliability and serviceability, but not the performance of alternative methods. In these cases, you must weigh the values of performance, reliability, and serviceability before making a decision.

The Small Computer System Interface (SCSI) was designed as a general-purpose interface for mass-storage devices. The SCSI interface is a standard maintained by the American National Standards Institute (ANSI). The SCSI standard allows up to eight devices to be placed on the interface. This design provides expandability for future system growth and the capability to transfer data at much higher speeds than a floppy controller or the QIC interface, which makes SCSI the interface of choice for current and future technology.

The SCSI adapter is actually a Host Bus Adapter (HBA). SCSI is a bus system standard just as the Industry Standard Architecture (ISA) and Micro Channel Adapter (MCA) are IBM bus standards. The SCSI interface is a converter that enables the different buses to communicate.

Media and Drive Types

Manufacturers supply many different media and recording methods. The most common methods are explained here to give you some general knowledge of the different types available.

QIC and cassette tapes are recorded in a back-and-forth manner. This method, as illustrated in figure 11.6, is called the *serpentine recording method* and enables multiple tracks to be recorded on the tape by moving the tape across a stationary recording head. These tapes can provide from 15M to 320M storage on a single tape depending on the tape type.

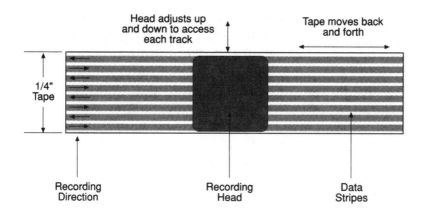

Figure 11.6

Serpentine recording method.

Helical scan technology is probably the most commonly used recording method today. This technology has been used in video equipment since the mid-1950s and is used in the common VCR. Helical scan tapes are available in 4mm and 8mm size, providing from 1.3G to 5G on a single tape cartridge. In this recording method, both the tape and the recording head move. The recording head is constructed as a drum and is placed at a five- to six-degree angle to the tape surface (see fig. 11.7). This positioning allows the recording head to write diagonal stripes on the tape.

Figure 11.7
Helical scan technology.

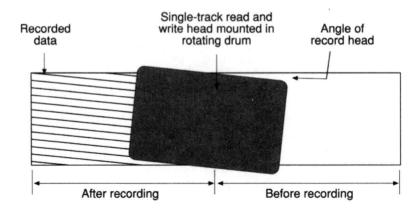

The 8mm tape cartridges are similar to those used in today's 8mm video camcorders, but with an important difference. The recording surface of videotape normally has some flaking of the oxide. In the video environment, this flaking might show up as a single speck of snow on the screen that might not even be visible to the viewer. But in the data environment, a single flake of oxide can represent extensive loss of data. To prevent oxide flaking, the data-specific tapes are manufactured to more stringent specifications, and the cost of these tapes generally reflects this higher quality. Currently, this technology is supplied by the Exabyte Corporation, which offers a 2.2G and a 5G version.

The 4mm or Digital Audio Tape (DAT), offering 1.2G and 2.0G storage, also is making its way into the technologically sophisticated tape-drive market. This tape format is similar to the 8mm technology. Both the 4mm and the 8mm tape systems provide high throughput and reliability along with a convenient, compact tape size.

Optical Drives

The family of optical disk drives includes the Compact Disk-Read Only Media (CD-ROM), Write Once Read Many (WORM), and Magnetic Optical (MO)—erasable optical disks. These removable drives provide very fast data access in a reliable format, if implemented properly.

Although the CD-ROM is a read-only device and is, therefore, not a backup device, it is rapidly becoming popular for fixed data storage.

This technology is reliable and is used as a storage device for large databases that do not change, but often are used as reference. CD-ROMs use a solid-state laser beam to read the surface.

WORM is similar to CD-ROM technology except that, although the CD-ROM information is written on the surface by the manufacturer, the WORM drive can write data to the disk. After this data has been added, however, it cannot be erased. The WORM disk is not susceptible to mechanical head crashes experienced by normal hard drives, because WORM disks have no read/write heads that come in contact with the surface. These disks also are not magnetic and, therefore, do not suffer from degradation due to electrical, magnetic disturbances. Figure 11.8 illustrates the CD-ROM and WORM technology.

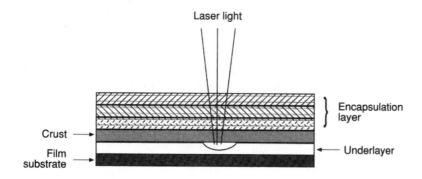

Figure 11.8

CD-ROM and WORM technology.

The MO disk is actually two technologies working together to provide an optically erasable disk that gives the performance of a low-end hard drive. As illustrated by figure 11.9, the magnetic optical disk operates by using a solid-state laser beam to heat the surface of the disk to allow a magnetic field to change the phase of the metallic structure of the coating on the disk's surface. The phase changes are then interpreted as digital 1s and 0s.

Figure 11.9
Magnetic optical technology.

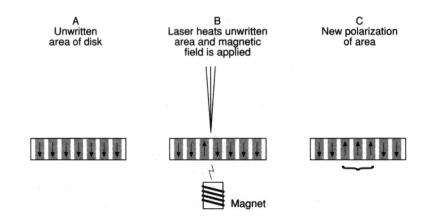

Optical drives also are available in automatic disk changers referred to as *jukeboxes*. These jukeboxes can provide many gigabytes of data but require special software to manage the robotic movements needed to perform the disk-change operations.

Software

Many high-quality tape and optical drives currently are available, but without good software, these drives are worthless. The software, not the hardware, directs the backup and manages the data. Ask the following questions when putting together the backup system right for you:

- Does it back up all NetWare security information?
- Does it allow password protection on the backup media?
- In what way does it handle a selective backup and restore?
- Can I redirect the data on a restore?
- Can it back up open files?
- What type of backup media management does it provide?
- In what way does the system handle backup media or tape spanning?

- In what way does it handle automatic or unattended backups?
- What method of reporting is used?

These questions are important when selecting a backup system. It also is important to add any questions that might be required to service your company's special needs.

When considering a backup system for a NetWare network, make sure that the system can back up all the NetWare bindery files and trustee information. Smaller software systems might not be able to do this backup, because they require the capability to close, back up, and reopen special invisible system files located on the file server.

Novell provides special API function calls to the programmer. The following calls back up the bindery files:

- CloseBindery
- OpenBindery

To back up Novell directory trustees, the function calls include the following:

- ScanDirectoryForTrustees
- AddTrusteeToDirectory

To maintain file attributes, the function calls are as follows:

- ScanFileInformation
- SetFileInformation

Novell API programming function-call information is available from Novell vendors in both OS/2, NLM, and DOS assembly and C libraries.

Security should be considered when selecting your tape-backup system. If your server has sensitive information, an unprotected tape can be a security hole. Some tape software systems have the capability of adding a password to the tape, which disarms the restore function without the proper password. The password, if used, is important, because most tape software packages cannot read the tape without it.

You also should consider the method used to back up files. Some tape software programs provide image, file-by-file, or both methods of backing up data. The *image method* is fast and can provide an efficient means of restoring the system in the event of a total failure, but the image method generally is cumbersome and it is sometimes impossible to restore a single file when needed. Most systems today use the *file-by-file* method of backup. This method reads each and every file separately while performing the backup, unlike the image method, which reads the disk partition from beginning to end.

The capability to redirect data during a restore can be a convenient feature. This capability can save many hours when replacing data to a different drive. Although most systems provide this feature, it might be worth your while to confirm that the system you are considering does.

Open files have always been a problem with tape software, because files open during backup do not get backed up. The usual way to deal with this problem is to skip the file, add an entry into the error log, and proceed. Some systems make use of the error report and attempt to back up open files after the main backup has finished. This feature works in some cases, as long as the files are not open due to an improperly logged-out workstation. Recently, a software package has come on the market that backs up open files. This software makes a "best attempt" service and is dependent on the way in which the file was opened. The integrity of these files is uncertain.

The capability to span tape is no longer as great a concern as it used to be. *Spanning* allows a backup to fill one tape and to continue on another. Many of the older technology systems did not provide this service. Current technology does provide spanning; make sure that the system you are considering does.

Currently, some backup software programs have trouble backing up large files or traversing large directory structures. If your system maintains a large database, avoid backup software that cannot back up large files. Traversing large directory structures also can be a problem but can be resolved by restructuring the directories. Large directory structures can cause a performance problem, and large files sometimes can prevent correct operation.

A little-known problem with DOS can occur on file servers or large DOS drives. DOS begins to experience performance problems with more than 500 files or directories at a single level. This problem can be contributed to the sequential manner in which DOS starts at the top of the File Allocation Table (FAT) and scans to the end in search of a file. More than 500 files in a subdirectory, or more than 500 subdirectories under a single directory, causes the problem. If this number reaches 1000, the problem becomes visible to the user; when the number reaches 2000 or more, serious performance problems occur when backing up these files or directories.

If the backup software builds a temporary table in memory, a large directory structure also can cause problems by running out of memory.

Another area of concern is documentation and the user interface. Any well-written program should include properly written user and administrator manuals. Both the manual and user interface should be clear and easy to understand.

The interface should have a system of double-checks and confirmations to prevent accidental damage to files. A functional on-line help system can be a great time-saver and, over time, is worth every dollar spent.

Although a well-written user interface with on-line help makes a system easy to use and understand, the capability to execute the backup from a command line also is important in some cases. The command line provides the inventive system administrator with the capability to implement various methods of starting and automating the backup procedure.

Chapter 11: NetWare 3.1x Advanced System Manager

Some systems provide batch or macro functionality in place of command-line utilities. This functionality also can be beneficial if the macro system is not overly complicated. You also should confirm that both the command-line and macro options provide a full set of functions available through the normal user interface.

Most backup software provides a scheme for starting the backup at a later time. These scheduling schemes vary greatly in their functionality; you should, however, make sure that the system you use maintains a level of security while waiting for the scheduled time to perform the backup. Some systems simply sit at the DOS prompt, logged in with supervisor rights, until backup time. This scheme can be a major security problem in some environments.

Some server-based backup systems currently are available. These systems enable the backup device to be connected directly to the file server and run as a valued-added process (VAP) or NetWare Loadable Module (NLM). Evaluate these systems as thoroughly as you would any standard workstation-based software.

Most server-based systems provide backup services without the use of a workstation and can supply high data throughput, because the data does not travel through the network cable. These functions are not automatic. One server-based system, for instance, requires a Windows application running on a workstation to perform a backup. This system transmits the data from the server to the workstation and back to the server, effectively eliminating most of the advantages of a server-based system, because it doubles network traffic rather than reduces it.

All backup software uses some kind of reporting method. Errors commonly occur during an unattended backup. Without a status report, these problems can go undetected and cause problems later.

Most backup software written today includes the capability to generate status reports. These reports vary in their level of detail, but most are more than adequate for tracking errors.

Novell provides a certification program for manufacturers who want to have their products tested as Novell-approved. This testing procedure confirms that products provide an adequate level of performance and are compatible with the Novell NetWare environment.

Copies of the Independent Product Testing (IPT) bulletins are available from any Novell vendor or CompuServe NetWire.

Backup Plans

After locating a suitable backup software and hardware system, you must develop a plan that effectively uses the equipment to obtain the level of protection required. This plan should at least answer the following questions:

- Who is responsible for the backup?
- When and how often do you back up?
- What method of rotating the backup media should be used?
- Which backup media should be taken off-site, and when?
- When and how often should backup media be tested?
- What type of plan do you need for a disaster?

An adequate backup system should account for these questions, and although each item might vary slightly in importance depending on your situation, none should be bypassed.

Your company also might require additional steps to be taken to ensure total protection. No one set plan fits everyone. Each company has different priorities and resources. A properly designed plan should provide a standard procedure and an alternative that does not allow the level of required protection to fail.

Responsibility

The person chosen to be responsible for maintaining the backup system must be sufficiently motivated to back up when planned.

Inconsistent backups allow periods of time when files might not be retrievable and can prove costly under the wrong circumstances.

Frequency

Because most backup software requires users to be logged out of the system, the most common time to perform backup is after business hours. This schedule generally requires an unattended backup system that provides adequate error reporting.

The frequency of the backup should be determined by the amount of data changed and the cost to reconstruct the data if lost. Most companies find that a backup once a day is adequate. Those companies that require more frequent backups usually do so because they have large systems that would require many hours of data entry to rebuild. The cost of this reconstruction should be calculated on a worst-case basis to determine if backups are required more often or if a dedicated backup device might be required.

Rotation Methods

Rotating the backup media is important to provide proper protection. Rotating the media provides multiple copies of data in the event of a natural disaster, such as a fire, or in the case of a physical backup media failure. You can rotate tapes in many ways. The following examples are the most commonly used and proven methods. Note that most of these methods assume your network primarily is used Monday through Friday, with little to no activity on Saturday or Sunday.

Grandfather Method

The grandfather method is fairly simple and provides an adequate level of protection to a small-to-midsize file server. This method requires 20 tape sets. A *tape set* is a set of tapes required to perform a backup. The grandfather method is simple to control if the total disk volumes can fit on a single tape and if the backup system can transfer all the data in an acceptable amount of time.

In the grandfather system, four daily tapes (or other media) are labeled Monday through Thursday, four Friday tapes are labeled to be used on Friday, and 12 monthly tapes are labeled January through December. The four daily tapes are used on the designated day with the weekly Friday1, Friday2, Friday3, or Friday4 tape being used on that week. The 12 monthly tapes are used on the last day of each month as labeled. This method provides current files Monday through Thursday and a weekly and monthly archive tape set.

If the file server to be backed up is larger than the maximum tape capacity, the number of tapes and the need to exchange tapes halfway through the backup become difficult to manage.

10-Tape Rotation

The *10-tape method* rotates all tapes evenly and provides a backup history of about 12 weeks. This system also becomes cumbersome if the data requires more than one tape to perform the backup.

Many companies only back up modified files on a daily basis to overcome the problem of the tape drive being too small. Most tape software can check the DOS Modified Attribute (the +A parameter sets the archive bit) to determine if the file has been changed since the last backup. This flag greatly reduces the number of files that require backup on a daily basis.

Managing this type rotation can be complicated and possibly hazardous if a mistake occurs. This method of backup also can increase greatly the time required to restore a system in the case of a failure. To restore more than a single file from this type of rotation might require all tapes to be restored. This restoration can take many hours using some software systems.

The 10-tape method uses a series of four-week cycles during a 40-week period. During a given four-week cycle, the same four tapes are used Monday through Thursday. This technique starts out much like the grandfather method. Each Friday of a four-week cycle, however, the number of the tape is increased by one. Also, at the start of each new four-week cycle, the Monday through Thursday tape numbers are increased.

The following example shows the different tape sets as they are used during the complete 40-week period. As you can see, this method can become confusing if multiple tapes are required for each backup session.

1-2-3-4-**5**-1-2-3-4-**6**-1-2-3-4-**7**-1-2-3-4-**8**

2-3-4-5-**6**-2-3-4-5-**7**-2-3-4-5-**8**-2-3-4-5-**9**

3-4-5-6-**7**-3-4-5-6-**8**-3-4-5-6-**9**-3-4-5-6-**10**

4-5-6-7-**8**-4-5-6-7-**9**-4-5-6-7-**10**-4-5-6-7-**1**

5-6-7-8-**9**-5-6-7-8-**10**-5-6-7-8-**1**-5-6-7-8-**2**

6-7-8-9-**10**-6-7-8-9-**1**-6-7-8-9-**2**-6-7-8-9-**3**

7-8-9-10-**1**-7-8-9-10-**2**-7-8-9-10-**3**-7-8-9-10-**4**

8-9-10-1-**2**-8-9-10-1-**3**-8-9-10-1-**4**-8-9-10-1-**5**

9-10-1-2-**3**-9-10-1-2-**4**-9-10-1-2-**5**-9-10-1-2-**6**

10-1-2-3-**4**-10-1-2-3-**5**-10-1-2-3-**6**-10-1-2-3-**7**

Tower of Hanoi Method

This method is named after a mathematical game in which the player must move a stack of different-sized rings in the proper order.

The tape sets are labeled A, B, C, and so on. A tape set generally has between five to eight tapes. The following example shows a typical rotation. The bold letters show the first use of a tape set.

A-**B**-A-**C**-A-B-A-**D**-A-B-A-C-A-B-A-**E**

A-B-A-C-A-B-A-D-A-B-A-C-A-B-A-**F**

A-B-A-C-A-B-A-D-A-B-A-C-A-B-A-E

A-B-A-C-A-B-A-D-A-B-A-C-A-B-A-**G**

This rotation method is one of the most difficult to maintain manually but can offer a wide range of file histories. The window of available files doubles each time a new tape set is introduced. A set of five tapes, for example, provides files up to 16 days old, six tapes 32 days, and seven tapes 64 days. You also can implement this system using a single tape for a whole week, which extends the window to 16 weeks, 32 weeks, and 64 weeks, respectively.

This rotation method recently has been implemented in a backup system that maintains a full database and handles the task of rotating tapes when needed. This system is one of the few that provides a full archive of file histories and enables the system administrator to restore from a list of versions in the archive. This particular system enables a spreadsheet or database to be restored as it was weeks or months ago.

Off-Site Backups

When examining the backup systems and rotation methods available, plan for multitape sets so that a complete set you can store off-site. A moderately current data set off-site protects you in the event of a building disaster, such as a fire or flood. A log book should be set so that others know where you last were in the rotation. This practice helps to keep the backup as consistent as possible. Tape sets should be scheduled to be stored off-site with plenty of time provided to retrieve them before needed. These off-site sets also should be second- or third-level copies that enable the most recent sets to remain on-site for immediate access, if needed. Generally, sets are moved on- and off-site every one to two weeks. This rotation might be done more frequently on a large system.

As networks become more complex and require a higher level of protection, backup systems need to be more versatile. Automatic expert systems are already starting to appear, providing full, intelligent solutions. One current system is not just a tape backup but a fully automated storage-management product. Providing fully automatic on- and off-site tape rotation schedules, these systems require a high level of knowledge to totally understand their flow of events.

Testing

It is critical that a backup system be tested from time to time. Many systems have experienced permanent data loss simply because the backup system was never tested. A backup is no good if you cannot restore it.

A simple way to test the backup is to create a dummy test directory that contains a few executable programs backed up at all times. This approach enables you to delete the directory structure and to restore from the backup media without losing important data. This restore test should be done after the initial system install and after any system change that can affect the operation of the backup device. Workstation hardware changes or DOS upgrades easily can cause a backup system to malfunction.

Disaster Recovery

A disaster-recovery plan should be a complete solution. This solution should include a backup system and a company plan to follow in the event of a total system failure. In most cases, disaster recovery is simply an afterthought, something that would have been handy. A backup system is required to maintain a complete set of data, as complete and current as possible. This data sometimes is required to re-create the system as it was after a major hardware problem.

A backup device is only a single part of what is generally needed to be properly protected. The following sections are intended as a guide to aid you in planning the proper system for your needs. Disaster-recovery systems or plans should be taken seriously if your company's data has any value. A written list of procedures, a list of support personnel, or a tape backup can make an adequate disaster recovery plan if it covers all your needs. Although most plans include some or all of these items, the key is to create a plan that provides your company with the necessary insurance.

Proper Preplanning

Proper preplanning of a recovery system easily can become overly complicated. The best plan is one that can be followed, fits the needs of your company, and provides an acceptable end result. A well-designed plan should have a backup schedule or log and a documented list of steps to take in the event of a problem and should include more than one responsible person.

Needed Equipment

Novell provides safety mechanisms for a first level of protection. NetWare's disk mirroring or disk duplexing can greatly reduce the cost of downtime in the event of a hard drive failure. NetWare provides a hot backup drive or complete disk channel that takes over in the event of a primary drive failure.

Many companies do not take advantage of this feature simply because of the cost of an additional hard drive. In most cases, the mere cost of a second hard drive is much less than the cost of downtime that might be experienced during a drive failure.

If implemented properly, Novell NetWare's disk duplexing can add as much as 50 percent to the disk-read performance. This additional performance alone can offset the cost of the extra hard drive and controller required.

By using disk mirroring or duplexing, you can schedule a failed hard disk for repair after normal business hours, eliminating user downtime completely.

Power Protection

A major source of file server data corruption is power loss. NetWare increases its performance by reading large amounts of data into a special portion of memory called a *cache*. The cache allows data to be read many times faster than if it were being read directly from the hard disk. The cache, however, is vulnerable to poor power conditions. If a power line spike or surge passes through the file server, data reliability is affected.

Many NetWare administrators are familiar with the General Protection Interrupt (GPI) or Non-Maskable Interrupt (NMI) errors at the file server console. These errors are displayed by an operating system task that constantly checks the integrity of the system memory. Both errors generally are traced to power or memory problems. And in most cases, a power-related problem makes the memory appear bad.

Power protection is important to the integrity of data on a file server. The minimum protection is a good surge strip to guard against spikes and surges.

A good quality Uninterruptible Power Supply (UPS) should be installed to prevent any unnecessary problems. A USP that has Novell communications capability can save many hours by making it unnecessary to repair data in the event of a power failure. Many vendors offer an interface that informs the file server when commercial power has been lost. When properly installed, these units can shut down the file server correctly, minimizing damaged data.

Available Utilities

The computer *virus* (vital information resources under siege) appears to be a growing problem. The first virus-like programs started out as a game, a battlefield between a few young geniuses writing self-repairing, roaming code. These programs had a mission to seek out and destroy the opponent. From these first amazing programs, the virus has developed into a special program designed to interfere with the normal operations of a computer. This interference varies from a simple message informing the user of its presence to the destruction of as much data as possible. Currently, more than 400 virus programs are known to exist, and more are added to the list daily.

Most viruses found today multiply by attaching to executable (EXE and COM) files and becoming memory-resident.

This spread of infectious programs prompted the growth of vaccine or virus detection and repair software. The capability of these programs to seek out and destroy the virus enables the system administrator to breathe more easily.

Although antivirus software has proven useful in the battle against viruses, do not think of it as an alternative to a properly designed network security system. Currently, no well-designed and properly administered Novell security system has been infected. The most dangerous and most common access point of a virus is through the user supervisor.

The special user supervisor and supervisor equivalents should be reserved for administrative tasks only. A user does not need the rights of the system supervisor to execute normal applications.

If a user has the right to change the read-only flag on all executable files, most new virus programs attack those files. If the user does not have the right to modify the flag, the file is protected.

Currently, the quality and methods of antivirus programs vary from one system to another. The best means of selecting a detection system is to follow trade magazines' software reviews or to contact a reputable software retailer.

Support Issues

Though network service persons are everywhere, an experienced and knowledgeable network service person is difficult to find.

A good, reputable service organization that can provide quality service and support is probably the most important key to a successful operation. Whether you are self-sufficient or totally dependent, you need a reliable source for replacement parts and assistance occasionally.

As part of your plan, a carefully planned service contract or agreement should be set up to supply the level of support your company might need in the event of a system failure. Include in the contract such items as on-site service, software, and hardware. The amount of on-hand parts and a reasonable time period should be specified as well. The service organization should be able to supply suitable replacement parts within the agreed time period and handle the problem with a suitable level of knowledge.

If your network is large, it might require an internal support staff. If so, Novell offers a *Network Support Encyclopedia* that can supply answers to a majority of your technical questions. This extensive database is available on floppy disk and CD-ROM. Novell provides a yearly subscription service that supplies updates.

Each main menu option offers submenus that enable administrators to narrow the search field or perform global searches on the complete database. The NSE database provides useful information that can be obtained quickly and is a practical addition to the NetWare toolbag.

Novell's NetWire, a special-interest group located on CompuServe, also is a good source of information. Through NetWire, you can communicate with other users, system administrators, and Novell technical persons. It is not uncommon to post a question in the evening and have a suggested solution waiting for you in the morning.

Training

As demonstrated in the industry, successful Novell networks are administered and run by highly competent people using Novell NetWare. The most cost-effective way to become familiar with the system is to receive professional training from an organization that can supply a working, hands-on environment. An experienced instructor can help you with both application and procedural issues. You can compensate for the cost of this training many times over by your improved ability to handle normal administrative issues internally.

Today's NetWare networks are not just an office of personal computers sharing printers. These networks have replaced many large, expensive corporate systems and have proven their capability to supply office automation.

Common problems are most often created by untrained employees and administrators. A simple, time-consuming problem like "My data was there before lunch" easily can be avoided by a knowledgeable administrator. A well-designed security system with a functional menu can prevent most accidental problems. In most cases, missing data files and programs are products of untrained users allowed to roam the system. These accidents usually stem from good intentions and can be prevented with proper user and administrator training.

Consultants

The network industry can supply professional consultants for any technical and administrative area needed. Many consultants are extremely good at what they do; some are not. As with selecting a service organization, a consultant should be selected based on experience and knowledge. You can train your staff to operate and administer your network. You should not be required to train your consultant to obtain the level of service you require.

Fixing Volumes Using VREPAIR

VREPAIR enables an administrator to attempt a software repair of a volume that appears to have problems. The most common use of VREPAIR is when the power to the file server has been cut off, causing data mirror mismatches or FAT (File Allocation Table) errors that prevent the server from booting.

In v3.1x, type **LOAD VREPAIR** and repair the dismounted volume.

Chapter 11: NetWare 3.1x Advanced System Manager

Use VREPAIR with discretion and always make sure that you have a current backup. When run on a good disk having FAT errors, VREPAIR is effective. If, however, the disk has hard-to-detect defects, VREPAIR might destroy data.

The VREPAIR NLM enables you to choose a volume to repair or set the VREPAIR options (see fig. 11.10). The options that you can set are as follows:

- Remove Name Space support
- Write the DET and FAT tables to disk
- Write changes at once to disk

Figure 11.10
The VREPAIR options screen.

```
Current Vrepair Configuration:
    Quit If A Required VRepair Name Space Support NLM Is Not Loaded
    Write Only Changed Directory And FAT Entries Out To Disk
    Keep Changes In Memory For Later Update

Options:
    1. Remove Name Space support from the volume
    2. Write All Directory And FAT Entries Out To Disk
    3. Write Changes Immediately To Disk
    0. Return To Main Menu
    Enter your choice:
```

VREPAIR checks the volume and attempts to repair file discrepancies with a valid File Allocation Table. Figure 11.11 shows the VREPAIR prompts. VREPAIR takes a considerable length of time if problems exist with the files. Avoid interrupting the VREPAIR process to allow sufficient time for the utility to complete the repair procedure.

Figure 11.11
VREPAIR on VOL1.

```
Total errors: 0
Current settings:
  Pause after each error
  Do not log errors to a file
Press F1 to change settings

Start 5:08:33 pm
Checking volume VOL1

FAT blocks>.............................................................<
Counting directory blocks and checking directory FAT entries
Mirror mismatches>......................................................<
Directories>............................................................<
Files>..................................................................<
Trustees>...............................................................<
Free blocks>............................................................<

Done checking volume
Total Time 0:00:10
<Press any key to continue>
```

Exploring the NetWare 3.1*x* Memory Model

NetWare 3.1*x* manages memory differently. NetWare 3.1*x* is dynamic and can vary or reallocate its memory as needed. NetWare 3.1*x* divides memory into memory pools. (A *memory pool* is an area of the file server's memory set aside for the server's use in processing request for services or for recording status of the server's various resources.)

A v3.1*x* file server requires at least 4M of system memory providing the disk drive is not larger than 80M, although it can address up to 4G of memory. These memory pools are divided into pools according to the way in which the memory is used. The pools as defined by NetWare are as follows:

- ◆ File Cache Buffer
- ◆ Cache Movable
- ◆ Cache Non-Movable
- ◆ Permanent
- ◆ Semi-Permanent
- ◆ Alloc Short Term

You must have an understanding of these memory pools to understand the many performance features available in NetWare 3.1x.

File Cache Buffer Memory Pool

All versions of NetWare make use of much of the system memory allocated as cache. This cache memory greatly speeds up the access time to the file server. Workstations can access information held in cache memory much faster than directly reading it from the system disk. When the NetWare 3.1x file server boots, any free memory is allocated as cache memory—the main memory pool used by NetWare 3.1x.

NetWare makes use of this cache memory in many ways. Cache memory is reallocated as system demands increase and memory is needed in other areas. The NetWare operating system uses memory from this pool to provide buffer resources to other areas when needed. The file cache buffer memory might be called upon to temporarily loan memory to the following processes:

- Cache buffers required by other applications (NLMs). This memory is returned to the Cache Buffer Pool after the NLM is unloaded.

- Cache buffers as needed to service user requests to access disk data.

- Cache buffers to build disk hash tables, FAT (file allocation tables), Turbo FAT, and DET (directory entry tables) tables.

All other pools obtain memory when needed in the file cache buffer memory pool. As memory is taken from this pool, the amount of memory available as file cache reduces. This process might result in some loss of performance, depending on the amount of total memory available to the system.

Cache Movable and Non-Movable Memory Pools

Both the Cache Movable Memory Pool and Cache Non-Movable Memory Pool give and take memory directly from the File Cache Memory Pool. These pools differ in that the movable pool moves or relocates itself to prevent memory fragmentation. Memory fragmentation, if excessive, can reduce overall file server performance.

The Cache Movable Memory Pool supplies memory to system tables such as FATs, DETs, and hash tables. Because of their dynamic nature, the size of these tables can grow and shrink quickly, resulting in memory fragmentation. (These tables are explained in the next section.) The Movable Memory Pool relocates itself when needed to minimize any fragmentation and, therefore, maintain optimum memory performance. Because of this feature, all tables maintained in cache movable memory are in a contiguous format. The tables maintained by this pool are relatively small in size and are dynamically expandable.

The Cache Non-Movable Memory Pool is used for larger memory buffers and tables as needed by NLMs. The memory used here is primarily for the loading and unloading of NLMs and is generally a short-term usage. The memory used from this pool is returned to the file cache buffer pool when no longer needed but is not relocated to prevent memory fragmentation. The tables and buffers that make use of the cache non-movable memory are not expandable and are held in noncontiguous memory blocks. An example of the usage of this pool is with the MONITOR and INSTALL NLMs. Each of these NLMs allocates memory from the Cache Non-Movable Memory Pool when loaded.

If cache non-movable memory is allocated and deallocated often by the loading and unloading of NLMs, memory can be fragmented to the point of appearing to be out of memory. Non-movable memory does not eliminate memory fragmentation and can become so bad that no contiguous block of memory is large enough to load NLMs. This problem generally only occurs with a file server short on system memory.

Permanent Memory Pool

The Permanent Memory Pool is the source drawn from for both the Semi-Permanent Pool and the Alloc Short Term Memory Pool. The Permanent Memory Pool is used for long-term necessities such as permanent tables and packet-receive buffers. NetWare loadable modules cannot make use of the memory in this pool. The Permanent Memory Pool takes additional memory from the File Cache Memory Pool, if necessary, but does not return it. This memory, however, is returned when the file server is brought down and back up.

Semi-Permanent Memory Pool

The Semi-Permanent Memory Pool is a secondary pool of the permanent pool. The Semi-Permanent Memory Pool is used by loadable modules such as disk and LAN card drivers when they are expected to make use of this resource for long periods. This memory is returned to the Permanent Memory Pool when no longer needed, but is not returned to the File Cache Buffer Memory Pool.

Alloc Short Term Memory Pool

The Alloc Short Term Memory Pool is used by many procedures and NLMs when memory is needed for short periods. This memory also is taken from the permanent pool when more resources are needed, but is not returned.

The Alloc Short Term Memory pool defaults to a minimum value of 2M in NetWare 3.11, but has a default value of 8M for NetWare 3.12. The maximum value is 32M in NetWare 3.12, an increase from NetWare 3.11. You can temporarily change the minimum value by entering a SET command at the server console command line or change it permanently by placing a SET command in the server's STARTUP.NCF or AUTOEXEC.NCF file as follows:

```
SET MAXIMUM ALLOC SHORTTERM MEMORY = value
```

Exploring the NetWare 3.1x Memory Model

Replace *value* with any value in the range of 50000 to 33554432 (32M).

After you change the Alloc Short Term Memory Pool size, allow the server to run for a few days, then check server to see if sufficient memory has been allocated or if you allocated too much memory to this pool. If memory pool information is set too low, you see messages indicating that an operation could not be completed because the memory pool has reached its allocated limit.

To check the memory, complete the following steps:

1. Load MONITOR.NLM at the server console.
2. Choose the Resource Utilization option.
3. View the Server Memory Statistics screen that appears.
4. Check the Alloc Memory Pool line. It tells you the number of bytes set for this memory pool. It also tells you the number of bytes in use. Compare the two figures.

The Alloc Short Term Memory Pool increases its size when needed but does not return the memory to the permanent memory pool or the file cache memory pool. After the Alloc Short Term Memory Pool increases in size, that memory remains in that pool until the server is rebooted. Thus, increase the Alloc Short Term Memory Pool if the comparison that you made in step 4 indicates that a high percentage (75 percent or more) of the Alloc Short Term Memory Pool is being used. This setup prevents requests for services from not being completed due to an insufficient amount of space in the memory pool.

Examples of processes or items that make use of the Alloc Short Term Memory Pool are as follows:

- ◆ Drive mappings
- ◆ Service requests
- ◆ File locks and open requests
- ◆ Service advertising and requests (SAPs and RIPs)
- ◆ User connection information

515

- Queue manager and NLM tables
- Message broadcasts pending

Now that you have a basic understanding of each memory pool, you can learn the way in which the pools are handled internally. This information is mostly for those interested and is not a necessity.

When a v3.1x file server is first booted, the operating system allocates as much memory as possible to the file cache buffers pool. It allocates the minimum amounts of memory for all others. You can adjust this allocation by using the console SET commands, but adjustment rarely is required. After the file server has been up and running and as users and applications make requests of the server, memory is allocated as needed. If the server is up for longer periods, you might notice that the total free cache blocks as shown on the MONITOR main screen changes. This change is a result of the dynamic allocation process.

Memory pools are allocated in one of two ways. Movable memory, or the Cache Movable Pool, is allocated from the bottom up, but the Cache Non-Movable, Permanent, and Alloc Short Term memory are allocated from the top down. The center of these areas is the File Cache Buffer Pool. NetWare maintains a minimum number of cache buffers (default of 20); without any, the file system cannot function.

Understanding NetWare 3.1x Memory Configuration

This section discusses ways in which you can determine the amount of memory your file server needs to perform properly by identifying the memory considerations particular to your installation. The issues to be considered are as follows:

- Minimum amount of memory to run NetWare
- Memory required by NLMs, including all drivers, name spaces, and communications devices

Understanding NetWare 3.1x Memory Configuration

- Total hard disk and volume sizes
- Number of directory entries (DET)
- Total memory required to properly cache volumes

Most NLMs require just enough memory to load; the memory needed is generally the size of the NLM. But many NLMs require the support of additional NLMs to operate. This requirement most often is true with communications NLMs, because they require buffer space. If so, the total size of all required NLMs must be considered. Some NLMs allocate additional memory as they are running. A simple method to determine memory requirements is to check memory before and after loading the NLM in the Resource Utilization option in the console MONITOR utility.

You can calculate estimated basic v3.1x file server memory requirements by using the following formulas. These numbers are estimated; each system has a different set of requirements because of the loads and expectations placed on the file server by its users.

```
M = .023 × VOLUME SIZE / BLOCK SIZE
```

The letter "M" is the memory required in megabytes.

If name space is added to a volume, then use the following:

```
M = .032 × VOLUME SIZE / BLOCK SIZE
TOTAL MEMORY = M1 + M2 + M3 + 2MB (ROUNDED TO THE HIGHEST M)
```

M1, M2, M3, and so on refer to each volume on the server.

If your file server has a 600M hard drive and you are setting it up to use the default of 4K blocks, for example, the following is true:

```
(600 × .023) / 4 = 3.45 + 2 = 5.45 or 6.0M
```

This number is rounded up to 6M, although most current PCs require you to go up in standard memory blocks of 4M, resulting in a server with 8M. With NetWare 3.1x, you should never be overly concerned with too much file cache as in NetWare 2.2. The memory concerns of NetWare 2.2 do not pertain to NetWare 3.1x. As a rule, in NetWare 3.1x, the more memory the merrier.

NetWare Tables and Buffers

NetWare makes use of tables and buffers to manage the attached disk drives. These tables and buffers enable NetWare to provide the high level of performance necessary to service many simultaneous users.

Each volume connected to a NetWare file server has two tables associated with it. The Directory Entry Table (DET) and File Allocation Table (FAT) both reside on the individual volumes and are loaded into cache buffers while running or mounted. NetWare 3.1x caches only the most recently used block of the DET. In earlier versions, the entire DET was cached.

Directory Entry Table (DET)

The DET contains all the directory entries for that particular volume. A *directory entry table* consists of data made up of items such as file and directory entries that include information on file name, owner, last date of update, and file location. The DET also contains entries for file trustees and directory trustees. Because NetWare 3.1x can span multiple hard disks, a disk might contain more than one DET. Directory Entry Blocks are always 4K regardless of the FAT blocks' settings. When a volume is first installed, six DET blocks are allocated. Each block can support 32 128-byte entries. The maximum number of DET blocks per volume is 65,536, which also reflects the maximum number of files per volume of 2,097,152. DET blocks are allocated automatically as needed.

File Allocation Table (FAT)

The File Allocation Table, or FAT, contains information corresponding to the location of disk blocks required to retrieve a file. This table is accessed from the DET. NetWare divides each volume into blocks or disk allocation blocks. You can configure these blocks during the installation process to have a block size of 4, 8,

16, 32, or 64K (the default is 4K). Each file stored on the volume has an entry in the FAT that lists all the blocks used to store the file.

File cache buffers are also an important feature of NetWare's performance. File cache buffers are blocks of memory where files are stored when being used.

 You can configure the size of these cache buffers, as in the FAT blocks, but never make them larger than the smallest disk allocation block.

These file cache buffers are the main memory used in the file server and make up the file cache buffer memory pool.

Directory Cache Buffers

Directory cache buffers are blocks of file server memory used to cache the DET blocks. NetWare allocates directory cache buffers as needed, taking them from the file cache buffer memory pool.

Packet Receive Buffers

Packet receive buffers are made up of file server memory areas set up as temporary holding areas for communications data coming in through the LAN interface. Data packets are held here until the file server can service them. During periods of heavy activity, data would be ignored and lost without this buffer area.

You can control these buffers by using a console SET command, and the MONITOR utility shows the number of buffers available for use.

Optimizing Memory and Performance

This section presents some of the more common concerns when configuring your file server memory and fine-tuning for performance. NetWare 3.1x provides many console SET commands to enable you to manually fine-tune your system. You should be aware, however, that in many cases simply adding file server memory eliminates the need to fine-tune or make adjustments. Novell has provided, as a default, a good set of rules if your file server is configured with the proper amount of memory.

NetWare 3.1x can support up to 4G of system memory. Resources are dynamically allocated as needed, and the system is designed to return memory no longer being used to the appropriate pools whenever possible.

Novell provides a basic tool to enable you to monitor the individual functions of the v3.1x file server. The MONITOR NLM provides many options and menus in which you can find performance-tuning information. The main information screen (statistics screen) of MONITOR displays some of the more important information when evaluating the performance of a file server.

The information as shown in figure 11.12 is informative when evaluating the basic condition of a file server. The following items are important to a properly operating file server. A basic understanding of these items is critical to understanding why a file server might be performing poorly.

- Total cache buffers
- Dirty cache buffers
- Packet receive buffers
- Directory cache buffers
- Service processes

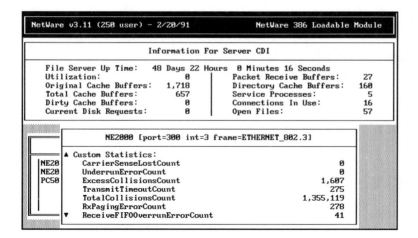

Figure 11.12
v3.1x Server Information screen.

Total Cache Buffers

The Total Cache Buffers field displays the total number of cache buffers currently available for use by the system. This number varies both up and down as NLMs and other processes require memory from the File Cache Memory Pool. If cache available buffers become too low, performance suffers. To determine the amount of memory available for cache buffers, check the Server Memory Statistics window found under the Resource Utilization option.

 If the Total Cache Buffers level gets to 20 percent or lower, add memory as soon as possible. An ideal level is 50 percent or better.

Dirty Cache Buffers

This field indicates the number of cache buffers that contain changed information and are waiting to be written to disk.

The number of dirty cache buffers should not reach more than 70 percent of the total cache buffers available.

If Dirty Cache Buffers consistently exceeds 70 percent, you can obtain some relief by setting the Maximum Concurrent Disk Cache Writes to a high number using the console SET command.

Packet Receive Buffers

This field shows the number of buffers configured to handle workstation requests. You also can configure this option by using the console SET commands. The SET commands are discussed later.

Directory Cache Buffers

This number indicates the number of cache buffers allocated to handle directory entries. You can modify this number as needed. If you have more than 100 buffers in use, you need to increase the minimum setting.

Service Processes

Service processes are "task handlers" configured to service workstation requests. These are dynamically configured as the load on the file server increases. You can configure the total maximum service processes with the appropriate console SET command.

File Server Statistics

You can monitor file server memory by selecting the Resource Utilization option from the main MONITOR screen. Here you are shown the way in which your file server's memory is allocated among the different pools. The two most important memory pools

Optimizing Memory and Performance

to monitor are the Alloc Memory Pool (the Alloc Short Term Memory Pool discussed earlier) and the cache buffers. If the Alloc Memory Pool reaches 2M, use the SET command to increase it by 1M. If this situation occurs, it can indicate a problem, and any third-party NLM developers should be contacted. The cache buffers should never fall below the level of 20 percent. If so, additional memory is required. Rebooting the server to recover memory from the permanent pools and unloading unnecessary NLM might provide temporary relief.

Many other options and resources can be monitored using NetWare's MONITOR utility. A few of the more important options are as follows:

- Resource Tags
- System Module Information
- Resource Utilization
- Processor Utilization

These options enable you not only to track your file server memory utilization, but also provide information on processes running on the server.

Resource Tags

This option displays a list of modules and tracked resources. This tool is helpful in determining if a particular NLM is not behaving properly. All NLMs are required to request resources from the operating system when they load. These resources should be returned after use. You can check this process by using this option.

System Module Information

System modules are NLMs. Selecting this option enables you to view the resources currently being used by a module.

Resource Utilization

The Resource Utilization option enables you to view the actual amount of memory being used in a pool by each resource. This option is useful in determining if a particular resource is consuming too much of the file server's memory.

Processor Utilization

This option of the MONITOR utility is only available when you load it using the -P command-line switch (LOAD MONITOR -P, for example). After you load MONITOR, select Processor Utilization from the main menu. You then are presented with a list of the currently loaded processes and interrupts being served by the CPU. To view a process or group of processes, simply use the NetWare standard function keys—F5 to mark and F3 to mark all. You then are shown a chart of the selected processes with information on Time, Count, and Load statistics. When viewing this screen, note that the Polling Process should represent most of the load.

If any NLM displays more than a 60-percent load, you should suspect a problem. NLMs that impose such a high load on the system can result in poor performance to all other users.

An example of the Resource Utilization screen appears in figure 11.13. Notice the load used by the polling process, which is normal.

Optimizing Memory and Performance

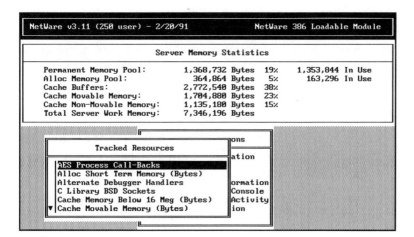

Figure 11.13
Resource Utilization screen.

Using Console SET Parameters

This section discusses some of the more common SET parameters used to adjust a v3.11 file server's performance. You can enter most of the parameters discussed here directly at the console prompt or place them in the AUTOEXEC.NCF and STARTUP.NCF files. The parameters covered in this section are grouped into the following categories:

- ◆ Communications
- ◆ Memory
- ◆ File caching
- ◆ Directory caching
- ◆ Miscellaneous

Many more SET parameters are supported by NetWare, but this book covers only the most important ones used in general system maintenance.

Communications

The following SET parameters pertain to network communications.

525

Maximum Packet Receive Buffers

This option enables you to configure the maximum number of packet receive buffers that the server can allocate.

Uses

If the current number of packet receive buffers is at the maximum, increase this number until you have one buffer per workstation. Increase this number in multiples of 10.

If you are using EISA or microchannel bus master boards in the file server, increase this number at least five buffers per board.

If you are receiving No ECB available count errors, increase this number at least 10 buffers per board.

Range

50 to 2000

Default

100

Placement

This option can be placed in the AUTOEXEC.NCF or entered at the console prompt.

Minimum Packet Receive Buffers

This parameter sets the minimum number of buffers the server immediately allocates upon booting.

Uses

Increase this number if the server is slow responding immediately after booting.

If you are using EISA or microchannel bus master boards in the file server, and you are receiving `No ECB available count` errors, increase this number at least five buffers per board.

Range

10 to 1000

Default

10

Placement

This option must be set in the STARTUP.NCF file.

Memory

The next few sections discuss SET parameters that pertain to memory.

Maximum Alloc Short Term Memory

This option enables you to set the amount of memory given to Alloc Short Term Memory.

Uses

Alloc Short Term Memory is responsible for drive mappings, NLM tables, user connection information, request buffers, open and locked files, and messages waiting to be broadcast.

Decrease this value if the server is allocating too much memory because of some temporary condition.

Increase this value if you receive error messages indicating that operations are not completed because this memory pool has reached its maximum.

Range

50000 to 16777216

Default

2097152

Placement

Place this option in the AUTOEXEC.NCF or type it at the console prompt.

Auto Register Memory Above 16 Megabytes

You can set this option to automatically see memory above 16M on an EISA bus machine.

Uses

Leave this option set to ON if you want the server to find memory above 16M.

Set this option to OFF if you have a network board that uses DMA or AT bus mastering. Leaving this option set to ON under these conditions corrupts file server memory.

Range

ON and OFF

Default

ON

Placement

This option must be set in the STARTUP.NCF file.

Cache Buffer Size

Use this option to set the size of the cache buffers.

Uses

If you are using block sizes greater than 4K, increasing the cache buffer size can improve performance.

If your volumes vary in size, set the cache buffer so that it is not larger than the smallest block size.

 The file server does not mount any volumes in which the block allocation size is smaller than the cache buffer size.

Range

4096, 8192, and 16384

Default

4096

Placement

This option must be set in the STARTUP.NCF file.

File Caching

The following SET parameter deals with file caching.

Minimum File Cache Buffers

All memory not being used by other processes is used for file caching. This option enables you to set the minimum number of file cache buffers needed on your system, thereby limiting the amount of memory given to requesting services.

Uses

If this number is set too high, you might have trouble loading additional NLMs into memory. Increase this value only when you need more memory for file caching.

Range

20 to 1000

Default

20

Placement

You can place this option in the AUTOEXEC.NCF or enter it at the console prompt.

Directory Caching

The next two SET parameters deal with directory caching.

Maximum Directory Cache Buffers

This option sets the maximum number of directory cache buffers the operating system is allowed to create.

Directory cache buffers are allocated permanently until the server is rebooted. This option helps to keep the number of unnecessary blocks down.

Uses

Increase this number if the file server is responding slowly when performing directory searches.

Decrease this number if you receive messages that the server is low on memory or if too much memory is being allocated to directory caching.

Range

20 to 4000

Default

500

Minimum Directory Cache Buffers

This option is set to allow a minimum number of directory cache buffers to be allocated for directory searches.

Uses

This number should be increased slightly when directory searches are slow immediately after booting the server. You must have enough buffers to perform searches quickly; you do not, however, want to over-allocate these buffers, because they do not go back into the memory pool. Unused directory cache buffers simply remain unused.

Range

10 to 2000

Default

20

Placement

You can set this option in the AUTOEXEC.NCF or STARTUP.NCF file or enter it at the console prompt.

Defining NetWare Name Service (NNS)

NetWare Name Service (NNS) is an item that you can purchase from Novell. Although it does not come automatically with NetWare 3.11, it is worth mentioning.

The first step to learning about NNS is defining the terms. The following sections define the words and phrases you encounter when exploring the potential benefits of NNS.

Domains

A *domain* is a group of servers networked together. Each domain can have up to a maximum of 400 file servers.

Profiles

A *profile* is a group of up to eight file servers in a domain. Because users can attach to a maximum of only eight servers (a universal NetWare limitation), *profiles* designate specific file server connections within a domain.

Synchronization

Each server in a domain has its bindery files and queues duplicated on all other servers. This process is called *synchronization* and is the engine by which NNS functions. A user can log in to any server in the domain with the same password. Because queues also are duplicated, the user does not have to specify a file server when printing, only the queue name. Logical queues are created on all servers in the domain, and print jobs are routed to the correct printer.

Filling in the Full Name field for each user is important. If two users have the same login name, synchronization is alerted if the full name is used.

Name Service Database

The Name Service Database is part of the binderies and contains information about users authorized to use the domain, their passwords, and their profile information.

Remember the following about NNS:

Domains

- Domains have a maximum of 400 file servers.

- A single file server can belong only to one domain.

- The domain login script replaces the system login script.

- User information and print queues are identical on all domain servers.

- Logical queues are created from the original on all other file servers in the domain.

- If all servers on the domain are NetWare 3.*x*, you can have up to 16 million users.

- If you have a mix of NetWare 2.*x* and NetWare 3.*x* servers, you can have only 5,000 users.

continues

continued

Profiles

- Each profile has a name.

- Each profile lists its members, which can be both users and groups.

- Profile login scripts are similar to user login scripts, but do not replace user login scripts.

- Each profile specifies up to eight file servers.

NETCON

When using NNS, the NETCON utility replaces SYSCON. The two utilities are similar.

For a workstation to run NETCON, you must have at least 640K of memory in the workstation.

Three major items have been added to NETCON as follows:

- **Change Current Domain.** This option is similar to Change Current Server in SYSCON. Change Current Domain enables you, if you have the appropriate rights, to look at information about another domain.

- **Domain Administration.** This option enables you to add and delete domain servers, to synchronize the user accounts and queues on the domain, and to edit the domain login script.

- **Profile Information.** This option enables you to set a full name for the profile, specify the domain managers, add members, modify the profile script, and designate up to eight servers for attachment.

When you purchase NNS, you receive several revised utilities. Do not replace these utilities with other versions after NNS is in place. The Name Service Database can become corrupt if non-NNS utilities are used. SYSCON is aware of NNS and alerts users that they should use NETCON.

Modified Utilities

The following sections discuss utilities and their parameters changed by NNS.

Printing Utilities

CAPTURE and NPRINT have added DO=*domain name* to specify a domain other than the default.

PCONSOLE now creates logical queues on all other servers whenever a new queue is added to the domain.

Connection Utilities

ATTACH, LOGIN, and LOGOUT have added @ *domain name* to specify which domain to attach to or log out of.

LOGIN has added /PRO=*profile* to specify which profile to use.

Examples of ways to use these files are as follows:

In the first example, INSTRUCT is the user attempting to attach to the domain CDI:

```
ATTACH INSTRUCT @ CDI
```

The next example logs in the user INSTRUCT to the domain CDI by using the profile EDUCATION. The profile designates to which file servers INSTRUCT attaches and executes the user's Profile Script.

```
LOGIN /PRO-EDUCATION INSTRUCT @ CDI
```

This following example logs the user out of the CDI domain.

```
LOGOUT @ CDI
```

User Utilities

SLIST and WHOAMI have added a /D parameter that specifies the domains available.

SETPASS has added the @ DOMAIN parameter to set your password on a domain.

MAKEUSER has added #DEFAULT_PROFILE to use when creating new users.

USERDEF now offers a Default Profile option.

The First NNS Server

The first server to utilize NNS becomes the template for all other servers and is considered the default server. For easy administration, the first server should be the one with the most users.

Passwords are set to expire automatically on the first domain server. Users must enter new passwords to maintain encrypted passwords. If you add more servers to the domain before users change their passwords, a random password is assigned to each user with an old password.

These items are not synchronized between domain servers:

- Directories and subdirectories
- Files
- Volume or disk space restrictions
- NetWare accounting
- Intruder detection
- Grace logins

Domain servers take up two grace logins whenever users decline a request to change passwords.

 A file is kept of the random passwords in SYS:SYSTEM/NEW.PWD.

Understanding Remote Management

NetWare 3.11 offers many features for remote file server management. File server access is available to LAN administrators connected directly to the LAN with a network interface and remotely through a modem. In this section, you are shown the different utilities supplied by Novell that allow this access.

Remote management enables you, as the system administrator, to perform the following tasks:

- Use file server utilities (NLMs)
- Search and edit files in DOS and NetWare directories
- Transfer files to a remote file server
- Install NetWare on a remote file server
- Add an existing file server to remote management
- Reboot a file server from a remote console

The first utility discussed here is RCONSOLE. RCONSOLE requires a total of three program modules to operate. Two of these modules are NLMs and operate on the file server; the third is a normal DOS-executable program. This utility communicates to the file server's console , enabling you to use the network cabling by using the NetWare SPX protocol. RCONSOLE provides complete access to the console, enabling you to use any NLM or console

Chapter 11: NetWare 3.1x Advanced System Manager

command. The RCONSOLE command is stored by default in volume SYS: under the SYSTEM directory to prevent any general user access to the utility itself. As a system administrator with supervisor privileges, this utility is available for your use.

For RCONSOLE to operate, you must first load the appropriate NLM modules on the file server. The first NLM to be loaded is REMOTE.NLM. This module provides the actual information exchange between the files server console and the remote administrator. The next NLM is RSPX.NLM, which supplies the communication layer that handles the actual connection through the SPX protocol and provides the advertisement of remote console capability to RCONSOLE users.

When loading the REMOTE.NLM, you are prompted for a password. This password is required for users who want to access the console by using the RCONSOLE DOS utility. When loading this NLM in the AUTOEXEC.NCF file, simply place the password on the command line as in the following example.

Simple AUTOEXEC.NCF statements are as follows:

```
LOAD REMOTE password
LOAD RSPX
```

The RCONSOLE utility provides complete access to the file server console along with the added features of scanning network directories and copying files to NetWare directories and DOS partitions.

Please note that the capability to copy files is in one direction only; you cannot copy from the network.

Upon executing the RCONSOLE utility, you are presented with a list of file servers advertising themselves as available for remote access. Select the file server you want to access, and you are

Understanding Remote Management

prompted for a password. This password can be either the password selected at the time the REMOTE.NLM was loaded, or the file server's SUPERVISOR password. At this time, the standard file server console screen appears.

If the keyboard is locked through the MONITOR utility, you are prompted to supply that password also.

Press the * key on the numeric keypad to open a menu of available options.

Press Shift+Esc to exit the remote console.

You can move between console screens by using both the + and - keys, also located on the numeric keypad.

From the available options menu, you can select one of the options shown in figure 11.14.

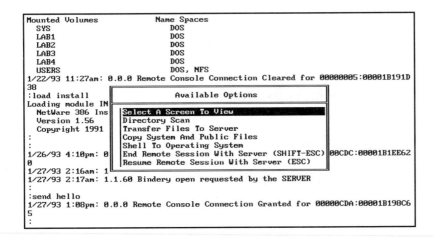

Figure 11.14
RCONSOLE available options.

Chapter 11: NetWare 3.1x Advanced System Manager

The RCONSOLE utility allows concurrent access to the file server. Thus, more than one system administrator can have access to the console at the same time. Although concurrent access can be beneficial when assisting a remote administrator through a problem, it also can cause confusion. If administrators using remote connections are working on different console screens, no conflicts arise. But if both users access the same console screen, keyboard entries can become mixed, creating confusion at first glance.

The Available Options menu of the RCONSOLE utility provides various functions that can assist you in your administrative tasks. The option Scan File Server Directories provides a way to scan or search both the DOS partition and NetWare volumes for any files about which you might be inquiring. If searching a DOS partition, make sure that you use the proper DOS drive letter, such as C. When searching NetWare volumes, make sure to use the full path including the volume label. This feature comes in handy for locating files you want to edit using the EDIT.NLM utility described later in this section.

The Transfer Files option enables you to copy files easily from your workstation to the file server. When you select this option, a screen appears requesting that you supply both the Source Path on Workstation and Target Path on Server. Each file is listed on the remote console screen as it is copied.

The next option is used to load or reload the original SYSTEM and PUBLIC utility files. This function is similar to that performed by the INSTALL.NLM with the exception that you must feed the floppy disks into your remote console.

 It is strongly recommended that loading of the utility files be performed only on RCONSOLE. The ACONSOLE utility, which is explained later, does not guarantee data delivery.

The option Resume Remote Session with Server enables you to return to the console screen after using any of the available options described here.

Understanding Remote Management

The End Remote Session menu option terminates the session in the same manner as all other Novell NetWare menu utilities. This option is one of many ways to properly exit the remote console operation. After selecting this option, a small menu box appears asking End Remote Console?. Selecting Yes or No determines the outcome. The remote console also can be exited by pressing Alt+F10 at the menu options. You also can press Shift+Esc, as instructed earlier, when you are in the remote console and bypass the menu options screen altogether.

ACONSOLE

ACONSOLE is NetWare's asynchronous remote console. This utility provides access to the file server through an asynchronous communications port by using a null modem cable or Hayes-compatible modem. You can use the ACONSOLE utility where support is provided over a large distance or as a redundant secondary link to the management workstation. This utility allows access to the file server even if the LAN cabling was not functional. If you intend to use ACONSOLE, the proper NLMs must be loaded at the file server. As with RCONSOLE, the REMOTE.NLM is loaded and a password is provided. Then the RS232.NLM is loaded with the parameters needed to communicate with your modem and COM port.

Please note that because of the communications speeds of asynchronous devices, file transfers are not recommended using ACONSOLE.

RSETUP.EXE

The RSETUP.EXE menu utility is designed to enable you to create a file server boot floppy. The RSETUP.EXE utility places all the required files and drivers, along with the AUTOEXEC.NCF and STARTUP.NCF, on the floppy. Although this utility is seldom used, you should be aware that it is available if needed.

EDIT.NLM

The EDIT.NLM utility is an ASCII text editor that enables you to edit files on NetWare volumes and file server DOS partitions. The EDIT command gives you the ability to modify NCF files while accessing the console. To use EDIT, simply use the console load command as in the following example:

LOAD EDIT oath/filename

This loads the EDIT utility with the specified file name. When you complete your file changes, press Esc and save your changes.

The Edit NLM searches directories created as search directories by using the console SEARCH command on the file server. By default, this directory is SYS:SYSTEM. You can have EDIT look to the file server's local drive as well.

You also can use the EDIT utility to create an NCF file that enables you to remotely reboot your file server. Create a file with the NCF extension and place the following command in it:

```
REMOVE DOS
DOWN
EXIT
```

You can use the EDIT.NLM to create various small (8K or smaller) files. When the file has an NCF extension, it can be used on the file server like a DOS batch file is used on a workstation.

Running this command from the file server console downs the server and automatically reboots. For this process to complete properly, you must have the server command in your AUTOEXEC.BAT file located on the C drive set up correctly.

Installing and Upgrading NetWare 3.12 Server and Client

You can install the NetWare 3.1x server from disk or, in the case of NetWare 3.12, from CD-ROM. Installing NetWare 3.1x enables you to install a new NetWare 3.1x server.

You also have the option of upgrading an existing NetWare server to NetWare 3.1x. Two utilities for upgrading current versions of NetWare are provided: MIGRATE.EXE and 2XUPGRDE.NLM. These utilities enable you to upgrade using three separate methods:

- Across-the-wire
- Same-server
- In-place

In addition to installing or upgrading your server, you also must install or upgrade clients (workstations).

An overview of server installation and upgrade, as well as client installation and upgrade, are discussed in this section.

Installing a NetWare 3.1x Server

You can run the NetWare 3.1x installation program by using the INSTALL disk or, in the case of NetWare 3.12, by running the INSTALL program from CD_ROM.

To run INSTALL from disk, place the disk in drive A of the computer on which you are installing NetWare 3.1x, then boot your computer.

 If you are installing NetWare 3.11, you can choose to install the files from an existing NetWare 3.11 server by entering **INSTALL J** rather than just INSTALL. Or, when you are prompted to copy the

continues

Chapter 11: NetWare 3.1x Advanced System Manager

continued

system and public files during the installation process, you can press F6 to select another drive letter from which to install.

If you are installing NetWare 3.12, the option to install files from other than drive A is assumed by default. Thus, the INSTALL J option used in NetWare 3.11 is not valid in NetWare 3.12, because it has already been incorporated into the installation program. The drive letter you choose can be a NetWare drive if you log in to a NetWare server and map drives before you start INSTALL.

To run install from CD-ROM, install the CD-ROM device and software, including the CD-ROM drivers, on to the computer. Make sure that the CD-ROM installation updated the CONFIG.SYS and AUTOEXEC.BAT files on the computer so that the CD-ROM drive is recognized on this system. Next, insert the NetWare 3.12 disc into the CD-ROM drive, and turn on the CD-ROM reader. Reboot the computer to make certain that the modified CONFIG.SYS and AUTOEXEC.BAT files are loaded. Change to the drive that represents the CD-ROM, then type **INSTALL** and press Enter.

Both of these installation startup processes load the installation interface that completes several tasks:

- Creating and formatting a DOS partition
- Copying system files for Novell DOS 6 to the created and formatted DOS partition
- Enabling you to enter a server name after the prompt
- Generating or assigning an IPX internal number
- Copying the server boot files to a server directory called SERVER.312
- Setting code page information
- Selecting to use the DOS file name format

- Creating the AUTOEXEC.NCF and STARTUP.NCF files
- Running the file that starts the server and loads it into memory—SERVER.EXE

Installation is provided through INSTALL.NLM. Figure 11.15 shows the INSTALL.NLM utility with screens open to specify a drive or directory for installing NetWare from other than drive A.

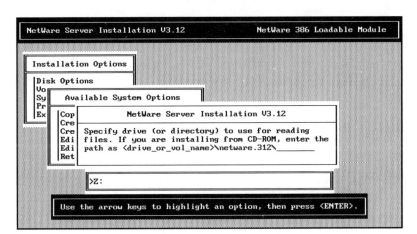

Figure 11.15
NetWare 3.12 INSTALL.NLM.

Creating and Formatting a DOS Partition

The first portion of the installation requires you to create and format a DOS partition on the hard drive of the computer onto which you are installing NetWare 3.1x. To accomplish this task, load the INSTALL NLM, choose Disk Options from the Installation Options screen, then select Format from the Available Disk Options screen. Formatting is optional; you do not need to do this step if the hard drive is already formatted.

By choosing Partition Tables from the Available Disk Options menu (see fig. 11.16), you can see if a DOS partition has already been created.

Figure 11.16

Partition Tables Option in Available Disk Options screen.

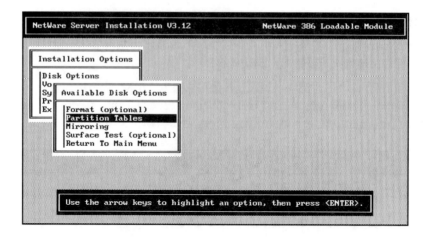

Copying System Files for Novell DOS 6

The NetWare 3.12 INSTALL disk includes two Novell DOS 6 system files, which are used to create partitions on the computer's hard disk. These files are FDISK.COM and FORMAT.COM. These files are included to make disk partitioning easier.

When partitioning the hard disk, you must allow a minimum DOS partition size of 2M, but Novell recommends using 5M as a minimum DOS partition size.

Naming the Server

The third main task to perform when installing NetWare 3.1x is to name the file server. Follow these rules when creating a name for the server:

- ◆ Give the server a name at least two characters long but that does not exceed 47 characters.

- ◆ Use only legal characters, which include any alphanumeric characters plus hyphens and underscores. Periods (.) and spaces cannot be used in a server name.

Some valid server names would include SERVER_1, ACCTG-1, S1, and S00147A.

Generating or Assigning an IPX Internal Network Number

Each NetWare 3.1x server has its own unique network number that identifies it from other servers on the network. The install program generates a random number for you during installation. You can use your own numbering system if you want.

An internal network number must consist of hexadecimal numbers. Using base 16, you can create an internal network number that contains the numbers 0 through 9 and/or the letters A through F. The internal network number must be no longer than eight digits, but can be as few as one digit. Consider the following examples:

- DAD
- BAD1
- 11111111
- 1BADCAD9

Set Code Page Information

NetWare 3.1x does not support multiple client languages. The install program, however, does enable you to choose a code page to set the language in which NetWare screens appear at the file server console.

Select DOS Filename Format

NetWare 3.12 does not require you to use only the standard DOS (eight characters plus a three-character dot extension) file naming convention. You have the option during install, therefore, to select the DOS filename format that you want to use. Novell, however, recommends that you select the DOS Filename Format and that you do not use extended characters.

Creating AUTOEXEC.NCF and STARTUP.NCF Files

Installation also creates AUTOEXEC.NCF and STARTUP.NCF files if you select the related Create option from the Available System Options menu.

To open the Available System Options menu, choose System Options from the Installation Options menu.

These two files control what happens when the server is first loaded. The AUTOEXEC.NCF file, for example, contains information that specifies in which time zone the server is located as well as the file server's name and IPX internal net number. This file also loads various files including the LAN board, and other information. Figure 11.17 shows the File Server AUTOEXEC.NCF File for a server called TSE-TSE.

Figure 11.17
File server AUTOEXEC.NCF file.

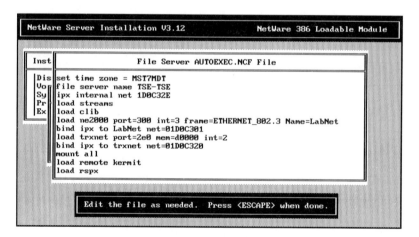

Load the Server (SERVER.EXE)

SERVER.EXE is the file that, when run on the computer, loads the NetWare 3.1x server.

Loading the server causes the AUTOEXEC.NCF and the STARTUP.NCF files to run. These files, as mentioned previously, perform such tasks as loading the LAN driver, binding the communication protocol to the LAN board, and loading NLMs such as MONITOR.NLM.

Upgrading Existing NetWare Servers

If your computer currently has an earlier version of NetWare 2.x or NetWare 3.x installed on it, two utilities are provided that enable you to upgrade that server to NetWare 3.12. These utilities are MIGRATE.EXE and 2XUPGRDE.NLM.

You run MIGRATE.EXE from a client attached to the network. The network requires both a source and a destination server in order to run this utility. (A *source server* is a server from which the files are being migrated, and a *destination server* is a server to which the files are being migrated.)

You run 2XUPGRDE.NLM at the server.

MIGRATE.EXE

MIGRATE.EXE enables you to upgrade the files on a NetWare 2.x or 3.x server to NetWare 3.12. This utility enables you to run two types of migrations:

- Across-the-wire migration
- Same-server migration

An *across-the-wire* migration is run from a DOS client. It takes files from a source server to a destination server using the network cabling system.

A *same-server migration* takes the bindery information on an existing NetWare server, copies it to a working directory on a network DOS client, translates (upgrades) the bindery information so that it is usable in a NetWare 3.1x format, then migrates it from the DOS client to the destination (NetWare 3.1x) server.

The MIGRATE.EXE utility enables you to perform a standard migration or a custom migration. If you have run the migration utility several times before and are very familiar with it, then you can run the Custom migration. Otherwise, Novell recommends that you run the Standard migration. Figure 11.18 shows the screens that appear when you choose Standard migration when running MIGRATE.EXE.

Chapter 11: NetWare 3.1x Advanced System Manager

The across-the-wire migration enables you to merge multiple-source servers to create a single, customized destination server. This option is particularly useful in an environment in which you have several older computers running older versions of NetWare that would be more useful to you if you combined their bindery files into one bindery on a more powerful computer.

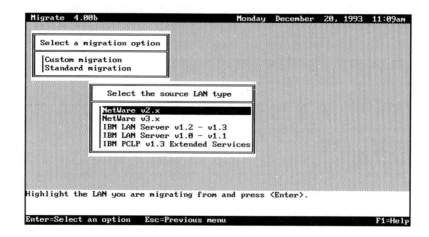

Figure 11.18
Standard migration option in MIGRATE.EXE.

When migrating source servers, you can let the system assign random passwords to the users whose accounts are migrated. Figure 11.19 shows the migration window that enables you to set a working directory for the migration files, define the NetWare source and destination servers, and even choose to assign random passwords to user accounts.

Regardless of whether you choose to let the system assign random passwords to user accounts, merging several source servers into one offers several other benefits. Some of those benefits include the following:

- ♦ You can establish a default account balance and account restrictions on the installed NetWare 3.1x destination server, which then is applied to the migrated accounts.

- ♦ You can set up other user restrictions on the destination server, which also are applied to the migrated accounts.

- You can preserve each user's individual account restrictions for each individual source server.

- You can merge users on different source servers into groups established on the single destination server.

- You can combine print queues and print servers to a single print queue that services multiple printers and let multiple queues service a single printer.

The across-the-wire upgrade is flexible and can help you overcome some networking restrictions. If the across-the-wire upgrade is not an option for you, however, you still can perform an in-place upgrade.

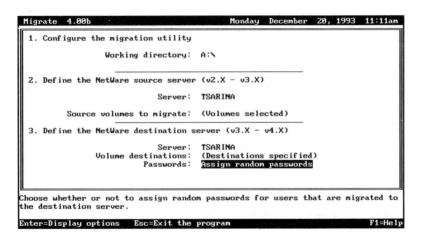

Figure 11.19
Migration configuration screen.

2XUPGRDE.NLM

The in-place upgrade uses the 2XUPGRDE.NLM, loaded at the server to be upgraded. The *in-place upgrade* enables you to upgrade an existing NetWare 2.1*x* server to a NetWare 3.1*x* server without the need for a second server. Your existing NetWare server must meet some minimum hardware requirements, however, including the following:

- An Intel 80386 processor
- 4M of RAM

Chapter 11: NetWare 3.1*x* Advanced System Manager

- ◆ The ability to be booted as a DOS device
- ◆ The ability to load SERVER.EXE

If your existing server can meet these minimum requirements, you can perform an in-place upgrade on this server.

Before running the in-place upgrade, however, you *must* back up your current server. A power failure or upgrade interruption at the wrong moment can cause you to lose your existing server information.

Novell considers the backup of your server before upgrading to be a very important step. So important, in fact, that one of the first screens you see after loading the 2XUPGRDE.NLM is a warning screen that prompts you to answer Yes or No to whether you have a recent backup of your server (see fig. 11.20). If you answer No to this prompt, the in-place upgrade is aborted.

Figure 11.20
The In-Place Upgrade Backup Prompt screen.

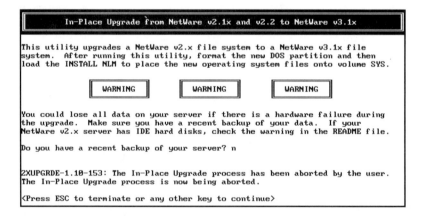

The in-place upgrade is run in four stages. First, an analysis of the system is performed to determine which disks are on the server and the amount of memory needed and available to complete an upgrade.

The second stage performs an analysis of the critical parts of the disks, looking in particular at the Hot Fix area, the File Allocation Tables, and the Directory Entry Tables. The FATs and DETs are then translated for the newer NetWare version, and directory attributes, file attributes, and Macintosh files are upgraded.

The third stage makes needed modifications to the disks, upgrades the partition table, adds the NetWare 3.1x files, and relocates data blocks as needed.

The fourth stage actually creates and updates the NetWare bindery.

The in-place upgrade has three limitations—it cannot upgrade any of the following:

- VAPs (*value-added processes*)
- Core printing services
- Volume and disk restrictions

Figure 11.21 shows the Phase Descriptions screen of the in-place upgrade. The purpose of this screen is two-fold. First, it shows you the process that NetWare goes through to upgrade your existing server. Understanding this process is important—if problems occur during the upgrade, you might have to restore your backup and start over.

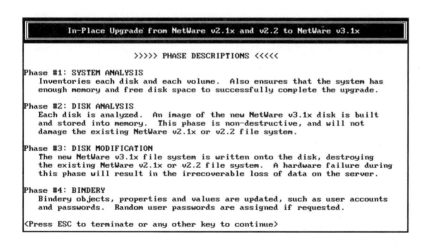

Figure 11.21

The In-Place Upgrade Phase Descriptions screen.

The second purpose of this screen is to give you another opportunity to exit the in-place upgrade before it begins—in case, after reading the Phase Descriptions screen, you realize you still need to do something before you start the in-place upgrade.

Installing a DOS Client

In addition to installing or upgrading a NetWare server, the DOS clients that use the server need to be updated as well. The DOS client installation is quick and easy to perform. Five steps are needed to update the DOS client. These steps appear as questions on the initial NetWare Client Install screen. These steps include the following:

1. Enter the target directory name for Client Installation. By default, the client files are installed to a directory called C:\NWCLIENT. You can change the location of these files if you need to.

2. Allow changes to the CONFIG.SYS and AUTOEXEC.BAT files. One line needs to be added to each of these files. To the CONFIG.SYS file, add LASTDRIVE=Z; to AUTOEXEC.BAT, add CALL STARTNET.BAT.

   The LASTDRIVE command makes it possible for your client to access all network drives, up through and including drive Z. If this entry is set to anything other than Z, your client only sees up to and including the drive letter that was set in this file. If no LASTDRIVE line exists in the CONFIG.SYS file, your client does not see any network drives.

   The CALL STARTNET.BAT line in the AUTOEXEC.BAT file calls another file that is added during the DOS client installation. This other file, STARTNET.BAT, is used to load the NetWare DOS Requester. (See Chapter 7 for more information on the NetWare DOS Requester.)

3. Choose whether to install support for Windows. If you do not run Windows on your client, choose No. If you run Windows on your client, choose Yes, then enter the path and directory name in which your Windows files are stored. Because this directory is usually C:\WINDOWS, it is the default. Change the default if the Windows files are stored elsewhere on this client.

Installing and Upgrading NetWare 3.12 Server and Client

4. Install a driver for your LAN board. If possible, the DOS client install program detects the installed LAN board and its settings and fills in this information for you. If the DOS client install program cannot detect the type of LAN card installed in this client, you must choose the card from a list of drivers and enter the configuration information manually.

5. Start the installation by pressing Enter with step 5 highlighted.

The DOS Client Installation also enables you to upgrade ODI files and drivers. If the installation program finds an existing ODI LAN driver, it tells you that a newer version of the driver is being installed.

Each update to the DOS Client Installation attempts to simplify the installation process. NetWare 3.11 simplifies the installation process by only requiring that you create a NET.CFG file. NetWare 3.12 does not have GENSH, SHELLGEN, or WSGEN utilities. In addition, NetWare 3.12 creates the NET.CFG file for you if one does not exist or automatically updates the one that does exist if you choose to have it do so.

If you have to upgrade several DOS clients that have similar hardware and software configurations, Novell provides two utilities to simplify that process:

- **WSUPGRD.** Upgrades IPX drivers currently using the IPX.EXE file, to make them ODI drivers.

- **WSUPDATE.** Updates workstation files such as NET.CFG and CONFIG.SYS when they already exist on your DOS clients and when the configurations set in these files are the same for many clients.

These two utilities should be used with caution, because a variety of network problems can result from incorrectly updating NET.CFG and CONFIG.SYS files in multiple clients with different configurations. (For more information about these two utilities, refer to *Workstation Basics and Installation* in the NetWare DOS Client kit documentation.)

Review Questions

1. Which of the following statements is true about NET.CPG?

    a. Link Driver Options should be at the top of the file and Cache Options should be at the end of the file.

    b. NET.CFG and SHELL.CPG are interchangeable.

    c. You need to define every option under the headings.

    d. Headings need to be left-justified; options need to be indented.

2. Which of the following statements about Shell options is false?

    a. INT64 and INT7A both default to ON.

    b. You should increase the number of IPX RETRY COUNT if the workstation is running PCONSOLE.

    c. SPX CONNECTIONS only needs to be increased to 60 if the workstation is running PSERVER.EXE.

    d. CACHE BUFFERS=n and FILE HANDLES=n belong in NET.CFG; BUFFERS=n and FILES=n belong in CONFIG.SYS.

3. Which SET parameter should be increased if the network is large and traffic is heavy or RPRINTER is used over routers?

    a. IPX RETRY COUNT
    b. SPX ABORT TIMEOUT
    c. SPX RETRY COUNT
    d. A and B
    e. B and C

4. Which of the following statements is correct for making certain that a workstation without a printer does not lock up if the user presses Shift+PrntScr?

    a. LOCAL PRINTERS=0
    b. LOCAL PRINTERS=NO
    c. CAPTURE
    d. A and C

5. If the print job you are sending to the printer contains an unusually high amount of initialization codes for the printer, which of the following statements should you increase?

    a. PRINT HEADER=*n*
    b. PRINT TAIL=*n*
    c. LOCAL PRINTER=*n*
    d. PRINTER INITIALIZE=*n*

6. Which of the following statements about SBACKUP terminology is false?

    a. A host also can be a target.
    b. A parent is a bindery or a directory.
    c. A child can be a file or an empty subdirectory.
    d. A target is any server backed up with SBACKUP.

7. Which of the following statements about SBACKUP NLMs is false?

    a. SBACKUP is comprised of three target modules and two host modules.

    b. SIDR is the data requester and uses SMSP.

    c. TSA links the data requester and the target.

    d. SBACKKUP.NLM is the user interface.

8. Which rotation method is the easiest to maintain?

    a. Two-Week Inverted

    b. Tower of Hanoi

    c. Ten-Tape Rotation

    d. Grandfather Rotation Method

9. How many tapes does the Grandfather Rotation Method require?

    a. 19 plus one fresh tape a month

    b. 20 for the year

    c. 10 tapes for the year

    d. 5 to 8 tapes a year

10. Which of the following statements about VREPAIR is true?

    a. You must have the appropriate VREPAIR for each name space that you want to remove.

    b. VREPAIR enables you to write the DET and FAT tables to a floppy disk.

    c. VREPAIR should be run occasionally to fix problems on the hard drive.

    d. VREPAIR should be run on a downed file server.

Review Questions

11. Which memory pool is responsible for pop-up menus like MONITOR?

    a. File Cache Buffer

    b. Cache Movable

    c. Cache Non-Movable

    d. Permanent

    e. Semi-Permanent

    f. Alloc Short Term

12. Which memory pool is responsible for FATs and DETs?

    a. File Cache Buffer

    b. Cache Movable

    c. Cache Non-Movable

    d. Permanent

    e. Semi-Permanent

    f. Alloc Short Term

13. From which memory pool are all other pools taken?

    a. File Cache Buffer

    b. Cache Movable

    c. Cache Non-Movable

    d. Permanent

    e. Semi-Permanent

    f. Alloc Short Term

Chapter 11:   NetWare 3.1x Advanced System Manager

14. Which memory pool is used to load and unload NLMs?

    a. File Cache Buffer

    b. Cache Movable

    c. Cache Non-Movable

    d. Permanent

    e. Semi-Permanent

15. Which memory pool can be reduced by limiting the number of network drive mappings users have?

    a. File Cache Buffer

    b. Cache Movable

    c. Cache Non-Movable

    d. Permanent

    e. Semi-Permanent

16. Which memory pool cannot be used by NLMs?

    a. File Cache Buffer

    b. Cache Movable

    c. Cache Non-Movable

    d. Permanent

    e. Semi-Permanent

17. Which memory pool is used when loading LAN and disk drivers?

    a. File Cache Buffer

    b. Cache Movable

    c. Cache Non-Movable

    d. Permanent

    e. Semi-Permanent

Review Questions

18. Which of the following statements about NNS is false?
    a. A file server can be in multiple domains.
    b. A file server can be in multiple profiles.
    c. A profile can include only eight servers.
    d. The domain login script replaces the system login script.

19. Which of the following statements about NNS is true?
    a. SYSCON should be used along with NETCON.
    b. NNS is not included with NetWare 3.11.
    c. Synchronization creates physical queues on each file server.
    d. Only one grace login is used when a user is asked to change his password and NNS is running.

20. Which of the following statements about Remote Management is false?
    a. The EDIT command is used to create the reboot file.
    b. RSETUP creates a bootable disk for the remote server.
    c. Typing **DOWN** reboots the server.
    d. RCONSOLE requires REMOTE.NLM and RSPX.NLM to be loaded in that order.

21. Which of the following is *not* an upgrade option?
    a. Across-the-wire
    b. Same-server
    c. Workstation-to-server
    d. In-place

Chapter 11:   NetWare 3.1x Advanced System Manager

22. Which install option has become part of the NetWare 3.12 INSTALL?

    a. INSTALL A

    b. INSTALL C

    c. INSTALL J

    d. INSTALL U

23. Which *two* Novell DOS 6 system files are copied to the DOS partition during INSTALL?

    a. FORMAT.EXE

    b. FORMAT.COM

    c. RDISK.COM

    d. FDISK.COM

24. Which of the following is *not* a legal server name?

    a. AMADMAN

    b. 123B4FAD

    c. 00712

    d. S_123BAD

25. Which of the following *cannot* be used in server names?

    a. Hyphen (-)

    b. Underscore (_)

    c. Space

    d. Hexadecimal characters

Review Questions

26. INSTALL randomly generates a(n) _____ that you can change.
    a. server name
    b. IPX internal number
    c. STARTUP.NCF
    d. SET SERVER=0

27. MIGRATE.EXE is run from:
    a. A NetWare 2.x server
    b. A NetWare 3.x server
    c. A dedicated file server
    d. A client

28. MIGRATE.EXE enables you to run which *two* types of migrations?
    a. Across-the-wire
    b. Same-server
    c. In-place
    d. DOS-client

29. Which of the following is *not* a benefit of merging several source servers into one?
    a. Default account balances can be established on the new server
    b. Users can be merged into groups
    c. Print queues and print servers can be combined
    d. You can use your existing Intel 80286 server

30. Which of the following is a minimum requirement of the destination server when running 2XUPGRDE.NLM?

   a. An 80486 Intel processor

   b. 6M RAM

   c. A DOS device

   d. Two different source and destination computers

31. The 2XUPGRDE.NLM can upgrade server files except:

   a. VAPs

   b. SERVER.EXE

   c. Core printing

   d. Users and groups

32. Which file is not updated during client install?

   a. STARTNET.BAT

   b. CONFIG.BAT

   c. AUTOEXEC.BAT

   d. CONFIG.SYS

Case Study

1. Create a NET.CFG file for a workstation on your network. Define each parameter.

PART 5

Appendixes

Appendix A
Answers to Review Questions

Appendix B
Test Objectives

Appendix C
Comparison Charts

Appendix D
NetWare 2.15

Answers to Review Questions

Chapter 3

1. B
2. C
3. C
4. A
5. B
6. B
7. A
8. B
9. D
10. D
11. C
12. D
13. B
14. C
15. A
16. B
17. D
18. A
19. A
20. B

Answers to Review Questions Chapters 4 – 6

Chapter 4

1. B
2. C
3. D
4. B
5. D
6. A
7. C
8. B
9. B
10. D
11. A
12. C
13. A
14. D
15. A
16. D
17. D
18. B
19. D
20. C

Chapter 5

1. A
2. B
3. D
4. C
5. B
6. A
7. D
8. B
9. D
10. A
11. B
12. A
13. B
14. C
15. C
16. A
17. D
18. B
19. C
20. D
21. A
22. C
23. A
24. B
25. D

Chapter 6

1. C
2. B
3. A
4. B
5. B
6. A
7. B
8. C
9. B
10. B
11. A
12. A
13. B
14. D
15. A
16. A
17. C
18. D
19. B
20. C
21. B
22. C
23. A
24. C
25. D

Chapter 7

1. B
2. A
3. D
4. A
5. C
6. D
7. C
8. A
9. D
10. C
11. A
12. A
13. B
14. C
15. A
16. C
17. B
18. A
19. D
20. D
21. C
22. A
23. C
24. B
25. A
26. D
27. B
28. A
29. D
30. D
31. B
32. A

Chapter 8

1. C
2. A
3. B
4. D
5. B
6. A
7. A
8. D
9. A&C
10. C
11. B
12. D
13. B
14. D
15. C
16. B
17. C
18. A
19. B
20. D
21. D
22. D
23. B
24. A
25. C

Answers to Review Questions Chapters 9 – 11

Chapter 9

1. B
2. C
3. C
4. D
5. B
6. D
7. A
8. E
9. C
10. A
11. B
12. B
13. A
14. D
15. C
16. B
17. D
18. A
19. B
20. D
21. D
22. C
23. A&B
24. B
25. C

Chapter 10

1. B
2. C
3. A
4. D
5. D
6. A
7. C
8. A
9. B
10. C
11. D
12. C
13. A
14. C
15. B
16. C
17. D
18. D
19. A
20. B
21. C
22. A
23. B
24. B

Chapter 11

1. D
2. B
3. D
4. D
5. A
6. C
7. A
8. D
9. B
10. A
11. F
12. B
13. A
14. C
15. F
16. D
17. E
18. A
19. B
20. C
21. C
22. C
23. B&D

Answers to Review Questions Chapters 11 – D

24. A
25. C
26. B
27. D
28. A&B
29. D
30. C
31. A&C
32. B

Appendix D

1. C
2. A
3. D
4. B
5. A
6. C
7. B
8. D
9. B
10. C

Test Objectives

This appendix contains Novell's list of test objectives. Before you take any test, consult this list as a final study measure. Make sure that you understand each point.

These objectives are current as of the publication of this book. The objectives are subject to change at Novell's discretion, and the presence of the objectives in this book does not constitute an endorsement by Novell, Inc. Readers are cautioned to obtain the current objectives from Novell when they begin to study for a course.

NetWare 2.2 System Manager: Test #50-20

1. List the responsibilities of a system manager.
2. Relate course topics to those responsibilities.
3. Fill in a NetWare log.
4. Use general system management resources provided by Novell.
5. Define a network.
6. List the hardware components of a network.
7. Choose the best option for expanding your network.
8. List the software components needed to access the network from the DOS environment.

Appendix B: Test Objectives

9. Choose and load IPX and the shell.
10. Create a distributed processing environment.
11. Use various tolerance features of NetWare 2.2.
12. Diagram the levels of the NetWare directory structure.
13. Name the required volume, the four required directories, and their contents and location in the directory structure.
14. Diagram possible directory structures given an organization and its needs.
15. Create an organized and efficient directory syntax.
16. Construct a directory path using the required syntax.
17. Work with DOS and NetWare commands related to directory structures and their contents.
18. Identify the default drive pointers in both the DOS and NetWare environments.
19. Use the MAP command to move through the directory structure.
20. Differentiate between drive mappings and search drive mappings.
21. Understand the effects of the DOS CD command on MAP.
22. List the levels of NetWare security.
23. Use command-line utilities to apply NetWare's security to a basic directory structure.
24. Understand security features implemented on the system through "user types."
25. Understand the correlation between NetWare command-line utilities and NetWare menu utilities.
26. Identify the workstation commands incorporated in these menus.
27. Recognize the specific tasks that can be accomplished within each menu utility.

28. Use the appropriate menu utility to create trustees, make trustee assignments, adjust all aspects of security, view directories and their contents, copy files, send messages, and manipulate drive pointers.
29. Describe the purpose of specific supervisor commands.
30. Identify the directory where supervisor commands are located and the limitations of other users to this directory.
31. Function within the special menu utilities reserved for supervisor use.
32. Recognize the function of console commands and where they are issued.
33. Identify the two printing services available.
34. Identify parameters for choosing the right service.
35. Create print queues.
36. Assign queues to printers.
37. Create spooler assignments.
38. Create a system AUTOEXEC.SYS file.
39. Print files by using CAPTURE, ENDCAP, and NPRINT.
40. Create, control, and monitor queues through PCONSOLE.
41. Determine application compatibility with NetWare.
42. Recognize the features necessary to allow multi-user access.
43. Determine the placement within a directory structure for easiest access and maintenance.
44. Perform the steps required by security to ensure safe and reliable results.
45. Contrast the three login scripts used on the network.
46. Identify and use login script commands to create a system and user login script.
47. Debug problems in login script logic.

48. Identify vital mappings that must exist in the system login script.
49. Customize a user environment using menus.
50. Recognize the menu option file format and syntax.
51. Create custom menus.
52. Execute custom menus.
53. List the functions of the NBACKUP utility.
54. Identify the rules for running NBACKUP.
55. List the basic steps for backing up a file server.
56. Identify the basic steps for restoring backed-up data.
57. Use NBACKUP to protect your data.
58. Configure a network.
59. Control security.
60. Organize login scripts.
61. Create menus.
62. Understand and use most of the commands introduced in this course.

NetWare 2.2 Advanced System Manager: Test #50-44

1. Choose the correct installation mode for your network environment.
2. Install NetWare 2.2 in the chosen mode.
3. Install the workstation software that best fits each user's needs.
4. Update workstation files from an earlier version of NetWare to be used on a NetWare 2.2 workstation.

5. Use multiple methods for creating and defining trustees.
6. Use multiple methods to restrict or control user access and use of your Novell network.
7. Use the FCONSOLE utility to master performance management techniques.
8. Expand your printing options and capabilities by installing and configuring a NetWare print server.
9. List the hardware requirements for a file server.
10. List the software requirements to install the operating system.
11. Understand the options available during operating system installations.
12. Choose the correct installation options for your network environment.
13. Install the NetWare 2.2 operating system in the chosen mode.
14. Understand the environment of the workstation.
15. Select the appropriate shell files for each workstation.
16. Use WSGEN to create the workstation files required for different environments.
17. Use WSUPDATE to update your shell and other files.
18. Define and create a router.
19. Create specialized configuration files for individual users' needs.
20. Restrict the number of workstations that can use the same login name at one time.
21. Restrict users to specific workstations.
22. Control minimum password length.
23. Control the frequency with which the password must be changed.
24. Restrict the times when users can be logged in.

Appendix B: Test Objectives

25. Restrict network disk storage by users.
26. Set parameters to help detect and deny intruder logins.
27. Use SYSCON to view the File Server Error Log.
28. Use NDIR to access network information on files and directories.
29. Use options of NDIR to find files with specific characteristics.
30. Establish resources for NetWare resource sharing.
31. Control and monitor the use of file server resources.
32. Create charges to be assessed against users for use of those resources.
33. Use the ATOTAL command to track summaries of file server resource use.
34. Use the PAUDIT command to view details of resource use.
35. Use advanced utilities to set up users.
36. Recognize which utility is best suited for a particular situation.
37. Establish defaults that fit your own users' needs.
38. Write the minimum and maximum memory requirements for NetWare 2.2.
39. Explain what a file service process is.
40. Explain the way in which DGroup memory affects the number of file service processes.
41. Change certain user-definable variables to possibly increase file service processes.
42. Use FCONSOLE to determine if there is enough memory in a file server to run efficiently.
43. Find other statistics in FCONSOLE to help manage memory and other functions of the network file server.

44. Determine if a network performance problem is indicated, given individual statistics from the Statistics Summary, Cache Statistics, and Disk Statistics screens.

45. Identify the possible course(s) of action to take when specific problems are indicated in the statistics screens.

46. Identify printing services and specifications.

47. Describe the purpose and functions of specific printing utilities.

48. Implement the appropriate steps in the NetWare 2.2 printing setup process.

49. Identify and use command-line utilities with the correct syntax for printing-related tasks.

50. Use PRINTDEF to create customized printer definitions, modes, and forms.

51. Use PRINTCON to create customized print jobs.

52. Print files using the jobs created in PRINTCON.

NetWare 3.11 System Manager: Test #50-91

1. Identify the responsibilities of a NetWare 3.11 system manager.

2. List the relationship of the course topics to those responsibilities.

3. Identify the relationships between the network operating system and the local operating system.

4. Describe the function of the shell/requester and the types of shells and support offered in v3.11.

5. List the method of processing used on a local area network.

6. Identify internal performance features.

Appendix B: Test Objectives

7. Identify system reliability features.
8. Describe procedures used to log in to the system.
9. Identify levels of the NetWare directory structure.
10. Name the required NetWare volume and the four system-created directories with their contents and locations in the directory structure.
11. Organize an efficient directory structure.
12. Write a NetWare directory path using the proper syntax.
13. Identify the functions of the DOS and NetWare commands related to directory structures.
14. Identify the default drive pointers in the DOS and NetWare environments.
15. Differentiate network drive mappings and search drive mappings.
16. Identify the appropriate parameters and syntax for using the MAP command to move through the directory structure.
17. Identify the levels and functions of network security.
18. Identify methods used at each security level to control access.
19. Compare the rights and responsibilities of the different types of managers and operators.
20. Identify the function and effect of each right.
21. List rights required for specified tasks.
22. Define security terms.
23. Determine effective rights for given cases.
24. Identify the function and effect of each attribute.
25. Select appropriate command-line utilities related to NetWare security.
26. Identify the purpose and capabilities of the SYSCON and FILER utilities.

27. Match related commands to specified tasks in a given utility.
28. Identify procedures needed to perform given tasks in SYSCON and FILER.
29. Identify the purpose and major capabilities of the SYSCON Accounting feature.
30. Identify procedures needed to create additional managers on the network.
31. Identify the purpose and functions of the MAKEUSER, USERDEF, DSPACE, and SALVAGE utilities.
32. Identify procedures needed to perform given tasks with the DSPACE and SALVAGE utilities.
33. Differentiate between console commands and NetWare loadable modules (NLMs).
34. Identify the functions of the remote management feature.
35. Identify the functions of major console commands.
36. Identify the purposes and functions of NLMs.
37. List tasks that can be performed by using specific NLMs.
38. Identify procedures for loading NLMs.
39. Identify printing services and specifications.
40. Describe the purposes and functions of specific printing utilities.
41. Identify appropriate steps in the NetWare 3.11 printing setup process.
42. Identify the pertinent utilities to implement the printing setup process.
43. Identify appropriate printing-related command-line utilities and proper syntax for given tasks.
44. Contrast the three types of login scripts used on the network.
45. Identify appropriate login script commands and proper syntax needed to create a system and user login script.

Appendix B: Test Objectives

46. Identify errors in login script logic for given cases.
47. Identify mappings that must exist in a user's login environment.
48. List specifications for creating custom menus.
49. Identify components of a turnkey system.
50. Identify proper menu option file format and syntax.
51. Follow procedures needed to execute custom menus.
52. Identify basic guidelines for selecting application software.
53. List basic steps to be completed when loading applications.
54. List the functions of the NBACKUP utility.
55. Identify rules for running NBACKUP.
56. List basic steps for backing up the file server.
57. Identify basic steps for restoring backed-up data.

NetWare 3.1x System Administration: Test #50-130

1. Describe the basic function and services of a network.
2. Identify the client types supported in NetWare 3.12.
3. Describe workstation communications with the network and list the files required to connect a DOS workstation to the network.
4. Describe the function of the software necessary to connect a workstation to the network, including local operating systems, NetWare DOS Requester, communications protocols, and network.
5. Connect a workstation to the network by loading the appropriate DOS workstation files.

NetWare 3.1x System Administration: Test #50-130

6. Explain and perform the login procedure.
7. Identify, navigate, and perform similar basic functions using a DOS text utility, a command-line utility, and graphical utility.
8. Activate and navigate Help for each type of utility.
9. Activate and navigate Novell ElectroText.
10. Explain the basic concepts of network file storage, including volume and directory structures.
11. Describe a volume and its technical specifications.
12. Describe a directory, including its main functions, hierarchical structure, directory name, and directory path.
13. List the system-created directories on the SYS: volume and describe their contents.
14. Access file systems by mapping network drives to volumes and directories.
15. Navigate volumes and directories by using network drives.
16. Access network applications by mapping search drives to application directories.
17. Display and modify the display of file system information on volumes, directories, and files.
18. Perform directory management tasks such as creating, deleting, and renaming directories.
19. Perform file management tasks such as copying, moving, deleting, salvaging, and purging files.
20. Identify the levels and functions of network security.
21. Describe login security including user account restrictions, time restrictions, station restrictions, and intruder detection.
22. Set up network user accounts and apply account restrictions.
23. Set up group accounts and user account management.
24. Describe packet signature.

Appendix B: Test Objectives

25. Describe NetWare 3.12 file system security, including the concepts of trustees, directory and file rights, inheritance, Inherited Rights Mask, and effective rights.
26. Make a trustee assignment and apply rights in SYSCON and FILER.
27. Calculate effective rights.
28. Describe directory and file attributes and their use in a file system security plan.
29. Implement a file system security plan using command-line and menu utilities.
30. Describe the function of the CONFIG.SYS, AUTOEXEC.BAT, and NET.CFG configuration files.
31. Alter workstation configuration files so that they contain all pertinent information to automate the process of connecting to the network, loading the DOS requester, and logging in to the network.
32. Perform a DOS and MS Windows client installation using the NetWare client installation software.
33. Describe the types of login scripts and how they coordinate at login.
34. Explain each login script command, propose standard procedures that are executed through login scripts, and plan a system of login scripts for user login.
35. Build and execute the plan using system and user login scripts.
36. Describe the components of a user menu system.
37. Describe NetWare 3.12 menu command language, and plan a simple user menu.
38. Build and execute a NetWare 3.12 menu.
39. Convert menu files from earlier versions of NetWare into the new menu utility.

40. Describe the function of a server, its interface, and its communication with the network.

41. Describe console commands, and identify the function of commands commonly used by administrators.

42. Describe NLMs, explain how they are loaded, and identify their types.

43. Identify the purpose and function of the major NLMs such as INSTALL, MONITOR, and UPS.

44. Describe remote console management, and list the steps necessary to set up a server for both SPX and asynchronous remote connections.

45. Use RCONSOLE.EXE to connect remotely to the server, and describe the purpose and function of the available options in RCONSOLE.

46. Implement console security features on the server by assigning a console password and placing the server in a secure location.

47. Describe the basic components of network printing and the way they interrelate in processing a print job. Describe the general steps necessary for setting up the components.

48. Set up a network printing environment by creating and configuring a related and functional print queue, printer, and print server.

49. Set up network printing hardware by bringing up a print server on a dedicated workstation or NetWare server and connecting a printer to the network through a NetWare server or a DOS workstation.

50. Send print jobs to network printers by redirecting print jobs with CAPTURE or NPRINT.

51. Perform basic network printing maintenance tasks such as viewing and modifying printing information in PCONSOLE.

52. Manage print jobs in the print queue by viewing their properties, pausing, rushing, delaying printing, and deleting jobs in the queue.

Appendix B: Test Objectives

53. Describe the way you use PRINTDEF and PRINTCON to customize print jobs.

54. Explain System Fault Tolerance (SFT) and describe the way to implement it.

55. Describe SMS and strategies for implementing successful storage management.

56. Use SBACKUP, NetWare's utility for implementing SMS, to perform a simple backup and restore.

57. Describe NetWare Basic Message Handling Service (MHS).

58. Describe the steps required to install Basic MHS on a NetWare server.

59. Perform administrative tasks, such as adding a user and creating a distribution list, using the Basic MHS Administration software.

60. Send, read, and file mail in First Mail.

61. Identify basic guidelines for selecting application software.

62. List basic steps to be completed when loading applications.

NetWare 3.11 Advanced System Manager: Test #50-82

1. Identify higher-level network management skills and strategies important for experienced NetWare 3.11 system managers.

2. List the relationships of the course topics to those skills and strategies.

3. Identify appropriate commands and syntax needed to track network information.

4. Identify and describe important configuration files used on the network.

5. Identify commands and options used to customize the appropriate configuration file.

6. Identify advanced commands and procedures used to accomplish a specific management task.

7. Describe the tables, performance features, blocks, and buffers important to the workings of file server memory.

8. Identify NetWare 3.11 memory pools and describe the features, content, resource use, and effect of each.

9. Identify performance monitoring procedures including MONITOR options and statistics and associated SET parameters.

10. List interactions between various parameter settings and considerations for changing settings.

11. Determine NetWare 3.11 memory requirements for given cases.

12. Identify procedures needed to analyze and optimize network performance and solve problems for given cases.

13. Identify the higher-level performance issues involved in measuring the time required for printing.

14. Determine the steps needed to perform printing maintenance tasks.

15. Identify advanced printing setup and management procedures.

16. Identify the PRINTDEF procedures needed to create customized printer definitions, modes, and forms.

17. Identify the PRINTCON procedures needed to create customized print jobs.

18. List the steps required to print files using the jobs created in PRINTCON.

19. Identify basic network printing troubleshooting procedures for given cases.

Appendix B: Test Objectives

20. Identify important features of the NetWare 3.11 remote management capability.
21. Describe management functions that can be performed through the remote management capability.
22. List access restrictions for remote management.
23. Identify software and hardware components and requirements for remote management.
24. Describe communication link types available for remote management and the uses for each.
25. Identify procedures needed to set up the remote console and perform given tasks.
26. Define ODI and identify its architecture and benefits to the NetWare system manager.
27. Describe ODI workstation software and associated files.
28. Identify the components and requirements involved in name space support.
29. Identify file server utilities associated with multiple protocol support including appropriate syntax and loading sequence.
30. Explain the components of OS/2 support.
31. Describe TCP/IP support including basic components, requirements, and associated systems.
32. Identify optional multiple protocol products used for file and print sharing.
33. Identify the value and tasks involved in following standard prevention and maintenance procedures for system management.
34. Describe utilities, login script commands, and procedures used to update NetWare shells.
35. Identify basic prevention strategies used to protect the network, and describe specific procedures for each area.

NetWare 3.11 OS Features Review Rev. 1.02: Test #50-45

1. Identify operating system features new with NetWare 3.1x.
2. List the relationship of course topics to those features.
3. Identify the functions of NetWare 3.11 features.
4. Explain the value of new features.
5. Identify the levels and functions of network security.
6. Identify methods used at each security level to control access.
7. Compare the rights and responsibilities of the different types of managers and operators.
8. Identify the function and effect of each right.
9. List rights required for specified tasks.
10. Define security terms.
11. Determine effective rights for given cases.
12. Identify the function and effect of each attribute.
13. List workstation utilities added with NetWare 3.x.
14. Identify the function of new NetWare 3.x workstation utilities.
15. Identify v3.x modifications to existing NetWare utilities.
16. Identify procedures needed to create additional managers on the network.
17. Identify procedures needed to perform given tasks using the DSPACE and SALVAGE utilities.
18. Differentiate between console commands and NetWare Loadable Modules (NLMs).
19. Identify the function of major console commands.

Appendix B: Test Objectives

20. Identify procedures for loading NLMs.
21. Identify the purposes and functions of NLMs.
22. Identify the functions of the remote management feature.
23. Identify printing services and specifications.
24. Describe the purposes and functions of specific printing utilities.
25. Identify appropriate steps in the NetWare 3.11 printing setup process.
26. Identify the pertinent utilities to implement the printing setup process.
27. Identify appropriate printing-related command-line utilities and proper syntax for given tasks.
28. List the functions of the NBACKUP utility.
29. Identify rules for running NBACKUP.
30. List basic steps for backing up the file server.
31. Identify basic steps for restoring backed-up data.
32. Define terms associated with the NetWare 3.1x installation process.
33. Identify the names and purposes of important installation files.
34. Identify installation specifications for file servers and workstations.
35. List the major steps in file server and workstation software installation.
36. Identify the appropriate utility used to upgrade a given version of NetWare.
37. Describe the purpose and functions of the UPGRADE utility.
38. Identify upgrade methods.
39. List basic steps for the given type of upgrade.

NetWare 3.1x Advanced Administration: Test #50-131

1. Identify and describe the server components.
2. Perform a server startup procedure.
3. Identify and describe server configuration files.
4. Identify commands and options used to customize the appropriate server configuration file.
5. Select the appropriate utility and edit the server configuration files.
6. Create server batch files that perform specific tasks, such as remotely downing the server.
7. Describe the communication and name space protocols supported by a NetWare server.
8. Identify the default Ethernet frame type and match the appropriate frame type to the communication protocol supported.
9. Identify the ODI support architecture and related files that are used at a NetWare server.
10. Describe the services provided by the NetWare protocol suite, including IPX, SPX, RIP, SAP, NCP, and Packet Burst.
11. Display and explain routing information with the TRACK ON utility.
12. Install TCP/IP support on a server.
13. Identify the components and requirements involved in name space support.
14. Install OS/2 and Macintosh name space support.
15. Identify optional multiple protocol products used for file and print sharing.

Appendix B: Test Objectives

16. Describe the tables, blocks, and buffers important to the workings of server memory.
17. Determine NetWare 3.12 server memory requirements for given cases.
18. Identify NetWare 3.12 memory pools, and describe the features, content, resource use, and effect of each.
19. Use MONITOR to view server memory statistics.
20. Describe server console commands related to memory.
21. Identify components that affect server and network performance.
22. Identify the relationships and balances needed between server memory components to maintain optimum server performance.
23. Use MONITOR to verify server and network performance and view resource and processor utilization.
24. List interactions between various SET parameters and the considerations for changing settings.
25. Select and implement the appropriate SET parameter needed to alter network performance based on a given case.
26. Describe the ways in which the LIP (Large Internetwork Packet) and Packet Burst protocol affect network performance.
27. Identify the performance implications associated with the NCP Packet Signature.
28. Identify the purpose and procedures of server maintenance utilities such as BINDFIX, BINDREST, VREPAIR, and SBACKUP.
29. Analyze the data presented on the disk information screen of MONITOR to determine the health of the server's hard disks.
30. Repair the server bindery using BINDFIX and BINDREST.
31. Describe the reasons you would use VREPAIR.

32. Use VREPAIR to remove name space support from a volume.
33. Back up and restore a server bindery and trustee assignments using SBACKUP.
34. Load the components needed to perform a client backup using SBACKUP.
35. Describe the utilities used to set time and time zone support.
36. Describe the utility used to support read-only devices.
37. Perform printing maintenance tasks with PCONSOLE and PSC.
38. Compare the steps required to set permanent and temporary settings for print queues and notification lists.
39. Use PRINTCON to create default print job settings to be used by CAPTURE and PCONSOLE.
40. Print a document using print job configurations that have been created in PRINTCON.
41. Identify advanced printing setup and management design considerations.
42. Summarize the capabilities of the NetWare DOS Requester modules.
43. Modify the NET.CFG file to configure the ODI environment.
44. Customize the NET.CFG file with parameters that affect the NetWare DOS Requester.
45. Identify the options available to load the NetWare DOS Requester.
46. Describe the changes made to a client station during the client installation for Microsoft Windows.
47. Update existing client files using WSUPDATE, and describe the procedures and login script commands used to automate the process.

Appendix B: Test Objectives

48. Describe the procedures used to protect against virus intrusion.
49. Describe the method used to support diskless client stations, and identify the files used with the method.

NetWare 2.2 Certified NetWare Administrator: Test #50-115

1. Define a network.
2. List the hardware components of a network.
3. Choose the best option for expanding your network.
4. Diagram the levels of the NetWare directory structure.
5. Name the required volume, the four required directories, and their contents and location in the directory structure.
6. Diagram possible directory structures given an organization and its needs.
7. Create an organized and efficient directory structure.
8. Construct a directory path using the required syntax.
9. Work with DOS and NetWare commands related to directory structures and their contents.
10. Identify the default drive pointers in the DOS and NetWare environments.
11. Use the MAP command to move through the directory structure.
12. Understand the effects of the DOS CD command on MAP.
13. List the levels of NetWare security.
14. Use command-line utilities to apply NetWare's security to a basic directory structure.

15. Understand the correlation between NetWare command-line utilities and NetWare menu utilities.
16. Identify the workstation commands incorporated in these menus.
17. Describe the purpose of specific supervisor commands.
18. Function within the special menu utilities reserved for supervisor use.
19. Identify the two printing services available.
20. Identify parameters for choosing the right service.
21. Determine application compatibility with NetWare.
22. Contrast the three login scripts used on the network.
23. Identify and use login script commands to create a system and user login script.
24. Customize a user environment using menus.
25. Recognize the menu option file format and syntax.
26. Create custom menus.
27. List the functions of the NBACKUP utility.
28. Identify the rules for running NBACKUP.
29. Select the appropriate shell files for each workstation.
30. Restrict the number of workstations that can use the same login name at one time.
31. Restrict users to specific workstations.
32. Control minimum password length.
33. Control the frequency with which the password must be changed.
34. Restrict the times when users can be logged in.
35. Restrict network disk storage by users.
36. Set parameters to help detect and deny intruder logins.
37. Use SYSCON to view the File Server Error Log.

Appendix B: Test Objectives

38. Identify printing services and specifications.
39. Describe the purposes and functions of specific printing utilities.
40. Implement the appropriate steps in the NetWare 2.2 printing setup process.
41. Identify and use command-line utilities with the correct syntax for printing-related tasks.

NetWare 3.11 Certified NetWare Administrator: Test #50-116

1. Identify the levels of the NetWare directory structure.
2. Name the required NetWare volume and the four system-created directories with their contents and locations in the directory structure.
3. Organize an efficient directory structure.
4. Write a NetWare directory path using the proper syntax.
5. Identify the default drive pointers in the DOS and NetWare environments.
6. Differentiate network drive mappings and search drive mappings.
7. Identify the appropriate parameters and syntax for using the MAP command to move through the directory structure.
8. Identify the levels and functions of network security.
9. Identify the methods used at each security level to control access.
10. Compare the rights and responsibilities of the different types of managers and operators.
11. Identify the function and effect of each right.

12. List rights required for specified tasks.
13. Define security terms.
14. Determine effective rights for given cases.
15. Identify the function and effect of each attribute.
16. Select appropriate command-line utilities related to NetWare security.
17. Identify the purpose and capabilities of the SYSCON and FILER utilities.
18. Identify procedures needed to perform given tasks in SYSCON and FILER.
19. Identify the functions of the remote management feature.
20. Identify printing services and specifications.
21. Describe the purposes and functions of specific printing utilities.
22. Identify appropriate steps in the NetWare 3.11 printing setup process.
23. Identify the pertinent utilities to implement the printing setup process.
24. Identify appropriate printing-related command-line utilities and proper syntax for given tasks.
25. Contrast the three types of login scripts used on the network.
26. Identify appropriate login script commands and proper syntax needed to create a system and user login script.
27. Identify errors in login script logic for given cases.
28. List specifications for creating custom menus.
29. Identify proper menu option file format and syntax.
30. Follow procedures needed to execute custom menus.
31. Identify basic guidelines for selecting application software.

Appendix B: Test Objectives

32. List the basic steps to be completed when loading applications.
33. List the functions of the NBACKUP utility.
34. Identify the rules for running NBACKUP.
35. List the basic steps for restoring backed-up data.
36. Identify the basic steps for backing up the file server.
37. Describe the tables, performance features, blocks, and buffers important to the workings of file server memory.
38. Identify NetWare 3.11 memory pools, and describe the features, content, resource use, and effect of each.
39. Determine NetWare 3.11 memory requirements for given cases.
40. Identify the higher-level performance issues involved in measuring the time required for printing.
41. Determine the steps needed to perform printing maintenance tasks.
42. Identify advanced printing setup and management procedures.
43. Identify the PRINTCON procedures needed to create customized print jobs.
44. List the steps required to print files using the jobs created in PRINTCON.
45. Identify basic network printing troubleshooting procedures for given cases.
46. Define ODI and identify its architecture and benefits to the NetWare system manager.
47. Describe ODI workstation software and associated files.
48. Identify file server utilities associated with multiple protocol support, including appropriate syntax and loading sequence.
49. Identify optional multiple protocol products used for file and print sharing.

50. Describe SBACKUP, and explain its value, associated terms, required NLMs, usage rules, and performance issues.

51. For SBACKUP, identify procedures for installation, backup, and restore.

Comparison Charts

APPENDIX C

Table C.1
Rights

v2.15	v2.2	v3.1x
Open		
Read	Read	Read
Write	Write	Write
Create	Create	Create
Modify	Modify	Modify
Delete	Erase	Erase
Search	File Scan	File Scan
Parental	Access Control	Access Control
		Supervisory

Appendix C: Comparison Charts

Table C.2
Rights and Attributes

v2.15	v2.2	v3.1x
Maximum Rights Mask	Inherited Rights Mask	Inherited Rights Mask
Directory Rights	Directory Rights	Directory Rights
		Directory Attributes
File Attributes	File Attributes	File Attributes
		File Rights

Table C.3
Minimum/Maximum File Server RAM Requirements

v2.15	v2.2	v3.1x
2M/16M	2.5M/12M	4M/4G

Table C.4
Maximum Disk Storage

v2.15	v2.2	v3.1x
2G	2.2G	32T

Table C.5
File Attributes

v2.15	v2.2	v3.1x
ALL	ALL	ALL
Normal (NsRw)	Normal (NsRw)	Normal (NsRw)
Shareable	Shareable	Shareable
Read/Write	Read/Write	Read/Write
Read Only	Read Only	Read Only
Modified Since Last Backup	Archive Needed	Archive Needed
Indexed	Indexed	
	Hidden	Hidden
	SYstem	SYstem
	Transactional	Transactional
	Read Audit	Read Audit
	Write Audit	Write Audit
		Purge
		Copy Inhibit
		Delete Inhibit
		Rename Inhibit

NetWare 2.15

APPENDIX D

This appendix discusses the features of NetWare 2.15. Although the NetWare 2.15 System Manager test is no longer available to take for credit toward a CNA, CNE, or ECNE, some organizations still run NetWare 2.15. This appendix, therefore, has been included for those who want to learn more about NetWare 2.15.

Many of the components of NetWare 2.15 are found in NetWare 2.2. You easily can compare these two systems. This appendix covers the following topics:

- Similarities between v2.15 and v2.2
- NetWare 2.15 security
- Printing
- Backup and Restore

Exploring v2.15 and v2.2 Similarities

The following items are virtually identical in these two versions of NetWare. Some features have been improved primarily for speed and reliability.

Binderies

The structure of the binderies is the same in NetWare 2.15 and 2.2. Two binderies are available: NET$BIND.SYS and NET$BVAL.SYS. These files are kept in the SYS:SYSTEM directory.

Mapping and Directory Structure

NetWare 2.15 creates four directories upon installation: SYSTEM, PUBLIC, LOGIN, and MAIL. All other directories are created by NetWare users and administrators.

The MAP command and all its parameters are available in v2.15. Earlier versions of NetWare do not support MAP NEXT or MAP ROOT, but after Novell's release of NetWare 2.15 revision C, these parameters are supported.

Major Utilities

SYSCON, FILER, SESSION, FCONSOLE, PRINTDEF, PRINTCON, and PCONSOLE are the same in v2.15 and v2.2.

System Fault Tolerance and Memory Management

NetWare System Fault Tolerance (SFT) features, such as Directory Caching and Hashing, File Caching, Elevator Seeking, and Hot Fix, are the same as v2.2.

Memory management is essentially the same. The only difference is the addition of Memory Pool D in v2.2. Previous versions of NetWare only had three memory pools. A portion of the first memory group in NetWare 2.15 was taken to form the new memory pool in v2.2.

Security

Security features common to v2.15 and v2.2 include the flow through of directory rights as well as using Maximum Rights Masks (MRM). Trustee rights are assigned to users and groups for the directory, and the MRM is assigned to the directory.

File attributes are similar. NetWare 2.15 uses Shareable, Nonshareable, Read Only, Read/Write, TTS, Hidden, System, and Indexed file attributes. NetWare 2.15 uses M for Modified since last backup, but v2.2 uses A for Archive needed. The function of M and A is the same.

Login Scripts and Menus

The creation of login scripts and menus remains the same between the versions. Even v3.*x* has not added much to change the way in which these two functions work.

Exploring NetWare 2.15 Security

Workgroup managers and account managers are not supported in v2.15. These classifications were not supported until v2.2.

The most obvious difference in v2.15 is trustee rights. NetWare 2.15 has four types of security divided into three different levels as shown in table D.1.

Table D.1
NetWare 2.15 Security

Type	Level
Login/Password	Initial Access
Directory	Directory Level
Trustee	Directory Level
File Attributes	File Level

Appendix D: NetWare 2.15

Passwords are encrypted at the file server in NetWare 2.15.

Access Rights

Table D.2 lists the access rights used by NetWare 2.15.

Table D.2
NetWare 2.15 Access Rights

Access Right	Function
Read	Enables the user to read open files
Write	Enables the user to write to open files
Open	Opens a file for reads and writes
Create	Creates files and subdirectories
Delete	Deletes files and subdirectories
Search	Enables the user to see files using DIR
Modify	Enables the user to change file attributes
Parental	Enables the user to assign rights to other users

If you need to read a file, you must have Read and Open (RO) rights. Likewise, you must have Write and Open (WO) rights to write to an existing file.

When using the GRANT command in v2.15, you must specify Write before Open. For example, **GRANT WO TO PAUL** is correct. If you entered **GRANT OW TO PAUL**, you actually give the Parental right to Paul, because the GRANT command uses OW to assign the person as OWNER.

To use the COPY or NCOPY command, you must have Write, Create, and Delete (WCD) rights in the destination directory. You must have Read, Open, and Search (ROS) rights in the source directory.

In versions of NetWare 2.1 through 2.12, you had to include the Open right with the Create right. NetWare 2.15 assumes the Open right when you assign Create.

Similarly, versions prior to v2.15 require the Parental right to make and delete files and subdirectories. NetWare 2.15 now uses Create and Delete.

To change a file's attributes from Nonshareable Read/Write (NRW) to Shareable Read Only (SRO), you must have Modify and Search (MS) rights to the directory in which the file resides.

To rename a file, you need the Modify (M) right in the subdirectory in which the file resides. To rename a directory, you must have the Modify (M) right in the parent directory.

To change the Maximum Rights Mask or Trustee Rights, you must have the Parental (P) right in that directory.

Default Rights

NetWare 2.15 assigns the following rights by default:

- The group EVERYONE gets ROS during login for the SYS:LOGIN directory. After they are logged in, these rights are removed. This group also gets WC to the SYS:MAIL directory and ROS to SYS:PUBLIC.

- Users are assigned ROSWCDM (every right except Parental) to the SYS:MAIL\USERID directory. These rights give the user permission to create and alter his own personal login script.

Exploring Printing in NetWare 2.15

Printing in NetWare 2.15 is similar to printing in v2.2. The biggest difference is in core printing. Core printing is set up when the operating system is installed and enables you to attach up to five printers to the file server without setting up a print server. Print Servers was an option added to NetWare 2.15, revision C, and functions the same as v2.2.

Using Backup and Restore

NetWare 2.15 offers several methods of backing up network files.

To archive files by using NetWare utilities, you must have the following rights in any directory you want to back up: Read, Open, Search, and Modify (ROSM).

To restore a file archived by a NetWare utility, you must have Write, Create, Open, Delete, and Search (WCODS) in the directory in which you want to restore the files.

When you use the archive utilities, a file called ARCHIVE.LOG is created on the medium to which you are backing up. This file must be intact to perform a restore. If you lose or corrupt this file, you cannot restore archived files.

ARCHIVE.LOG contains the following information:

◆ Which files are backed up

◆ Which file server the files come from

Using Backup and Restore

- If the files are hidden or system files
- The way in which the files are split to fit onto the backup medium

LARCHIVE and LRESTORE

LARCHIVE backs up network files to a local device such as a floppy disk or a workstation hard drive. LARCHIVE breaks files into smaller segments to fit the files onto floppy disks smaller than the file size.

Type **F:SYSTEM>LARCHIVE** to back up the current directory and all its subdirectories.

Type **F:SYSTEM>LARCHIVE G:** to back up the indicated drive—in this case G:—and all its subdirectories.

Type **F:SYSTEM>LARCHIVE SYS:** to back up the indicated volume—in this case SYS:—and all directories and subdirectories.

Type **F:SYSTEM>LARCHIVE SYSTEM** to archive all directories on the network to which you have rights. If you are a supervisor or a supervisor equivalent, you can use this command to archive the entire network.

LRESTORE is used to retrieve files archived by LARCHIVE.

NARCHIVE and NRESTORE

NARCHIVE uses the same syntax as LARCHIVE. NARCHIVE, however, enables you to back up the files onto a network drive. This command is useful if you have multiple servers and you want to back up one server onto the other.

NRESTORE is used to retrieve files archived by NARCHIVE.

Appendix D: NetWare 2.15

BACKUP and RESTORE

If your file server supports an internal tape backup system, these commands back up and restore the entire disk. They are found on the NetWare disk labeled TAPEEXE.

 BACKUP and RESTORE can be used only after the file server has been downed. These commands cannot be run if the file server is running.

MACBACK

This utility prepares files created on an AppleShare network for archiving. To back up these files by using LARCHIVE or NARCHIVE, you must run MACBACK. MACBACK envelopes the Macintosh file's resource and data forks in a DOS format.

Third-Party Support

The most important thing to check for when using another vendor's tape backup system is compatibility with your NetWare version. The following criteria must be met for a secure backup:

- The backup system must back up the bindery files.
- NetWare uses several files always held open. A good backup system can ignore open files and still complete the backup.
- The backup system must be written to Novell's call sequences and stipulations.

Review Questions

1. Which of the following is the correct set of bindery files for v2.15?

    a. NET$BIND.SYS, NET$VAL.SYS

    b. NET$OBJ.SYS, NET$PROP.SYS, NET$VAL.SYS

    c. NET$BIND.SYS, NET$BVAL.SYS

    d. None of the above

2. Which directory is not created automatically in v2.15?

    a. SYS:ETC

    b. SYS:LOGIN

    c. SYS:MAIL\mailid

    d. SYS:PUBLIC

3. Which menu utility is not included with NetWare 2.15?

    a. PCONSOLE

    b. FCONSOLE

    c. FILER

    d. DSPACE

4. Which of the following is a feature of NetWare 2.15?

    a. Inherited Rights Mask

    b. Maximum Rights Mask

    c. Directory Attributes

    d. File Rights

5. Which of the following is the correct set of trustee rights for NetWare 2.15?

    a. RWOCDSPM

    b. RWCEMFAS

    c. RWCEMFA

    d. None of the above

6. Which rights do you need to use NCOPY in NetWare 2.15?

    a. RF in destination, C in source

    b. C in destination, RF in source

    c. WCD in destination, ROS in source

    d. ROS in source, WCD in destination

7. Which set of default rights is correct?

    a. ALL to Home directory

    b. WC in SYS:MAIL and ALL but P in SYS:MAIL\userid

    c. ROS in SYS:PUBLIC and SYS:LOGIN (during login only)

    d. B and C

8. Which statement about printing in v2.15 is true?

    a. You can use PSERVER.EXE or PSERVER.VAP.

    b. You can have up to five printers attached to the file server if set up during installation.

    c. PRINTDEF and PRINTCON are the same as in v2.2.

    d. All of the above

9. Which statement about backing up v2.15 files is true?

    a. You can back up Macintosh files using MACBACK.

    b. You can use LARCHIVE to back up to a local drive or NARCHIVE to back up to a network drive.

    c. You can use SBACKUP.VAP at the server.

    d. None of the above

10. Which statement about archiving in v2.15 is true?

    a. ARCHIVE.LOG is necessary only if you use LARCHIVE.

    b. Deleting ARCHIVE.LOG is not a problem, because NetWare can sense if it is missing and re-create it if necessary.

    c. The ARCHIVE.LOG file is found on the medium to which it was backed up and is necessary for restoring.

    d. The ARCHIVE.LOG file is found in SYS:SYSTEM.

Case Study

1. Create a comparison chart for v2.2 and v2.15 that lists all similar features.

2. Create a comparison chart for v2.2 and v2.15 that lists all different features.

616

Index

Symbols

(pound sign) in commands, 292
#ACCOUNT_EXPIRATION (MAKEUSER) keyword, 176
#ACCOUNTING (MAKEUSER) keyword, 176
#CLEAR (MAKEUSER) keyword, 176
#CONNECTIONS (MAKEUSER) keyword, 176
#CREATE (MAKEUSER) keyword, 176
#DEFAULT_PROFILE (MAKEUSER) keyword, 176
#DELETE (MAKEUSER) keyword, 177
#GROUPS (MAKEUSER) keyword, 177
#HOME_DIRECTORY (MAKEUSER) keyword, 177
#HOME_SERVER (MAKEUSER) keyword, 177
#LOGIN_SCRIPT (MAKEUSER) keyword, 177
#MAX_DISK_SPACE (MAKEUSER) keyword, 177
#NO_HOME_DIRECTORY (MAKEUSER) keyword, 177
#PASSWORD_LENGTH (MAKEUSER) keyword, 177
#PASSWORD_PERIOD (MAKEUSER) keyword, 177
#PASSWORD_REQUIRED (MAKEUSER) keyword, 177
#PROFILES (MAKEUSER) keyword, 177
#PURGE_USER_DIRECTORY (MAKEUSER) keyword, 178
#REM (MAKEUSER) keyword, 178
#RESET (MAKEUSER) keyword, 176
#RESTRICTED_TIME (MAKEUSER) keyword, 178
#STATIONS (MAKEUSER) keyword, 178
#UNIQUE_PASSWORD (MAKEUSER) keyword, 178
% (percent)
   identifier variables, 285
   submenus, 299
* (asterisks) on forms, 248
? (question mark) flag, 246
^ (carat) in commands, 313
{} (braces) in commands, 313
10-tape method, 501-502
2XUPGRDE.NLM, 551-553

A

ABort flag, 261
ABORT REMIRROR command, 452
aborting print jobs, 248, 261
Access Control right, 103, 360-361, 433
access rights (NetWare 2.15), 608-609
accessing
   directories, 50, 79-81
   LOGIN directory, 54
Account Balance (SYSCON) option, 150-151
Account Restrictions (SYSCON) option, 151-153
Accounting (SYSCON) menu, 127-135
   Blocks Read Charge Rates option, 129
   Blocks Written Charge Rates option, 129
   Connect Time Charge Rates option, 129
   Disk Storage Charge Rates option, 129
   Service Requests Charge Rates option, 130
accounts
   charge rates, 132-134
   limiting balances, 134-135
   setting up, 130-132
   unlocking, 146
ACONSOLE command, 442
ACONSOLE utility, 541
across-the-wire migration, 446-447, 549-550
Active condition (print jobs), 218
adaptive tests, 22, 38
ADD NAME SPACE TO VOLUME command, 452

Adding condition (print jobs), 219
ADMIN utility, 442-443
administrators, 508-509
Advanced Administration: Test #50-131 (NetWare 3.1x), 591-594
Advanced Installation option (INSTALL program), 385-393
Advanced System Manager: Test #50-44 (NetWare 2.2), 576-579
Advanced System Manager: Test #50-82 (NetWare 3.11), 586-588
Alloc Short Term Memory Pool, 515-516
ALLOW command, 443-444
ALTERNATE option (Link Driver), 475
answers (review questions), 567-571
antivirus software, 506-507
applications
   directories, 64-65
   directory structures, 276-277
   flagging files, 277
   installing, 61, 64, 277
   memory managers, 278
   NetWare compatibility, 276
   NetWare-aware applications, 276
   network-compatible applications, 275-276
   single-user applications, 275
   stand-alone applications, 274-275
   technical support, 276
   user access, 278-279
Archive Needed attribute, 105, 436
ARCHIVE.LOG file, 610-611
ArcServer (Cheyenne Software), 485

ASCII (American Standard Code for Information Interchange), 253
asterisks (*) on forms, 248
asynchronous remote console, 541
ATOTAL command, 58
ATOTAL utility, 132
ATTACH command, 293, 339
attaching file servers, 53-54
attributes
   Archive Needed, 105, 436
   Copy Inhibit, 438
   Delete, 438
   directory, 439-440
   Execute Only, 105, 436
   files, 603
      searching, 75-76
   Hidden Directory, 439
   Hidden File, 106, 436
   NetWare 2.15, 602
   NetWare 2.2, 602
   NetWare 3.1*x*, 602
   Nonshareable, 107, 437
   Purge, 439
   Purge Directory, 440
   Read Audit, 106, 437
   Read Only, 106, 437
   Read/Write, 106
   Rename, 439
   Shareable, 107, 437
   System Directory, 439
   System File, 107
   Transactional, 107, 438
   Write Audit, 106, 437
Auto Register Memory Above 16 Megabytes parameter (SET command), 528-529
Autoendcap flag, 244
AUTOEXEC.BAT file, 336
AUTOEXEC.NCF file, 116, 548

Available Options menu (RECONSOLE utility), 216, 540-541

B

BACKUP command, 612
backups, 105, 482-483
   bindery files, 495
   disaster recovery plans, 504-507
   drive types, 491-492
   file-by-file method, 496
   frequency, 500
   grandfather method, 500-501
   hardware, 488-489
   image, 496
   interface adapters, 489-490
   media types, 491-492
   memory pools, 511-512
      Alloc Short Term Memory Pool, 515-516
      cache memory, 512
      Cache Movable Memory Pool, 513
      Cache Non-Movable Memory Pool, 513
      Permanent Memory Pool, 514
      Semi-Permanent Memory Pool, 514
   NetWare 2.15, 610-612
   off-site, 503-504
   optical drives, 492-494
   responsibility for, 499
   rotation method, 500-503
   SBACKUP utility, 483-488
      ArcServe, 485
      host modules, 484
      target modules, 484
   software, 494-499
   tapes, 495-496
   technical support, 507-508

testing backup systems, 504
Tower of Hanoi method,
    502-503
UPS (Uninterruptible Power
    Supply), 505-506
viruses, 506-507
banner pages, 243
**Basic Installation option
    (INSTALL program), 380-385**
Basic MHS, 442-443
**Batch File Missing error message,
    302**
BIND command, 452-453
BIND.VLM, 335
binderies
    Name Service Database,
        533-534
    NetWare 2.5, 606
bindery files, 59-60
    backups, 495
    creating, 59
BINDFIX command, 59
BINDREST command, 60
blank status (file servers), 53
**Blocks Read Charge Rates
    (SYSCON) option, 129**
**Blocks Written Charge Rates
    (SYSCON) option, 129**
boot image file, 55
braces ({ }) in commands, 313
BREAK ON/OFF command, 288
bridges, 338
**Broadcast Console Message
    (FCONSOLE), 395**
**BROADCAST message
    command, 359**
buffered print jobs, 239
buffers
    cache buffers, 409
    communication buffers, 403, 412
    directory cache buffers, 519

packet receive buffers, 519
routing buffers, 412
statistics on incoming packets,
    403
**BUFFERS option (Link Support),
    477**
byte-stream printing, 242

C

**-C: Configuration Complete
    installation option, 379**
cable numbers, 453
**Cache Buffer Size parameter
    (SET command), 529**
cache buffers
    Directory Cache Buffers field,
        522
    Dirty Cache Buffers field,
        521-522
    NetWare 2.2 memory
        requirements, 409
    Packet Receive Buffers field,
        522
    Total Cache Buffers field, 521
**CACHE BUFFERS option
    (SHELL.CFG), 481**
cache hits, 398
cache memory, 512
cache misses, 398
**Cache Movable Memory Pool,
    513**
**Cache Non-Movable Memory
    Pool, 513**
caching
    directories, 428
        *Maximum Directory Cache
            Buffers parameter, 530-531*
        *Maximum File Cache Buffers
            parameter, 530-532*

Minimum Directory Cache Buffers parameter, 531-532
NetWare 2.2 memory requirements, 408
files, 428
Minimum File Cache Buffers parameter, 529-530
NetWare 2.2 memory requirements, 409
statistics (FCONSOLE), 398-399
calculating memory requirements (NetWare 2.2), 407-412
calling menus, 302-303
Cancel Down flag, 261
CAPTURE command, 232, 236-238
capturing print jobs, 245
caret (^) in commands, 313
CD command, 67, 87-88
CD-ROM (Compact Disc Read-Only Memory), 493
Certification Assessment Diskette, 22-23
certification programs, 9-10
   classes, 24
   CNA (Certified NetWare Administrator), 17-21, 40
   CNE (Certified NetWare Engineer), 11-16, 39
   ECNE (Enterprise Certified NetWare Engineer), 16-17
   NTS (Novell Technical Support), 11
   paths, 39-40
   studying, 37-43
   tests, 21-24, 43
Certified NetWare Administrator, *see* CNA
Certified NetWare Administrator: Test #50-115 (NetWare 2.2), 594-596
Certified NetWare Adminstrator: Test #50-116 (NetWare 3.11), 596-599
Certified NetWare Engineer (CNE) training, *see* CNE
Change Current Server (SESSION) menu, 198-199
Change Current Server (SYSCON) menu, 136
Change Password (SYSCON) option, 154
charge rates, 132-134
Cheyenne Software, ArcServe, 485
child file server, 484
CHKDIR command, 68, 444
CHKVOL command, 69
CLEAR MESSAGE command, 359
CLEAR STATION command, 359
clearing screen, 453
clients, 554-556
CLS command, 453
CNA (Certified NetWare Administrator), 17, 40
   benefits, 20-21
   DOS (Disk Operating System), 18
   hardware technicians, 18
   NAEC (Novell Authorized Education Center), 19
   requirements, 18-20
   tests, 19
CNE (Certified NetWare Engineer), 39
   benefits, 13-17
   CNE logo, 15
   CNEPA (CNE Professional Association), 15-16
   continuing education, 12
   DATC (Drake Authorized Testing Centers), 11

DOS (Disk Operating System), 11
elective credits, 31-36
NAEC (Novell Authorized Education Centers), 12
Network Support Encyclopedia (NSE), 13-14
progress map, 28-30
requirements, 11-12
techinical support, 15
COLORPAL utility, 299
COM file extension, 105
command-line parameters, 293
command-line switches, 331
command-line utilities, 58-60
    GRANT command, 109
    REMOVE command, 110-111
    REVOKE command, 109
    RIGHTS command, 108
    TLIST command, 108
COMMAND.COM Not Found error message, 284
commands, 67
    ABORT REMIRROR, 452
    ACONSOLE, 442
    ADD NAME SPACE TO VOLUME, 452
    ALLOW, 443-444
    ATOTAL, 58
    ATTACH, 293, 339
    BACKUP, 612
    BIND, 452-453
    BINDFIX, 59
    BINDREST, 60
    BREAK ON/OFF, 288
    CAPTURE, 232, 236-238
    CD, 67, 87-88
    CHKDIR, 68, 444
    CHKVOL, 69
    CLS, 453
    command windows (menus), 308
    COMPATIBLE, 294
    COMSPEC, 290
    console, 452-459
    control commands, 312
    COPY, 67, 71
    COPY CON, 67
    DEL, 67
    DISABLE TTS, 453
    DISPLAY, 288-289
    DISPLAY NETWORKS, 453-454
    DISPLAY SERVERS, 454-455
    DOS commands
        BREAK, 290
        DIR, 107
        SET, 290
        VERIFY, 290
    DOWN, 455
    DRIVE, 290
    ENABLE TTS, 453
    ENDCAP, 238
    essential system login script commands, 294
    EXIT, 291, 455
    FDISPLAY, 288-289
    FIRE PHASERS, 286
    FLAG, 166
    FLAGDIR, 166
    flags, 239-251
    GETx, 315
    GOTO, 291
    IF-THEN-ELSE statement, 286-288
    INCLUDE, 289
    IPX, 323
    LARCHIVE, 611
    LIST DEVICES, 455
    LISTDIR, 69-71
    LOAD, 455
    LOGIN, 324
    !LOGOUT, 302
    LOGOUT, 302, 340

LRESTORE, 611
MAGAZINE, 456
MAP, 83-84, 282-284
MAP DEL, 86-87
MD, 67
MEDIA, 456
MEMORY, 456
MIRROR STATUS, 456
MODULE, 456
NCOPY, 71-72, 277
NDIR, 72-77, 107
NetWare 3.12 menuing system commands, 313-314
NETX, 323
NPRINT, 236, 239
organizational commands, 312
PAUDIT, 58
PAUSE, 286
PRINTCON, 256-263
PRINTDEF, 252
PROTOCOL, 456
PSC, 260-263
RD, 67
REGISTER MEMORY, 457
REMIRROR PARTITION, 457
REMOVE DOS, 457
RENDIR, 77
RESET ROUTER, 457
RESTORE, 612
RPRINTER, 236
RPRINTER.EXE, 215
SCAN FOR DEVICES, 457
SEARCH ADD, 458
SEARCH DEL, 458
SECURE CONSOLE, 458
SECURITY, 58
SET, 459, 525-532
SET TIME ZONE, 459
SORT, 73
SPEED, 459
UNBIND, 452-453
VERSION, 459
VOLINFO, 77-79
WRITE, 284-285
communication buffers, 403
  NetWare 2.2 memory requirements, 412
communication protocols, 338-339
Compact Disc Read-Only Memory, *see* **CD-ROM**
COMPATIBLE command, 294
compiling menus, 315-316
COMPSURF.EXE file, 376
COMSPEC command, 290
CONFIG.SYS file, 336
configuration files, 336
  single-user applications, 275
configuration files (ODI)
  NET.CFG
    Link Driver hardware options, 472-474
    Link Driver software options, 475-477
    Link Support options, 477
    Protocol Selection parameters, 478
  SHELL.CFG, 479-482
configuring memory, 516-519
  DET (Directory Entry Table), 518
  FAT (File Allocation Table), 518-519
Connect Time Charge Rates (SYSCON) option, 129
connecting protocols, 452-453
connections, 353
Connections Information Menu, 395
connectivity, 34
CONNECTOR DIX option (Link Driver), 473
console commands, 452-459

CONSOLE operators, 100
consultants (technical support), 509
Control (trustee rights), 360
conventional memory, 404
Copies flag, 242
COPY command, 67, 71
COPY CON command, 67
Copy Inhibit attribute, 438
copying
   files, 67, 71, 277
   print jobs, 259
   system files, 438
core printing, 362
   NetWare 2.15, 610
   NetWare 2.2, 364-366, 387
Create flag, 245
Create right, 103, 360, 432
creating
   bindery files, 59
   directories, 62, 67
   files, 67
   routers, 181
Current Directory Information (FILER) menu, 165-167
customizing
   menus, 297-316
   printers, 229, 251-256
cut-and-paste (login scripts), 282

D

DAT file extension, 316
data directories, 66-67
database files, 438
DATC (Drake Authorized Testing Centers), 11
dedicated file servers, 355, 382
dedicated protected routers, 182-187
dedicated routers, 182

Default Account Balance/Restrictions (SYSCON) option, 145
default login scripts, 281
default print jobs, 258
default queue, 232
default rights, 609
default status (file servers), 53
Default Time Restrictions (SYSCON) option, 145
Defined Printers screen, 230
DEL command, 67
Delete flag, 244, 438
DELETED.SAV directory, 449
deleting
   directories, 67
   drive mappings, 86-87
   files, 67
   print jobs, 218
   system files, 438
departmental directories, 66
DET (Directory Entry Table), 358, 518
determining charge rates, 132-134
device modes, 252
directories, 62-67
   accessing, 50
      drive mappings, 79-81
   application directories, 64-65
   attributes, 439-440
   cache buffers, 519
   caching, 428
      Maximum Directory Cache Buffers parameter, 530-531
      Maximum File Cache Buffers parameter, 530-532
      Minimum Directory Cache Buffers parameter, 531-532
      NetWare 2.2 memory requirements, 408
   creating, 62, 67

data directories, 66-67
DELETED.SAV, 449
deleting, 67
directory rights, 104, 361
entries, 407-408
hiding, 76
HOME directories, 62-66
information, 444
login scripts, 283
managing, 60-62
menus, 302
NetWare 2.5, 606
network shells, 317
parameters, 72-77
paths, 49
statistics, 68
structures, 48, 68-79, 276-277
subdirectories, 77
switching, 67
SYS: volume
    LOGIN directory, 52-55, 61
    MAIL directory, 55-57, 61
    PUBLIC directory, 57, 61
    SYSTEM directory, 58-61
volumes, 49-50
Directory Cache Buffers field, 522
Directory Contents (FILER) menu, 167-170
Directory Disk Space Limitation Information data entry box, 445
Directory Entry Table (DET), 358, 518
directory supervisors, 104
Dirty Cache Buffers field, 521-522
DISABLE TTS command, 453
disaster recovery plans (backups), 504-507
DISK command, 359
disk drivers, 444-445

disk storage, 357
Disk Storage Charge Rates (SYSCON) option, 129
diskless workstations, 55
disks
    duplexing, 358, 505
    Hot Fix blocks, 399-400
    I/O error count, 399-400
    INSTALL, 543-544
    mirroring, 358, 505
    partitions, 452
DISPLAY command, 288-289
DISPLAY NETWORKS command, 453-454
DISPLAY SERVERS command, 454-455
distributed processing, 355
DMA channel number option (Link Driver), 473
domain servers, 536-537
domains, 532
DOS (Disk Operating System)
    CNA (Certified NetWare Administrator), 18
    CNE (Certified NetWare Engineer), 11
    commands, 290
    DOS redirection, 335
    DOS Requester, 333-337
    logging into networks, 323-327
        EMSNETX file, 326
        IPX.COM file, 325-326
        NetBIOS, 327
        NETX file, 326
        XMSNETX file, 326
    printing, 244
DOS commands, 67
    BREAK command, 290
    DIR command, 107
    SET command, 290
    VERIFY command, 290
DOWN command, 359, 455

Drake Authorized Testing
  Centers (DATC), 11
Drake Training and
  Technologies, 21
DRIVE command, 290
drive mappings, 79-81, 278-279
  deleting, 86-87
  local, 82-83
  network, 83-84
  search drives, 81, 85-86
  setting up, 82
  switching, 87-88
Drive Mappings (SESSION)
  menu, 199
drivers
  non-ODI, 479-482
  ODI, 472-478
  WSGEN utility, 319
drives
  disk mirroring, 358
  hard drives, 377
  local, 82-83
  network, 83-84
  optical, 492-494
  search drives, 85-86
DSK (NLM), 460
DSPACE utility, 444-445
duplexing disks, 505
duplicate FATs, 358
dynamic memory pools, 403,
  413-414

E

-E: Expert—Advanced
  Installation option, 378
ECNE (Enterprise Certified
  NetWare Engineer), 16-17
  benefits, 17
  elective credits, 31-36
  progress map, 30-31
  requirements, 17
Edit System AUTOEXEC File
  (SYSCON) option, 145
EDIT.NLM utility, 542
editing
  device modes, 252
  files, 542
  IRMs, 443-444
  print devices, 251
effective rights, 104, 361-362
elective tests, 31-36
  connectivity, 34
  discontinued tests, 36
  internetworking, 34
  operating systems, 32-33
  reseller authorization tests, 33
  TCP/IP, 34
  troubleshooting, 34
  UNIX, 35
elevator seeking, 428-429
ELSs (entry-level solutions), 354
EMSNETX file, 326
ENABLE TTS command, 453
end users, 101
  HOME directories, 62-64
ENDCAP command, 238
entering queues, 216
Enterprise Certified NetWare
  Engineer (ECNE), see ECNE
entry-level solutions (ELSs), 354
environments (NetWare 3.1x), 427
Erase right, 103, 360, 432
error messages
  Batch File Missing, 302
  COMMAND.COM Not Found,
    284
  File not found, 81
  Invalid COMMAND.COM,
    284, 295
  Missing COMMAND.COM,
    295

essential environmental
  components, 294
essential system login script
  commands, 294
EXE file extension, 105
executable files, 376-377
Execute Only attribute, 105, 436
EXIT command, 291, 455
exiting
  login scripts, 291
  menus, 302
expanded memory, 407
exporting print devices, 251
extended memory, 406

F

-F: File Server Definition
  installation option, 379
fatal unload error (uploading
  files), 332
FATs (file allocation tables), 358,
  518
  NetWare 2.2 memory
    requirements, 409
FCONSOLE operators, 99
FCONSOLE utility, 99, 394-397
  Broadcast Console Message,
    395
  cache statistics, 398-399
  Connections Information
    Menu, 395
  disks, 399-400
  file servers, 400-403
  Hot Fix blocks, 399-400
  Logical Record Locks option,
    397
  Open Files/Physical Records
    option, 396-397
  semaphores, 397
FDISK.COM file, 546

FDISPLAY command, 288-289
File (trustee rights), 360
file allocation tables (FATs),
  see FATs
file handles, 410
FILE HANDLES option
  (SHELL.CFG), 481
File not found error message, 81
File Scan right, 103, 432
File Server Console Operators
  Option (SYSCON) option, 145
File Server Error Log (SYSCON)
  option, 147
File Server Information
  (SYSCON) menu, 136
file servers, 393-394
  accessing hard drives, 356
  ATTACH command, 293
  attaching, 53-54
    additional servers, 339
  bridges, 338
  buffer statistics, 403
  child, 484
  commands, 359-360
  dedicated, 355, 382
  dynamic memory pools, 403
  FCONSOLE utility, 394-397
  hosts, 484
  listing, 54
  logging in to networks, 53-54,
    324
  logging out, 340
  memory, 404-414
  memory configuration, 516-519
  naming, 48-49
  NetWare 2.2, 354-360
  nondedicated, 355, 383
  parent, 484
  print queues, 223-224
  printing, 214, 362-365

processes, 401-402, 454
remote management
   ACONSOLE utility, 541
   EDIT.NLM utility, 542
   RCONSOLE utility, 537-541
   RESETUP.EXE utility, 541
requests, 402
requirements (NetWare 3.1x), 425
routers, 338
software, 279
statistics, 400-403, 522-523
status types, 53
target, 484
tokens, 71
troubleshooting, 520-524
VAPs (value-added processes), 356

File Service Process (FSP), 412
file names, 547
FILER utility
  Current Directory Information menu, 165-167
  Directory Contents menu (FILER) menu, 167-170
  Select Current Directory menu, 170
  Set Filer Options menu, 170-172
  Volume Information menu, 172-173
files
  2XUPGRDE.NLM, 551-553
  ARCHIVE.LOG, 610-611
  attributes, 603
    Archive Needed, 105
    Execute Only, 105
    Hidden File, 106
    Nonshareable, 107
    Read Audit, 106
    Read Only, 106
    Read/Write, 106

    searching, 75-76
    Shareable, 107
    System, 107
    Transactional, 107
    Write Audit, 106
  AUTOEXEC.BAT, 336
  AUTOEXEC.NCF, 116, 548
  backups, 105, 610-612
  bindery files, 59-60
    backups, 495
  boot image file, 55
  caching, 428
    cache hits, 398
    cache misses, 398
    Minimum File Cache Buffers parameter, 529-530
    NetWare 2.2 memory requirements, 409
    statistics (FCONSOLE), 398-399
  COM file extension, 105
  COMPSURF.EXE, 376
  CONFIG.SYS, 336
  configuration files (ODI)
    NET.CFG, 472-478
    SHELL.CFG, 479-482
    single-user applications, 275
  copying, 67, 71, 277
  creating, 67
  DAT file extension, 316
  databases, 438
  deleting, 67
  directory structure, 276-277
  displaying on-screen, 288-289
  editing, 542
  EXE file extension, 105
  executable, 376-377
  FDISK.COM, 546
  FORMAT.COM, 546
  GO*.BAT, 301
  help, 57

hiding, 76
INSTOVL.EXE, 376
IPX.COM, 316, 325-326
LOGIN directory, 55
MENUCNVT.EXE, 312
MENUMAKE.EXE, 312
menus, 301
MIGRATE.EXE, 549-551
MNU file extension, 301
MONITOR.NLM, 520-524
NET$OS.EXE, 377
NET.CFG, 327, 336-337
NMENU.BAT, 312, 447
parameters, 72-77
PDF file extension, 252
piracy, 106
printer definition, 57
PSERVER.NLM, 225
PSERVER.VAP, 225
Read/Write, 437
RESTART*.BAT, 301
restoring, 449-452
security, 105-107
SERVER.EXE, 548
shareable, 437
SRC file extension, 315
STARTNET.BAT, 336
STARTUP.NCF, 548
storing, 63
system, 438
transferring, 71-72
trustee rights, 103-105
TTS (Transaction Tracking System), 107
uploading, 332
viewing, 450-451
VLMs (Virtual Loadable Modules), 333-337
VREPAIR.EXE, 377
wild cards, 239
ZTEST.EXE, 376
FIRE PHASERS command, 286

First Mail, 443
FLAG command, 166
FLAGDIR command, 166
flagging application files, 277
flags
   commands, 239-251
   PSC flags, 261
   see also attributes
floppy interface, 489
Folio View (NSE), 14
Form Feed flag, 243, 262
Form flag, 241
form tests, 22
FORMAT.COM file, 546
formats (filenames), 547
formatting
   menus, 298-301
   partitions, 545
forms (printers), 241, 247, 255-256
   definitions, 255
   positioning, 262
Forms and Form Definition screen, 255
FRAME option (Link Driver), 475
FSP (File Service Process), 412
Full Name (SYSCON) option, 139, 154

G

GETx command, 315
GO*.BAT file, 301
GOTO command, 291
grace logins, 153
grandfather method of backups, 500-501
GRANT command, 109
Group Information (SYSCON) menu
   Full Name option, 139
   Managed Users and Groups option, 139

Managers option, 139
Member List option, 139-140
Trustee Directory Assignments
  option, 140-143
Group List (SESSION) menu, 200
**Groups Belonged To (SYSCON)
  option, 154**

H

hackers, 102
hard drives, 356
  boot track, 377
hardware
  backups, 488-489
  requirements (NetWare 3.1x),
    427-428
  settings, 320-322
  technicians, 18
hashing tables, 408
Held condition (print jobs), 218
helical scan technology, 491-492
help files, 57
HELP utility, 195-196
hexadecimal format, 253
Hidden Directory attribute, 439
Hidden File attribute, 106, 436
hiding directories, 76
HOME directories, 62-66
hops, 454
**horizontal placement (menus),
  300**
hosts, 484
Hot Fix, 357
  blocks, 399-400
  tables, 408

I

I/O error count, 399-400
**identifier variables, 283, 289,
  295-297**

**IF-THEN-ELSE statement,
  286-288**
image backups, 496
importing print devices, 251
incidents (technical support), 15
INCLUDE command, 289
**Independent Product Testing
  bulletins, 499**
**Inherited Rights Mask (IRM),
  105, 430-435**
input variables (menus), 308-311
INSTALL disk, 543-544
INSTALL program
  installation options, 377-380
    *-E: Expert—Advanced
      Installation, 378*
    *-C: Configuration Complete
      installation option, 379*
    *-F: File Server Definition
      installation option, 379*
    *-L: Linked or Linking Complete,
      378*
    *-M: Maintenance installation
      option, 379*
    *-N: No Linking installation
      option, 379*
    *-U: Upgrade installation
      option, 379-380*
  main menu, 380
Installation manual, 440
installing
  applications, 61, 64, 277
  clients, 554-556
  NetWare 2.2, 375-377
    *advanced installation option,
      385-393*
    basic installation, 380-381
    core printing, 387
    *executable files, creating,
      376-377*
    ISA disk controllers, 388-389

options, 377-380
step-by-step guide to basic installation, 382-385
servers, 543-548
  AUTOEXEC.NCF file, 548
  DOS partitions, 545
  filename formats, 547
  IPX internal network numbers, 547
  names, 546
  SERVER.EXE file, 548
  STARTUP.NCF file, 548
INSTOVL.EXE file, 376
INT interrupt request number option (Link Driver), 474
INT64 option (SHELL.CFG), 480
INT7A option (SHELL.CFG), 480
interface adapters, 489-490
interfaces, 489
Internetwork Packet Exchange (IPX), 316
internetworking, 34
interrupting login scripts, 288
Intruder Detection/Lockout (SYSCON) option, 146
Intruder Lockout Status (SYSCON) option, 155-156
Invalid COMMAND.COM error message, 284, 295
IPX (Internetwork Packet Exchange), 316
IPX command, 323
IPX internal network numbers, 547
IPX RETRY COUNT option (SHELL.CFG), 480
IPX.COM file, 316, 325-326
IRM (Inherited Rights Mask), 105
  editing, 443-444
  Supervisory rights, 430
  trustee rights, 433-435
  version 3.1x, 430-431
ISA controllers (NetWare 2.2), 388-389

J–K

Job flag, 241

Keep flag, 245
keywords (MAKEUSER utility), 174-181

L

-L: Linked or Linking Complete installation option, 378
LAN (NLM), 460
LANs, 537-542
LARCHIVE command, 611
Large Internet Packets (LIPs), 339
launching print servers, 232
limiting account balances, 134-135
Link Driver (NET.CFG file)
  hardware options, 472-474
  Protocol Selection parameters, 478
  software options, 475-477
LINK STATIONS option (Link Driver), 476
Link Support (NET.CFG file) options, 477
Link Support Layer (LSL), 328
LIPs (Large Internet Packets), 339
LIST DEVICES command, 455
LISTDIR command, 69-71
listing
  file servers, 54
  flags, 246
  print jobs, 257

LITE.VLM, 335
LOAD command, 455
loading VAPs (value-added processes), 357
local drives, 82-83
Local Port flag, 245
LOCAL PRINTERS option (SHELL.CFG), 481
logging in to networks, 316-337
   diskless workstations, 55
   DOS, 323-327
      EMSNETX file, 326
      IPX.COM file, 325-326
      NetBIOS, 327
      NETX file, 326
      XMSNETX file, 326
   file servers, 53-54, 324
   hardware settings, 320-322
   ODI drivers, 327-332
      LSL (Link Support Layers), 328
      MLID (Multiple Link Interface Driver), 329
   VLMs (Virtual Loadable Modules), 333-337
logging out, 340
logical disk partitions, 452
Logical Record Locks option (FCONSOLE), 397
login (grace), 153
LOGIN command, 324
LOGIN directory, 52-55
Login Script (SYSCON) option, 156-157
login scripts
   # (pound sign) in commands, 292
   calling menus, 302-303
   command-line parameters, 293
   commands, 282-297
   cutting and pasting, 282
   default login scripts, 281
   directories, 283
   essential system login script commands, 294
   exiting, 291
   guidelines, 281
   identifier variables, 281-283, 295-297
   interrupting, 288
   map commands, 279
   remark statements, 292
   required statements, 294-295
   script parameters, 281-282
   system login scripts, 279-280
   user login scripts, 280
login/password-level security, 102
!LOGOUT command, 302
LOGOUT command, 302, 340
LONG MACHINE TYPE option (SHELL.CFG), 481
LRESTORE command, 611
LSL (Link Support Layer), 328

M

-M: Maintenance installation option, 379
MACBACK utility, 612
MAGAZINE command, 456
Magnetic Optical (MO) disks, 493
mail, 442-443
MAIL directory, 55-57
MAKEUSER utility, 173-178
Managed Users and Groups (SYSCON) option, 139, 157-158
Manager (SYSCON) option, 139, 158
managing
   directories, 60-62
   directory structure, 68-79

manuals (NetWare 3.1x), 440-441
MAP command, 83-84, 282-284
map commands, 279
MAP DEL command, 86-87
mapping, drives
    local, 82-83
    network, 83-84
    search, 85-86
MArk flag, 262
MAX BOARDS option (Link Support), 477
MAX FRAME SIZE option (Link Driver), 476
MAX STACKS option (Link Support), 478
MAX TASKS option (SHELL.CFG), 481
Maximum Alloc Short Term Memory parameter (SET command), 527-529
Maximum Directory Cache Buffers parameter (SET command), 530-531
Maximum Packet Receive Buffers parameter (SET command), 526
Maximum Rights Mask (MRM), 105
MD command, 67
MEDIA command, 456
MEM option (Link Driver), 474
Member List (SYSCON) option, 139-140
memory, 404-414
    configuring, 516-519
    conventional, 404
    disk storage, 602
    expanded, 407
    extended, 406
    NetWare 2.2, 407-412

    optimization, 520-524
        Directory Cache Buffers field, 522
        Dirty Cache Buffers field, 521-522
        file server statistics, 522-523
        MONITOR.NLM, 520
        Packet Receive Buffers field, 522
        service processes, 522
        Total Cache Buffers field, 521
    RAM, 602
    requirements
        operating systems, 410
        VAPs, 412
    SET command parameters, 527-529
    upper, 405
MEMORY command, 456
memory managers, 278
memory pools, 511-512
    Alloc Short Term Memory Pool, 515-516
    cache memory, 512
    Cache Movable Memory Pool, 513
    Cache Non-Movable Memory Pool, 513
    dynamic, 403, 413-414
    Permanent Memory Pool, 514
    Semi-Permanent Memory Pool, 514
MEMPOOL option (Link Support), 478
MENU utility, 301
MENUCNVT.EXE file, 312
MENUMAKE.EXE file, 312
menus, 297-316
    Available Options (RECONSOLE utility), 540-541
    calling, 302-303

command windows, 308
Connections Information
  Menu, 395
directories, 302
exiting, 302
FILER utility, 165-167
formats, 298-301
input variables, 308-311
INSTALL program, 380
mappings, 305
menu options, 304-306
naming, 299
NetWare 3.12, 311-316
numbering options, 305
placing on-screen, 299
submenus, 299
syntax, 300
SYSCON utility
  Accounting, 127
  Change Current Server, 136
  File Server Information, 136
  Group Information, 137-143
  Supervisor Options, 144-148
  User Information menu,
    148-165
trustee rights, 301
utilities, 126-127
messages
clearing from screen, 453
sending, 395
MIGRATE utility, 446-447
MIGRATE.EXE file, 549-551
**Minimum Directory Cache
Buffers parameter (SET
command), 531-532**
**Minimum File Cache Buffers
parameter (SET command),
529-530**
**Minimum Packet Receive
Buffers parameter (SET
command), 526-527**

MIRROR STATUS command,
  456
mirroring disks, 505
Missing COMMAND.COM error
  message, 295
MLID (Multiple Link Interface
  Driver), 329
mnemonics, 42-43
MNU file extension, 301
MO (Magnetic Optical) disks,
  493
Modify right, 103, 360, 432
modifying print jobs, 248-249
Module 1: Operating System
  Generation, 376
Module 2: Linking and
  Configuring, 376-377
Module 3: Track Zero Test, 377
Module 4: File Server Definition,
  377
MODULE command, 456
MONITOR number command,
  359
MONITOR.NLM, 520-524
MOunt Form flag, 262
MRM (Maximum Rights Mask),
  105, 361
Multiple Link Interface Driver
  (MLID), 329

N

-N: No Linking installation
  option, 379
NAECs (Novell Authorized
  Education Centers), 12, 23-24
  Certification Assessment
    Diskette, 23
  CNA (Certified NetWare
    Administrator), 19
NAM (NLM), 460

Name Service Database, 533-534
naming
   file servers, 48-49
   menus, 299
   servers, 546
   volumes, 51
navigating utilities, 126-127
NBACKUP utility, 187-192
NCOPY command, 71-72, 277
NCP (NetWare Core Protocol) packets, 338
NCP packet signature, 111-117
   changing settings, 116-122
   process, 112
   security levels, 113-115
   version 3.1*x*, 429
NDIR command, 72-77, 107
NDS.VLM, 335
NEAPs, 12, 23-24
NET$OS.EXE file, 377
NET.CFG configuration file, 472-478
NET.CFG file, 327
   DOS Requester, 336-337
   Link Driver
      hardware options, 472-474
      Protocol Selection parameters, 478
      software options, 475-477
   Link Support options, 477
NetBIOS, 327
NETCON utility, 534-535
NetWare 2.15
   ARCHIVE.LOG file, 610-611
   attributes, 602
   backing up files, 610-612
   commands
      LARCHIVE, 611
      LRESTORE, 611
      RESTORE, 612
   file attributes, 603
   MACBACK utility, 612
   printing, 610
   RAM requirements, 602
   rights, 601-602
   tape backup system compatibility, 612
NetWare 2.2
   Advanced System Manager: Test #50-44, 576-579
   attributes, 602
   Certified NetWare Adminstrator: Test #50-115, 594-596
   CNE (Certified NetWare Engineer), 40
   core printing, 363-365
   DETs (directory entry tables), 358, 408
   disks
      duplexing, 358
      mirroring, 358
      storage, 357
   duplicate FATs, 358
   FATs, 410
   file attributes, 603
   file servers, 354-360
      FCONSOLE utility, 394-403
      management, 393-394
   hot fix, 357
   installing, 375-377
      advanced installation, 385-393
      basic installation, 380-381
      core printing, 387
      executable files, 376-377
      ISA controllers, 388-389
      options, 377-380
      step-by-step guide to basic installation, 382-385
   memory, 407-412
   Module 1: Operating System Generation, 376

Module 2: Linking and
  Configuring, 376-377
Module 3: Track Zero Test, 377
Module 4: File Server Definition, 377
printing, 233
RAM requirements, 602
Read-After-Write Verification, 357
rights, 601-602
System Manager: Test #50-20, 573-576
tests, 28
TTS (Transaction Tracking System), 358
VAPs (value-added processes), 356-357

NetWare 2.15
binderies, 606
directories, 606
security, 607-609
System Fault Tolerance, 606
utilities, 606

NetWare 3.1, 264

NetWare 3.11
Advanced System Manager: Test #50-82, 586-588
Certified NetWare Adminstrator: Test #50-116, 596-599
OS Features Review Rev. 1.02: Test #50-45, 589-590
System Manager: Test #50-91, 579-582

NetWare 3.12
LIPs (Large Internet Packets), 339
menus
  commands, 313-314
  compiling, 315-316
  control commands, 312
  creating menus, 312-315
  organizational commands, 312
Novell ElectroText, 440
Packet Burst, 338-339
upgrading servers, 549-553

NetWare 3.1x
Advanced Administration: Test #50-131, 591-594
attributes, 435-440, 602
caching directories, 428
CNE (Certified NetWare Engineer), 39
elevator seeking, 428-429
environment support, 427
file attributes, 603
file server requirements, 425
hardware requirements, 427-428
installing
  clients, 554-556
  servers, 543-548
IRM (Inherited Rights Mask), 430-431, 433-435
new utilities, 441-452
OSs, 427
RAM requirements, 602
reference manuals, 440-441
rights, 601-602
security
  NCP Packet Signature, 429
  passwords, 429
  trustee rights, 433-435
  user rights, 430-433
System Administration: Test #50-130, 582-586
tests, 29-31
workstation compatibility, 426

NetWare 4.0, 31
NetWare Applications Notes, 402
NetWare Buyers Guide, 14
NetWare Concepts Manual, 440

NetWare Core Protocol (NCP) packets, 338
NetWare for Macintosh protocol, 471
NetWare Loadable Modules, *see* NLMs
NetWare Name Services, *see* NNS
NetWare Requester for OS/2 protocol, 471
NetWare-aware applications, 276
NetWire special interest group, 15
network drives, 83-84
Network File System (NFS) protocol, 471
network numbers
   displaying, 453
   IPX internal network numbers, 547
network shells, 317
Network Support Encyclopedia (NSE), 13-14, 508
network-compatible applications, 275-276
NETX command, 323
NETX file, 326
NLMs (NetWare Loadable Modules), 459-460
   2XUPGRDE.NLM, 551-553
   REMOTE.NLM, 538
   RSPX.NLM, 538
   starting, 455
NMENU.BAT file, 312, 447
NNS (NetWare Name Services)
   domains, 532
   Name Service Database, 533-535
   profiles, 532
   server templates, 536-541
   synchronization, 532-533

   utilities, 535-536
     connection, 535-536
     NETCON, 534-535
     printing, 535-536
     user, 536
No Autoendcap flag, 244
No Banner flag, 243
No Form Feed flag, 243
No Tabs flag, 242
NODE ADDRESS option (Link Driver), 474
nodes, 71
nondedicated file servers, 355, 383
nondedicated routers, 181-182
Nonshareable attribute, 107, 437
Novell Authorized Education Centers (NAEC), 12
Novell ElectroText, 440-441
Novell Technical Support (NTS), 11
NPRINT command, 232, 236, 239
NSE (Network Support Encylopedia), 13-14
NTS (Novell Technical Support), 11
numbering menu options, 305

O

ODI configuration files
   NET.CFG, 472-478
   SHELL.CFG, 479-482
ODI (Open Data Link Interface), 469-470
ODI drivers, 327-332
   LSL (Link Support Layers), 328
   MLID (Multiple Link Interface Driver), 329

Open Data Link Interface (ODI), 469-470
Open Files/Physical Records option (FCONSOLE), 396-397
Operating System Generation, 386
operating systems
   NetWare 2.2, 28, 40
   NetWare 2.2 memory requirements, 410
   NetWare 3.1x, 29-31, 39
   NetWare 4.0, 31
   tests, 32-33
operators, 77
optical drives, 492-494
organizational commands, 312
OS Features Review Rev. 1.02: Test #50-45 (NetWare 3.11), 589-590
OS/2, 264
OSs (NetWare 3.1x support), 427
Other Information (SYSCON) option, 158-159
overlay files, 57
overriding PCONSOLE command, 261

P

Packet Burst, 338-339
packet receive buffers, 519
Packet Receive Buffers field, 522
packets, 338-339
parameters, 74
   Protocol Selection (NET.CFG file), 478
   searching
      directories, 72-77
      files, 72-77
   SET command, 525-532
   SHELL.CFG file, 479-482
   sorting, 73-74
parent file server, 484
partitions
   creating, 545
   disks, 452
   formatting, 545
passing token (file servers), 71
passwords, 102, 324
   domain servers, 536
   version 3.1x, 429
PAUDIT command, 58
PAUSE command, 286
PAUse flag, 262
pausing printers, 248, 262
PCONSOLE menu, 216-225
PCONSOLE operators, 100
percent (%)
   identifier variables, 285
   submenus, 299
Permanent Memory Pool, 514
pirating files, 106
PORT option (Link Driver), 474
ports, 245, 363
pound sign (#) in commands, 292
power supply (UPS), 358
practice tests, 22-23
PREFERRED SERVER option (SHELL.CFG), 482
Print Device Options screen, 251
PRINT HEADER option (SHELL.CFG), 482
Print Job Configuration screen, 222, 258
Print Queue Entry Information screen, 219
Print Queue Information menu, 216
print queue operators, 100
Print Server Configuration menu, 227
Print Server manual, 440
print server operators, 100, 246

print servers, 224-226, 246-250
   launching, 232
   printer status, 262
   printing options, 248-249
   PSC command, 260-263
   PSC flags, 261
   setup, 225
   specifications, 249
   SPX (sequenced packet exchange), 233
PRINT TAIL option (SHELL.CFG), 482
PRINTCON command, 256-263
PRINTCON menu utility, 241
PRINTDEF menu utility, 241, 251-256
printer definition files, 57
printers
   advancing, 262
   customizing, 229
   device modes, 252
   forms, 255-256
      definitions, 255
      positioning, 262
   multiple queues, 226
   pausing, 248, 262
   print devices, 251-254
   printer numbers, 233
   remote printers, 225, 229, 262
   status, 262
   stopping, 263
printing, 214-215, 362-365
   aborting print jobs, 248, 261
   banner pages, 243
   buffered print jobs, 239
   byte-stream printing, 242
   capturing print jobs, 245
   copying print jobs, 259
   default print jobs, 258
   disconnected workstations, 245
   file servers, 214, 223
   flags (commands), 239-251
   form feed, 243
   forms, 241, 247, 255-256
   in NetWare 2.15, 610
   listing
      flags, 246
      print jobs, 257
   modifying print jobs, 248-249
   NetWare 2.2, 233
   options, 248-249
   OS/2, 264
   overriding PCONSOLE command, 261
   pausing printers, 248
   ports, 245, 363
   print jobs
      configurations, 256-263
      parameters, 241
   print servers, 225-226, 246-250
      launching, 232
      setup, 225
      specifications, 249
      SPX (sequenced packet exchange), 233
   printing to screen, 284-285
   queues, 214-225, 364
      adding jobs, 222-223
      default queue, 232
      deleting jobs, 218
      entering, 216
      multiple printers, 227
      print servers, 224
      printer numbers, 233
      printers, 226
      queue operators, 224
      queue priority, 230
      queue status, 223
      routing jobs, 233
      service modes, 249
      subdirectories, 224
      users, 225
      viewing jobs, 217-223

resuming, 262
setup, 236-246
    CAPTURE command, 237
    NPRINT command, 239
shelling out to DOS, 244
workstations, 215
privileges, 103-105
processes (file servers), 401-402
Processor Utilization option (MONITOR), 524
professional associations, 15-16
profiles, 532
progress maps
    CNE (Certified NetWare Engineer), 28-30
    ECNE (Enterprise Certified NetWare Engineer), 30-31
    electives, 32-36
PROTOCOL command, 456
PROTOCOL option (Link Driver), 476
protocol stacks, 329
protocols
    connecting, 452-453
    NetWare for Macintosh, 471
    NetWare Requester for OS/2, 471
    Network File System (NFS), 471
    ODI (Open Data Link Interface), 469-470
    TCP/IP, 471
PSC command, 260-263
PSC flags, 261
PSERVER.EXE program, 215
PSERVER.NLM file, 225
PSERVER.VAP file, 225
PUBLIC directory, 57
Purge attribute, 439
Purge Directory attribute, 440

Q

Quarter Inch Cartridge (QIC) interface, 489
question mark (?) flag, 246
queues, 214-225, 364
    adding jobs, 222-223
    default queue, 232
    deleting jobs, 218
    entering, 216
    file servers, 224
    multiple printers, 227
    print servers, 224
    printer numbers, 233
    printers, 226
    queue operators, 224
    queue priority, 230
    queue status, 223
    routing jobs, 233
    service modes, 249
    subdirectories, 224
    users, 225
    viewing jobs, 217-223

R

RAM
    memory requirements, 602
    menus, 311
RCONSOLE utility, 448, 537-541
    concurrent access, 540
    file servers, 538-539
    NLMs, loading, 538
RD command, 67
Read Audit attribute, 106, 437
Read Only attribute, 106, 437
Read right, 103, 360, 431
Read-After-Write Verification, 357

Read/Write attribute, 106
Read/Write files, 437
Ready condition (print jobs), 219
RECONSOLE utility, 540-541
REGISTER MEMORY command, 457
REM (MAKEUSER) keyword, 178
remark statements, 292
REMIRROR PARTITION command, 457
remote file server management, 537-542
remote printers, 225, 229, 262
REMOTE.NLM, 538
REMOVE command, 110-111
REMOVE DOS command, 457
Rename attribute, 439
renaming subdirectories, 77
RENDIR command, 77
repairing volumes, 509-512
requests (file servers), 402
reseller authorization tests, 33
RESET ROUTER command, 457
RESETUP.EXE utility, 541
Resource Tags option (MONITOR), 523
Resource Utilization option (MONITOR), 522-524
Resource Utilization screen display, 524
RESTART*.BAT file, 301
RESTORE command, 612
restoring files, 449-452
review question answers, 567-571
REVOKE command, 109
rights
   access, 608-609
   Access Control, 433
   Create, 432
   default, 609

Erase, 432
File Scan, 432
Modify, 432
NetWare 2.15, 601-602
NetWare 2.2, 601-602
NetWare 3.1x, 601-602
Read, 431
Supervisory
   IRMs, 430
   NetWare 3.1x, 433
trustee, 140-143, 433-435
user, 430-433
Write, 431-432
RIGHTS command, 108
rotation method (backups), 500-503
ROUTEGEN utility, 181-187
routers, 338
   creating, 181
   dedicated, 182
   dedicated protected, 182-187
   nondedicated, 181-182
routing
   buffers, 412
   print jobs, 233
RPRINTER command, 236
RPRINTER.EXE command, 215
RSPX.NLM, 538

S

Saber menu system, 311-316
SALVAGE utility, 449-452
same-server migration, 446, 549
SAPS option (Link Driver), 477
SBACKUP utility, 193-195, 483-488
   ArcServe, 485
   host modules, 484
   target modules, 484
Scan right, 360

SCAN FOR DEVICES command,
  457
screen displays
  Cache Statistics (FCONSOLE),
    398
  Disk Statistics, 399
  File Server Statistics Summary,
    400
  Resource Utilization, 524
  User Disk Space Limitation
    Information, 445
screens
  clearing, 453
  Defined Printers, 230
  Forms and Form Definition,
    255
  Print Device Options, 251
  Print Job Configuration, 222,
    258
  Print Queue Entry Information,
    219
script parameters, 281-282
  identifier variables, 281,
    295-297
    MAP command, 283
SEARCH ADD command, 458
SEARCH DEL command, 458
search drives (drive mappings),
  81, 85-86
Search Mappings (SESSION)
  menu, 201-211
searching
  attributes, 75-76
  directories, 72-77
  files, 72-77
  operators, 77
SECURE CONSOLE command,
  458
security
  backups, 482-483
    bindery files, 495

  disaster recovery plans,
    504-507
  drive types, 491-492
  file-by-file method, 496
  frequency, 500
  grandfather method, 500-501
  hardware, 488-489
  image, 496
  interface adapters, 489-490
  media types, 491-492
  memory pools, 511-512
  off-site, 503-504
  optical drives, 492-494
  responsibility for, 499
  rotation method, 500-503
  SBACKUP utility, 483-488
  software, 494-499
  tape, 495-496
  technical support, 507-508
  ten-tape method, 501-502
  testing backup systems, 504
  Tower of Hanoi method,
    502-503
  UPS (Uninterruptible Power
    Supply), 505-506
  viruses, 506-507
bindery files, 59
command-line utilities, 107-111
files, 105-107
hackers, 102
IRM (Inherited Rights Mask),
  105
MRM (Maximum Rights
  Mask), 105, 361
NCP packet signature
  changing settings, 116-122
  process, 112
  security levels, 113-115
NetWare 2.5, 607-609
NetWare 3.1x
  IRM (Inherited Rights Mask),
    430-435

NCP Packet Signature, 429
passwords, 429
trustee rights, 433-435
user rights, 430-433
passwords, 102
SECURE CONSOLE command, 458
session keys, 112
training, 508-509
trustee rights, 103-105, 360-362
user levels, 97-101
SECURITY command, 58
Security Equivalences (SYSCON) option, 159-161
Select Current Directory (FILER) menu, 170
self-evaluation tests, 22-23
semaphores, 397
Semi-Permanent Memory Pool, 514
sending
messages, 395
tokens (file servers), 71
sequenced packet exchange (SPX), 233
serpentine recording method, 491
SERVER.EXE file, 548
servers
domain servers, 536-537
file servers, 393-394
 buffer statistics, 403
 child, 484
 dedicated, 382
 dynamic memory pools, 403
 FCONSOLE utility, 394-397
 hosts, 484
 memory, 404-414, 516-519
 nondedicated, 383
 parent, 484
 processes, 401-402, 454
 remote management, 537-542
 request statistics, 402
 requirements for NetWare 3.1x, 425
 statistics summary, 400-403
 target, 484
 troubleshooting, 520-524
installing, 543-548
 AUTOEXEC.NCF file, 548
 DOS partitions, 545
 filename formats, 547
 IPX internal network numbers, 547
 SERVER.EXE file, 548
 STARTUP.NCF file, 548
naming, 546
upgrading
 2XUPGRDE.NLM, 551-553
 MIGRATE.EXE file, 549-551
service modes (queues), 249
service processes, 522
service protocols (VLMs), 335
Service Requests Charge Rates (SYSCON) option, 130
session keys, 112
SESSION utility
Change Current Server menu, 198-199
Drive Mappings menu, 199
Group List menu, 200
Search Mappings menu, 201-211
SET command, 459, 525-532
Set Filer Options (FILER) menu, 170-172
SET TIME ZONE command, 459
setting up
accounts, 130-132
drive mappings, 82
HOME directories, 63
print servers, 225
Shareable attribute, 107, 437
Shareable Read Only option, 277

shared data directories, 66
SHared flag, 262
SHELL.CFG configuration file, 479-482
SHOW DOTS option (SHELL.CFG), 482
SIGs (special interest groups), 15
single-user applications, 275
SLOT option (Link Driver), 474
same-server migration, 447
socket numbers, 156
software
   antivirus, 506-507
   backups, 494-499
   installing, 274-279
   see also applications
SORT command, 73
sorting parameters, 73-74
source users, 259
special-interest groups (SIGs), 15
SPEED command, 459
SPOOL command, 359
SPX (sequenced packet exchange), 233
SPX ABORT TIMEOUT option (SHELL.CFG), 481
SPX CONNECTIONS option (SHELL.CFG), 481
SRC file extension, 315
stand-alone applications, 274-275
STARt flag, 262
starting
   First Mail, 443
   NLMs, 455
STARTNET.BAT file, 336
STARTUP.NCF file, 548
Station Restrictions (SYSCON) option, 161
STATus flag, 262
status types (file servers), 53
STop flag, 263

storing files, 63
studying, 37-43
subdirectories
   flow-through, 108
   print queues, 224
   renaming, 77
   trustee rights, 103
submenus, 299
supervisor equivalents, 99, 216, 224
Supervisor Options (SYSCON) menu
   Default Account Balance/ Restrictions option, 145-211
   Default Time Restrictions option, 145
   Edit System AUTOEXEC File option, 145
   File Server Console Operators Options option, 145
   File Server Error Log option, 147
   Intruder Detection/Lockout option, 146
   System Login Script option, 147
   Workgroup Managers option, 148
supervisors, 99, 106
Supervisory right, 104
   IRMs, 430
   version 3.1*x*, 433
switching
   directories, 67
   drive mappings, 87-88
SYS: volume, 51-60
SYSCON Supervisor Options, 365
SYSCON utility, 127-164
   Accounting menu, 127-135
      Blocks Written Charge Rates option, 129

Connect Time Charge Rates
option, 129
Disk Storage Charge Rates
option, 129
Service Requests Charge Rates
option, 130
Change Current Server menu,
136
File Server Information menu,
136
Group Information menu,
137-143
Supervisor Options menu,
144-148
 Default Account Balance/
 Restrictions option, 145
 Default Time Restrictions
 option, 145
 Edit System AUTOEXEC File
 option, 145
 File Server Console Operators
 Options option, 145
 File Server Error Log option,
 147
 Intruder Detection/Lockout
 option, 146
 System Login Script option,
 147
 Workgroup Managers option,
 148
User Information menu,
148-165
 Account Balance option,
 150-151
 Account Restrictions option,
 151-153
 Change Password option, 154
 Full Name option, 154
 Groups Belonged To option,
 154

Intruder Lockout Status option,
 155-156
Login Script option, 156-157
Managed Users and Groups
 option, 157-158
Manager option, 158
Other Information option,
 158-159
Security Equivalences option,
 159-161
Station Restrictions option, 161
Time Restrictions option,
 161-162
Trustee Directory Assignments
 option, 162-163
User Volume/Disk Restrictions
 option, 163-211
**System Administration manual,
440**
**System Administration: Test #50-
130 (NetWare 3.1x), 582-586**
system administrators
 training, 508-509
 user login scripts, 280
SYSTEM directory, 58-62
System Directory attribute, 439
**System Fault Tolerance
(NetWare 2.15), 606**
**System Fault Tolerance (NetWare
2.2), 358-359**
System File attribute, 107
system files, 438
**System Login Script (SYSCON)
option, 147**
system login scripts, 279-280
**System Manager: Test #50-20
(NetWare 2.2), 573-576**
**System Manager: Test #50-91
(NetWare 3.11), 579-582**
**System Module Information
option (MONITOR), 523**

T

Tabs flag, 242
tape backups, 495-496
target file server, 484
target users, 259
TCP/IP, 34
TCP/IP protocol, 471
technical support
  applications, 276
  backups, 507-508
  CNE (Certified NetWare Engineer), 15
  consultants, 509
terabytes, 51
tests, 21-24, 43
  adaptive tests, 22, 38
  CNA (Certified NetWare Administrator), 19
  CNE (Certified NetWare Engineer), 11
  discontinued tests, 35
  Drake Training and Technologies, 21
  electives, 31-36
  form tests, 22
  NetWare 2.2
    Advanced System Manager: Test #50-44, 576-579
    Certified NetWare Adminstrator: Text #50-115, 594-596
    System Manager: Test #50-20 573-576
  NetWare 3.11
    Advanced System Manager: Test #50-82, 586-588
    Certified NetWare Adminstrator: Test #50-116, 596-599
    OS Features Review Rev. 1.02: Test #50-45, 589-590
    System Manager: Test #50-91, 579-582
  NetWare 3.1x
    Advanced Administration: Test #50-131, 591-594
    System Administration: Test #50-130, 582-586
  operating systems, 32-33
  reseller authorization, 33
  review question answers, 567-571
  self-evaluation tests, 22-23
  studying, 37-43
ticks, 454
Time Restrictions (SYSCON) option, 161-162
Timeout flag, 244
TLIST command, 108
Total Cache Buffers field, 521
Tower of Hanoi method of backups, 502-503
Transaction Tracking System, (TTS), 107, 358, 453
Transactional attribute, 107, 438
transferring files, 71-72
Transport Control Protocol/Internet Protocol, see TCP/IP
transport protocols (VLMs), 335
troubleshooting, 34
  File not found error message, 81
  file servers, 520-524
Trustee Directory Assignment list, 56
Trustee Directory Assignments (SYSCON) option, 140-143, 162-163

trustee rights, 103-105, 140-143, 360-361
  directory rights, 361
  effective rights, 362-363
  menus, 301
  version 3.1x, 433-435
TTS (Transaction Tracking System), 107, 358, 453

U

-U: Upgrade installation option, 379-380
UNBIND command, 452-453
Uninterruptible Power Supply (UPS), 358, 505-506
UNIX, 35
unlocking accounts, 146
UPGRADE utility, 448
upgrading
  clients, 554-556
  DOS Requester, 335-350
  MIGRATE, 446-447
  servers, 543-553
    2XUPGRDE.NLM, 551-553
    AUTOEXEC.NCF file, 548
    DOS partitions, 545
    filename formats, 547
    IPX internal network numbers, 547
    MIGRATE.EXE file, 549-551
    names, 546
    SERVER.EXE file, 548
    STARTUP.NCF file, 548
  UPGRADE utility, 448
uploading files, 332
upper memory, 405
UPS (Uninterruptible Power Supply), 358, 505-506
user account managers, 100
User Disk Space Limitation Information screen, 445
User Information (SYSCON) menu, 148-165
  Account Balance option, 150-151
  Account Restrictions option, 151-153
  Change Password option, 154
  Full Name option, 154
  Groups Belonged To option, 154
  Intruder Lockout Status option, 155-156
  Login Script option, 156-157
  Managed Users and Groups option, 157-158
  Manager option, 158
  Other Information option, 158-159
  Security Equivalences option, 159-161
  Station Restrictions option, 161
  Time Restrictions option, 161-162
  Trustee Directory Assignments option, 162-163
  User Volume/Disk Restrictions option, 163
user login scripts, 280
user rights (NetWare 3.1x), 430-433
User Volume/Disk Restrictions (SYSCON) option, 163-211
USERDEF utility, 178-180
users, 97-101
  application access, 278-279
  directory supervisors, 104
  end users, 62-64, 101
  FCONSOLE operators, 99
  limiting disk space, 444-445
  PCONSOLE operators, 100
  print queues, 225

print server operators, 246
queue operators, 224
sending messages to, 395
source users, 259
supervisor equivalents, 99, 216, 224
supervisors, 99, 106
system administrators, 280
system login scripts, 279-280
target users, 259
user account managers, 100
workgroup managers, 100
utilities, 125-211
   ACONSOLE, 541
   ADMIN, 442-443
   ATOTAL, 132
   COLORPAL, 299
   command-line, 58-60, 107-111
   DSPACE, 444-446
   EDIT.NLM, 542
   FCONSOLE, 99, 394-397
      Broadcase Console Message, 395
      cache statistics, 398-399
      Connections Information Menu, 395
      file server statistics summary, 400-403
      Hot Fix blocks, 399400
      Logical Record Locks option, 397
      Open Files/Physical Records option, 396-397
      semaphores, 397
      statistics, disks, 399-400
   FILER, 165-173
      Current Directory Information menu, 165-167
      Directory Contents menu, 167
      Select Current Directory menu, 170
      Set Filer Options menu, 170-172
      Volume Information menu, 172-173
   HELP, 195-197
   MACBACK, 612
   MAKEUSER, 173-178
   MENU, 301
   menus, navigation keys, 126-127
   MIGRATE, 446-447
   NBACKUP, 187-193
   NETCON, 534-535
   NetWare 2.5, 606
   NetWare 3.1*x*, 441-452
   PCONSOLE menu, 216-225
   PRINTCON menu, 241
   PRINTDEF menu, 241, 251-256
   RCONSOLE, 448, 537-541
      concurrent access, 540
      file servers, selecting, 538-539
      NLMs, loading, 538
   RESETUP.EXE, 541
   ROUTEGEN, 181-187
   SALVAGE, 449-452
   SBACKUP, 187, 193-195, 483-488
      ArcServe, 485
      host modules, 484
      target modules, 484
   SESSION, 197-202
      Change Current Server menu, 198-199
      Drive Mappings menu, 199
      Group List menu, 200
      Search Mappings menu, 201-211
   SYSCON, 127-164
      Accounting menu, 127-135
      Change Current Server menu, 136

File Server Information menu, 136
Group Information menu, 137-143
Supervisor Options menu, 144-148
User Information menu, 148-165
UPGRADE, 448
USERDEF, 178-181
VREPAIR, 509-512
WSGEN utility, 316-322
WSUPDATE, 202-204
Utilities Reference manual, 440

V

value-added processes, *see* VAPs
VAP command, 360
VAPs (value-added processes), 353, 356-357
   loading, 357
   NetWare 2.2 memory requirements, 412
VERSION command, 459
vertical placements (menus), 300
viewing
   directory
      information, 444
      satistics, 68
      structure, 69-71
   files, 450-451
   system files, 438
   volume information, 69, 77-79, 444
viruses, 506-507
VLMs (Virtual Loadable Modules), 333-337
VOLINFO command, 77-79

volume bit maps, 408
Volume Information (FILER) menu, 172-173
volumes, 49-50
   information, 444
   naming, 51
   repairing, 509-512
   statistics, 69, 77-79
   SYS: volume, 51
VOLUMES command, 459
VREPAIR utility, 509-512
VREPAIR.EXE file, 377

W

Waiting condition (print jobs), 219
WATCHDOG command, 360
wild cards, 239
workgroup managers, 100
Workgroup Managers (SYSCON) option, 148
workstation tables, 410
workstations, 354
   bridges, 338
   COMSPEC command, 290
   disconnecting during printing, 245
   distributed processing, 355
   DOS Requester, 335
   hardware options, 319
   logging into networks, 316-337
   NetWare 3.1*x* compatibility, 426
   printing, 215
   routers, 338
   SPX (sequenced packet exchange), 233
WORM (Write Once Read Many) drive, 493
Write Audit attribute, 106, 437

WRITE command, 284-285
Write Once Read Many (WORM)
  drive, 493
Write right, 103, 360, 431-432
WSGEN utility, 316
  hardware settings, 320-322
  network shells, 317
  selecting driver, 319
WSUPDATE utility, 202-204

X–Y–Z

XMSNETX file, 326

ZTEST.EXE file, 376

WANT MORE INFORMATION?

CHECK OUT THESE RELATED TITLES:

	QTY	PRICE	TOTAL
Inside Novell NetWare, Third Edition. This #1 selling tutorial/reference is perfect for beginning system administrators. Each network management task is thoroughly explained and potential trouble spots are noted. The book also includes a disk with an extremely easy to use workstation menu program, an MHS capable e-mail program, and workgroup management tools. ISBN: 1-56205-257-8.	____	$34.95	_____
NetWare 4: Planning and Implementation. The ultimate guide to planning, installing, and managing a NetWare 4.0 network. This book explains how best to implement the new features of NetWare 4.0 and how to upgrade to NetWare 4.0 as easily and efficiently as possible. ISBN: 1-56205-159-8.	____	$27.95	_____
Downsizing to NetWare. Get the real story on downsizing with *Downsizing to NetWare*. This book identifies applications that are suitable for use on LANs and shows how to implement downsizing projects. This book lists the strengths and weaknesses of NetWare—making it perfect for managers and system administrators. ISBN: 1-56205-071-0.	____	$39.95	_____
LAN Operating Systems. Learn how to connect the most popular LAN operating systems. All major LAN operating systems are covered, including: NetWare 3.11, Appleshare 3.0, Banyan VINES 5.0, UNIX, LAN Manger 2.1, and popular peer-to-peer networks. The following client operating systems are covered as well: MS-DOS, Windows, OS/2, Macintosh System 7, and UNIX. This book clears up the confusion associated with managing large networks with diverse client workstations and multiple LAN operating systems. ISBN: 1-56205-054-0.	____	$39.95	_____

Name _____

Company _____

Address _____

City _____ State _____ ZIP _____

Phone _____ Fax _____

☐ Check Enclosed ☐ VISA ☐ MasterCard

Card #_____ Exp. Date _____

Signature _____

Prices are subject to change. Call for availability and pricing information on latest editions.

Subtotal _____

Shipping _____

$4.00 for the first book and $1.75 for each additional book.

Total _____
Indiana residents add 5% sales tax.

New Riders Publishing 201 West 103rd Street • Indianapolis, Indiana 46290 USA

Orders/Customer Service: 1-800-428-5331
Fax: 1-800-448-3804

NetWare Training Guide: Managing NetWare Systems

REGISTRATION CARD

Fill out this card to receive information about future NetWare books and other New Riders titles!

Name _____ **Title** _____

Company _____

Address _____

City/State/ZIP _____

I bought this book because: _____
_____

I purchased this book from:
☐ A bookstore (Name _____)
☐ A software or electronics store (Name _____)
☐ A mail order (Name of Catalog _____)

I purchase this many computer books each year:
☐ 1–5   ☐ 6 or more

I currently use these applications: _____
_____
_____
_____

I found these chapters to be the most informative: _____
_____

I found these chapters to be the least informative: _____
_____

Additional comments: _____
_____

☐ I would like to see my name in print! You may use my name and quote me in future New Riders products and promotions. My daytime phone number is: _____

New Riders Publishing   201 West 103rd Street • Indianapolis, Indiana 46290 USA

Fold Here

PLACE
STAMP
HERE

New Riders Publishing
201 West 103rd Street
Indianapolis, Indiana 46290
USA